THE POWER OF ASTROLOGY:

Uncover the Secrets of All 12 Zodiac Signs & Their Influence on Your Life

By
Sofia Visconti

CLICK HERE

Or Visit Below:

https://www.subscribepage.com/svmyth

Or Simply Scan The Qr Code To Join

ARIES:

A COMPLETE GUIDE TO THE ARIES ASTROLOGY STAR SIGN

Contents

INTRODUCTION 1

Aries Overview 1

CHAPTER 1: HISTORY AND MYTHOLOGY 4

Babylonians and Sumerians 5

Ancient Egyptians 5

Ancient Greeks 6

Evolution of "Aries" 6

Historical events 7

CHAPTER 2: LOVE & COMPATIBILITY 10

Aries Approach to Love 10

Compatibility With Other Zodiac Signs 12

Tips for Dating and Nurturing Relationships with Aries 15

General Tips for Dating and Relationships with Aries 16

CHAPTER 3: FRIENDS AND FAMILY 18

Aries as a Friend 18

Aries in Family Dynamics 20

Challenges in Friendships and Family 22

Developing Relationships 24

CHAPTER 4: CAREER AND AMBITIONS 25

Aries Career Preferences and Professional Goals 25

Aries Strengths in the Workplace 27

Challenges faced by Aries and strategies to overcome them 28

CHAPTER 5: SELF-IMPROVEMENT 32

Embracing Aries Strengths and Overcoming Weaknesses 32

Personal Development 34

CHAPTER 6: ARIES IN THE YEAR AHEAD 37
Horoscope Guide For Aries 38
Key Themes for the Year 38
Astrological Influences on Aries 39
CHAPTER 7: FAMOUS ARIES PERSONALITIES 42
Charlie Chaplin 42
Diana Ross 43
Robert Downey Jr. 43
Lucy Lawless 43
Thomas Jefferson 44
Mariah Carey 44
Eric Clapton 44
Lady Gaga 45
Elton John 45
J. P. Morgan 45
Maria Sharapova 46
Aretha Franklin 46
CONCLUSION 48

INTRODUCTION

Astrology has fascinated humanity for centuries. It explores the positions and movements of the planets and stars to identify their impact on human behavior and events here on Earth. Essentially astrology is a belief system that suggests a connection between the cosmos and our personal lives. In this book we embark on a journey to delve into one of the twelve zodiac signs, Aries. Inside we seek to uncover its secrets and gain valuable insights from it. The objective of this book is to offer readers an in depth exploration of the Aries zodiac sign. It aims to provide an understanding of the characteristics, traits and tendencies associated with individuals born under this fiery and dynamic sign.

Whether you are an Aries yourself or have friends or loved ones who fall under this zodiac sign, this book endeavors to assist you in navigating through their qualities and confronting any challenges that may arise.

ARIES OVERVIEW

- **Date**; Aries spans from March 21st to April 19th marking the beginning of the zodiac calendar.
- **Symbol**; Represented by the Ram. The powerful horns of a Ram symbolizes strength, determination and leadership qualities.
- **Element**; Aries is associated with the Fire element representing passion, energy and assertiveness.
- **Planet**; Mars, the planet known for action, aggression and desire governs Aries. This planetary influence amplifies their courage and competitive spirit.
- **Color**; Red.

PERSONALITY TRAITS

Aries individuals are recognized for their fearless nature. They possess the following personality traits.

- **Fearless**; Aries individuals fearlessly venture into new territories and embrace risks.
- **Energetic**; They radiate energy and enthusiasm often initiating ventures and exciting experiences.
- **Independent**; Aries value their independence and prefer to carve out their own path.
- **Leadership**; Aries are leaders at heart. They have a knack for inspiring and leading others.
- **Optimistic**; Aries maintains an optimistic outlook on life. Even in the face of challenges.

STRENGTHS

- **Brave**; Aries confronts challenges with courage and resilience.
- **Determined**; They possess unwavering determination to achieve their goals.
- **Initiators**; Aries takes initiative and excels at catalyzing beginnings.

WEAKNESSES

- **Impulsive**: Aries can be impulsive, often acting without thinking through the consequences.
- **Impatient**: Patience is not a virtue commonly found in Aries. They want things to happen immediately. They can become frustrated when things don't move as quickly as they'd like.
- **Competitive**: While being competitive can be a strength, for Aries, it can sometimes be a weakness. Their strong desire to be the best can lead to unnecessary stress and conflict, particularly in collaborative or team environments.

In the opening of this book we have delved into the realm of astrology with an emphasis on the Aries zodiac sign. So far we have gained knowledge about the aspects that define Aries including their birth dates, symbol, element and their ruling planet.

We have also explored the personality traits, strengths and weaknesses that distinguish individuals born under the sign of Aries. From their independent nature to moments of impulsiveness and impatience, Aries personalities are both inspiring and complex.

ARIES

As we progress further into this book's core content you can anticipate a detailed exploration of Aries. We'll delve into its roots, connections as well as provide practical insights that will help you understand and appreciate the Aries individuals in your life. Together we will unravel the mysteries surrounding this zodiac sign by uncovering its stories, characteristics and compatibility factors. Join us on this journey as we unlock the secrets of Aries!

CHAPTER 1: HISTORY AND MYTHOLOGY

The constellation known as Aries, has a captivating history that spans thousands of years. It has deeply influenced civilization with its origins intertwined in the records and observations made by various ancient cultures. To truly grasp the importance of Aries we must take a journey through time. Here we will explore how different civilizations perceived and depicted this marvel on their star maps.

In ancient times when the night sky served as both a storytelling canvas and a navigational aid Aries stood out prominently among the constellations. Its position in the heavens made it an integral part of tales crafted by cultures to explain the mysteries of the universe.

As we delve further into history and mythology we will uncover the tapestry of Aries revealing its role as a guiding light in the sky, a source of inspiration and a symbol representing cosmic awe for countless generations. Join us on this expedition to unravel the enigmas and meanings behind the constellation of Aries.

BABYLONIANS AND SUMERIANS

The Babylonians and Sumerians who lived in Mesopotamia during ancient times (c. 5400 BC) are credited with the earliest known observations of the Aries constellation. They associated this constellation with the cycles that were crucial to their society. Aries was commonly linked to the equinox. This marked the onset of spring and the beginning of their year. This event held great importance for their pursuits as it marked the commencement of the planting season. This was a time when they could sow crops with anticipation of a fruitful harvest, in due course. Consequently Aries became closely intertwined with rebirth and thus marked a new beginning for farming activities.

ANCIENT EGYPTIANS

The ancient Egyptians had an understanding of Aries, which played a key role in their belief systems and mythologies. Aries held a place in their worldview closely associated with the revered deity Amon Ra. Amon Ra, the powerful sun god was often depicted with the distinct curved horns of a ram. These horns were not just symbolic. This represented the connection between Amon Ra and the constellation Aries. The Egyptians saw Aries as an embodiment of power and the life giving force of the sun. The ram, symbolizing strength and protection, was considered a manifestation of Amon Ras' might. The image of the ram adorned temples, amulets and tombs—acting as both guardian and symbol of resilience.

Interestingly the ancient Egyptians approached astronomy differently from how we classify constellations in astronomy. Instead individual stars and groups of stars were linked to gods, legends and cosmic events. The stars, within the region we now know as Aries, were part of a tapestry that played a role in Egyptian religious and astronomical practices. This interconnected network of stars and their celestial narratives contributed to the mystical worldview of the Egyptians blurring the line between the earthly realm and the divine through the wonders of the night sky.

ANCIENT GREEKS

According to Greek mythology Aries is often linked to the captivating tale of the Golden Fleece and the adventures of Jason and the Argonauts. The story revolves around a ram adorned with a fleece that Jason and his crew eagerly pursued. This ram had been sent by Hermes and Athena to rescue Phrixus and Helle who were facing persecution from their stepmother. As a gesture of gratitude Phrixus sacrificed the ram upon reaching Colchis hanging its fleece on a tree as a symbol of appreciation. The Golden Fleece became an emblem of power and authority.

Furthermore Ares (the equivalent of the god Mars) known as the god of war in Greek mythology is often associated with the assertive and energetic qualities attributed to individuals born under the sign of Aries.

OTHER CULTURES

Various other cultures, such as the Persians and Indians had their own interpretations of Aries within their unique mythologies and knowledge of stars. These interpretations often touched upon themes of fertility, rejuvenation and seasonal transitions.

Overall the historical origins of the Aries constellation have deep roots, in various observations and interpretations made by civilizations. Whether seen as a symbol of renewal or associated with quests or divine protection Aries has carried diverse meanings across cultures enriching its celestial legacy in our night sky. To sum it up, ancient mythologies featuring Aries frequently symbolize courage, renewal and divine intervention. These mythical connections continue to infuse depth and symbolism into our understanding of Aries today.

EVOLUTION OF "ARIES"

Over time our perception and understanding of Aries in astrology has undergone many changes. Ancient civilizations primarily linked this sign with symbolism and mythology. However in modern astrology there has been a shift, towards psychological interpretations focusing on personality traits. Let's explore some key points that highlight this evolution.

Ancient Interpretations

In ancient times civilizations such as the Babylonians, Greeks and Egyptians associated Aries with cycles, mythical narratives and symbols of divinity. They emphasized its significance in terms of renewal and fertility.

Modern Astrology

Modern astrology offers insights into compatibility with zodiac signs as well as guidance regarding careers and relationship dynamics. This allows individuals to gain an understanding of themselves and make choices in their lives. In modern astrology Aries is considered one of the twelve zodiac signs that represent various personality traits and characteristics. Contemporary astrology delves into the aspects related to individuals born under the sign of Aries. It explores their strengths, weaknesses and potential life paths while emphasizing self awareness and personal growth.

To summarize, our understanding of Aries in astrology has transformed from symbolism to a modern perspective focused on psychology. While courage and initiative remain integral to its representation, contemporary astrology provides individuals with tools for self discovery and personal development in today's world.

HISTORICAL EVENTS

Throughout history many significant events have taken place during the season of Aries. The Aries zodiac sign is associated with qualities, like courage, initiative and leadership. Here are a few noteworthy historical events that occurred during this time and their possible astrological connections.

- **The American Revolution (1775 1783)**; The American Revolution, which saw the signing of the Declaration of Independence, on July 4 1776 took place during the Aries season. This period reflects the pioneering spirit of Aries as American colonists fought for their independence.
- **Apollo 11 Moon Landing (1969)**; The iconic Apollo 11 mission, where astronauts Neil Armstrong and Buzz Aldrin became the first humans to walk on the moon on July 20 1969 aligns with the Aries characteristic of pushing boundaries and venturing into territories.
- **The Fall of the Berlin Wall (1989)**; The fall of the Berlin Wall began on November 9 1989 leading to the reunification of East and West Germany. This event embodies the Aries trait of breaking barriers. Taking actions that bring about transformative change.

Historical figures

Throughout history there have been numerous figures born under the Aries zodiac sign who have left a lasting impact. Let's explore a few examples.

- **Leonardo da Vinci (April 15 1452)**; Leonardo da Vinci, a Renaissance man was born under the Aries sign. Made significant contributions to the fields of art, science and engineering. His genius and pioneering spirit truly embodied the qualities associated with Aries.
- **Thomas Jefferson (April 13 1743)**; Thomas Jefferson, one of the Founding Fathers of the United States and the principal author of the Declaration of Independence, leadership and determination that are often associated with Aries within the context of American history.
- **Maya Angelou (April 4 1928)**; Maya Angelou, a poet and civil rights activist born under Aries fearlessly used her voice to inspire and uplift others. Her assertiveness embodies one of the defining traits attributed to individuals born under this sign.

In conclusion we have delved into a captivating collection of tales and historical significance linked to Aries – a ram – throughout this chapter. From the search for the Golden Fleece to Amun Ra's symbolism Aries has stood as an emblem of bravery, rejuvenation and pioneering spirit across human history. These stories and mythologies have played a role in shaping this zodiac sign's enduring heritage.

Aries' impact is not limited to stories; it extends into the world of astrology today. The essential qualities of Aries – bravery, leadership and a vibrant passion for life – still hold relevance in helping individuals understand themselves and navigate the complexities of the era. Aries guides us in embracing starts taking daring steps and connecting with our warriors.

For those interested in exploring the history and mythology of Aries here is a curated collection of sources ancient texts and contemporary writings;

- **"The Almagest"** by Claudius Ptolemy; An ancient text that offers valuable insights into the depiction and explanation of the Aries constellation's celestial significance.
- **"The Golden Fleece"** by Robert Graves; A literary journey delving into the legendary quest for the Golden Fleece and its connection to Aries in Greek mythology.
- **"The Oxford Guide to Classical Mythology**, in the Arts 1300 1990s" edited by Jane Davidson Reid; An reference work that provides perspectives on how Aries and other zodiac signs have influenced art, literature and culture throughout history.

- **"Astrology; Unraveling the Birth Chart"** written by Kevin Burk is a handbook that delves into the astrological dimensions of Aries and the complete zodiac providing valuable insights into its ongoing importance in modern astrology.

These references provide an, in depth comprehension of the captivating past, mythology and astrological implications associated with Aries.

CHAPTER 2: LOVE & COMPATIBILITY

In the tapestry of the zodiac we welcome you into the captivating world of Aries individuals and their experiences, with love and compatibility. Exploring their dynamic nature we uncover their unique approach to romantic relationships. All this plus how they connect with zodiac signs. Join us as we navigate through Aries multifaceted love life and uncover the secrets of their compatibility. Whether you're an Aries seeking self discovery or looking to understand Aries in love, this chapter promises to be an enlightening journey.

ARIES APPROACH TO LOVE

Aries individuals embrace their qualities and fiery personality traits when it comes to matters of the heart. Here's a closer look at how.

- **Passionate and Intense**; Aries is renowned for its passion. When they fall in love they do so with enthusiasm and intensity. When it comes to romance, Aries individuals possess an intense passion. They are unafraid to openly express their feelings.
- **Fearless Pursuit**; Aries individuals have an inclination towards leadership. They don't hesitate when it comes to pursuing someone they are interested

in. They enjoy the excitement of chasing after someone. For them they take pleasure in being the initiator who makes the first moves in a relationship.

- **Spontaneity and Adventure**; Aries thrives on excitement and adventure which also reflects in their approach to love. They are spontaneous by nature. They take delight in surprising their partners with outings, grand gestures and thrilling escapades. Routine and predictability simply don't fit into their love vocabulary.
- **Independence and Freedom**; Aries highly values their independence. As such they expect the same level of freedom from their partner. They need room to pursue their passions without feeling tied down. In a relationship they look for a partner who can match their lifestyle filled with activity.
- **Fiercely Loyal**; While Aries may enjoy seeking out experiences once they commit to a relationship they display loyalty. In turn they stand firmly by their partner's side through thick and thin, always protective of those they love.
- **Direct Communication**; A known among Aries individuals is their directness, in communication. They prefer straightforwardness without beating around the bush or playing games. They value honesty and expect their partner to do the same. They don't enjoy playing mind games in relationships, preferring honest conversations, about their feelings and expectations.
- **Quick to Forgive;** Aries spontaneous nature can sometimes lead to conflicts or disagreements within a relationship. However they are quick to forgive and move forward from disputes as they don't hold grudges. Their ability to bounce back from disagreements with optimism is a characteristic.
- **Craving Challenges**; Aries individuals thrive when faced with challenges and this extends to their love life. They may seek partners who intellectually and emotionally stimulate them, keeping the relationship dynamic and exciting.
- **Physical Intimacy**; Physical attraction and intimacy are crucial for Aries in a relationship. They are lovers who enjoy expressing their emotions, desiring a partner who shares their enthusiasm for physical connection.

In conclusion Aries approaches love and romance with passion, intensity and an unwavering pursuit of excitement. Their direct communication style, loyalty and thirst for adventure make them captivating partners. However it's important to remember that each individual is unique so while these traits generally apply to Aries individuals, the specifics of how they approach love may vary from person to person.

COMPATIBILITY WITH OTHER ZODIAC SIGNS

When it comes to astrology compatibility is a key concept to consider. The compatibility between Aries individuals and other zodiac signs depends on elements, including the qualities of each partner and the dynamics of their relationship. Here's an overview of how Aries tends to interact with other zodiac signs.

ARIES AND ARIES

- Compatibility; A connection between two Aries individuals can be quite thrilling because of their shared sense of adventure and vitality. They truly understand each other's desire for freedom. As such they can inspire one another in many ways.
- Challenges; However there might be some challenges arising from both partners being strong willed and competitive. Power struggles or conflicts may occasionally occur. For this relationship to flourish it is crucial for them to find a common ground through compromise and effective communication.

ARIES AND TAURUS

- Compatibility; A pairing of an Aries and a Taurus can be intriguing due to their differences. While Aries brings excitement and spontaneity. Taurus offers stability and grounding. Their contrasting qualities have the potential to complement one another effectively.
- Challenges; Nevertheless the impulsive nature of Aries might clash with the need for security and routine that Taurus seeks. To make this relationship work harmoniously, patience and understanding play important roles.

ARIES AND GEMINI

- Compatibility; When it comes to an Aries and Gemini pairing you'll find a love for stimulation, communication and social activities. Engaging conversations are likely as they both enjoy exploring varied concepts.
- Challenges; However at times Gemini's indecisiveness may test the patience of an action oriented Aries partner. Similarly Gemini might perceive Aries as being impulsive. Striking a balance between excitement and stability becomes essential in maintaining harmony in this relationship.

ARIES AND CANCER

- Compatibility; Although Aries and Cancer may have their differences they can actually complement each other well. Aries' energetic nature can help

Cancer break out of their shell. Meanwhile Cancer's nurturing qualities can offer support to Aries.

- Challenges; However it's important for Aries to be mindful of how their directness may hurt Cancers feelings. Likewise Aries should take care not to misunderstand or overlook the sensitivity that Cancer possesses. Effective communication and empathy are essential in navigating these challenges.

ARIES AND LEO

- Compatibility; When it comes to Aries and Leo they share a passion for life along with an adventurous spirit. Their relationship tends to be filled with excitement. This creates a fiery quality.
- Challenges; Both signs have a tendency towards dominance and driven behavior, which can sometimes lead to power struggles between them. Learning how to share the spotlight and avoiding conflicts fueled by ego is crucial in maintaining harmony.

ARIES AND VIRGO

- Compatibility; In the case of Aries and Virgo there is a dynamic at play. Aries has the ability to inspire Virgo to embrace spontaneity and adventure. Meanwhile Virgo brings practicality and organization into the mix – effectively balancing one another.
- Challenges; However it's worth noting that Aries impulsive nature might occasionally clash with Virgo's preference for orderliness. Additionally due to Virgo's tendencies there is a possibility that they could unintentionally undermine Aries self confidence. Patience, alongside acceptance are attributes needed in addressing these challenges effectively.

ARIES AND LIBRA

- Compatibility; Aries and Libra go well together because Aries is action oriented while Libra values harmony and balance. They can enjoy a loving life together.
- Challenges; Aries may sometimes find Libra hesitant in decision making. Similarly Libra might perceive Aries as being impulsive. It's important for them to find ground and be willing to compromise.

ARIES AND SCORPIO

- Compatibility; Aries and Scorpio share an intense connection. They have a physical bond often displaying unwavering loyalty towards each other.
- Challenges; Both signs can be stubborn and possessive leading to power struggles. Building trust through communication is crucial for maintaining a happy relationship.

ARIES AND SAGITTARIUS

- Compatibility; Aries and Sagittarius are both individuals who cherish their freedom. Together they delight in exploring life's wonders based on shared interests.
- Challenges; Their mutual love for independence may occasionally cause conflicts. However they can usually find ways to compromise without dampening their enthusiasm.

ARIES AND CAPRICORN

- Compatibility; Aries ambitious nature often aligns well with Capricorn's drive for success in life. They can greatly motivate each other to achieve their goals together.
- Challenges; Aries impatience may not always align with Capricorn's practical approach. It is important for them to find a common ground between taking calculated risks and making decisions.

ARIES AND AQUARIUS

- Compatibility; Aries and Aquarius value individuality and innovation which can lead to a fulfilling connection. They both enjoy embarking on new adventures.
- Challenges; Aries spontaneous nature may sometimes clash with Aquarius' desire for unpredictability. Meanwhile Aquarius' tendency to be detached might pose a challenge for Aries. Open communication plays an important role in overcoming these obstacles.

ARIES AND PISCES

- Compatibility; Aries and Pisces have differences that can either complement or create conflicts, within their relationship. The strength of Aries combined with the sensitivity of Pisces can foster a nurturing dynamic.
- Challenges; Aries straightforwardness may unintentionally hurt the feelings of Pisces. Meanwhile, the dreamy nature of Pisces could confuse Aries. Building trust and emotional understanding are important aspects for their relationship to thrive.

Note that it's important to keep in mind that while astrology can offer insights into compatibility factors such as personality, life experiences and communication skills play a role in determining the success of a relationship. Many successful relationships thrive between individuals with energies indicating that astrological signs alone do not determine compatibility.

TIPS FOR DATING AND NURTURING RELATIONSHIPS WITH ARIES

Dating and nurturing relationships with Aries individuals can be an fulfilling experience. However it's essential to understand their qualities and needs. Whether you're a man or a woman here are some tips for establishing and sustaining a bond with an Aries.

TIPS FOR MEN DATING ARIES WOMEN

- **Confidence is Key**; Aries women are drawn to confidence and assertiveness. Display confidence by making decisive actions and choices.
- **Respect Their Independence**; Aries women highly value their independence and freedom. Encourage their pursuits and passions while also maintaining your own interests and independence.
- **Embrace Adventure**; Aries women thrive on excitement and spontaneity. Plan thrilling dates that keep the relationship vibrant and dynamic.
- **Honesty and Transparency**; Aries women value honesty and straightforwardness. It's important to communicate your feelings and intentions to establish trust.
- **Show Support**; Aries women are ambitious and driven. Show support for their goals and dreams. Be their cheerleader during challenging times.

TIPS FOR WOMEN DATING ARIES MEN

- **Respect Their Need for Independence**; Aries men highly value their independence. Give them space to pursue their interests without overwhelming them with attention.

- **Appreciate Their Initiatives**; Aries men are leaders and initiators. Appreciate their efforts in planning dates and making decisions.
- **Be Confident and Self Assured**; Aries men are attracted to partners who exude confidence. Believe in yourself and showcase your abilities. Overall this will make you more attractive to them.
- **Engage in Physical Activities**; Aries men enjoy being active and participating in physical activities. Join them in sports, workouts or outdoor adventures to bond over shared enthusiasm.
- **Communicate Openly**; Aries men appreciate communication. If you have any concerns or desires express them clearly as they prefer honesty and straightforwardness.

GENERAL TIPS FOR DATING AND RELATIONSHIPS WITH ARIES

- **Embrace Spontaneity**; Aries individuals thrive on spontaneity and excitement. Be open, to impromptu plans or adventures that keep the relationship alive.
- **Practice Patience**; Aries people tend to act on impulse, which can occasionally lead to disagreements. It's important to practice patience and find compromises in order to resolve conflicts.
- **Finding a balance is key**; Strive to strike a balance, between giving them space for independence and nurturing your bond with them. Encourage their growth while cherishing the connection you share.
- **Celebrate their accomplishments**; Aries individuals are highly motivated by success. Take the time to celebrate their achievements, even the small ones as it will bring them happiness.
- **Don't forget about your interests**; While nurturing the relationship remember to maintain your passions and pursuits. Aries individuals appreciate partners who have their own hobbies and goals.
- **Respect boundaries**; Aries individuals have boundaries so it's crucial to respect their limits. Open communication about your boundaries will contribute to creating a respectful partnership.

Remember that astrology provides insights. Individual personalities and compatibility are influenced by various factors beyond zodiac signs. Building a relationship with an Aries individual requires understanding, compromise and open communication. Just like any other relationship.

In conclusion of the chapter "Love & Compatibility " we have explored the passionate nature of Aries individuals when it comes to matters of the heart.

From the fearless way they approach love and romance to their intense energy, individuals born under the sign of Aries bring a dynamic and thrilling presence to their relationships.

We have delved into the complexities of Aries compatibility, with zodiac signs discovering the chemistry and challenges that arise when an Aries pairs up with different celestial counterparts. Whether they find harmony with Fire signs, engage in stimulating connections with Air signs or navigate the depths of emotional intimacy with Water signs, Aries romantic journey is marked by excitement, personal growth and occasional clashes of will.

As we wrap up this chapter one thing remains crystal clear; Aries individuals approach love and relationships with unwavering courage and boundless enthusiasm. They are determined to conquer any challenges that come their way and are eager to experience the thrill of connection.

CHAPTER 3: FRIENDS AND FAMILY

This chapter explores the loyalty and leadership that Aries brings to their friendships well as the profound impact they have on family dynamics. With their inclination for leadership and fierce protectiveness Aries individuals establish connections, inspire those around them and navigate challenges in their pursuit of harmonious relationships.

Here we delve into the qualities and challenges that arise for Aries individuals as they balance their assertive caring nature in both friendships and family relationships. Whether you are an Aries seeking an understanding of your role in these relationships or a curious reader interested in gaining insight into the world of Aries connections, this chapter promises an enlightening journey through the intricate bonds and dynamics within friends and family.

ARIES AS A FRIEND

Being friends with an Aries is an invigorating experience full of vibrancy. Aries friends possess a combination of qualities that make them loyal and exhilarating companions. Here's what you can expect when befriending an Aries;

- **Loyalty and Reliability**; Aries friends display loyalty and reliability. When Aries individuals commit to a friendship they are unwavering in their loyalty and support. You can always count on them to have your back no matter the circumstances.
- **Spontaneity**; One remarkable quality of Aries friends is their spontaneous spirit. They have a thrilling nature that makes every experience exciting and new. With them there's never a dull moment.
- **Leading**; Aries friends naturally take charge to lead the way. They are proactive, in planning outings, gatherings and activities. Their ability to rally the group and make things happen is truly admirable.
- **Honesty**; Honesty is highly valued by Aries individuals when it comes to friendships. They appreciate direct communication from their friends without any sugar coating. In return they expect the same level of transparency.
- **Supportive**; Supporting your dreams and ambitions is something Aries friends excel at. They are incredibly supportive. They will motivate you to reach your goals while helping you overcome obstacles along the way.
- **Enthusiasm**; Aries friends bring an enthusiastic vibe wherever they go. Their infectious energy adds excitement to gatherings inspiring others to join in on the fun.
- **Solutions focused**; Problem solving comes naturally to Aries individuals. Whenever their friends face challenges or difficulties they quickly offer solutions with a helping hand.
- **Forgiving**; Forgiveness is a virtue that Aries' friends possess. They have a nature that allows them to solve conflicts or misunderstandings, for the sake of maintaining strong friendships. Aries ' friends may get angry quickly. But they are just as quick to forgive and move on from disagreements. They don't hold grudges and prefer to maintain a friendship.
- **Protective Nature**; Aries friends have an instinct to protect their loved ones and will go to great lengths to ensure their safety and well being.
- **Independence and Freedom**; Aries' friends value their independence and expect their friends to respect their need for personal space and freedom. They appreciate friends who support their pursuits.

While Aries friends bring qualities into your life it's important to remember that their assertiveness and occasional impatience can lead to conflicts. However these conflicts are usually short lived as Aries forgiving nature ensures that friendships remain strong.

In conclusion, having an Aries friend means having an adventurous and supportive companion by your side. Their dynamic personality and zest for life can add excitement and vitality to your friendship creating a memorable connection.

ARIES IN FAMILY DYNAMICS

Aries individuals bring their unique qualities and characteristics into family dynamics influencing the atmosphere within the household as well as interactions, among family members. Understanding the role of Aries in family life can provide key insights into how they contribute, face challenges and shape family dynamics.

- **Natural Leaders**; Aries individuals often step into leadership positions within their families. They are proactive and assertive, taking charge of decision making and problem solving. They may naturally gravitate towards being the spokesperson for the family or organizing family events.
- **Protectors and Defenders**; Aries individuals possess an instinct to protect especially when it comes to their loved ones. They are fiercely loyal and will stand up for their family members if they perceive any threat or injustice.
- **Independence and Autonomy**; Aries highly value their independence and autonomy which can sometimes create conflicts within family dynamics. They may resist controlling or restrictive family settings. Overall they prefer to have a certain level of personal freedom.
- **Sibling Rivalry**; Aries assertiveness and desire to excel may lead to rivalries with their brothers or sisters. While healthy competition can be beneficial it's important for parents to promote cooperation and teamwork among siblings.
- **Parenting Approach**; Aries parents tend to be energetic and actively involved in their children's lives. They encourage independence and self confidence from an early age nurturing a sense of empowerment in their kids.
- **Teaching Resilience**; Aries parents and family members demonstrate resilience by exemplifying courage when faced with challenges. They impart the belief that setbacks are opportunities for growth and learning experiences.
- **Conflict Resolution**; Although Aries family members may sometimes have tempers, their ability to forgive and move on swiftly contributes to maintaining a happy atmosphere. It is crucial for them to work on communication skills and conflict resolution techniques.
- **Celebrating Achievements;** Aries individuals take pride in acknowledging their families accomplishments and milestones. With enthusiasm they

celebrate birthdays, graduations and other significant achievements making family gatherings truly memorable.

- **Spontaneous Adventures;** Aries family members infuse an element of spontaneity into their shared experiences. They welcome outings and adventures ensuring that family activities remain exciting and dynamic.
- **Supportive and Encouraging**; Aries family members provide unwavering support to their loved ones. They actively encourage family members to pursue their dreams and passions fostering a sense of self belief, within the unit.

Overall, within the dynamics of a family Aries assertiveness and protective nature contribute to creating a sense of security and empowerment among its members. While they may encounter challenges related to independence or conflicts at times. Overall their ability to forgive and move forward ensures the strength of bonds remains intact. Ultimately Aries brings an active presence to family life promoting growth, resilience and a strong sense of individuality, among family members.

CHALLENGES IN FRIENDSHIPS AND FAMILY

Although Aries individuals bring beneficial qualities to their friendships and family relationships they may also encounter certain challenges due to their assertive and dynamic nature. Here are some common difficulties they might face.

- **Spontaneity**; Aries individuals are known for their spontaneous nature. While this can lead to nice experiences it can also result in decisions or actions that may have negative consequences in both friendships and family relationships. Taking a moment to consider the potential outcomes can be beneficial.
- **Assertiveness vs. Aggression**; Sometimes Aries assertiveness can be mistaken for aggression, which could lead to conflicts in both friendships and family dynamics. Learning how to balance their assertiveness with diplomacy and sensitivity can help them avoid misunderstandings.
- **Independence and Personal Space**; Aries values their independence and the need for space. Striking a balance between their desire for freedom and the expectations of relationships can be challenging, particularly if friends or family perceive them as distant or unavailable.
- **Impatience**; Aries individuals often prefer results. As such they may become impatient when things don't go according to plan or meet their expectations. Such impatience can put a strain on relationships both with friends and family, especially if they expect others to keep up with their pace.
- **Resolving Conflicts**; Aries individuals are not afraid to address conflicts. Their direct and sometimes confrontational communication style can be overwhelming, for others. Learning to approach conflicts with patience and empathy can lead to resolutions.
- **Balancing Priorities**; Aries individuals feel a sense of responsibility towards their family. Their active social lives can sometimes make it challenging to find a balance. Managing time effectively is important in order to fulfill family commitments while also nurturing friendships.
- **Competitiveness**; Aries competitive nature, in friendships with Aries or competitive family members can lead to rivalry and tension. Encouraging cooperation and celebrating each other's successes is crucial in maintaining relationships.
- **Stubbornness**; Aries individuals tend to be stubborn when they believe they are right. This stubbornness can result in disagreements and conflicts within familial relationships. Learning to compromise and be open minded towards others perspectives is essential.
- **Forgiveness**; While Aries individuals may get angry quickly they also have the ability to forgive swiftly. However it's important to recognize that not

everyone processes their emotions at the pace as them. Patience and understanding play a role, in resolving conflicts.

- **Burnout**; Aries' boundless energy levels have the potential to lead to exhaustion, which can impact their ability to maintain bonds with friends and family. It is important for them to recognize the value of self care and taking breaks when necessary in order to avoid burning out.

To sum it up, Aries individuals bring enthusiasm, leadership and loyalty into their friendships and family relationships. On the other hand they also face challenges related to acting on impulse and overly asserting themselves. By acknowledging these challenges and focusing on growth and effective communication Aries individuals can cultivate better connections with their loved ones.

In our exploration of "Aries; Friends And Family " we have delved into the dynamics that Aries individuals contribute to their friend circles and familial ties. Their unwavering loyalty, leadership qualities and passionate nature leave an impact on the lives of those they hold dear. However as with any aspect of life there is always room for improvement, maintenance and growth within these relationships. Here are some final tips to enhance, nurture and develop relationships.

ENHANCING RELATIONSHIPS

- **Embrace Patience**; Aries individuals tend to be impulsive and quick, in their actions. To enhance their relationships they can work on slowing down, actively listening to others perspectives and considering the consequences before making decisions.
- **Improve Communication**; Although Aries tends to be direct, honing their communication skills can help them express their thoughts and feelings. Overall this will help in reducing misunderstandings and conflicts.
- **Embrace Flexibility**; Aries enthusiasm, for spontaneity is great. It's equally important to be adaptable to others schedules and preferences. Being flexible promotes interactions.

NURTURING RELATIONSHIPS

- **Quality Time**; Continue prioritizing quality time with friends and family. Regular get-togethers and meaningful conversations will help nurture connections.
- **Consistent Support**; Offering support and encouragement to loved ones ensures that relationships remain nurturing and reliable.

- **Respect Boundaries**; Show respect for others boundaries while also communicating your own. Healthy relationships are built on respect for space and independence.

DEVELOPING RELATIONSHIPS

- **Cultivate Empathy**; Aries individuals can benefit from cultivating empathy. Understanding others' emotions and perspectives fosters deeper connections.
- **Emphasize Cooperation**; Encourage cooperation, then competition in friendships and family dynamics. Collaborating strengthens bonds while minimizing conflicts.
- **Reflect and Learn**; Take time to reflect on interactions and relationships. Learning from both successes and challenges can lead to growth and stronger connections.

To sum up, Aries individuals have the potential to create friendships and maintain family relationships by practicing patience, effective communication and a willingness to adapt. By fostering these relationships with care and commitment Aries individuals will discover that their distinct attributes enrich the lives of their loved ones resulting in lasting and loving ways.

CHAPTER 4: CAREER AND AMBITIONS

This chapter uncovers the ambitious nature of Aries individuals in their financial endeavors. It explores how Aries approaches their career path, goals and the strategies they employ to achieve success. Here we also delve into the strengths and challenges that Aries faces on their journey. From their ability to lead to their inclination for decision making, we examine what sets them apart. Whether you're an Aries seeking an understanding of your career and financial aspirations or a curious reader interested in gaining insights into how Aries thinks about money. This chapter offers an exploration of how Aries pursues success, stability and prosperity.

ARIES CAREER PREFERENCES AND PROFESSIONAL GOALS

Aries individuals are known for being dynamic and ambitious which significantly shapes their career preferences and professional goals. Let's take a look at what drives and motivates them in the world of work.

- **Leadership Roles**; Aries individuals have an inclination towards leadership positions. They gravitate towards careers that allow them to take charge, make decisions and guide others. They thrive when given authority roles such as managers or team leaders.
- **Solutions based**; Thriving in stimulating work environments is where Aries individuals shine. They find their energy through competition problem solving and conquering hurdles. Careers in sales, marketing and entrepreneurship hold an appeal for them. Aries people have a knack for solving problems. In addition they thrive in careers that demand thinking, adaptability and the ability to make decisions under pressure.
- **Independence**; Independence holds value to Aries individuals. They gravitate towards careers that allow them to work independently or grant them the freedom to make decisions and set goals. Pursuing freelancing opportunities consulting roles or venturing into entrepreneurship are paths for them.
- **Entrepreneurship**; The entrepreneurial spirit runs strong in Aries individuals. They embrace risks. Eagerly pursue ideas. Starting their businesses or working in startup environments aligns perfectly with their desire for independence and innovation.

- **Driven**; Being goal oriented is a defining trait of Aries individuals. They set targets for themselves. Tirelessly they work towards achieving them. Careers that offer milestones and avenues for growth hold allure.
- **Adventurous;** Aries adventurous nature often leads them towards professions that involve travel, exploration or physical challenges. Their inclinations draw them towards fields such as adventure sports, travel blogging or outdoor guiding.
- **Competitive**; Competition fuels the fire within Aries individuals, who relish being acknowledged for their accomplishments. Often gravitating towards careers, in sports, entertainment or fields where they can showcase their talents and receive recognition.
- **Continuous Learning**; Aries individuals have a thirst for knowledge and enjoy acquiring new skills. They might pursue careers in technology, research or fields where they can continually expand their expertise.
- **Making a Difference**; Many Aries individuals are driven by the desire to create an impact on the world. They may choose careers in activism, social justice or advocacy to channel their passion for change.

While an Aries individual's career preferences and professional aspirations are influenced by their traits and characteristics it's important to remember that individual personalities vary. Some Aries individuals may find fulfillment in careers aligned with these preferences while others may explore alternative paths. Ultimately Aries determination, energy and leadership skills make them valuable assets in endeavors where they can pave the way and achieve remarkable success.

ARIES STRENGTHS IN THE WORKPLACE

Aries individuals possess a set of strengths and qualities that propel them towards success, in the workplace. Notably, Aries individuals possess an assertive nature that sets them apart as contributors. Let's explore some strengths that contribute to their success, in careers;

- **Leadership Skills**; Aries has a talent for leadership exhibiting confidence and taking charge of situations. Their ability to inspire and guide others proves valuable in leadership positions
- **Proactive Approach**; Aries individuals are known for their nature, always eager to take the initiative rather than waiting for instructions. This quality makes them efficient workers.
- **Unyielding Determination**; Aries is renowned for their determination. Once they set their sights on a goal they pursue it relentlessly often overcoming obstacles through willpower.
- **Fearlessness**; Aries individuals fearlessly embrace risks and challenges. They approach situations with courage. Eagerly seize opportunities that others may shy away from. This fearlessness often leads to innovation and groundbreaking achievements.
- **Competitive Spirit**; Aries thrives on competition viewing challenges as opportunities to demonstrate their abilities and excel. Their competitive drive propels them to consistently improve themselves and surpass expectations.
- **Swift Decision Making**; Aries individuals possess the ability to make decisions under high pressure circumstances. Their decisive nature enables them to navigate situations. The skill of thinking is valuable, in fast paced work environments.
- **Problem Solving Abilities**; Aries demonstrates intellect and problem solving skills. They excel at analyzing issues, identifying solutions and implementing them.
- **Independence**; Aries highly values their independence. Thrives in situations where they can work autonomously. They are self motivated, require supervision and can handle tasks and projects independently.
- **Productive**; Aries individuals possess levels of energy and productivity. They have a drive to efficiently accomplish tasks without getting fatigued.
- **Innovation**; Aries' innovative mindset and willingness to explore ideas contribute significantly to their success. They are open to experimenting with new approaches and finding creative solutions when faced with challenges.

- **Resilience**; Aries individuals quickly bounce back from setbacks. They view failures as opportunities for growth remaining undeterred by career obstacles.
- **Charisma**; Many Aries individuals possess a personality that enables them to communicate effectively and negotiate skillfully. Their ability to influence others makes them valuable in many professions.
- **Passion**; Aries is deeply passionate about their work. Their enthusiasm and dedication inspire both themselves and their colleagues to strive for excellence.
- **Time Management**; Aries individuals are adept at managing their time. They prioritize their tasks. Maintain an approach ensuring that they meet deadlines and achieve their goals.
- **Being a team player**; Although Aries individuals enjoy taking on leadership roles they also excel as team players. Their competitive-spirit drives them to collaborate with others in order to accomplish shared objectives.

These strengths, combined with Aries innate determination and assertiveness make them valuable assets, in the workplace. They thrive in positions that require leadership, innovation and the ability to tackle challenges head on. Aries individuals are highly motivated to achieve success and their dynamic work approach often leads to accomplishments in their careers.

CHALLENGES FACED BY ARIES AND STRATEGIES TO OVERCOME THEM

While Aries individuals possess strengths that can propel them towards career success they also face specific challenges due to their assertive and dynamic nature. Understanding these challenges and implementing strategies to overcome them can result in a fulfilling and well balanced professional life;

Impulsivity

- Challenge; At times Aries individuals may act impulsively by making decisions without considering the potential consequences.
- Strategy; Before making decisions take a moment for reflection. Carefully evaluate all available information. Seek input from trusted colleagues or mentors to ensure an informed choice.

Impatience

- Challenge; Aries impatience can sometimes lead to frustration when they don't see results or when their colleagues work at a pace.

- Strategy; It's important for Aries to practice patience and understand that not all projects or processes will deliver outcomes. Setting expectations and focusing on progress is key.

Conflict Resolution

- Challenge; Aries individuals have a tendency to be direct and confrontational which can create conflicts with their colleagues or superiors.
- Strategy; Developing conflict resolution skills involves listening to others perspectives and finding common ground. Diplomacy and tact are valuable in maintaining working relationships.

Burnout

- Challenge; Aries high energy levels can sometimes lead to burnout if they neglect self care.
- Strategy; Prioritizing self care is essential for Aries. Incorporating breaks, exercise and relaxation techniques into their routine helps recharge their energy levels and sustain long term productivity.

Balancing Independence and Teamwork

- Challenge; While independence is important for Aries they also need to work within teams.
- Strategy; Embracing collaboration is crucial, for Aries. Recognizing the strengths of colleagues and understanding that teamwork often leads to outcomes and personal growth is vital.

Delegation

- Challenge; Delegating tasks may be challenging for Aries as they prefer handling everything themselves.
- Strategy; Aries individuals should consider the benefits of delegation. Trusting others with tasks allows them to focus on responsibilities while fostering a sense of teamwork. Be patient, in advancing your career;

Rushing

- Challenge; Aries strong desire to quickly climb the ladder may lead to frustration if promotions or opportunities do not materialize swiftly as expected.
- Strategy; Establish career objectives. Work steadily towards achieving them. Understand that career growth often requires patience and continuous development of skills.

Embrace diplomacy

- Challenge; Aries straightforwardness may sometimes be perceived as abrupt or confrontational in environments.
- Strategy; Practice the art of diplomacy by choosing your words and considering the impact your communication may have. Foster an atmosphere of respect and cooperation.

Recognize the value of experience

- Challenge; Aries may underestimate the importance of experience becoming overly focused on pursuing challenges.
- Strategy; Acknowledge the wisdom that comes with experience and seek guidance from professionals. By combining enthusiasm with experience you can achieve success.

Maintain a work life balance

- Challenge; Aries dedication to their careers can occasionally disrupt their work life balance.
- Strategy; Prioritize maintaining a work life balance by setting boundaries and making time for family, relaxation and personal interests.

Introspection and awareness ultimately leads to improved performance. By acknowledging and addressing these obstacles individuals born under the zodiac sign Aries can effectively utilize their strengths. As such they can navigate their careers, with success and fulfillment. Overcoming these challenges can result in a sustainable professional journey.

In this chapter we have discovered the dynamic nature of Aries individuals as they pursue their professional goals and financial aspirations. Their unwavering determination, inherent leadership qualities and competitive spirit make them formidable contenders in the realms of career and finance.

We have also explored the difficulties they encounter such as impulsiveness and impatience along with strategies to overcome them. The path that Aries individuals embark upon in terms of their career and finances is characterized by enthusiasm, ambition as a pursuit of personal success both financially and professionally.

As we bring this chapter to a close it becomes evident that individuals born under Aries are fueled by a desire to accomplish their objectives, ascend the career ladder and secure their future. Their dynamic approach coupled with a willingness to adapt and grow, positions them for excellence.

CHAPTER 5: SELF-IMPROVEMENT

With their ambitious nature Aries are always motivated to refine their strengths, address weaknesses and strive for achievements. This chapter delves into the path of self improvement for Aries individuals providing guidance and exercises tailored to their unique personality traits. Whether you're an Aries seeking growth or a curious reader intrigued by the world of the Ram, this chapter guarantees an inspiring exploration of the relentless pursuit of self improvement and excellence.

EMBRACING ARIES STRENGTHS AND OVERCOMING WEAKNESSES

Like every zodiac sign, Aries individuals possess a unique set of strengths and weaknesses. To maximize their potential for success and personal growth Aries can leverage their strengths while working on overcoming weaknesses. Here's a guide on how to accomplish that.

UTILIZING STRENGTHS;

- **Leadership Skills**; Embrace leadership roles, in both personal and professional spheres. Utilize your ability to inspire others and provide guidance to foster change.
- **Taking Initiative**; Keep embracing challenges by taking initiative and actively seeking out projects. Your ability to take initiative and motivate yourself sets you apart and contributes to your success.
- **Determination**; Focus your determination, on setting goals and staying committed to achieving them. Your unwavering dedication is an asset.
- **Fearlessness**; Embrace calculated risks. View them as opportunities for growth and innovation. Your willingness to take risks can lead to breakthroughs.
- **Competitive Spirit**; Use your competitive nature as motivation to set professional benchmarks. Let competition drive you towards self improvement.

OVERCOMING WEAKNESSES

- **Impulsivity**; Practice mindfulness and take a moment to pause before taking action. Developing patience will help you make better decisions.
- **Impatience**; Cultivate patience by setting timelines and understanding that success often takes time and perseverance. Be patient in your career advancement by setting goals and keeping track of your progress. Remember that climbing the career ladder often requires time and experience.
- **Conflict Resolution**; Work on improving your diplomacy skills and actively listening to others during conflicts. Approach disagreements with empathy for seeking common ground.
- **Burnout**; Prioritize self care to prevent burnout. Schedule regular breaks, engage in hobbies. Overall maintain a work life balance.
- **Balancing Independence and Teamwork**; Embrace collaboration with colleagues recognizing their strengths while acknowledging the benefits of teamwork for growth and better outcomes.
- **Delegation**; Learn to trust others capabilities by delegating tasks within your team or organization allowing yourself more time for responsibilities.
- **Practice diplomacy**; Choose your words and consider how they will impact others. Create an atmosphere of respect and collaboration through communication.
- **Recognize the value of experience**; Seek guidance from professionals. Combining enthusiasm with wisdom gained from experience can lead to more success.

- **Set boundaries**; Prioritize maintaining a work life balance by setting boundaries and making time for relaxation, family and personal interests. A balanced life contributes to overall well being and enhanced performance.

By embracing their strengths and actively working on improving their weaknesses Aries individuals can unlock their full potential. Overall they can achieve greater success in both personal and professional domains. Self awareness along with a commitment to growth plays an important role in thriving in all aspects of life.

PERSONAL DEVELOPMENT

Aries individuals are known for their ambition which makes personal growth an essential part of their journey. To evolve and flourish Aries can focus on areas of self improvement while harnessing their strengths. Here's a personalized guide to help Aries individuals grow.

- **Self Reflection**; Take the time to reflect on yourself and gain an understanding of your strengths, weaknesses and motivations. Having self awareness is crucial for growth and development.
- **Cultivating Patience**; Develop patience by practicing mindfulness and recognizing that not everything happens instantly. Embracing patience allows you to make better decisions and effectively navigate challenges.

- **Emotional Understanding**; Nurture your intelligence by listening to others. Empathize with their feelings and understand the impact your words and actions have on those around you.
- **Resolving Conflicts**; Work on your skills. Learn effective conflict resolution strategies. Address conflicts with empathy, patience and the intention of finding solutions.
- **Effective Time Management;** Improve your time management skills to maintain a balance in your lifestyle. Prioritize. Allocate time for work, personal life and self care to avoid burnout.
- **Fostering Empathy**; Cultivate empathy as it helps you better understand others and connect with them on a level. Individuals who are empathetic often have happier relationships and can inspire others more effectively.
- **Embracing Collaboration**; Recognize the value of collaboration and teamwork by embracing the input of others in generating insights and ideas. Balancing independence with collaboration leads to improved outcomes.
- **Lead with Compassion;** Apply your leadership skills with compassion and empathy taking into consideration the needs and emotions of others. Guide them on their journeys.

By dedicating yourself to growth and development in these aspects individuals born under the sign of Aries can tap into their strengths and become even more dynamic, understanding and successful human beings. Remember that personal growth is a process and every step you take contributes to a meaningful and purposeful life.

To recap, in this chapter we have delved into the path of growth that defines individuals born under the sign of Aries. With their determination, natural leadership qualities and ambitious nature Aries individuals possess huge potential for self improvement.

Throughout this chapter we have discussed a variety of exercises and practices tailored specifically to address both the strengths and challenges to Aries. These include techniques, strategies and exercises. By embracing these, Aries individuals can fully utilize their qualities while also addressing areas that may require further development.

The future holds endless possibilities for individuals born under the sign of Aries.

Their unwavering pursuit of excellence coupled with their dedication to self improvement positions them for a future marked by accomplishment, satisfaction and personal development. As they further refine their leadership abilities, foster connections with others and navigate challenges with skillfulness, they have the potential to unlock their fullest capabilities. In turn they can make a lasting impact on the world around them.

Ultimately, the journey of self improvement is an endless adventure and Aries individuals possess the qualities to embark on this path with eagerness, resilience and a vibrant spirit. As they continue to grow and evolve they are bound to inspire those in their presence and attain lasting success.

CHAPTER 6:
ARIES IN THE YEAR AHEAD

Welcome to a fresh new chapter! Here we will delve into how the celestial forces will shape the experiences, aspirations and obstacles that Aries individuals may encounter in the year ahead. Known for their assertive nature as the sign of the zodiac Aries is always ready to embrace new adventures and face challenges head on. Within this chapter we will dive into the influence of events on Aries love life, career path, financial matters, health, personal growth and much more. By highlighting dates and time periods of importance our aim is to provide insights and guidance that will assist you in navigating through these currents.

The year ahead presents a tapestry woven with opportunities for growth, self reflection and transformation. So buckle up for this celestial journey to uncover what lies ahead for you under the stars in the coming year.

HOROSCOPE GUIDE FOR ARIES

The year ahead has much in store for Aries. Here is a closer look of what to expect.

- **January - March (Aries Season);** The year starts off with your season Aries! It's a time to set goals and take the lead, in all aspects of life. Focus on your aspirations. You'll see your determination bear fruit.
- **April - June;** During this period relationships and partnerships become important. Be open to collaborating and finding common ground. Balancing assertiveness with diplomacy will be key.
- **July - September;** Mid year brings many opportunities for career growth and recognition. Your leadership abilities will flourish. You may receive deserved praise or even promotions.
- **October - December;** As the year comes to a close it's a moment to reflect on your objectives. Pay attention to budgeting and term financial planning for securing your future.

KEY THEMES FOR THE YEAR

- **Career Advancement**; This year presents opportunities for reaching new heights in your journey through ambition and determination. Embrace leadership roles, set goals and seize growth prospects.
- **Relationship Dynamics**; Give importance to both professional relationships. Strive for a balance between assertiveness and empathy while seeking connections.
- **Financial Planning**; Take a look at your finances. Consider long term goals as you plan ahead. Responsible management of your finances and making investments will pave the way for a prosperous financial future.
- **Personal Growth**; Keep nurturing your growth and development. Cultivate patience, practice mindfulness and work on improving your skills in diplomacy and conflict resolution.
- **Exploration**; Fulfill your spirit by exploring horizons be it through travel learning new things or pursuing exciting hobbies.
- **Health and Wellbeing**; Make self care a priority. Maintain a balance between work and personal life. Regular exercise, relaxation techniques and a balanced diet are crucial for your well being.
- **Creativity and Innovation**; Allow your creativity to flow freely this year. Channel that energy into projects or ventures that showcase your talents.
- **Family and Home**; Strengthen the bonds with your family members while creating a nurturing home environment. Your leadership qualities can serve as a source of support and inspiration for your loved ones.

- **Networking and Connections**; Expand your network by connecting with new and old connections. New friendships or partnerships may open up opportunities for you.

Remember that astrology provides guidance but doesn't determine your destiny entirely. Your choices and actions play a role in shaping the course of your life.

Embrace the opportunities and challenges that come your way with confidence and enthusiasm and you'll make the most of your year Aries!

ASTROLOGICAL INFLUENCES ON ARIES

Throughout the year Aries individuals, who are known for their assertive nature will be influenced by notable astrology events. These celestial happenings can shape their experiences, moods and opportunities. Here are some important astrological events and how they may impact Aries.

- **Aries Season (March 21. April 19);** During the period when the sun moves through your sign in the Aries season your energy and motivation reach their peak. It's a time for rejuvenation, self exploration and setting goals for the year.
- **Venus in Aries (February 20 to March 16) ;** When Venus, the planet associated with love and relationships transits through Aries it gives a boost to your life as well as social interactions. You may feel more assertive in pursuing your desires and forming connections.
- **Mars Retrograde (periodic) ;** Mars is considered your ruling planet so its retrogrades can have an impact on you. During Mars retrograde periods you might experience a decrease in energy levels and assertiveness compared to times. This is an opportunity for reflection and practicing patience.
- **Full Moon (monthly);** Every month when the full moon appears it can bring about new emotions. It will shed light on your relationships and personal life. It's a moment to let go of what does not serve you and make adjustments, in different aspects of your life.
- **Arrival of a New Moon (monthly);** The arrival of a new moon each month signifies starts and opportunities to set intentions. As an Aries individual you can use these moments to initiate projects, embark on ventures or make changes in your life.
- **Mercury Retrograde (periodic) ;** Periodically during Mercury retrograde phases be cautious about communication and travel. It's advisable for Aries individuals to double check plans. Exercise care in their interactions during these periods to avoid misunderstandings.

- **Jupiter and Saturn (periodic);** Throughout the year pay attention to the movements of Jupiter and Saturn as they traverse zodiac signs. These transitions can have an impact on your long term goals and personal growth. They may present opportunities for expansion as discipline.
- **Eclipses (periodic);** The times of year when eclipses occur signify shifts in your life and will alter your perspective on things. Be prepared for events that may arise during these times and be open to uncovering truths about yourself or situations around you.
- **Retrograde of other Planets (periodic);** At times throughout the year keep an eye out for retrograde planets like Venus, Mars or Jupiter. These planetary retrogrades might prompt you to reassess relationships, career choices or personal beliefs that are important to you.
- **Solar and Lunar Eclipses (Twice a Year);** Aries individuals may experience noticeable effects during lunar and solar eclipses. These celestial events have the potential to bring about moments that motivate them to take action or make life decisions.

In conclusion Aries individuals are renowned for their dynamic personality traits. Being the sign of the zodiac they embody the essence of beginnings and fresh starts. Aries people are driven, enthusiastic and always prepared to embrace challenges. Their fearless approach to life often leads them to accomplishments and triumphs.

Remember that it's important to understand that astrology provides guidance and insights. Ultimately our actions and choices shape our destiny. Aries individuals can utilize celestial events, as tools, for self awareness and personal growth adapting to the changing energies in order to lead fulfilling and purposeful lives.

Looking ahead to the upcoming year, Aries individuals can utilize their energy and determination to pursue their goals and aspirations. This may involve setting intentions, refining their leadership abilities and directing their spirit towards positive endeavors. It is also crucial for Aries individuals to nurture their relationships as sometimes their spirited nature can lead to conflicts.

Overall the year ahead is a time for reaching new levels of success, while inspiring those around them with their fearlessness and adventurous spirit. Of course we wish you the very best

CHAPTER 7:
FAMOUS ARIES PERSONALITIES

In this chapter we embark on a journey exploring the lives and accomplishments of some of the world's most famous individuals who were born under the zodiac sign of Aries. Aries individuals are well known for their assertive nature, which often drives them to achieve greatness. From actors and musicians, to leaders and visionaries, personalities born under the Aries sign have made significant contributions to the world. Their legacies continue to inspire us and shape our world.

As we delve into the stories of these Aries individuals we will explore their concise biographies and distinctive Aries traits that define their impact. Join us as we celebrate the spirit and accomplishments of these individuals born under the sign of Aries.

CHARLIE CHAPLIN

- Date of Birth; April 16 1889.
- Brief Biography; Charlie Chaplin was a legend in silent films who gained worldwide recognition for his comedic brilliance and unforgettable character. He achieved fame through his groundbreaking contributions to cinema by revolutionizing storytelling through films.
- Aries Traits; Assertive and creative.

- Impact; Chaplins legacy lives on as a trailblazer, in the realm of film comedy. He is a revered cultural icon.
- Personal Life; Chaplin led a life marked by multiple marriages and controversies. However he left an enduring imprint on the entertainment industry.

DIANA ROSS

- Date of Birth; March 26 1944.
- Brief Biography; Diana Ross is an singer, actress and record producer renowned for her powerhouse voice and contributions to Motown. Through her role as the vocalist of The Supremes and her successful solo career she has achieved many chart topping hits.
- Aries Traits; Energetic and determined.
- Impact; Diana Ross holds influence in the music industry as an embodiment of empowerment.
- Personal Life; Ross enjoys a fulfilling family life alongside a career that spans decades.

ROBERT DOWNEY JR.

- Date of Birth; April 4 1965.
- Brief Biography; Robert Downey Jr. Is an actor acclaimed for his versatility in roles and exceptional talent. He garnered worldwide acclaim for his portrayal of Tony Stark/Iron Man, in the Marvel Cinematic Universe.
- Aries Traits; Charismatic, adventurous and creative.
- Impact; Downeys performances have made a lasting impression on film leaving a significant mark.
- Personal Life; In his personal life he has overcome many challenges and is well known for his philanthropic endeavors.

LUCY LAWLESS

- Date of Birth; March 29 1968.
- Brief Biography; Lucy Lawless is an actress and singer from New Zealand. She is most famous for her portrayal of Xena in the television series "Xena; Warrior Princess."
- Aries Traits; Fearlessness, determination and charisma.
- Impact; Lawless has become a symbol of empowerment. She has paved the way for the inclusion of powerful women characters in the entertainment industry.

- Personal Life; In her personal life she continues to act while also advocating for social and environmental causes.

THOMAS JEFFERSON

- Date of Birth; April 13 1743.
- Brief Biography; Thomas Jefferson was one of America's Founding Fathers serving as the author of the Declaration of Independence and later becoming the nation's President.
- Aries Traits; Intellectuality, visionary thinking and determination.
- Impact; Jefferson's legacy includes expanding the nation through the Louisiana Purchase while strongly championing liberties.
- Personal Life; Thomas Jefferson had personal interests in architecture, science and farming.

MARIAH CAREY

- Date of Birth; March 27 1969.
- Brief Biography; Mariah Carey is a singer, songwriter and actress who is widely recognized for her extraordinary vocal range. Throughout her career she has produced chart topping hits and solidified herself as one of the most influential female artists in the music industry.
- Aries Traits; Known for being creative, ambitious and independent.
- Impact; Mariah Carey's musical contributions have left an indelible mark on the industry. Her vocal prowess is highly acclaimed by critics and fans. Additionally she has won numerous Grammy Awards.
- Personal Life; She has found fulfillment in her personal life with a loving family.

ERIC CLAPTON

- Date of Birth; March 30 1945.
- Brief Biography; Eric Clapton is a guitarist, singer and songwriter celebrated for his exceptional skills on the guitar. With a legendary status in rock music history he has played with influential bands like The Yardbirds and Cream before establishing himself as a successful solo artist.
- Aries Traits; Recognized as determined, passionate and innovative.
- Impact; Eric Clapton's mastery of the guitar has permeated generations of musicians. He is widely regarded as one of the greatest guitarists of all time due to his influence on the genre.

- Personal Life; Eric Clapton has led a life, marked by his musical achievements, as a highly regarded guitarist and songwriter. However he has also faced challenges such as addiction and turbulent relationships. In addition he has been active in philanthropy.

LADY GAGA

- Date of Birth; March 28 1986.
- Brief Biography; Lady Gaga, whose real name is Stefani Joanne Angelina is a singer, actress and songwriter known for her unique style and popular music. Throughout her career she has received numerous awards and recognition for her contributions to pop culture.
- Aries Traits; Known for her bold and pioneering spirit, as well as her confidence, creativity, and determination.
- Impact; Lady Gaga is also an advocate for self expression and inclusivity.
- Personal Life; Lady Gaga's personal life is defined by her career as a singer, actress and activist.

ELTON JOHN

- Date of Birth; March 25 1947.
- Brief Biography; Elton John is a singer songwriter, pianist and composer renowned for his music and flamboyant stage presence. His illustrious career spans decades of timeless hits and multiple accolades that have solidified his status as a music legend. In addition to his achievements
- Aries Traits; Elton John possesses Aries qualities such as ambition, creativity and a captivating stage presence. These attributes have greatly influenced his music career and philanthropic endeavors.
- Impact; Elton John has made contributions to the LGBTQ+ community through both his artistry and philanthropic endeavors.
- Personal Life; Elton John's had struggles with addiction and mental health. He is notable for his philanthropy.

J. P. MORGAN

- Date of Birth; Born on April 17 1837.
- Brief Biography; J. P. Morgan was a financier, banker and philanthropist who played an important role in shaping the financial system of the United States.
- Aries Traits; determined and strategic.

- Impact; Morgans influence in finance and industry had a major effect on the growth of the United States.
- Personal Life; He was widely recognized both in the world and American society as a pioneer of finance.

MARIA SHARAPOVA

- Date of Birth; Born on April 19 1987.
- Brief Biography; Maria Sharapova is a retired tennis player who achieved prominence as one of the top athletes in her sport. She secured Grand Slam titles and gained a reputation for her fierce competitive spirit.
- Aries Traits; Competitive, determined and confident.
- Impact; Sharapova's success and international recognition significantly contributed to the rise in popularity of women's tennis.
- Personal Life; Following her tennis career she ventured into business pursuits.

ARETHA FRANKLIN

- Date of Birth; Born on March 25 1942.
- Brief Biography; A Musical Legend, Aretha Franklin was a singer, songwriter and pianist who earned the title of "Queen of Soul." Throughout her career she captivated audiences with her iconic voice and unforgettable songs.
- Aries Traits; Aretha Franklin, showcased Aries qualities of determination, confidence and a strong pioneering spirit.
- Impact; Her talent and passion led to awards and accolades solidifying her status as a legend in the music industry. She also actively participated in causes making contributions to the civil rights movement.
- Personal Life; Aretha Franklin actively participated in the civil rights movement. Unfortunately she faced health challenges, including diabetes before her passing in 2018.

In summary, this chapter explored how individuals born under this zodiac sign have left a legacy in the world. Their determination, creativity and unwavering passion have propelled them to greatness in fields. As we conclude our exploration of these Aries figures across entertainment, politics, sports and more; it is evident that they have not influenced our culture but also inspired generations with their unique journeys. Their unwavering determination and fearless approach to challenges have not only propelled them towards success. It has also created a lasting impact that continues to influence and inspire many more people.

As we acknowledge the achievements of these individuals born under the Aries zodiac sign, let their stories remind us of the qualities associated with this sign. Bravery, leadership and an unwavering pursuit of their dreams. These traits possess the potential to lead to accomplishments and contribute to change in our world.

Whether you share the Aries sign or simply appreciate the resilience and creativity of these individuals, their journeys ignite within you a pursuit of your own aspirations leaving an indelible mark on the fabric of life. As we bid farewell to this chapter let us carry the spirit of Aries with us as we face our own challenges, with determination and boundless enthusiasm.

CONCLUSION

We have reached the conclusion of our journey across Aries. Let us now take a moment to revisit the points we've discussed throughout this book. We want to appreciate the qualities of Aries individuals and offer them encouragement to embrace their traits. Before that let's summarize what we've learned about Aries.

Aries being the sign of the zodiac is known for its courage, assertiveness and unwavering pursuit of goals. Throughout this book we have uncovered the origins, history and mythology of Aries in various cultures. We have explored how they approach love, friendships and family dynamics. We have also delved into their career aspirations and personal growth while catching a glimpse into what lies ahead for them in the year. Additionally we have celebrated personalities who were born under the sign of Aries and left an impact on the world.

As we bring this book to a close it's time to wrap up everything we've covered and provide a sense of completion. We have journeyed through chapters each offering a perspective on the multifaceted nature of individuals born under Aries;

- **In Chapter 1** we traced back Aries through history and mythology unearthing ancient tales and beliefs associated with this sign.
- **In Chapter 2** we explored how Aries approaches love by providing insights into their compatibility and relationships.
- **In Chapter 3** we explored the dynamics of Aries when it comes to friendships and family, thereby providing guidance on how to nurture these connections.
- **In Chapter 4** we delved into Aries career preferences, strengths and challenges offering insights into their goals.
- **In Chapter 5** our focus shifted to Aries journey of self improvement. We provided exercises and guidance for personal growth and development.
- **In Chapter 6** we provided a glimpse into what the upcoming year ahead holds for Aries. We discussed key events and their potential impact.
- **In Chapter 7** we celebrated personalities who shared the Aries sign and explored their lasting legacies.

Our aim throughout these pages has been to honor the qualities of Aries individuals, inspire self awareness and offer insights into their multifaceted nature. We promised a guide to all aspects of Aries. From their origins to their love life family dynamics, career aspirations, personal growth journeys and encounters with astrological influences. If there's one thing we want you as a reader to take away from this book is this; Embrace your Aries spirit, with confidence and authenticity. Recognize that your assertiveness, passion and fearlessness are assets as you navigate through life.

The Aries zodiac sign, with its complexities, plays an important role in the vast tapestry of the universe. By understanding your qualities and embracing the spirit of Aries you can effectively navigate life's obstacles and achieve success in your endeavors. In conclusion it is important to keep in mind that astrology serves as a tool for self discovery and personal development. Ultimately the actions and decisions you take will shape your life.

We sincerely appreciate your participation in this journey alongside us. As you move forward may the knowledge gained from these pages continue to provide guidance while the celestial stars above illuminate your path towards an fulfilling life. May your cosmic expedition be filled with moments of discovery, personal growth and an enhanced connection to the universe surrounding us. Best wishes to you, Aries!

TAURUS:

A COMPLETE GUIDE TO THE TAURUS ASTROLOGY STAR SIGN

Contents

INTRODUCTION 1
Overview the Taurus Zodiac Sign 2
CHAPTER 1: HISTORY AND MYTHOLOGY 4
Earliest Observations of Taurus 4
Notable Historical Events under "Taurus" 6
CHAPTER 2: LOVE & COMPATIBILITY 9
Love language of Taurus 10
Compatibility between Taurus and other zodiac signs 11
Relationships with Taurus Individuals 13
CHAPTER 3: FRIENDS AND FAMILY 16
Taurus as a friend 17
Family 18
Challenges in Relationships with Family and Friends 19
CHAPTER 4: CAREER AND AMBITIONS 22
Career Aspirations 23
Strengths that make Taurus individuals stand out in the workplace 24
Common career challenges with strategies to overcome them 25
CHAPTER 5: SELF-IMPROVEMENT 28
Embracing Taurus Strengths and Overcoming Weaknesses 29
CHAPTER 6: THE YEAR AHEAD 33
Horoscope Guide for Taurus 33
Key Themes for the Year 34
Astrological Influences 35
Key Areas of Consideration 36

CHAPTER 7: FAMOUS "TAURUS" PERSONALITIES ---------- 39
Elizabeth II 39
Barbra Streisand 39
Audrey Hepburn 40
Melania Trump 40
Adele 41
Cher 41
William Shakespeare 41
Stevie Wonder 42
George Clooney 42
Pope John Paul II (Karol Józef Wojtyła) 42
Mustafa Kemal Atatürk 43
Mark Zuckerberg 43

CONCLUSION ---------- 45

INTRODUCTION

Throughout history, humans have always looked up at the night sky with a sense of wonder and curiosity. For centuries astrology has been a trusted companion, offering insights into our personalities, relationships and the mysteries of life. At its essence astrology is based on the belief that celestial bodies like planets and stars have an influence on affairs and natural phenomena through their positions and movements.

The zodiac acts as a map of astrology consisting of twelve signs that provide a framework for understanding the distinct qualities and tendencies associated with individuals born under each sign. Each astrological sign possesses its own characteristics, strengths and obstacles. Astrologers use the study of these signs to provide guidance and promote self awareness. Astrology serves as a tool in navigating the landscapes of life, relationships and personal development.

In this book we embark on an exploration of one constellation within the zodiac; Taurus. As we delve into the realm of astrology and explore the Taurus sign we'll uncover a wealth of knowledge spanning history, mythology, psychology, personal development and much more. Our exploration will encompass understanding the personalities, strengths and challenges that define those born under this sign. By gaining insights into Taurus individuals both within ourselves and in our relationships we can foster a complete understanding.

Whether you are a follower of astrology or simply curious about it, our journey through the realm of Taurus promises to be both enlightening and enriching. This book aspires to equip you with knowledge that empowers self awareness while cultivating an appreciation for how cosmic influences shape our existence. As we embark on this journey together let us open our minds and hearts to the realm of Taurus that lies ahead.

OVERVIEW THE TAURUS ZODIAC SIGN

- **Date**; Taurus season starts from April 20th and extends until May 20th, marking a time of the year where the spring is in full bloom in the northern hemisphere. It is a time when the earth starts to show its bountifulness, symbolizing the Taurus traits of growth and stability.
- **Symbol**; The Bull, representing Taurus, symbolizes strength, tenacity, and a grounded nature.
- **Element**; As an Earth sign, Taurus is deeply connected to the physical world and material things. This element represents solidity, stability, and practicality.
- **Planet**; Ruled by Venus, the planet of love, beauty, and money. Taurus individuals often have an appreciation for art, aesthetics, and the pleasures of the senses..
- **Color**; Green, symbolizing growth, harmony and the beauty of the world. It also reflects their connection to the earth's abundance.
- **Traits**; Taurus, is often associated with stability, practicality and a strong connection to the world. Individuals born under this sign are recognized for their determination and resolute nature.

STRENGTHS

- **Reliability**; Taureans are renowned for their reliability and they can be relied upon to honor their commitments.
- **Determination**; Once a Taurus sets their sights on a goal they pursue it with determination.
- **Practicality**; Taurus possess a sense of practicality and approaches life's challenges with grounded perspectives.
- **Sensuality**; Being ruled by Venus, the planet of love and beauty, Taureans often have an appreciation for life's pleasures and aesthetic delights.
- **Loyalty**; Taureans have a sense of loyalty, towards their friends and loved ones forming lasting bonds.

WEAKNESSES

- **Stubbornness**; Taurus individuals can be quite stubborn and resistant to change often preferring the comfort of what they know.
- **Possessiveness**; They may tend to be possessive in relationships valuing security and stability in their connections.

- **Materialism**; Their affection for the material world can sometimes lean towards materialism placing importance on possessions.
- **Resistance to Change**; Taurus individuals can be hesitant when it comes to embracing change, which might result in missed opportunities for growth.
- **Indulgence**; Their sensual nature can occasionally lead them to overindulge in food, luxury or other pleasures.
- **Compatibility**; Taurus is known to have compatibility with earth signs like Virgo and Capricorn as well as water signs such as Cancer, Scorpio and Pisces. These signs often share values and priorities in relationships and life.

In essence individuals born under Taurus are characterized by stability and practicality. They bring reliability and determination to their endeavors while being driven by a rooted desire for security and sensuality.

In the beginning of our exploration, into the Taurus zodiac sign we set off on an adventure through the realm of astrology, where it is believed that the positions of celestial bodies have an impact on human affairs. We discovered that Taurus, represented by the steadfast bull, holds a unique position in this tapestry. Now we will delve further into the realm of Taurus in an attempt to unlock its secrets and unravel its mysteries. Our journey will transport us across time and cultures as we explore the origins and mythical tales surrounding Taurus. We will also delve into the personalities, strengths and weaknesses exhibited by those born under this sign. By doing so, we aim to offer insights into both Taurus individuals who are part of our lives and our own self discovery. Our goal is to empower you with knowledge, self awareness and a profound appreciation for the influences that shape our existence. So dear reader join us as we turn the pages and delve deeper into the world of Taurus.

CHAPTER 1: HISTORY AND MYTHOLOGY

In the realm of astrology each zodiac sign carries a tapestry of history, mythology and symbolism. Among these entities Taurus, symbolized by the steadfast bull stands strong. In this chapter we embark on a journey, through time and culture to explore the narratives and mythological tales that surround the Taurus sign.

Taurus has inspired humanity for centuries as it occupies a prominent position in the zodiac. From ancient civilizations like Mesopotamia and Egypt to the worlds of Greece and Rome, the bull has always held great significance in our collective imagination.

As we dive into the history and mythology surrounding Taurus we will uncover stories about seduction, seasonal changes and the profound connection between phenomena and earthly affairs. We will explore how ancient civilizations interpreted Taurus mythologically while reflecting on how this celestial entity shaped their beliefs and practices.

Furthermore our exploration will include an examination of how perceptions and understandings of Taurus have evolved over time. The transition, from interpreting Taurus through mythology to gaining personal insights has expanded our understanding of this constellation. Without further ado, join us on a journey through time as we delve into the enduring impact of Taurus in history and mythology.

EARLIEST OBSERVATIONS OF TAURUS

Dating back thousands of years, ancient civilizations such as the Mesopotamians, Egyptians and Greeks recorded their observations of the Taurus constellation. These ancient cultures gazed at the night sky and identified patterns among the stars while attributing cultural significance to them.

MESOPOTAMIA

Considered by many as the cradle of civilization, Mesopotamia associated the Taurus constellation with Marduk, their god. In star maps, the mighty deity was often portrayed as a divine bull. This representation symbolized strength and fertility. Moreover the positioning of this constellation in the night sky played an important role in agriculture and calendars. Its appearance marked the arrival of spring. A time for sowing seeds and beginning cycles.

ANCIENT GREECE

The Ancient Greeks assimilated elements of Egyptian astronomy into their understanding of the night sky. In Greek Mythology Taurus is closely linked to the tale of Europa and the Bull. According to this myth Europa, a princess from Phoenicia encountered a bull while picking flowers near the sea. Unbeknownst to her this bull was none other than Zeus himself disguised as a creature. Europa was captivated by the nature of the bull so she decided to climb onto its back. Taking advantage of the opportunity Zeus swiftly whisked her away, to Crete, an island filled with enchantment and mystery. This ancient myth holds symbolism exploring themes of abduction, transformation and the divine essence found within the Taurus constellation. It highlights how the bull represents power and sensuality, Zeus attempt to seduce Europa.

ANCIENT EGYPT

In Ancient Egypt, the Taurus constellation was linked to Hathor, their goddess who was often depicted with cow horns. Hathor personified love, music, fertility and motherhood. The presence of Taurus in the sky correlated with events like flooding of the Nile River. This was an important event for agriculture and civilization. Its connection reinforced the bulls association with abundance and prosperity.

MODERN ASTROLOGY

The Taurus constellation contains objects such as the Hyades star cluster and the Pleiades star cluster, which continue to captivate astronomers and stargazers alike. To sum up, the Taurus constellation boasts a diverse history that traces back to ancient civilizations observations and interpretations. Over time it has been linked with fertility, mythology and seasonal changes contributing to humanity's tapestry and our ongoing fascination with the wonders of the night sky.

Throughout mythologies Taurus, represented by the bull, encompasses a multitude of symbolic meanings such, as strength, fertility, sensuality and transformation. This constellation holds importance as it served as a marker for seasonal events due to its prominent position in the night sky. While specific myths and interpretations varied among cultures Taurus remained a celestial entity that influenced the beliefs and practices of these ancient civilizations.

The perception and understanding of Taurus has undergone significant changes throughout history. In ancient civilizations Taurus was often associated with concepts like fertility, agriculture and the cyclical nature of seasons. In modern astrology there has been a transition away from relying on mythological interpretations of zodiac signs, towards incorporating psychological insights into personality analysis. Taurus is now frequently linked to personality traits such as determination, stability and an appreciation for life.

NOTABLE HISTORICAL EVENTS UNDER "TAURUS"

Throughout history various significant events have occurred during the period associated with Taurus. It is important to note that astrology lacks proof; however some individuals believe that celestial alignments may influence affairs. During the Taurus season some notable events took place, each with its potential astrological significance.

- **The Signing of the United States Declaration of Independence (May 1776)**; The signing of the Declaration of Independence occurred during the Taurus season. This document holds importance as it symbolizes determination and resilience. Both are known traits of Taurus.
- **The End of World War II in Europe (May 1945);** The surrender of Nazi Germany coincided with the Taurus season marking the conclusion of World War II in Europe. This event can be seen as a transition towards a peaceful era aligning with the stability often linked to Taurus.
- **Apollo 11 Moon Landing (May 1969)**; Neil Armstrong and Buzz Aldrin's historic moon landing happened during the Taurus season. This remarkable achievement showcased beauty and aesthetics which are connected to Venus, the ruling planet of Taurus.

Additionally there have been notable historical figures born under the sign of Taurus. While astrology cannot definitively explain their impact, some believe that certain personality traits attributed to Taurus may have contributed to their success.

- **William Shakespeare (April 23 1564)**; This renowned playwright and poet is widely regarded as one of the most famous writers ever. His works have had a lasting impact on literature and culture.

- **Karl Marx (May 5 1818)**; Known as a philosopher and political theorist Marx's ideas have profoundly influenced political thought through Marxism.

For those who want to delve further into the historical and mythological aspects of Taurus, below is a list of primary sources, ancient texts and contemporary writings.

Ancient Texts and Sources;

- **"The Epic of Gilgamesh"**- An ancient Mesopotamian epic that explores celestial events of significance including the prominent role played by the constellation Taurus.
- **"Metamorphoses"** by Ovid - A Roman narrative poem that includes the captivating myth of Europa and the Bull. This tale significantly contributes to our understanding of Taurus.
- "The Pyramid Texts". - An Ancient Egyptian religious text discovered within the pyramids that mentions Taurus.

Modern Writings on Astrology and Taurus;

- **"The Only Astrology Book You'll Ever Need"** by Joanna Martine Woolfolk. A comprehensive work that provides insights into Taurus personalities and astrological interpretations.
- **"The Secret Language of Birthdays"** by Gary Goldschneider and Joost Elffers. A resource offering personality profiles, for each zodiac sign, including a rich exploration of Taurus.

CHAPTER 2: LOVE & COMPATIBILITY

In the world of astrology the Taurus zodiac sign is known for its blend of sensuality, loyalty and unwavering determination. Nowhere do these traits shine brighter, than in matters of the heart. In this chapter we embark on an exploration of how Taurus approaches love and compatibility with other signs of the zodiac.

Love, which is universally understood as the language of the heart, takes on a unique flavor when experienced by individuals born under the Taurus sign. Their steadfast commitment, kind nature and appreciation for life weaves together to form a unique tapestry of love. As we delve into the world of Taurus individuals we will explore their unwavering loyalty in matters of love.

Furthermore we will venture into the intricacies of how Taurus pairs up with other zodiac signs by examining their challenges faced together. In addition to the potential strengths that arise when these celestial energies intertwine. Whether you're a Taurus looking to understand your tendencies or someone curious about the Taurus in your life this chapter offers an exploration of love and compatibility.

LOVE LANGUAGE OF TAURUS

The way Taurus approaches love and romance is characterized by an appreciation for sensuality, loyalty and a strong desire for stability in relationships. Taurus individuals embrace love with genuine intentions and practicality. Here is more on how Taurus approaches love.

- **Stability and Security;** Stability and security hold high value, for individuals born under the sign of Taurus when it comes to relationships. They seek partners who can provide them with a sense of safety and dependability. Once they commit to a relationship they are typically committed for the long term. As such they are willing to invest time and effort into making it thrive.
- **Sensuality and Passion**; Taurus individuals, ruled by Venus, the planet associated with love and beauty possess an inclination towards sensuality and physical pleasures. They often express their affection through touch. Romance holds a significance for Taurus individuals as it captivates all of their senses.
- **Loyalty and Devotion**; Known for their loyalty Taurus individuals exhibit unwavering commitment once they fall in love. They become partners who are willing to go to great lengths to support and safeguard their loved ones.
- **Practicality in Love**; When it comes to matters of the heart Taurus individuals approach love with practicality. They don't rush into relationships. Rather they take their time to evaluate the compatibility with potential partners and examine the long term prospects of the relationship.
- **Material Comfort**; The connection Taurus has with the material world sometimes translates into a desire for creature comforts. They appreciate gifts as tokens of affection. Often they enjoy sharing these delights with their partners. However it's important to note that their inclination towards materialism is often driven by creating a cozy environment for their loved ones.
- **Conflict Avoidance**; In relationships Taurus individuals tend to steer clear of conflict or unnecessary drama. They have a preference for maintaining harmony and peace. They possess the skill to find compromises and solutions when disagreements arise. However their occasional stubbornness can lead to prolonged disagreements if their core values are challenged.

In summary Taurus individuals approach love and romance with a focus on stability, sensuality, loyalty and practicality. As such they seek partners who can offer security and create a sense of home. Although they may be cautious in matters of love, once they commit to someone they wholeheartedly invest themselves in building enduring and fulfilling relationships based on trust, comfort and deep emotional connections with their partners.

COMPATIBILITY BETWEEN TAURUS AND OTHER ZODIAC SIGNS

TAURUS AND ARIES

These two signs exhibit notable differences. Taurus is known for being patient and valuing stability. Aries tends to be adventurous and values independence. Taurus might perceive Aries as hasty or impulsive. Aries may view Taurus as boring. However if both partners can recognize each other's strengths they can find common ground. Communicating effectively their differences, they can actually work together in a complementary way.

TAURUS AND TAURUS

Of course these two have key similarities such as a shared love for stability, sensuality and material comforts. They both highly value loyalty and are partners who create a strong bond. However their stubbornness might occasionally cause conflicts because they both resist change. In such situations, patience and understanding become crucial in resolving any disputes that arise.

TAURUS AND GEMINI

Taurus individuals tend to be grounded and practical in their approach to life and relationships. On the other hand Geminis are known for being curious and adaptable. This fundamental difference might make it challenging for Taurus to deal with Gemini's unpredictability or need for variety. Meanwhile Gemini may perceive Taurus as too focused on routines. A successful relationship between these signs requires compromise from both sides along with an appreciation of each other's qualities.

TAURUS AND CANCER

This is considered a strong pairing due to their shared values of emotional connection, family bonds and security. Taurus brings stability along with practicality to the relationship. Cancer offers depth well as nurturing qualities. Together they create a foundation based on understanding. Their shared desire for a secure home life can foster a long lasting relationship.

TAURUS AND LEO

Taurus and Leo have varying approaches to life and love. Taurus seeks stability and security while Leo craves attention and admiration. Taurus might feel overwhelmed by Leo's need for the spotlight. Leo might perceive Taurus as overly cautious. Building a successful relationship would involve finding a balance between meeting Leo's need for recognition and fulfilling Taurus' desire for stability.

TAURUS AND VIRGO

This pairing is highly compatible as both signs share a nature of practicality and a fondness for paying attention to details. Taurus appreciates Virgo's mindset and nurturing qualities while Virgo admires Tauruss reliability and stability. Their shared values along with their dedication to each other can result in a bond that stands the test of time.

TAURUS AND LIBRA

There are some noticeable differences between Taurus and Libra. Taurus values practicality and stability. Libra emphasizes harmony and fairness. Taurus may perceive Libra as indecisive while Libra might see Taurus as rigid. Open communication along with willingness to compromise is crucial in order to find common ground that leads to a balanced relationship.

TAURUS AND SCORPIO

The connection between Taurus and Scorpio can be intense and passionate because both signs deeply desire intimacy. Tauruss stability complements the intensity of Scorpio while Scorpios loyalty aligns with Tauruss values. However it is important to note that both signs have a tendency to be possessive. Trust and open communication are vital in order to avoid issues related to jealousy and control.

TAURUS AND SAGITTARIUS

Taurus and Sagittarius approaches to life differ significantly. Taurus seeks stability in life. Sagittarius craves adventure and freedom. Taurus may perceive Sagittarius as spontaneous and unreliable while Sagittarius might view Taurus as overly cautious. In order for their relationship to thrive, understanding each other's perspectives and finding a compromise becomes essential.

TAURUS AND CAPRICORN

Compatibility between these two is quite high. Both signs share a love for stability, practicality and long term goals. Taurus appreciates Capricorn's ambition and determination. Capricorn highly values the loyalty and reliability of Taurus. Their shared values create a foundation for a lasting partnership.

TAURUS WITH AQUARIUS

Taurus with Aquarius exhibit varying approaches towards life and love. Taurus cherishes tradition and security. Aquarius seeks innovation and independence. This divergence may lead to challenges in their relationship. Taurus might find Aquarius too unconventional while Aquarius could perceive

Taurus as too traditional. Building a relationship often involves finding a common ground between these different perspectives.

TAURUS AND PISCES

This combination can be quite harmonious since both signs value connection, sensitivity and a feeling of security. Taurus offers practicality and stability. Pisces brings creativity and emotional depth to the relationship. However there may be instances where Taurus practical nature clashes with Pisces disposition. In such cases open communication and understanding become crucial.

To summarize the compatibility between Taurus and other zodiac signs varies depending on how they understand, appreciate and balance their differences. While astrology can provide insights into compatibility, individual personalities and experiences also play roles in determining the success of any relationship.

RELATIONSHIPS WITH TAURUS INDIVIDUALS

Taurus individuals are renowned for their dependability, sensuality and loyalty when it comes to relationships. Whether you're currently dating or in a relationship with a Taurus here are some tips for both men and women.

TIPS FOR A RELATIONSHIP WITH A TAURUS MAN

- **Reliability;** Appreciate the reliability of Taurus men in your life whether its support or emotional stability.

- **Aspire;** Share your hopes and dreams with them as they appreciate partners who open up about their aspirations.
- **Cultivate Patience;** Taurus men value taking their time when making decisions. Therefore it's important to avoid rushing them into commitments or pushing for changes in the relationship. Give them space to feel comfortable and secure.
- **Show Your Appreciation;** Taurus men love feeling valued. Let them know that you admire their qualities and efforts. This will boost their confidence and strengthen your bond.
- **Be Patient with Their Stubbornness;** Taurus men can be quite stubborn at times. When confronting them, try to find common ground and compromise when disagreements arise.
- **Share Your Emotions;** Although Taurus men may not always openly express their feelings they appreciate it when their partners do so. Share your emotions with them. Create a space for vulnerability.
- **Respect Their Need for Routine;** Taurus men often value routines as they provide stability and predictability in their lives. Be understanding of this need. Support them in maintaining it.
- **Respect Their Need for Space;** Personal space holds significance for Taurus individuals; they cherish moments of solitude as an opportunity to recharge. It is vital to understand that their need for time should not be interpreted as rejection but as an essential aspect of who they are.

TIPS FOR A RELATIONSHIP WITH A TAURUS WOMAN

- **Celebrate Special Moments;** Taurus women enjoy celebrations and meaningful gestures. Remember dates, such as anniversaries or birthdays. Make an effort to celebrate them with thoughtful gifts or shared experiences.
- **Appreciate Their Loyalty;** Taurus women are partners who stand by your side through thick and thin. Show gratitude for their support making sure they understand how much you value their commitment.
- **Demonstrate Consistency;** Winning a Taurus's heart requires showcasing reliability and consistency. Ensure that you keep your promises arrive punctually and establish yourself as someone they can rely on.
- **Freedom;** Avoid being overly possessive or controlling as Taurus women value their independence and personal interests.
- **Delight Their Senses;** Since Taurus people possess an affinity for the material world indulging their senses can be particularly enchanting. Plan romantic outings that cater to their pleasures—think dining experiences, soothing massages or cozy movie nights at home.

- **Foster Trust;** Trust forms the bedrock of any relationship with a Taurus person. Thus it is crucial to maintain honesty and open communication at all times since even the slightest hint of dishonesty can undermine their trust in the relationship.

These guidelines will assist you in strengthening a connection with your Taurus partner. Keep in mind that while these tips can offer guidance every person is unique. A successful relationship with a Taurus individual like any other relies on communication, understanding and mutual respect. Love isn't solely determined by one zodiac sign. Rather it encompasses how different energies interact between individuals.

In wrapping up the chapter we have explored the aspects of love and compatibility within the Taurus zodiac sign. Throughout this chapter we have delved into how Taurus individuals approach matters of the heart and examined the complexities of their preferences. From their sensuality, to their loyalty Taurus individuals bring a beautiful blend of love into their relationships. They appreciate the comforts that life has to offer and place value on the security and stability that love provides. Their ability to create a harmonious environment along with their dedication to their partners makes them cherished companions in the journey of love.

CHAPTER 3:
FRIENDS AND FAMILY

In the tapestry of life our connections with friends and family play an important role weaving together to create a mosaic of our existence. For those who are born under the Taurus zodiac sign these relationships bring their qualities of loyalty, stability and sensuality to the forefront. This chapter takes us on an exploration of how Taurus individuals approach friendships and family dynamics.

Taurus individuals offer a constant and reliable presence, in the lives of those they hold dear. However, like any zodiac sign, they encounter unique challenges when it comes to relationships. In this discussion we will delve into these challenges in order to better understand how to navigate them and foster healthier and more harmonious connections. Join us on this journey as we delve into the connections that define the Taurus experience within the realm of friends and family.

TAURUS AS A FRIEND

Taurus individuals are friends who can be relied upon. Just as they are renowned for their loyalty, in relationships their steadfast and trustworthy nature also extends to their friendships. Here's what you can anticipate when you have a Taurus as a friend.

- **Loyalty**; Taurus friends exhibit loyalty. They will stand by your side through thick and thin consistently offering support when you need it most. Their loyalty is unwavering, making them trusted companions.
- **Dependability**; When it comes to reliability Taurus friends are unmatched. They are individuals who will never leave you hanging in any situation. When Taurus individuals promise to be there, they genuinely mean it.
- **Stability**; People born under the Taurus zodiac sign highly value stability and have a knack for bringing a sense of calmness to their friendships. They are the anchors in your life providing support and a feeling of security.
- **Generosity**; Taurus friends are known for their generous nature. Often they find much joy in sharing life's pleasures with their companions. Whether it's treating you to a meal or presenting gifts they express their affection through acts of generosity.
- **Attentive Listeners**; Taurus individuals make great listeners. They exhibit patience and attentiveness when you need someone to talk to. They create a non-judgmental space where you can freely share your thoughts and emotions.
- **Appreciation for Sensory Delights**; Taurus friends often possess an appreciation for sensory pleasures like delicious food, music and relaxation. They can introduce you to experiences or help you relish life's simple joys.
- **Conflict Resolution Skills**; While Taurus friends prefer harmony they also excel at resolving conflicts. They approach problem solving with practicality and groundedness which proves beneficial when issues arise.
- **Honesty**; Honesty and trust hold significance for Taurus individuals, in their friendships. You can count on them to provide advice while keeping your confidence intact.
- **Shared Bonds**; Taurus friends often find joy in establishing and sharing traditions and routines. Whether it's a movie night, a getaway or other shared activities they value the continuity and connection that arise from these experiences.

Although Taurus friends possess qualities that enrich your life it's worth noting that their determination can occasionally lead to disagreements. Nevertheless their loyalty and dedication to the friendship usually help overcome such challenges. If you have a Taurus friend, treasure the stability and steadfast support they provide.

FAMILY

Taurus individuals contribute key qualities and dynamics to family life. Their strong sense of stability, loyalty and practicality typically influence relationships and interactions. Let's take a closer look at how Taurus influences family dynamics.

- **Stability**; Like the oak tree in the family forest, Taurus serves as a reliable foundation for their loved ones. They are key members of the family often playing the role of the anchor that keeps the family grounded.
- **Loyalty**; Taurus individuals exhibit loyalty, towards their family. They develop long lasting bonds with their parents, siblings and extended relatives. Family gatherings and traditions hold great importance to them as they cherish the feeling of unity and belonging they bring.
- **Caring and Protective**; Taurus individuals often take on a nurturing role within their family. They naturally gravitate towards caring for children and elderly members displaying a nurturing and protective nature. Creating a harmonious home environment brings them much joy.
- **Appreciation for Comfort**; Taurus individuals have an affinity for material comforts, which is reflected in their desire to create a cozy and visually appealing home. Providing their family with a sense of security in an inviting atmosphere is something they truly enjoy.
- **Embracing Tradition**; Taurus individuals value family values highly. Family dinners, celebrations and customs hold significance for them. Family traditions and routines play a role in their lives as they provide continuity and foster connection.
- **Promoting Harmony**; Taurus individuals prioritize maintaining harmony within the family unit often taking on the role of peacemaker during conflicts. They approach conflict resolution by emphasizing compromise and seeking ground.
- **Generosity**; Taurus is known for their generous nature especially when it comes to their family. They willingly provide support or lend a helping hand whenever their loved ones need it. They often take charge in organizing family get-togethers. There they ensure that everyone's well being is taken care of.
- **Parenting Style**; When it comes to being parents Taurus individuals are nurturing. They create a secure environment for their children emphasizing the importance of responsibility and practical life skills.

- **Cherished Family Traditions;** Family traditions hold significance for Taurus. Whether it's celebrating holidays, hosting family reunions or passing down treasured heirlooms they actively preserve the legacy of family history and customs.
- **Maintaining Family Bonds;** Taurus recognizes the importance of keeping connections alive with family members. They make efforts to nurture relationships with aunts, uncles, cousins and other relatives fostering a sense of unity within the family.

While Taurus's positive qualities greatly contribute to family dynamics it is essential to acknowledge that their stubbornness can sometimes lead to disagreements due to resistance towards change or strong opinions within the family. However the loyalty and dedication that Taurus individuals possess towards their family bonds often enable them to overcome difficulties. This fosters a sense of unity and security that is deeply cherished by their loved ones.

CHALLENGES IN RELATIONSHIPS WITH FAMILY AND FRIENDS

Although Taurus individuals bring qualities to their friendships and family relationships they may also face specific challenges due to their inherent traits and tendencies. Here are some common hurdles that Taurus individuals might encounter.

- **Stubbornness**; Taurus individuals are renowned for their determination and unwavering resolve. While this can be an asset it can sometimes manifest as stubbornness. They might be resistant to change or unwilling to consider perspectives leading to conflicts and strained relationships. This aspect of their personality can pose challenges in relationships that require adaptability. As such they may struggle with transitions or exhibit reluctance towards new experiences. Meeting others halfway can be a way forward.
- **Possessiveness**; Tauruss loyalty and desire for security can occasionally result in possessiveness within friendships and family ties. They may become overly protective of their loved ones, which can feel suffocating and restrict growth.
- **Materialism**; Due to their connection with the material world and affinity for material comforts, Taurus individuals might occasionally develop an emphasis on possessions. This might be misunderstood, as materialism by friends and family which could potentially cause tensions regarding priorities.
- **Apathy**; Taurus individuals can find it challenging to express their emotions. They tend to be reserved when it comes to sharing their feelings, which can be frustrating for loved ones who desire connection and communication.
- **Avoidance**; While Taurus desire for harmony is a trait it can sometimes lead to avoiding conflicts. They may suppress their emotions. Avoid addressing issues within relationships in order to maintain peace resulting in unresolved conflicts.
- **Hesitance**; Taurus individuals may hesitate to seek help or advice when it's necessary. They prefer solving problems which can lead to prolonged issues or missed opportunities for growth.
- **Overindulgence**; Their fondness for pleasures and comfort sometimes leads them to overindulgence – whether it's overindulging in food, luxury items or other pleasures. These factors can have a negative impact on their well being. It can also strain their relationships with concerned individuals.
- **Slow to Forgive**; Taurus people tend to hold grudges or harbor resentments for a long time. Their reluctance to forgive and move on can hinder the process of healing in relationships and perpetuate negativity.

It's worth noting that these challenges are not impossible to overcome and Taurus individuals can develop strategies to address them. Being self aware, maintaining communication and being willing to adapt are crucial in overcoming these challenges. Additionally the support and understanding from friends and family members can play a role in helping Taurus individuals navigate these dynamics effectively.

In the dance of life Taurus individuals serve as pillars of stability steadfastly devoted to their loved ones. In this chapter we have delved into the realm of Taurus friendships and family dynamics discovering the influence they have on the lives of those enough to be part of their circle.

As friends Taurus individuals bring unwavering loyalty, reliable support and a deep appreciation for life's pleasures, into their relationships. They are the ones you can rely on through thick and thin forging bonds that endure the trials of time.

Within a family Taurus individuals play a role, as a pillar of tradition, stability and unwavering commitment. They highly value family gatherings, cherished traditions and the comforting atmosphere of home that fosters the growth and prosperity of each generation.

However just like any aspect of life, friendships and family relationships present their share of challenges. Tauruss willed nature, resistance to change and occasional possessiveness can sometimes create hurdles in maintaining harmony. It is essential to acknowledge these challenges with empathy and engage in communication to address them effectively.

As we wrap up this chapter let's keep in mind that Taurus individuals bring a combination of stability, loyalty and sensuality to their relationships, with friends and family. By recognizing their strengths and challenges and by nurturing empathetic connections Taurus individuals can build lasting, meaningful and harmonious relationships that enhance both their own lives and the lives of those they care about.

CHAPTER 4: CAREER AND AMBITIONS

When it comes to careers and finances, Taurus individuals truly stand out as reliable and hardworking professionals. They bring a hard working ethic, a commitment to excellence and a keen focus on security. In this chapter we delve into the connection between Taurus individuals, their career aspirations and how they handle money matters.

For Taurus individuals choosing a career is not just about earning a living; it's also an expression of their values and desires. The pursuit of stability, financial security and practicality significantly influences the path they choose in their lives. Known for their determination, meticulous attention to detail and unwavering dedication to their work, Taurus individuals thrive in various fields.

As we delve into the realm of Taurus and their ambitions, in the professional spheres we'll gain an understanding of their unique qualities and the values that shape their choices in the world of work and money. So dear reader, come along as we explore how individuals with the Taurus star sign approach their careers and finances.

CAREER ASPIRATIONS

Taurus individuals tackle their careers with determination, practicality and steadfastness. Furthermore they have distinct preferences and aspirations that reflect their distinctive personality traits. Now let's take a closer look at Tauruss career inclinations and professional goals.

- **Stability**; Taurus individuals hold stability and financial security in high regard when it comes to their careers. They are drawn to professions that offer a steady income stream with long term prospects.
- **Practicality**; Individuals with Taurus traits possess an inclination towards practicality and realism. Often they gravitate towards careers that align with these tendencies, such as finance, accounting, real estate or healthcare. They excel in roles that demand attention to detail along with a pragmatic approach.
- **Materialism**; People born under the Taurus zodiac sign have an admiration for the material world, which often influences their career choices towards fields related to assets. They may find fulfillment in professions involving luxury goods, fashion, interior design or culinary arts.
- **Nurture**; Given their nurturing side Taurus individuals are well suited for professions that involve caring for others and making an impact on people's lives. This makes them suitable for careers in healthcare, education or caregiving.
- **Creativity**; Due to their appreciation of beauty and sensory pleasures many Tauruses are drawn towards creative outlets. They may choose careers in art, music, theater or design where they can express their talents and create pleasing experiences.
- **Patience**; Tauruses tend to make progress at a steady pace, rather than rushing things. They exhibit patience and hold the belief that hard work and determination will ultimately lead to success.
- **Prudence**; Financial prudence is another trait commonly found among Taurus individuals. They prioritize saving and investing aligning with their term goals and desire for security.

To summarize, Taurus individuals are attracted to careers that offer stability, financial security and the chance to work with assets or in nurturing roles. Their practicality, patience and dedication make them valuable contributors across many fields. While they excel in some roles. Finding a balance between their resistance to change and potential for growth is a consideration on their journey.

STRENGTHS THAT MAKE TAURUS INDIVIDUALS STAND OUT IN THE WORKPLACE

- **Reliability**; Taurus individuals are well known for their reliability. When they make a commitment you can trust them to follow through. This characteristic is highly valued in work settings because colleagues and supervisors can rely on them to keep their promises and meet deadlines consistently.
- **Strong Work Ethic**; Taurus individuals have a dedication to their work. They are willing to put in the necessary effort to excel in their roles. They approach tasks with determination and persistence often going above and beyond to achieve results.
- **Attention to Detail**; Their meticulous attention to detail is an asset in professions that require precision and accuracy. Taurus individuals shine in roles that involve data analysis, quality control, research or any task that demands an eye for specifics.
- **Practical Problem Solving**; Taurus individuals have a practical approach when it comes to solving problems. They excel at identifying challenges and finding solutions. Their down to earth perspective often leads to problem resolution.
- **Consistency**; Taurus individuals thrive in environments that offer stability and routine. They are well suited for roles that require consistency and the ability to handle tasks patiently and precisely. Their constant presence in the workplace contributes to creating a harmonious environment.
- **Perseverance**; Taurus individuals possess a sense of determination. When faced with obstacles or challenges they persistently work towards their goals making them valuable team members in projects that span over periods.
- **Financial Expertise**; Many Taurus individuals have a talent for financial matters. They excel in roles related to finance, accounting, budgeting and investments.
- **Organized**; Taurus individuals are often highly organized. They thrive in hierarchical environments where they can efficiently manage their tasks and responsibilities. Their organizational skills contribute to productivity and efficiency at work.
- **Conflict Resolution**; Taurus desire for harmony extends to their ability to handle conflicts. They approach disagreements with a calm demeanor while seeking compromises and solutions that maintain a harmonious work atmosphere.

- **Growth Perspective**; Taurus individuals typically have a long term outlook on their careers. They possess patience. Understand the value of steady progress. Taurus individuals with their commitment to achieving their goals often experience long term success and accomplishments.

COMMON CAREER CHALLENGES WITH STRATEGIES TO OVERCOME THEM

While Taurus individuals bring many strengths to the workplace it's important to acknowledge that they may also face challenges. By recognizing and addressing these challenges head on, Taurus individuals can truly thrive in their careers.

Resistance Towards Change

- Challenge; One of the traits of Taurus individuals is their resistance towards change due to a preference for stability and a familiar routine. This tendency might hinder adaptability in paced or rapidly evolving work environments.
- Strategy; To overcome this challenge it is beneficial for Taurus individuals to gradually embrace change. By exposing themselves consistently to novel experiences they can build confidence in adapting to unfamiliar situations.

Stubbornness

- Challenge; Sometimes Taurus individuals' determination and strong opinions can make it difficult for them to collaborate with others or consider other viewpoints.
- Strategy; Taurus individuals can work on being more open minded, by listening to other perspectives and being open to feedback. Engaging in discussions and being willing to compromise can lead to more harmonious work relationships.

Risk Aversion

- Challenge; Taurus individuals often prioritize security and may be hesitant to take calculated risks or explore career paths.
- Strategy; While it is important to maintain stability Taurus individuals can assess the benefits of calculated risks and consider exploring new career opportunities. Gradually introduce calculated risks into career plans allowing them to explore opportunities without jeopardizing their security.

Overemphasis on Materialism

- Challenge; Tauruss strong affinity for the material world may result in a focus on rewards potentially overshadowing other aspects of career satisfaction.
- Strategy; Taurus individuals should strive for a balance between security and overall career fulfillment. By identifying roles or projects that align with their passions and values they can find job satisfaction, beyond considerations.

Resistance, to Changing Careers

- Challenge; Taurus individuals often find themselves getting comfortable in their roles because they prefer stability.
- Strategy; To overcome this challenge Taurus individuals can set career goals and regularly evaluate whether their current position aligns with their aspirations and values. Seeking guidance from mentors, expanding their network and considering alternative career paths can offer fresh perspectives.

Hesitation in Pursuing Advancement

- Challenge; Tauruss patient and determined nature sometimes results in a reluctance to actively pursue career advancement or seek promotions.
- Strategy; Taurus individuals can address this challenge by communicating their career objectives to supervisors and actively seeking opportunities for skill enhancement and upward mobility within the organization. Building connections can also open doors to new possibilities.

Persevering Despite Discontentment

- Challenge; Tauruss persevering nature may cause them to persist in a career that no longer brings them satisfaction or fulfillment.
- Strategy; Taurus individuals should periodically assess their level of job satisfaction. Take action if they find themselves in unfulfilling roles. Exploring options such as career counseling, mentorship programs or further education can assist them in aligning their careers with their passions and aspirations.

Throughout this chapter we have explored the relationship that Taurus individuals have with their aspirations and approach to wealth. For them, careers go beyond the grind. They are a reflection of their core values. Their pursuit of stability, financial security and a comfortable life underlies their choices. They are professionals who pay attention to detail and excel. Their natural financial acumen, discipline and ability to plan for the term serve them well in building a brighter future.

As we wrap up this chapter we hope you now have a good understanding of how Taurus individuals approach career growth and money. Ultimately Taurus people serve as a reminder that success goes beyond the amount of money in your bank account. It also encompasses the stability, security and satisfaction that comes from choosing a career you love.

CHAPTER 5: SELF-IMPROVEMENT

In the pursuit of discovering oneself and growing personally each zodiac sign possesses unique qualities and characteristics that shape their journey. For those born under the Taurus zodiac sign their path towards self improvement is defined by a commitment to stability, practicality and reliability. In this chapter we will explore how they can utilize their traits to become the best versions of themselves.

Taurus individuals are renowned for their hard work and affinity for materialistic pursuits. When it comes to self improvement they approach it with the determination they apply to their careers and finances. Their practical nature and steadfast loyalty to their values serve as guiding principles on their growth journey.

However, like individuals from all zodiac signs, Taurus faces both challenges and opportunities while striving for self improvement. Their resistance to change and occasional stubbornness can hinder progress. Within this chapter we will explore strategies and practices that can assist Taurus individuals in embracing self improvement. So my dear reader join us as we delve into the journey of Taurus individuals towards self improvement.

EMBRACING TAURUS STRENGTHS AND OVERCOMING WEAKNESSES

Taurus individuals possess a unique blend of strengths and weaknesses that shape their personality. To lead a fulfilling life it is crucial to leverage these strengths while working on areas that need improvement. Here's a helpful guide on achieving that.

UTILIZING STRENGTHS

- **Reliability**; Taurus reliability is an asset. Use it to establish trust in both professional and personal relationships. Keep your promises consistently through your actions.
- **Strong Work Ethic**; Make the most of your strong work ethic by excelling in your career endeavors. Take on tasks, work diligently and strive for excellence. Your dedication will not go unnoticed.
- **Attention to Detail**; Your meticulous attention to detail can be advantageous, in roles that require precision. Consider exploring professions that involve working with data analysis, quality control or research. These fields can benefit greatly from your attention to detail. Focus on specifics.
- **Practical Problem Solving**; Your practical approach to problem solving is incredibly valuable. Use this skill to identify challenges, break them down into tasks and find solutions. Your practical mindset can lead to outcomes.
- **Consistency and Stability**; Embrace your preference for stability and routine. Establishing a routine can enhance productivity and reduce stress levels. Your consistency can bring comfort not only, to yourself but to those around you.

OVERCOMING WEAKNESSES

- **Resistance to Change**; While valuing stability is a strength it's important to acknowledge that change is a part of life. Practice flexibility by introducing experiences into your daily routine. Embrace change as an opportunity for growth.
- **Openness and Flexibility**; Work on being more receptive to perspectives by actively listening during discussions. Engage in conversations. Be willing to find compromises when necessary. An open minded approach leads to better interactions.
- **Managing Risk Aversion**; Challenge yourself by taking calculated risks both in your life. Start with small steps. Gradually increase your tolerance

for risk taking activities. Understand that taking some level of risk is essential for growth and achieving success.

- **Developing oneself**; Growing as an individual is a journey that applies to Taurus individuals well. Embracing the qualities of being a Taurus, such as practicality and steadfastness while also being open to change and self improvement can lead to a satisfying and harmonious life.
- **Avoiding focus on possessions**; Although it's important to have comfort in life it's essential not to equate material things with happiness alone. Practicing gratitude and directing attention towards relationships, experiences and personal development can bring greater fulfillment.
- **Being open to career changes**; It's beneficial for Taurus individuals to periodically evaluate their career satisfaction levels and remain receptive to opportunities. Seeking guidance from mentors, networking with professionals from fields and considering education can broaden horizons.
- **Taking action - even when dissatisfied**; If you find yourself in an unfulfilling career situation taking action steps towards change is crucial. Exploring challenges, pursuing your passions and contemplating career paths are all worthwhile endeavors. Remember that pursuing long term happiness is always worth it.

By leveraging your strengths while actively working on areas that need improvement Taurus individuals can embark on a journey of growth and self improvement. This approach allows for a rewarding and successful life. Here are some more tips and growth strategies.

Take Change Slowly;

- Challenge for Taurus; Taurus individuals have a tendency to be resistant to change and prefer stability.
- Growth Approach; While it's important to maintain stability, try embracing change in steps. By exposing yourself to new experiences bit by bit you can become more adaptable over time.

Foster Open Mindedness;

- Challenge for Taurus; Stubbornness can sometimes hinder mindedness and flexibility.
- Growth Approach; Make an effort to genuinely listen to other perspectives and engage in discussions with an open heart and mind. Take the time to consider alternative viewpoints and be willing to adapt your beliefs when presented with new information.

Step Beyond Your Comfort Zone;

- Challenge for Taurus; Taurus individuals often stick within their routines and comfort zones.
- Growth Approach; Challenge yourself by trying out activities exploring interests or taking calculated risks. Stepping beyond your comfort zone can lead to growth. Broaden your horizons.

Set Ambitious Objectives;

- Challenge for Taurus; The love of stability may sometimes result in complacency or resistance towards setting goals.
- Growth Approach; Identify long term goals and aspirations both in your personal life. Create a plan on how you'll achieve them while remaining open, to adjusting those goals as you continue growing and evolving.

Developing Communication Skills;

- Challenge for Taurus; One challenge that Taurus individuals may face is the tendency to hold back their emotions or thoughts.
- Growth Approach; To overcome this challenge it is beneficial to practice assertive communication. Sharing your feelings, needs and opinions with your loved ones and colleagues can lead to relationships and personal growth.

Exploring Creativity;

- Challenge for Taurus; Another challenge for Taurus individuals is prioritizing practicality over self expression.
- Growth Approach; To nurture your side engage in activities such as art, music, writing or any other form of creative expression. Embracing your creativity can be a fulfilling experience.

Personal Development Opportunities;

- Challenge for Taurus; Taurus individuals may sometimes fall into complacency when it comes to growth.
- Growth Approach; To counter this challenge make an effort to seek opportunities for self improvement. Attend workshops, read books. Participate in activities that intellectually and emotionally challenge you.

Practicing Mindfulness and Patience;

- Challenge for Taurus; Taurus individuals may have a tendency to rush through life without appreciating the moment.

- Growth Approach; To cultivate mindfulness and patience in your life consider practicing gratitude exercises or engaging in meditation or yoga. These practices can help you stay present and enjoy the journey, rather than solely focusing on reaching your goals.

Maintaining a balance, between materialism and inner fulfillment;

- Challenge for Taurus; Sometimes being strongly connected to the material world can overshadow the importance of finding fulfillment.
- Growth Strategy; While it is important to have material comfort it is equally essential to prioritize well being, nurturing relationships and personal growth. Strive for a pursuit of both material goals and the pursuit of happiness and self discovery.

Ultimately personal growth involves embarking on a journey of self reflection, adapting to changes and continuously learning. Taurus individuals can leverage their strengths while working on their challenges in order to lead a life filled with fulfillment and personal development. By embracing change and remaining open to experiences, Taurus individuals can unlock their potential and achieve holistic personal growth.

As Taurus individuals contemplate their prospects, for growth and personal evolution it is important to remember that self improvement is a journey that unfolds gradually with purpose. There is endless potential for growth and self improvement among Taurus individuals. By embracing change, being open minded and stepping out of their comfort zones, Taurus individuals can unlock their full potential. This path is grounded in their determination and is guided by self awareness offering the promise of an enriched life.

CHAPTER 6:
THE YEAR AHEAD

As a Taurus your year ahead will be shaped by the changing cosmos, where celestial events influence the ups and downs of your life. This chapter acts as your guide to the stars. In the following pages we will explore dates and periods that hold significance. From Venus movements to solar eclipses we will uncover how these celestial happenings may affect your journey in the year ahead.

So dear Taurus, as you dive into this tapestry that awaits you in the year, always remember that the stars are here to guide you. Opportunities for growth and fulfillment are abundant like the universe itself. Embrace this journey. May the celestial energies align in your favor throughout the year.

HOROSCOPE GUIDE FOR TAURUS

Welcome, aboard Taurus! As you embark on your journey through the year there are promises of stability, personal growth and the potential to bring your dreams to life. Being an earth sign ruled by Venus, your practicality, determination and appreciation for life's pleasures are well known. This comprehensive yearly horoscope guide is designed to assist you in navigating the influences and making the most of what lies ahead.

- **January to March;** Evaluating priorities. The year commences with a focus on reevaluating your priorities regarding your career and relationships. Take some time to establish goals and lay a foundation for your endeavors. Trust your intuition when making decisions. Be willing to let go of anything that no longer serves you.
- **April to June;** Building financial security. During this period concentrate on building financial security while exploring opportunities for growth. Your practical nature and strong work ethic will guide you in making investments and financial choices. Consider long term goals. Set a plan in motion that includes saving.
- **July to September;** Broadening horizons. The months of the year encourage you to expand your horizons through travel, education or personal development. Embrace the new. Step out of your comfort zone. Seek inspiration, from cultures and perspectives as a means of widening your worldview.

- **October to December;** Strengthening connections. As the year comes to a close it's a time to strengthen your relationships whether it's with your partner or your family and friends. The key lies in communication and finding compromises when conflicts arise. Your loved ones will truly appreciate your loyalty and dedication.

KEY THEMES FOR THE YEAR

- **Balance and Harmony**; Strive for balance in all areas of your life by taking care of yourself while pursuing your goals. It's important to nurture both your well being and aspirations.
- **Self Expression**; Explore your expressive side this year. Give voice to your inner thoughts and emotions. Engaging in creative activities can be particularly fulfilling.
- **Financial Growth**; Utilize your knowledge to secure a better financial future for yourself. Consider long term investments and savings plans that align with your goals.
- **Personal Growth**; Embrace change and personal development as you move forward. Don't shy away from experiences that push you out of your comfort zone. Keep a journal as a means of tracking progress on this journey of growth.
- **Reality**; Stay grounded in reality while trusting yourself and following your instincts.
- **Open mind**; Be open minded, adaptable and willing to adjust when faced with changing circumstances.
- **Nurture**; Prioritize self care to ensure both health and emotional well being. Nurture your relationships by being present, attentive and maintaining communication.

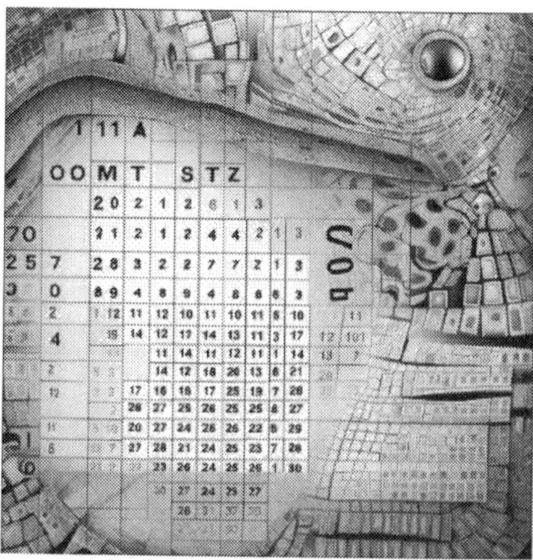

Remember, Taurus the stars are aligned in favor of opportunities, for growth, stability and personal fulfillment in the year! Have confidence in your abilities, embrace the opportunities for change and take pleasure in the joys of life. Your unwavering determination and practical approach will lead you towards success and fulfillment.

ASTROLOGICAL INFLUENCES

Astrological events can have an impact on your energy levels, emotions and life journey. Here are some significant astrological events to keep an eye on and their potential effects on individuals born under Taurus.

- **Venus Retrograde (January 1. January 29);** At the beginning of the year your ruling planet Venus goes retrograde. This period might encourage you to reassess your relationships and financial matters. Take time to contemplate your values when it comes to love and money.
- **Taurus Season (April 20. May 20);** During Taurus season you will feel more connected to your core traits emphasizing your determination and practicality. You will experience a sense of grounding and focus during this time making it an ideal period for setting goals and pursuing them.
- **Lunar and Solar Eclipse in Taurus (periodic);** A lunar eclipse occurring in your sign may bring about intensity and transformative changes in your life. The eclipse has the potential to bring about transformations, in your life urging you to let go of patterns and embrace personal growth.
- **Retrograde of other Planets (periodic)**; Jupiter, known as the planet of expansion, moves into Pisces. This influences your social life. During this period expect your social circle to expand, providing avenues for spiritual growth through connections with others.
- **Mercury Retrograde (periodic);** Be mindful of Mercury retrogrades that may impact communication and decision making processes at times. Take caution when dealing with contracts or important conversations during these periods. Instead use these times for reflection and review before making any decisions.

Throughout the year Saturn remains in Aquarius putting a spotlight on your career and public life. While you continue to work towards achieving your career goals it's crucial to remain open minded towards innovation and be willing to adapt as changes arise along your path.

KEY AREAS OF CONSIDERATION

LOVE AND RELATIONSHIPS

For Taurus individuals your romantic life and relationships will be influenced by astrological occurrences in the coming year. Pay attention to the following;

- **Venus Retrograde** (January 1. January 29); During this period you may find yourself contemplating relationships and reassessing your values when it comes to love. It's a time for self exploration and gaining insights into your desires.
- **Lunar Eclipse in Taurus (Periodic);** This celestial event holds significance, for matters of the heart. A lunar eclipse has the potential to bring about changes and transformations in your romantic life. It may lead to shifts in your relationships allowing you to let go of patterns and embrace growth.
- **Venus (May 2nd to May 27th);** Venus will grace your sign of Taurus. This period will enhance your qualities and charm creating an opportunity for building or nurturing a deep connection with your partner.

CAREER AND FINANCES

Taurus individuals can expect key events throughout the year that will influence their career and finance. Here are some key moments to keep an eye on.

- **Saturn's presence;** Saturn will continue its presence in Aquarius throughout the year emphasizing your life. Be prepared for work and potential rewards along your career path.
- **Jupiter's transit;** Jupiter's transit through Pisces will focus on friendships and social connections. This period can bring opportunities for career growth through networking and collaborations.
- **Mercury retrograde;** During dates when Mercury goes into retrograde it is advisable to exercise caution with decisions and contracts. Utilize these periods, for review and planning purposes.
- **Mars in Taurus**; During the period of Mars in Taurus, you will find yourself driven and motivated to take on career challenges and financial goals with a sense of determination.

HEALTH AND WELLNESS

Taurus individuals can expect key events throughout the year that will influence their health and wellness. Here are some key moments to keep an eye on.

- **Lunar Eclipse;** When the Lunar Eclipse occurs be prepared for heightened intensity. Use this time to focus on self care and adopt stress management techniques.
- **Venus in Taurus**; An opportunity for indulging in self care and pampering. Make sure you pay attention to both your emotional well being during this period.
- **Saturn;** Throughout the year Saturn will present to remind you of the importance of maintaining a work life balance. It is crucial not to overwork yourself but prioritize relaxation and rest.

GROWTH AND SELF DISCOVERY

Throughout the year Taurus individuals can leverage astrological events to their advantage. Here are some tips for making the most of what lies ahead.

- **Venus Retrograde;** During Venus Retrograde take time for introspection regarding your values in love and relationships. Use this period as an opportunity to gain an understanding of your desires.
- **Eclipse;** Align with growth and self discovery. Embrace new experiences that resonate with yourself.

As we come to the end of this section we have embarked on a journey through the stars exploring the forces and cosmic energies that will shape the path of Taurus individuals. As you navigate through events and astrological influences always remember that you possess inner strength to overcome obstacles and wisdom to seize opportunities. Your journey in the coming year holds potential for love, success in career well being and personal growth. By staying attuned to influences and being open to change and self discovery you can make the most of opportunities that come your way. Trust in your qualities and ability to adapt and you'll see that the universe supports your efforts.

Remember that astrology can be a tool for self awareness and guidance. It's ultimately your choices and actions that shape your future. As you move forward into the year use the energy of the cosmos to make your dreams come true.

Taurus, this is your chance to shine!

CHAPTER 7: FAMOUS "TAURUS" PERSONALITIES

In the realm of astrology, the Taurus zodiac sign is often associated with qualities, like determination, practicality, loyalty and a passion for enjoying life's pleasures. People born under Taurus are known for their dedication to their goals and their ability to create stability in their lives. Within this chapter we cordially invite you to explore the lives and accomplishments of famous individuals who share the Taurus star sign. From domains like entertainment, politics, sports and more these famous Taurus personalities have left an imprint on history. In fact they continue to inspire us with their qualities and contributions.

As we dive into the stories of these individuals you will uncover how the traits commonly associated with Taurus have played a role in shaping their path towards success. These icons exemplify the core essence of being a Taurus in diverse and captivating ways. Come along on a journey through their lives as we gain an understanding of how Taurus, astrological influences have shaped their destinies.

ELIZABETH II

- Date of Birth: April 21, 1926.
- Brief Biography: Queen Elizabeth II was the longest-reigning monarch in British history. She ascended to the throne in 1952 and presided over the United Kingdom and the Commonwealth with grace and dedication.
- Taurus Traits: Queen Elizabeth II embodied Taurus traits like determination and an unwavering commitment to her royal duties.
- Impact: Her reign witnessed significant historical events, making her a symbol of continuity and stability.
- Personal Life: Queen Elizabeth II was known for her dedication to public service and her close-knit royal family.

BARBRA STREISAND

- Date of Birth: April 24, 1942.
- Brief Biography: Barbra Streisand is an iconic American singer, actress, and filmmaker. She is known for her powerful voice and numerous achievements in the entertainment industry.

- Taurus Traits: Her determination and pursuit of excellence align with Taurus qualities, contributing to her long-lasting success.
- Impact: Streisand has won multiple Grammy Awards, Academy Awards, and Tony Awards for her contributions to entertainment.
- Personal Life: She is also known for her philanthropic efforts and advocacy for various causes.

AUDREY HEPBURN

- Date of Birth: May 4, 1929.
- Brief Biography: Audrey Hepburn was a beloved British actress and humanitarian known for her elegance and grace on and off the screen. She won an Academy Award for her role in "Roman Holiday" and starred in iconic films like "Breakfast at Tiffany's."
- Taurus Traits: Hepburn's determination, poise, and enduring popularity reflect Taurus qualities.
- Impact: She remains an enduring symbol of timeless beauty and style, and her humanitarian work continues to make a positive impact.
- Personal Life: Hepburn was also dedicated to UNICEF and worked tirelessly for children's rights.

MELANIA TRUMP

- Date of Birth: April 26, 1970.

- Brief Biography: Melania Trump is a former First Lady of the United States and a former model. She served as First Lady from 2017 to 2021, focusing on initiatives such as children's well-being and online safety.
- Taurus Traits: Melania Trump's practicality and determination are evident in her approach to her role as First Lady.
- Impact: Her time in the White House saw various initiatives aimed at making a positive impact on society.
- Personal Life: Melania Trump is known for her privacy and her family life with former President Donald Trump.

ADELE

- Date of Birth: May 5, 1988.
- Brief Biography: Adele is a British singer and songwriter known for her soulful and powerful voice. She gained worldwide recognition for her albums, including "21" and "25."
- Taurus Traits: Her determination and practicality are evident in her dedication to her craft and her ability to connect with audiences.
- Impact: Adele has won numerous Grammy Awards and has achieved record-breaking album sales.
- Personal Life: She has been open about her personal experiences, which often inspire her music.

CHER

- Date of Birth: May 20, 1946.
- Brief Biography: Cher is an American singer, actress, and cultural icon known for her versatile career in music and film.
- Taurus Traits: Cher's enduring success and resilience align with Taurus qualities of determination and loyalty.
- Impact: She has won an Academy Award, Grammy Awards, and an Emmy, among other accolades.
- Personal Life: Cher's career has spanned decades, and her personal life has often been in the public eye.

WILLIAM SHAKESPEARE

- Date of Birth: April 26, 1564.
- Brief Biography: William Shakespeare was an English playwright and poet widely regarded as one of the greatest writers in the English language. His

works, including "Romeo and Juliet," "Hamlet," and "Macbeth," are considered timeless classics of literature.

- Taurus Traits: Shakespeare's enduring legacy reflects the determination and creativity associated with Taurus.
- Impact: His contributions to literature and the arts have had a profound and enduring influence on culture and language.
- Personal Life: While details of his personal life are limited, his literary achievements continue to inspire generations.

STEVIE WONDER

- Date of Birth: May 13, 1950.
- Brief Biography: Stevie Wonder is an American singer-songwriter, musician, and record producer known for his groundbreaking contributions to music. He has won multiple Grammy Awards and is celebrated for albums like "Songs in the Key of Life."
- Taurus Traits: Stevie Wonder's determination and artistic creativity align with Taurus qualities.
- Impact: His music has touched the hearts of millions and inspired social change through his lyrics and activism.
- Personal Life: Despite blindness from infancy, he has overcome obstacles to become a musical legend.

GEORGE CLOONEY

- Date of Birth: May 6, 1961.
- Brief Biography: George Clooney is an American actor, filmmaker, and philanthropist known for his charm and versatility in Hollywood. He has won Academy Awards as both an actor and a producer and is known for films like "Ocean's Eleven."
- Taurus Traits: George Clooney's success and commitment to humanitarian causes reflect Taurus qualities.
- Impact: He has used his platform to advocate for various humanitarian efforts and remains a prominent figure in entertainment.
- Personal Life: Clooney is known for his advocacy and his marriage to human rights lawyer Amal Clooney.

POPE JOHN PAUL II (KAROL JOZEF WOJTYLA)

- Date of Birth: May 18, 1920.

- Brief Biography: John Paul II, born Karol Józef Wojtyła, was the head of the Roman Catholic Church as Pope from 1978 until his passing in 2005. He was the second-longest-serving Pope in history and a pivotal figure during the Cold War era.
- Taurus Traits: His steadfast dedication to his role as Pope and his commitment to peace align with Taurus traits like determination and practicality.
- Impact: John Paul II' had a profound impact on the Catholic Church and global politics, earning him recognition as a spiritual leader and advocate for human rights.
- Personal Life: As Pope, his personal life was deeply intertwined with his religious and pastoral duties.

MUSTAFA KEMAL ATATÜRK

- Date of Birth: May 19, 1881.
- Brief Biography: Mustafa Kemal Atatürk, born Mustafa Kemal, was the founder of modern Turkey and its first President. He led sweeping reforms that transformed Turkey into a secular and modern nation-state.
- Taurus Traits: Atatürk's determination to reshape Turkey and his practical approach to nation-building align with Taurus qualities.
- Impact: He is celebrated as a national hero in Turkey and is recognized for his enduring influence on the country's politics, culture, and identity.
- Personal Life: His personal life was deeply tied to his role as a statesman and leader of the Turkish people.

MARK ZUCKERBERG

- Date of Birth: May 14, 1984.
- Brief Biography: Mark Zuckerberg is an American computer programmer and entrepreneur who co-founded Facebook, one of the world's most prominent social media platforms.
- Taurus Traits: His determination, practicality, and steadfast commitment to the growth of Facebook align with Taurus qualities.
- Impact: Facebook has had a profound influence on global connectivity and communication, shaping the way people interact online.
- Personal Life: Zuckerberg is known for his philanthropic efforts and his role as the CEO of Meta Platforms, the parent company of Facebook.

As we wrap up this chapter highlighting individuals born under the Taurus zodiac sign we have embarked on a journey through the lives of individuals who exemplify Taurus traits. From captivating stages in the entertainment industry to positions of power and influence. These individuals have showcased how determination, practicality and loyalty can shape their paths to success.

May the stories of these Taurus figures ignite a sense of inspiration within you to embrace your unique strengths and navigate a path towards personal achievement and fulfillment. Just as constellations illuminate our night sky, so too do Taurus individuals shine brightly with their talents and aspirations continuing to leave a lasting impact on our world.

CONCLUSION

Dear reader, we have reached the conclusion of this book. Together we have embarked on a voyage through the aspects of Taurus delving into its rich history, captivating mythology, distinct traits and the countless ways it shapes the lives of those born under its influence. As we approach the concluding pages of this book let us pause for a moment to reflect on the wisdom and invaluable lessons we have absorbed.

Throughout our exploration we have unraveled the tapestry that's Taurus. We've discovered its origins in history, explored its impact on matters of love and relationships. We have examined its dynamics within friendships and families, analyzed its aspirations in careers and finances. We also delved into its potential for growth and development. Moreover we've celebrated individuals embodying the spirit of Taurus who have left a mark on our world. Now we shall distill these insights into a radiant constellation of knowledge—providing you with a comprehensive overview encapsulating the essence of Taurus!

As we come to the end of our exploration of the Taurus zodiac sign we find ourselves at a crossroads, in the cosmos. Here history, mythology, love, friendships, family, career aspirations, personal growth, future prospects and the influential presence of known Taurus personalities intersect. At this junction of knowledge and awe inspiring wonders we offer you a conclusion that encapsulates the wisdom we have discovered throughout these chapters. Let us summarize what we learned in each.

- **Chapter 1; History and Mythology;** In Chapter 1 we embarked on a captivating journey into the past as we unraveled the origins and legendary tales that shaped the Taurus constellation. From ancient civilizations to enduring myths and legends, Taurus has served as a source of inspiration across countless generations.
- **Chapter 2; Love & Compatibility;** Moving on to Chapter 2 we delved into matters of the heart by exploring how individuals born under the sign of Taurus approach love and relationships. We uncovered insights into their compatibility with zodiac signs—revealing intricate nuances that govern romantic connections guided by its celestial influence.
- **Chapter 3; Friends and Family;** In Chapter 3 we celebrated the cherished roles played by Taurus individuals as friends and family members. We explored their dynamics within relationships while offering insights, into both challenges and rewards found in familial bonds and friendships.

- **Chapter 4; Career and Finance;** In Chapter 4 we delved into the realms of career and finances exploring the preferences, strengths and challenges that Taurus individuals often encounter. We discussed how they strive for stability and achievement through their work ethic.
- **Chapter 5; Self Improvement;** Chapter 5 took us on a journey of self improvement and personal development uncovering how Taurus individuals can utilize their strengths to overcome obstacles and become the versions of themselves.
- **Chapter 6; The Year Ahead;** In Chapter 6 we gazed into the crystal ball to gain insights into what the upcoming year may hold for Taurus individuals. From shifting events in the stars to cosmic guidance we provided a roadmap, for navigating the year ahead.
- **Chapter 7; Famous Taurus Personalities;** Throughout Chapter 7 we celebrated personalities who were born under the Taurus zodiac sign. From Queen Elizabeth II to Mark Zuckerberg, their remarkable journeys shed light on how celestial influences have shaped their lives.

As we conclude this voyage together our hope is that you not only gained a deeper understanding of what it means to be a Taurus but also recognized your limitless potential. The universe has granted you an identity and your journey serves as a testament to the brilliance of the cosmos itself.

To all our readers born under the sign of Taurus we extend words of encouragement. Embrace your qualities with pride and conviction. Your traits serve as guiding stars illuminating your extraordinary journey forward. Your individual cosmic identity holds a wellspring of strength, creativity and resilience. As you navigate through the changing landscape of life, always remember that the universe has bestowed upon you remarkable gifts.

In the spirit of unity and appreciation, for the zodiac we encourage individuals from all signs to embrace and celebrate their qualities. Like each constellation in the night sky possesses its brilliance, so do our individual qualities and traits that define us. Within this tapestry every star radiates its own light contributing to the beauty and wonder of our universe.

As we say our goodbyes, may you continue exploring the enigmas of the universe finding inspiration in constellations above and embracing possibilities. The cosmos is your guiding force and your journey has only just begun. Throughout this odyssey we have ventured into realms of Taurus zodiac sign uncovering its secrets and celebrating its characteristics. As we reflect upon our expedition let us distill the essence of our exploration once again to reaffirm our commitment and offer a guiding star to illuminate your path.

We embarked on this expedition with a pledge to unravel Taurus' rich tapestry. From its origins to its impact on love, family dynamics, career paths and personal growth. We have fulfilled our promise by providing a range of insights, guidance and inspiration to help you navigate the twists and turns of life. Our mission was to shed light on your journey of self discovery. We have accomplished that by revealing the map that defines your Taurus identity.

If there's one thing we hope you take away from this book, it's the importance of self awareness and the timeless enchantment of astrology. Embrace your qualities whether you belong to Taurus or any other zodiac sign. Utilize the wisdom of the stars to navigate through this cosmic voyage.

The characteristics of Taurus, determination, loyalty and practicality have undeniably made a mark on humanity's tapestry. As you move forward may the stars remain as your guiding lights. May you forever draw inspiration from the marvels that envelop us. Embrace your identity and let the magnificence of the cosmos illuminate your path on this remarkable journey we call life.

GEMINI:

A COMPLETE GUIDE TO THE GEMINI ASTROLOGY STAR SIGN

Contents

INTRODUCTION -- 1
Overview of Gemini -- 2

CHAPTER 1: HISTORY AND MYTHOLOGY.. 4
Earliest Observations in Ancient Civilizations -- 5
Historical Events Under the Gemini Sign -- 7
Further Reading and References -- 8

CHAPTER 2: LOVE & COMPATIBILITY -- 10
Gemini's Love and Compatibility with Other Zodiac Signs -- 10
Tips for Relationships with Gemini -- 14

CHAPTER 3: FRIENDS AND FAMILY -- 16
Gemini as a Friend -- 16
Gemini in Family Dynamics -- 18
Challenges in Friendships and Family Relations -- 19
Key Insights Recap -- 20

CHAPTER 4: CAREER AND AMBITIONS -- 22
Career Preferences and Professional Aspirations -- 23
Strengths in the workplace -- 24
Professional Challenges and Strategies to Overcome Them -- 25

CHAPTER 5: SELF-IMPROVEMENT -- 28
Personal Growth and Self-Development -- 28
Harnessing Strengths and Overcoming Weaknesses -- 30

CHAPTER 6: THE YEAR AHEAD -- 34
Key Astrological Events and Their Impact on Gemini -- 37
Key areas of interest -- 39

CHAPTER 7: FAMOUS "GEMINI" PERSONALITIES -------------------- 42
Donald Trump ---------- 42
Paul McCartney ---------- 43
Marilyn Monroe ---------- 43
Queen Victoria ---------- 44
Clint Eastwood ---------- 44
Anne Frank ---------- 44
Tupac Shakur ---------- 45
Johnny Depp ---------- 45
Kylie Minogue ---------- 45
Angelina Jolie ---------- 46
Tim Berners Lee ---------- 46
Alanis Morissette ---------- 46

CONCLUSION ---------- 48

INTRODUCTION

For centuries astrology has captured the imagination of humanity. A canvas where stars and planets intertwine to tell the tales of our existence. At its core astrology explores the movements and positions of celestial bodies. From this it explores their impact on our affairs and the world. This ancient practice transcends time and cultures by offering insights into personality traits, relationships, life events and much more.

The essence of astrology lies in the belief that an individual's character and destiny are shaped by the alignment of stars and planets at the moment of their birth. Each zodiac sign corresponds to a period within a year. Each carries distinct characteristics and attributes. The twelve signs form a belt encircling the sky, are divided into segments named after their respective constellations.

In this book we delve into one constellation, Gemini. Our journey, through these pages, aims to unravel the qualities, characteristics and background of those born under the influence of Gemini's star sign. The purpose of this book is to serve as a guide for Geminis who want to gain self awareness and for those who wish to understand the Geminis in their lives. Whether you are a Gemini yourself or have a connection with one. This book will offer insights into the strengths, challenges and potentials associated with this zodiac sign.

OVERVIEW OF GEMINI

- **Date**; May 21st - June 20th. This period marks the transition from spring to summer in the Northern Hemisphere. This is a time, associated with the blossoming of ideas and the joy of learning.
- **Symbol**; The symbol of Gemini is the Twins, which represents the duality inherent in this sign.
- **Element**; Gemini is an Air sign. Air signs are characterized by their intellectual, communicative and analytical abilities.
- **Planet**; Mercury, the planet associated with intellect, communication skills and agility.
- **Color**; Yellow represents energy, a positive outlook and an open mind.
- **Traits**; Individuals born under Gemini are renowned for their agile nature, sociability and intelligence.

STRENGTHS

- **Adaptability**; Geminis are skilled at adapting to various situations.
- **Communication Skills**; They excel in expressing themselves and understanding others.
- **Intellect**; Geminis naturally gravitate towards learning and exploring intellectual concepts.
- **Sociability**; They are individuals who thrive on social interactions.

WEAKNESSES

- **Indecisiveness**; Geminis can find it challenging to make decisions due to their indecisive nature.
- **Impulsiveness**; Their curiosity sometimes leads them to act without thought.
- **Inconsistency**; Their diverse range of interests can result in a lack of focus at times.
- **Compatibility;** Geminis generally get along well with air signs (Libra, Aquarius) and fire signs (Aries, Leo, Sagittarius) as they share similar energy and perspectives on life.

In our introduction we explored the captivating world of the Gemini star sign offering an exploration of its multifaceted nature. It begins by placing Gemini within the context of astrology, emphasizing how celestial bodies have long been believed to influence lives. Subsequent chapters in the book promise an in depth exploration of Gemini. By combining insights, practical tips and captivating narratives this book aims to offer an accessible guide for comprehending and appreciating the complexities as well, as the allure of the Gemini zodiac sign.

CHAPTER 1:
HISTORY AND MYTHOLOGY

In this chapter we will explore the history and mythological origins of Gemini. This exploration will not only deepen our understanding of Gemini, it will also shed light on the profound influence that celestial events have had on humanity. The constellation of Gemini has captivated people, across cultures and time. Let's embark on a journey through history and mythology to uncover the stories behind this sign.

We will begin by examining how ancient civilizations observed and documented Gemini. From the ancient gods in Mesopotamia to Greek and Roman mythology, each tale reflects both the astronomical knowledge and the cultural beliefs of those times. As we move forward in time we will discover how various cultures interpreted and depicted Gemini in their star maps. These interpretations offer a range of meanings for the twins. From being protectors and patrons, to representing duality, intelligence and communication.

This chapter not only provides an overview but also immerses us in captivating mythological narratives that have shaped our understanding of Gemini. We will encounter figures associated with this zodiac sign whose stories echo themes of brotherhood, intellect and adaptability. Come along with us on this journey as we unveil the secrets and legends surrounding Gemini. A sign that has fascinated humans for centuries.

EARLIEST OBSERVATIONS IN ANCIENT CIVILIZATIONS

MESOPOTAMIA

The Mesopotamians were among the first to record and associate the Gemini constellation with the Great Twins, Gilgamesh and Enkidu. These twins held a significance in star mythology. They were protectors. This association highlights the Geminis themes of duality and finding balance.

ANCIENT GREECE

Moving to Ancient Greece, Gemini was linked to the twin brothers Castor and Pollux collectively known as the Dioscuri. They were regarded as patrons of sailors symbolizing both brotherhood and navigation. When Castor tragically lost his life Pollux felt grief. He pleaded with Zeus to grant him immortality so that he could be reunited with his twin. Touched by this display of love Zeus immortalized them both as the constellation Gemini, in the night sky. This tale beautifully portrays themes of brotherhood, loyalty and an unbreakable bond that transcends death. All deeply resonating with the relational connection associated with Gemini.

ANCIENT ROME

The ancient Romans followed suit by incorporating Gemini into their lore. They associated this constellation with Romulus and Remus, founders of Rome. Together they represent the city's beginnings and divine protection. The Romans revered them as protectors of the city. Throughout times of war and conflict people often turned to the concept of unity and cooperation as a symbol of strength.

CHINESE ASTRONOMY

Chinese astronomy integrated the stars of Gemini into constellations within their own system. One notable example is their inclusion in the White Tiger of the West formation. Unlike other interpretations centered around twins, Chinese cosmology offered a new perspective on these stars.

INDIA ASTRONOMY

In the astronomy of India, the stars of Gemini were viewed as a pair of physicians known as Ashvins who served as gods. They were regarded as symbols of good health, fortune, rejuvenation and healing.

INDIGENOUS CULTURES

Indigenous cultures also had their own interpretations of the stars within the Gemini constellation. For instance in American traditions these stars might have been seen as a pair of animals or other significant figures from their cultural stories and mythologies.

Across the cultures mentioned above, it is evident that the Gemini constellation consistently represents concepts such as duality, connection and transformation. Whether portrayed as brothers or celestial twins, or even protective deities themselves; the Gemini constellation has always been more than two stars, in the night sky. It has been a reflection that mirrors the intricate complexities and dualities embedded within human experiences.

The historical journey of the Gemini constellation demonstrates how various cultures throughout time have gazed upon the stars and deciphered their own narratives. Whether depicting twins, celestial patrons or symbols of healing, how Gemini is represented on star maps and in folklore reflects the tapestry of human culture and its profound connection with the universe.

From ancient times to the Middle Ages the concept of Gemini was surrounded by stories often portrayed as twins or brothers in different cultures. This symbolism was closely associated with ideas of duality, brotherhood and the transition between spring and summer.

As the Renaissance and Enlightenment periods unfolded our understanding of astronomy deepened. However astrological interpretations of Gemini still heavily relied on celestial symbols. In the modern era astrology has taken a psychological approach. Contemporary discussions about Gemini often focus on agility, communication skills and its ability to adapt to situations, highlighting its dual nature. This shift from mythological to interpretations is representative of a trend in astrology. It has evolved from a myth based practice into an introspective and therapeutic tool that helps explore personality traits, identity formation and human relationships.

HISTORICAL EVENTS UNDER THE GEMINI SIGN

Gemini season has witnessed many events throughout history. These occurrences are often interpreted in astrology as reflections of Gemini's qualities of adaptability, communication and intellect. Below are some notable historical events during Gemini season

- **Advancements in Science**; Many crucial scientific discoveries and events have taken place during the Gemini season. These align with Gemini's association with intelligence and curiosity. For instance we can mention the telegraph communication by Samuel Morse on May 24 1844 and the historic launch of Valentina Tereshkova as the first woman in space on June 16 1963.
- **Political Milestones**; Gemini has also witnessed political events that mirror it's adaptable nature and duality. This period has seen the signing of treaties and declarations including the adoption of the Magna Carta on June 15 1215.

- **Historical Figures Born Under Gemini;** Gemini has given birth to notable figures such as John F. Kennedy (born on May 29 1917) Marilyn Monroe (born on June 1 1926) and Anne Frank (born on June 12 1929). Their impact on society and culture resonates with the multifaceted nature associated with Gemini traits. In addition brilliant scientific thinkers, such as Alan Turing (born on June 23 1912) are often linked to the Gemini trait of having an intellect.

As we wrap up this chapter we reflect on the captivating collection of stories, myths and historical accounts associated with the Gemini constellation. From the ancient Greeks and Romans, to civilizations like Mesopotamia and beyond. Gemini has symbolized duality, connection and transformation. These cultures showcase the depth and complexity of human relationships as well as our dualistic nature.

FURTHER READING AND REFERENCES

For those interested in exploring the history and mythology of Gemini in greater detail, the following sources offer a wealth of information.

Primary Ancient Texts

- "Theogony" by Hesiod: Provides insight into early Greek mythology, including the story of Castor and Pollux.
- "Metamorphoses" by Ovid: A classical source that explores various Greek and Roman myths, including those associated with the Gemini constellation.

Astronomical and Astrological Texts

- "Almagest" by Ptolemy: An ancient Greek text on astronomy, offering early observations of the Gemini constellation.
- "Brihat Samhita" by Varahamihira: An influential work in Indian astrology, which includes references to the Ashvins and Vedic interpretations of Gemini.

Modern Astrological Writings

- "The Only Astrology Book You'll Ever Need" by Joanna Martine Woolfolk: A contemporary guide that provides insights into modern interpretations of Gemini.
- "Parker's Astrology" by Julia and Derek Parker: A comprehensive guide to astrology, offering a detailed look at the Gemini sign and its traits.

- "Astrology & Numerology" by Sofia Visconti offers a fresh perspective on Astrology and Numerology.

Cultural and Mythological Studies

- "The Greek Myths" by Robert Graves: A detailed exploration of Greek mythology, offering context and stories related to the Gemini constellation.
- "Mythology: Timeless Tales of Gods and Heroes" by Edith Hamilton: A classic text that covers a wide range of myths, including those associated with Gemini.

These sources, ranging from ancient texts to modern interpretations, offer a deeper understanding of the Gemini constellation and its place in both historical and contemporary astrology. Through them, readers can continue to explore the fascinating and multifaceted world of Gemini.

CHAPTER 2:
LOVE & COMPATIBILITY

In this chapter we will embark on a journey to explore how the Gemini sign navigates the realms of romance. Geminis are known for their deep thinking, communication skills and a love for variety. All of which bring a unique and dynamic flavor to their romantic experiences. As we delve into this chapter we will uncover the characteristics that define how Geminis approach love. We will discuss their preference for meaningful connections, playful banter and their deep seated need for understanding. By exploring these traits we will gain insights into how they shape their interactions with their partners.

Compatibility plays an important role in a Gemini's love life. We will also examine which zodiac signs harmonize best with Gemini's versatile nature. This exploration will reveal the complexities of compatibility while highlighting the synergy between Gemini individuals and potential partners. Furthermore we will discuss both the challenges and triumphs that Geminis encounter in their quest for love.

Overall our goal in this chapter is to offer an understanding of how Geminis romantic inclinations align with the stars. Whether you're a Gemini seeking insights into your love life or someone interested in forming a bond with a Gemini. This exploration will provide perspectives on love, relationships and astrological compatibility. Join us as we explore the dynamic world of love and compatibility for Geminis.

GEMINI'S LOVE AND COMPATIBILITY WITH OTHER ZODIAC SIGNS

GEMINI AND ARIES

Aries and Gemini usually have a lively relationship. Aries brings passion and determination which aligns well with Gemini's love for stimulation and social interaction. Both signs value their independence creating a balanced partnership.

However sometimes Aries impulsiveness may clash with Gemini's tendency to be indecisive. Effective communication becomes essential in navigating these differences.

GEMINI AND TAURUS

Taurus offers stability and a practical perspective, which can both ground and occasionally frustrate the adventurous Gemini. The intellectual curiosity of Gemini may sometimes clash with Tauruss preference for routine. Differences in energy levels and interests can pose obstacles that require compromise and understanding from both sides.

GEMINI AND GEMINI

When two Geminis come together they often engage in stimulating conversations and enjoy activities together. They recognize each other's need for personal space and variety. Their similar qualities enhance the relationships energy levels and foster creativity. However their shared tendency, towards inconsistency or lack of focus might lead to instability if not properly managed.

GEMINI AND CANCER

Cancer's depth of emotions can bring warmth to Gemini. However conflicts may arise due to Gemini's love for freedom and variety conflicting with Cancers desire for security and stability in relationships. There may be instances of miscommunication that require Gemini to be more empathetic while Cancer needs to understand Gemini's need for expression.

GEMINI AND LEO

Leo's charismatic and lively personality blends well with Gemini's communicative nature. Both enjoy being in the limelight leading to a fun filled and dynamic relationship of excitement and adventure. It is important for them to ensure that they share the spotlight equally as both signs thrive on attention.

GEMINI AND VIRGO

Both signs are ruled by Mercury. These signs share a love for creative pursuits. However there might be clashes between Virgo's attention to detail and Gemini's broader range of interests. A flourishing and happy relationship requires respect and understanding between the two.

GEMINI AND LIBRA

Compatibility is high between these two, as both are air signs. Gemini and Libra naturally connect through their shared affinity for communication and social interaction. Naturally this makes for a great relationship. Keep building upon their strengths and a lasting love is guaranteed.

GEMINI AND SCORPIO

Compatibility is not the best. But it is not the worst either. Gemini might find Scorpios intensity and depth intriguing. Sometimes it can be a bit overwhelming. Scorpio on the hand might see Gemini's lightheartedness, as being a bit superficial. Building trust and emotional depth requires effort. Scorpio needs connection while Gemini values their freedom.

GEMINI AND SAGITTARIUS

Both signs share a love for adventure, learning and exploration. Sagittarius' philosophical approach to life complements Gemini's curiosity leading to an expanding relationship. They both need to strike a balance between independence and commitment in order to maintain a relationship.

GEMINI AND CAPRICORN

Not the best match but there is always potential for these two. Capricorn's practicality and ambition can add structure to Gemini's diverse ideas. However Capricorn's serious nature may clash with Gemini. It is important for them to understand and respect each other's approaches to life and goals in order to create harmony.

GEMINI AND AQUARIUS

Being both air signs there is an understanding and connection between Gemini and Aquarius. Aquarius' innovative ideas complement Gemini's curiosity leading to a forward thinking partnership. Since both signs value their independence, establishing a grounded relationship can present a challenge.

GEMINI AND PISCES

Pisces brings depth and emotional insight to the partnership with Gemini. Meanwhile Gemini adds depth and intellectual stimulation to Pisces. This combination can be enriching yet also pose challenges. The emotional sensitivity of Pisces may overwhelm Gemini at times while Gemini's rational approach might perplex Pisces. Emotional understanding and effective communication are crucial for navigating these differences.

TIPS FOR RELATIONSHIPS WITH GEMINI

Dating a Gemini whether it's a man or a woman can be an exhilarating and intellectually stimulating experience. Geminis are known for their wit, curiosity and dynamic personalities, which bring excitement and diversity to relationships. Here are some personalized tips for dating and maintaining relationships with Gemini individuals.

DATING GEMINI MEN

- **Engage His Mind**; Have engaging conversations that stimulate his intellect. Share your thoughts. Be open to discussing any topics. Gemini men enjoy having a partner who can keep up with their quick thinking.
- **Embrace Adventure**; Gemini men often crave variety and excitement. Be open to new experiences and adventures together. This will keep the relationship vibrant and captivating for them.
- **Respect His Independence;** Gemini men highly value their freedom. It's crucial to respect their need for space and independence without taking it. Trust them. Give them the room to be themselves.
- **Adaptability;** Remain flexible as Gemini men can be unpredictable at times frequently changing their minds. Being adaptable is essential in maintaining harmony in the relationship.
- **Share Laughter;** A good sense of humor is an excellent way to connect with a Gemini man. Heartedness and playful banter can make your time together more enjoyable.
- **Avoid Falling into a Monotonous Routine;** It's important to steer away from getting stuck in a boring routine. Gemini men thrive on diversity and new experiences so it's essential to keep things varied.

DATING GEMINI WOMEN

- **Effective Communication is Key;** Gemini women love engaging in conversations and expressing themselves. It's crucial to participate in discussions and actively listen. Building a relationship with a Gemini woman revolves around communication.
- **Appreciate Her Intellectual Abilities;** Show interest in her ideas and thoughts. Gemini women value partners who recognize and appreciate their intellect as those who can engage them in intelligent conversations.
- **Embrace Social Interactions;** Gemini women often enjoy social settings. Be open to attending gatherings and meeting new people.
- **Respect Her Need for Independence;** Just like their male counterparts, Gemini women highly value their independence. Respect her desire for space.
- **Nurture Emotional Connection;** While intellectual compatibility is important it's equally important not to neglect the bond. Despite their independent nature Gemini women also crave emotional connections.
- **Be Patient with Dualities;** Gemini women can have personalities that may seem contradictory, at times. It's important to be patient, understanding and accepting of the facets of her character.

Overall remember it's essential to understand that each individual is unique. The secret to building a connection with a Gemini regardless of gender lies in effective communication and empathy. The key takeaway from this chapter is the significance of communication and flexibility within relationships involving Geminis. Partners who are willing to engage in honest conversations embrace change gracefully and appreciate the nature of Gemini will discover a deeply fulfilling relationship.

Gemini individuals may appear lighthearted and playful, on the surface. However they are capable of forming emotional connections. The challenge for Geminis lies in finding a balance between their nature and their emotions. When they discover a partner who appreciates this duality and creates an environment where both sides can coexist, Geminis can experience fulfilling romantic relationships.

To summarize Geminis approaches love and romance from angles making it an evolving journey. Their relationships thrive on stimulation, effective communication and the desire for both variety and independence. Recognizing and embracing these characteristics can lead to partnerships that stand the test of time.

CHAPTER 3:
FRIENDS AND FAMILY

This chapter explores the friends and family of Geminis. As we delve into the lives of Geminis we uncover the nuances of their interactions with friends and family. Known for their eloquence, adaptability and insatiable curiosity Geminis bring a unique flavor to their relationships. They are great connectors often becoming the life and soul of any gathering. However this same liveliness and love for diversity can occasionally result in inconsistency. Or a hesitation to explore emotional connections.

In terms of friendship Geminis excel as stimulating companions who're always open to ideas and experiences. Nevertheless their need for variety and intellectual stimulation can sometimes clash with the desire for relationships grounded in consistency. Within the family context, Geminis display versatility by taking on roles ranging from peacemakers to problem solvers. However their yearning for space and independence can sometimes create tension with family expectations.

Through insights and observations we will examine Geminis' approaches to their loved ones to harmonize these intricate dynamics. By doing so, we aim to nurture relationships that are fulfilling and long lasting. Join us as we dive into the realm of Gemini;. family and friends. Together lets unravel the mysteries and embrace the joys that come with these vibrant connections.

GEMINI AS A FRIEND

Having a Gemini as a friend is truly captivating and intriguing. Truly they embody the duality represented by their twins. Here are some key aspects of being friends with a Gemini.

- **Engaging**; Geminis thrive on stimulating discussions delving into topics ranging from scientific breakthroughs to the nuances of various art forms.
- **Social**; Geminis effortlessly navigate social circles. Their ability to mingle and engage with groups makes them exceptional companions at gatherings.
- **Versatile**; Geminis are individuals who easily embrace new situations. Whether it's embarking on an adventure or trying something they make great travel companions for exploring uncharted territories.

- **Inconsistency**; One negative aspect of having a Gemini friend is their inconsistency. They may change plans or flip flop, on opinions. It stems from their curious and exploratory nature.
- **Humor**; Geminis typically possess a fantastic sense of humor. With their sharp wit they effortlessly find humor in situations making them enjoyable and entertaining friends.
- **Empathetic**; They possess an ability to comprehend diverse perspectives making them empathetic companions who can provide meaningful guidance.
- **Independence**; Geminis highly value their independence. Occasionally they require some time to explore their individual interests. It's important not to mistake this trait for a lack of interest in friendship.
- **Loyal**; Despite their inclination towards variety and change Geminis are loyal friends. Once they establish a bond they are loyal and supportive, willing to go above and beyond to assist their friends.
- **Inquisitive**; A Gemini friend is always eager to learn. They possess an open mind making them wonderful companions for exploring ideas and diverse cultures.

To sum up, a Gemini friend embodies energy, wit and intellect. Their presence brings excitement and diversity to friendships albeit their need for change and stimulation can sometimes present challenges. Understanding and appreciating their nature can lead to a friendship filled with depth.

GEMINI IN FAMILY DYNAMICS

Gemini individuals, known for their caring nature represented by the twins, bring a positive dynamic to family relationships. Let's see how a Gemini might interact within the family.

- **Great Communicators**; Geminis excel in communication. They are usually the ones who keep the dialogue going during family gatherings and can effectively resolve misunderstandings through discussions.
- **Adaptable**; In family dynamics Geminis are highly adaptable. They can effortlessly switch roles acting as mediators, entertainers or advisors based on what the situation calls for.
- **Wide Range of Interests**; With their range of interests Geminis can easily connect with family members on different levels. For instance they may share a love for sports with one sibling while appreciating music with another.
- **Craving Intellectual Stimulation**; Geminis actively encourage discussions and debates on topics which keeps the family atmosphere dynamic and engaging.
- **Inconsistency**; Their moods may fluctuate at times which can be challenging for some family members to understand.
- **Independence**; Geminis value their independence. They tend to encourage the same among their family members. They value the pursuits and independence of each family member showing their support.
- **Playful**; Geminis bring an youthful energy to the family. They often lighten the atmosphere, adding a sprinkle of humor to family interactions.
- **Avoidance**; Geminis may tend to avoid getting emotionally entangled which can sometimes be misunderstood as detachment. It's crucial for family members to acknowledge that this is part of who they are.
- **Flexibility**; They are individuals who willingly adapt to changing dynamics within the family. Whether it's taking charge during times or stepping back to allow others to lead, Geminis can smoothly adjust their roles as needed.

In conclusion Geminis inject vibrancy, effective communication and adaptability into family life. Their desire for stimulation and variety can greatly contribute to a dynamic family environment. However it's important for other family members to understand and accommodate their fluctuating moods and need for space. Embracing these traits can make the familial experience more fulfilling and harmonious.

CHALLENGES IN FRIENDSHIPS AND FAMILY RELATIONS

Gemini presents their own challenges when it comes to friendships and family relationships due to their inherent traits. Understanding these challenges can help Geminis and their loved ones navigate their relationships effectively.

CHALLENGES IN FRIENDSHIPS

- **Unpredictability**; Geminis love for variety and change can sometimes result in random behavior. Friends may find it challenging to keep up with their changing interests and moods which can lead to misunderstandings.
- **Communication Overflow;** While Geminis excel at communication their constant need to share and discuss things can overwhelm some friends who prefer reflective interactions.
- **Fear of Emotional Intensity;** Geminis may shy away from connections or serious conversations, which could be misinterpreted as shallowness or a lack of commitment to the friendship.
- **Distractibility**; Their natural curiosity and desire to explore everything can occasionally make them appear distracted or less fully engaged in the moment, which might mistakenly be seen as disinterest.
- **Indecisiveness;** Geminis have a tendency towards indecisiveness, which might frustrate friends who rely on them for making decisions or providing opinions.

CHALLENGES IN FAMILY RELATIONS

- **Need for Independence**; Geminis highly value their independence, which can sometimes clash with family expectations. For example in close knit families where collective decision making is the norm.
- **Avoidance;** When it comes to family situations Geminis may tend to avoid delving into emotional conversations. This behavior might make them appear empathetic or engaged in family issues.
- **Juggling Multiple Roles;** Gemini's adaptability, in switching between roles within the family dynamic can sometimes lead to feelings of exhaustion or being misunderstood. Family members may not always recognize their efforts to strike a balance between these roles.

- **Unpredictable Mood Swings;** The dual nature of Geminis can result in mood swings that are challenging for family members to comprehend or anticipate. This can create a sense of instability during interactions within the family.
- **Craving Variety versus Routine;** Gemini individuals desire for change and variety may clash with the stability. Routine typically found in family life. Consequently they might experience restlessness or a feeling of being confined.

As we wrap up our exploration of how Geminis interact in the realms of friendship and family it becomes clear that this journey is as diverse and complex as the sign itself. Geminis, with their duality and appreciation for diversity bring an energy to their relationships. However maintaining harmony and depth in these connections requires mindfulness and effort. Lets recap some of the key points.

KEY INSIGHTS RECAP

- **Embrace Open Communication**; Geminis thrive on communication. It's important to encourage honest dialogue during emotionally charged situations. This not only helps misunderstandings but also strengthens trust and understanding.
- **Respect Individuality**; Both friends and family members of Geminis should respect their need for space and independence. Understanding this allows Geminis to feel valued and respected, fostering connections.
- **Patience with Inconsistencies**; Recognizing and accepting the fluctuating interests and moods of Geminis can help prevent conflicts. Patience and empathy play roles in nurturing these relationships.
- **Encourage Emotional Expression**; Geminis may benefit from encouragement to explore their emotions deeply. Creating an environment for expression can deepen the bond between individuals.
- **Find Balance**; Geminis should strive to strike a balance, between engagements and personal time. It is essential for individuals to set aside time, for introspection and self care in order to maintain their well being.
- **Growth mindset**; When it comes to relationships with Geminis there is a potential for growth and learning. Embracing their curiosity and thirst for knowledge can lead to shared experiences that enhance these bonds.
- **Flexibility and adaptability**; These are crucial for both Geminis and their loved ones. Being able to adapt to changing circumstances and accommodate each other's needs is key in maintaining a relationship.

- **Self awareness**; To nurture their relationships Geminis should focus on self awareness and understanding how their nature impacts others. It's important for them to recognize any tendencies towards superficiality or indecisiveness and work on improving those aspects, which can result in fulfilling relationships.

In conclusion the relationships involving Geminis resemble dances of energy, change and adaptability. By embracing the qualities that make Geminis unique while also addressing challenges along the way these relationships have the potential to evolve into lasting connections. Embarking on a journey with a Gemini entails conversations, joyful laughter and valuable opportunities for growth and knowledge. It is an experience that combines enrichment and enlightenment. Enjoy the journey for every step is worth it.

CHAPTER 4:
CAREER AND AMBITIONS

Geminis, known for their duality and intellect, stands apart in the zodiac constellation. This chapter explores the connection between Geminis and their professional lives which are as multifaceted as the sign itself. They bring a combination of adaptability, strong communication skills and curiosity to their work. However these very qualities that propel them forward can also present challenges when it comes to maintaining focus and consistency.

Join us on an exploration of the professional realm of Gemini, where we delve into the impact of astrology, on their career paths and financial behavior. This journey will unveil insights into how this adaptable and intellectually driven zodiac sign can unlock their potential in the professional world.

CAREER PREFERENCES AND PROFESSIONAL ASPIRATIONS

Gemini individuals often exhibit key preferences and ambitions in their lives. Naturally they are influenced by their inherent qualities of adaptability, effective communication skills and intellectual curiosity. Here is a brief overview of the career preferences and aspirations for someone born under the Gemini zodiac sign.

- **Versatile and Diverse Roles**; Geminis thrive in careers that offer a range of tasks and opportunities. They prefer roles that're dynamic allowing them to tackle projects and avoid monotony. In terms of their aspirations They often strive for a range of experiences throughout their career. They may explore roles within the field or even switch careers altogether in order to fulfill their desire for variety.
- **Communication Oriented Jobs**; With their ability to communicate effectively Geminis excel in professions that involve writing, speaking or other forms of communication. Careers in journalism, writing, public relations or broadcasting often appeal to them.
- **Stimulating Environments**; They gravitate towards careers that challenge their intellect and provide learning opportunities. Roles involving research, analysis or problem solving can be particularly attractive to them.
- **Social Interaction**; Geminis enjoy working in environments where they can interact with groups of people. Careers involving teamwork, networking or public engagement align with their nature. They commonly aspire to communication based roles where they can use their skills to influence, educate or entertain others. This could manifest as becoming a journalist, an author or even establishing themselves as a media personality.
- **Autonomy**; They value flexibility in their work environment. Careers that offer a degree of autonomy along with work hours or the option to work remotely tend to be highly appealing to them.
- **Creative**; Fields that require creativity and innovation such as advertising, graphic design or digital media are particularly attractive to Gemini individuals due to their inclination towards being creative and inventive.
- **Growth**; Continuous learning and personal development play roles in the growth of Geminis. They actively seek out opportunities for training, education and new experiences to keep expanding their knowledge and keeping their minds engaged.

In conclusion Gemini individuals pursue careers that're vibrant, intellectually engaging and provide chances for social engagement. Their career goals are fueled by a craving for diversity, ongoing learning and the urge to express their creativity and thoughts. Thanks to their adaptability and strong communication abilities they excel as professionals who can thrive in various industries and positions.

STRENGTHS IN THE WORKPLACE

Gemini individuals possess a set of strengths that contribute to their success, in professional settings. These strengths are rooted in their ability to adapt, think on their feet and communicate effectively. Let's take a look at the strengths that Geminis bring to their workplaces.

- **Adaptability**; Geminis demonstrate adaptability effortlessly adjusting to changing situations and workplace dynamics. Their flexibility proves invaluable in roles that involve handling shifts or diverse tasks.
- **Strong Communication Skills**; Geminis naturally excel in communication. They have a knack for expressing their thoughts persuasively making them highly effective in roles that involve negotiation, presentations or team coordination.
- **Intellectual Curiosity**; Geminis possess a curiosity that drives them to learn and explore new ideas. This quality proves invaluable in industries characterized by evolution since they thrive on staying up to date with the trends and information.
- **Problem Solving**; Known for their analytical minds Geminis approach problems, from various perspectives and devise innovative solutions. Their ability to think outside the box makes them excellent problem solvers.
- **Social Skill**s; With their social nature Geminis are great at networking. They excel at building and maintaining professional relationships, which can greatly benefit any career.
- **Ability to Handle Multiple Tasks**; Geminis have an impressive talent for multitasking. They can effortlessly manage responsibilities simultaneously without compromising the quality of their work.
- **Enthusiasm and Energy**; Geminis often bring a sense of enthusiasm and vitality to the workplace. Their energetic presence has a motivating and uplifting effect on the team.
- **Versatility**; Thanks to their range of interests and skills Geminis are adaptable employees. They can easily adjust to roles or tasks making them valuable assets in dynamic work environments.
- **Quick Learning**; Gemini individuals possess intellects that enable them to grasp concepts and acquire new skills rapidly. This makes them quick learners who can swiftly adapt to roles or technologies.

- **Effective Team Players**; While they appreciate their independence Geminis also excel as team players. They understand how group dynamics work. Make contributions to collaborative efforts.

In summary Gemini individuals bring together a combination of adaptability, communication skills, creativity and intellectual curiosity. These strengths make them well suited for dynamic work environments that require flexibility, problem solving abilities and effective communication skills. Their aptitude for learning and effective collaboration both as contributors and team players renders them invaluable assets, in any professional environment.

PROFESSIONAL CHALLENGES AND STRATEGIES TO OVERCOME THEM

Gemini individuals will encounter many challenges in their professional journeys. Understanding these challenges and employing strategies can aid Geminis in navigating the realm of work successfully.

CAREER CHALLENGES

- **Inconsistency and Difficulty Maintaining Focus**; Geminis occasionally struggle with maintaining consistency. Their ranging interests may result in a lack of focus on a task or project which can impact productivity and hinder career advancement.
- **Impatience**; Their quick thinking nature can sometimes manifest as impatience in situations that require a methodical and deliberate approach. This impatience can lead to frustration in work environments that emphasize attention to detail and patience.
- **Challenges with Routine**; Geminis often find tasks uninspiring, which can contribute to dissatisfaction in jobs lacking diversity and opportunities for creativity.
- **Taking on too much**; With their enthusiasm and willingness to tackle responsibilities Geminis may occasionally take on more than they can handle leading to stress and exhaustion.
- **Communication Overload**; Although Geminis are skilled, at communication there may be times when they overwhelm their colleagues or clients with an abundance of information. They might also struggle to listen as they speak.
- **Avoidance of In depth Tasks**; Geminis tend to prefer tasks that offer variety and stay on the surface, which can sometimes hinder their ability to engage deeply with detailed work.

STRATEGIES FOR OVERCOMING CAREER CHALLENGES

- **Organize**; Geminis can benefit from using tools and techniques that help them prioritize tasks and manage their time effectively. By setting goals and deadlines they can bring structure and focus to their work.
- **Mindfulness and Patience Training**; Practices like mindfulness can assist Geminis in developing patience and the ability to concentrate on the task at hand. These qualities are crucial for long term projects requiring attention to detail.
- **Seek Variety within Structure**; Finding roles that offer a mix of tasks within an environment can satisfy Gemini's need for change while still allowing them to maintain focus. This could involve taking on projects within a job position.
- **Set Realistic Commitments**; It's essential for Geminis to realistically assess their workload and establish boundaries in order to avoid overcommitment. Learning how to say no or delegate tasks when necessary becomes crucial in maintaining balance.
- **Develop Active Listening Skills**; While Geminis excel at expressing themselves, focusing on enhancing their listening skills can make them effective communicators overall transforming them into well rounded professionals.
- **Embrace the Power of Deep Work**; Geminis have the ability to gradually train themselves to engage in work. They can start by setting aside time for these tasks and gradually increasing the duration.

- **Consider Career Flexibility**; Geminis can keep themselves engaged and motivated by exploring careers that offer flexibility, such as freelancing or roles with responsibilities.

To sum up, while Geminis may face challenges in their careers due to their love for variety and quick thinking nature, there are strategies they can implement to overcome these obstacles. By organizing their workload, practicing patience and enhancing their listening skills Geminis can not only navigate their careers successfully but also thrive professionally. They can then leverage their strengths to their advantage and make significant progress in their professional endeavors.

In essence, this chapter illuminates the path for Geminis to transform their potential career challenges into stepping stones for success. With an arsenal of strategies like meticulous organization, cultivated patience, and honed listening skills, Geminis are well-equipped to navigate the professional labyrinth with grace and acumen. By embracing these tactics, they can effectively harness their innate gifts of versatility and quick thinking, paving the way to a flourishing and prosperous career journey that sparkles with the unique Gemini brilliance.

CHAPTER 5: SELF-IMPROVEMENT

This chapter dives into the world of Gemini exploring the paths and practices that lead to growth and fulfillment. We will delve into how Geminis can harness their strengths like adaptability, quick thinking and social finesse to excel in life. Simultaneously we'll address strategies to overcome their weaknesses such as inconsistency, restlessness and a tendency to avoid emotional commitments.

Join us on a journey of self improvement tailored specifically for those born under the Gemini zodiac sign. This adventure guarantees to be both fulfilling and eye opening as it uncovers the potential for growth and transformation that lies within this captivating astrological symbol.

PERSONAL GROWTH AND SELF-DEVELOPMENT

Personal growth and self-development, for individuals born under the Gemini zodiac sign, represented by the symbol of twins, revolves around embracing their duality and harnessing their strengths. The journey towards growth for Geminis encompasses many important aspects.

- **Embracing Dual Nature**; Geminis often exhibit a mix of sociability and solitude, seriousness and playfulness. Personal growth entails recognizing these opposing qualities and harmoniously integrating them.
- **Self Understanding**; Geminis will greatly benefit from introspection, meditation or journaling to gain an understanding of their multifaceted nature. Exploring their thoughts and emotions can be enlightening.
- **Intellectual Advancement**; Geminis possess a thirst for knowledge. Personal growth is nurtured by pursuing education reading extensively or delving into hobbies and skills.
- **Cultivating diverse experiences**; Broadening perspectives through exposure to various experiences is key. Traveling to new places, attending workshops or immersing oneself in cultures can be highly enriching.
- **Social Development**; While Geminis are famed for their intellectual approach it's important to cultivate emotional depth as well. Practices, like mindfulness or seeking counseling contribute to developing intelligence.

COMMUNICATION SKILLS

- **Improving Listening Skills**; While Geminis are great at expressing themselves they can enhance their communication skills by listening and empathizing with others gaining an understanding of different perspectives.
- **Honest Communication**; It's important for Geminis to work on communicating their needs, boundaries and thoughts in an honest and clear manner. This is crucial for growth.
- **Strengthening Relationships**; Geminis have an opportunity for growth when it comes to building meaningful connections. They can focus on being more present during their interactions and investing in their relationships.

CAREER AND PERSONAL ASPIRATIONS

- **Setting Goals**; Geminis may sometimes struggle with finding a direction due to their range of interests. Setting short term and long term goals can help them focus their energy and stay motivated.

- **Balance**; Learning how to balance ambition with finding contentment in the moment is essential for fulfillment. It's about appreciating the present while striving towards aspirations.

HEALTH AND WELLNESS

- **Exercise and Relaxation**; Engaging in activities and relaxation techniques can aid Geminis in managing their occasionally restless energy. Activities like yoga, meditation or participating in sports can be particularly beneficial.
- **Establishing Routine and Structure**; Despite their preference, for variety establishing a routine in daily or weekly schedules can provide a sense of stability and grounding.

In conclusion Geminis can experience growth by finding a balance between their intellectual curiosity, emotional and social well being and overall health. By embracing their multifaceted nature and prioritizing these aspects of life Geminis have the opportunity to embark on a successful journey of self discovery and personal development.

HARNESSING STRENGTHS AND OVERCOMING WEAKNESSES

To make the most of Gemini individuals strengths and address their weaknesses it's important to understand their nature and appreciate their qualities. Geminis have a range of strengths that can be capitalized on while their weaknesses offer chances for growth and development. Let's take a look.

HARNESSING STRENGTHS

- **Leveraging Strong Communication**; Geminis have a talent for communication. They can make the most of this strength by pursuing careers or roles that involve writing, speaking, teaching or negotiation. Their ability to express ideas clearly makes them effective in positions that require persuasion or explanation.
- **Embracing Adaptability**; Gemini's inherent adaptability makes them well suited for dynamic work environments and roles that demand thinking and flexibility. They thrive in situations where they need to adjust to changing circumstances.
- **Nurturing Intellectual Curiosity**; Geminis should embrace their love for learning and exploration. Engaging in education whether through channels

or self directed pursuits allows them to stay intellectually stimulated and stay ahead in their respective fields.

- **Maximizing Social Skills**; With their social nature Geminis excel at networking and building relationships. They should seize opportunities to connect with others as this can lead to professional growth.
- **Creative Problem Solving**; Gemini's ability to view things from perspectives gives them an edge in problem solving. They are excellent at finding solutions by considering multiple angles. Gemini individuals can take advantage of this during brainstorming sessions and, in roles that value creative solutions.

OVERCOMING WEAKNESSES

- **Prioritizing Consistency**; One of the hurdles for Geminis is their inclination towards inconsistency. To tackle this they can establish routines. Or set goals to maintain focus. Utilizing tools such as planners and to do lists can also be helpful in ensuring consistency in both professional aspects of their lives.
- **Cultivating Patience**; Geminis tend to have a high level of impatience. Engaging in mindfulness practices and exercises that build patience can prove beneficial for them. It's important for them to be present and fully engaged in the moment especially when dealing with situations that require an approach.
- **Managing Indecisiveness;** Geminis often struggle with making decisions due to their many interests. To address this challenge they should strive to make informed choices and stick to them by setting deadlines for decision making.
- **Deepening Emotional Connections**; While Geminis excel at surface level interactions they could work on forging deeper connections. This can be accomplished through honest communication well as investing quality time in meaningful conversations.
- **Balancing Enthusiasm with Realism**; Geminis naturally possess enthusiasm but sometimes lean towards excessive optimism. It is crucial for them to strike a balance between enthusiasm and realism particularly when it comes to planning and executing tasks.

In conclusion individuals born under the sign of Gemini can maximize their potential by embracing their communication skills, adaptability, curiosity and sociable nature. To overcome their weaknesses they should work on being consistent. They can develop patience and decisiveness, nurturing depth and finding a balance between enthusiasm and realism. By doing this Geminis can tap into their talents and also experience personal growth. Overall they can achieve a well rounded and satisfying life.

As we wrap up this exploration of the self improvement journey undertaken by individuals born under the Gemini zodiac sign it becomes evident that the path they traverse is as diverse and dynamic, as their nature. By embracing their qualities and harnessing their strengths Geminis can unlock a realm of possibilities in both their professional lives.

The future looks promising for Geminis when it comes to self improvement. They have an ability to adapt, think quickly and communicate effectively which positions them for success, in many aspects of life. By embracing the exercises and techniques outlined in this chapter, they can make use of their strengths and overcome challenges. Naturally this will lead to a more satisfying and balanced life.

Remember that the journey of self improvement for Geminis is ongoing and ever evolving. As they learn to balance their nature, embrace their curiosity and channel their energies productively they open themselves up to many possibilities. The key is to remain receptive to change and growth while allowing their inherent talents to flourish. At the same time, continuously work on areas that need improvement.

In summary the path towards self improvement for Geminis involves finding harmony within their contrasting characteristics and leveraging their versatility as a strength. By committing themselves to growth and being open minded to explore alternative approaches Geminis can develop remarkable self awareness and find fulfillment in their journey. The future holds huge potential, for those who embrace this path guiding them towards an enriched life.

CHAPTER 6: THE YEAR AHEAD

As the alignment of stars begins a new cycle, in the zodiac individuals born under the sign of Gemini find themselves on the brink of a year filled with possibilities. Renowned for their intellect, adaptability and strong communication skills, Geminis are poised to navigate through aspects of life that will require these qualities. This chapter aims to unravel the tapestry that awaits those who belong to this sign. By combining foresight with advice we will embark on a journey through key astrological events that are destined to influence Gemini's love life and relationships, career, finances, health and much more.

From Mercury's retrogrades (as it's their ruling planet) to Venus and Jupiter's transits, each movement of these celestial bodies carries its own significance that will shape Gemini's experiences and opportunities. We will explore how these cosmic shifts can impact their lives. Throughout each section we delve into here, Geminis will gain insights on how to harness the influences brought by these celestial forces. They will also learn how to navigate any challenges that may arise.

Overall our goal in this chapter is to equip Geminis with the tools and knowledge to make the most out of the year ahead. So join us as we embark on a journey through the year for Geminis. A year filled with opportunities for growth, self discovery and a deeper understanding of how the cosmic forces influence their daily lives.

A YEARLY HOROSCOPE GUIDE FOR GEMINI

When it comes to creating a horoscope guide, for Gemini individuals the focus lies in providing insights and forecasts for various aspects of their life such as career, relationships, personal growth and health. It's important to remember that while astrology can offer some guidance and entertainment value it shouldn't be seen as a substitute for advice in any field. Here's a general outline for a horoscope guide specifically tailored to Geminis.

FINANCES

- **Start of the Year;** The beginning of the year will place emphasis on career development. There may be chances for advancement or taking on new projects. From a financial perspective it's wise to plan and budget accordingly for the changes.
- **Mid Year**; The middle of the year could bring some challenges. However by staying adaptable and utilizing your communication skills effectively you'll be able to navigate through them. This period also presents opportunities for networking and exploring career paths.
- **End of Year**; As the year draws to a close all your hard work will start paying off. You might receive recognition. Even you could find yourself on the path, towards promotion. Financial stability is on the rise creating conditions for investments or major purchases.

RELATIONSHIPS AND SOCIAL LIFE

- **Start of the Year**; The beginning of the year brings opportunities for new connections and friendships. For those currently in relationships effective communication plays an important role during this period.
- **Mid Year**; The middle of the year may bring some misunderstandings in relationships. It's important to maintain openness and honesty in your communication. Singles might find this a unique time to explore romantic interests.
- **End of Year**; As the year comes to an end, harmony prevails in your relationships. It's a time to deepen bonds and reconnect with loved ones. Social gatherings and celebrations take center stage.

PERSONAL GROWTH AND HEALTH

- **Start of the Year**; The start of the year focuses on development. It presents an opportunity for Geminis to acquire skills or engage in hobbies. In terms of health, maintaining a balanced lifestyle is key.
- **Mid Year**; The middle of the year calls for self reflection. It's a period to reassess goals and aspirations. Prioritizing well being becomes crucial during this time; practices such as meditation or yoga can be beneficial.
- **End of Year**; As the year draws to an end you will experience renewed purpose and clarity. Maintaining health is important so make sure to not overlook check ups.

TRAVEL AND EXPLORATION

- **Throughout the Year**; There are many travel opportunities available, at different times throughout the year. Overall it's more favorable to go on short trips rather than long journeys. These short trips can offer both relaxation and opportunities for growth.

In conclusion for Gemini individuals this year will bring chances for professional development alongside challenges that will test and enhance your abilities. Being adaptable, communicative and open, to learning will be skills to navigate this year successfully. Embrace the changes that come your way. You'll find it to be a fulfilling journey.

KEY ASTROLOGICAL EVENTS AND THEIR IMPACT ON GEMINI

Different zodiac signs can be influenced in various ways by key astrological events. In the case of Gemini individuals, specific astrological occurrences throughout the year can have an impact on aspects of their lives including emotions and decision making processes. Here's an overview of some key astrological events and how they might affect Gemini.

Mercury Retrograde

- Impact; Since Mercury is the ruling planet for Gemini its retrograde periods can have a significant influence on them. During these times communication issues, misunderstandings and travel disruptions are common. Geminis may also experience a reflective state.
- Advice; It's advisable for Geminis to double check all forms of communication. Avoid initiating projects during Mercury retrograde. It's also an opportunity to revisit and revise projects.

Solar and Lunar Eclipses

- Impact; Eclipses often bring about changes and revelations. For Gemini individuals solar eclipses can signal beginnings in areas such as growth and relationships while lunar eclipses may bring closure or emotional climaxes.
- Advice; Embrace the changes brought about by eclipses. Solar eclipses present circumstances for Geminis to embark on ventures or foster relationships while lunar eclipses are ideal moments to let go of what no longer serves them.

Venus Transit

- Impact; Venus governs love and finance; thus its transit can affect Gemini's relationships and financial matters.
- Advice; During this time Geminis often find clarity in their relationships. May feel compelled to reevaluate their strategies. My advice would be to focus on maintaining balance in your budget and being open and honest with your loved ones. It's an opportunity for Geminis to resolve any lingering conflicts with those to them.

Mars Transit

- Impact; The transit of Mars can have an impact on energy levels and ambition for Geminis. It has the potential to enhance drive in career related endeavors and physical activities.
- Advice; Be cautious of impulsiveness or getting into conflicts. Make use of this energy by pursuing goals and engaging in physical activities that bring you fulfillment.

Jupiter's Transit

- Impact; Jupiter's transit can bring about luck and expansion for Geminis. It opens doors for growth and abundance in areas of life such as career, education and travel opportunities.
- Advice; seize these chances for development by exploring education options, embarking on exciting travels or considering expanding your professional horizons.

Saturn's Transit

- Impact; Saturn's transit is known for its influence on structure and discipline. During this period Geminis might face increased responsibilities along with lessons in the realms of career growth and personal development.
- Advice; Stay disciplined, focused and embrace the challenges that come your way. This is a time when Geminis need to put in work and stay determined as it holds the promise of long term rewards.

New Moon and Full Moon

- Impact; During the New Moon and Full Moon phases Geminis can experience noticeable impacts. The New Moon can inspire them to embark on projects or make changes in their lifestyles. On the other hand the Full Moon may bring about a culmination or fulfillment of aspects of their lives.
- Advice; Utilize the energy of the New Moon for setting intentions and starting endeavors. As for the Full Moon it's a time for self reflection. Witnessing the results of your efforts. By staying aware of these events and understanding their effects Geminis can navigate through life more smoothly while making use of any opportunities that come their way.

KEY AREAS OF INTEREST

LOVE AND RELATIONSHIPS

The impact of astrology on the love life of Gemini individuals is set to bring changes in the year. Important astrological events, such as the movement of Venus and Mars will play key roles.

Venus, known as the planet of love, will enter a position that enhances Geminis charm and social skills. This period creates conditions for forming connections or strengthening existing relationships. Geminis will feel more open to love and establishing bonds.

When Mars influences Gemini's love life there may be a surge of passion and impulsive behavior. It is important for Geminis to navigate this time carefully in order to avoid conflicts within their relationships.

Mercury, which governs Gemini, goes retrograde periodically. During these phases misunderstandings or communication issues might arise within relationships. It is crucial for Geminis to practice patience and ensure communication during this time.

Strategies for Love and Relationships

- **Open Communication;** During Mercury retrograde periods it is vital for Geminis to prioritize honest communication in order to prevent misunderstandings.
- **Embrace Romantic Opportunities;** The transit of Venus presents an opportunity for Geminis to explore romantic possibilities or rekindle existing relationships.
- **Managing Impulsiveness;** During the time when Marss, in transit Geminis need to be mindful of their nature when it comes to matters of the heart.

CAREER AND FINANCES

Gemini's financial aspects will be influenced by planetary movements this year. The movement of Jupiter, the planet associated with expansion indicates growth and opportunities in career and finances. This period is favorable for advancing in one's job and making investments. Then, Saturn's movement might bring about challenges and increased responsibilities at work requiring Geminis to practice discipline and hard work.

Career and Financial Strategies

- **Seizing Opportunities**; Make use of the period when Jupiter is in transit to broaden your career prospects and explore avenues for growth.
- **Maintaining Discipline;** During Saturn's transit focus on long term goals. Stay disciplined to overcome any obstacles that may arise.

HEALTH AND WELLNESS

Gemini's well being will be subtly influenced by movements throughout the year. Lunar cycles during the New Moon and Full Moon phases can have an impact on Gemini's emotional well being as well as physical health. These periods call for self care practices that help maintain balance.

Advice on Health and Well being

- **Achieving Physical Balance;** Incorporate the cycles into your focus on emotional well being and physical health. Engage in practices such as meditation and regular exercise as they can have effects.
- **Regular Health Check ups;** It is advisable to undergo health check ups to keep track of your well being.

PERSONAL GROWTH AND SELF DISCOVERY

The astrological events throughout the year provide opportunities for personal growth and self discovery especially for individuals born under the Gemini zodiac sign. Mercury Retrograde periods are ideal for introspection reflecting on goals and reevaluating them. During Jupiter and Saturn Transits, expand your knowledge and skills. Be sure to also incorporate discipline and structure into your growth endeavors.

Strategies for Personal Growth

- **Reflecting and Reevaluating**; Take advantage of the energy during Mercury retrograde to engage in self reflection and set goals.
- **Embrace Learning;** The transit of Jupiter presents an opportunity to pursue pursuits or develop new skills.
- **Develop Discipline;** Utilize Saturn's influence to establish discipline in activities related to self improvement.

By understanding these influences and aligning with them Gemini individuals can navigate the year with greater awareness and purpose. This will allow them to make the most of opportunities for growth in areas such, as love, career, health and personal development.

As we wrap up our exploration of what lies for Gemini in the year it's evident that the upcoming months will present a mix of challenges, opportunities and significant moments of growth. With Gemini's diverse nature and the unique influences, from the realm we can expect a dynamic and diverse year that reflects the essence of this zodiac sign.

It is important for Geminis to embrace the journey that awaits them with a balanced mind and adaptability. The astrological events throughout the year will require a balance between flexibility and decisiveness as Geminis navigate through both sailing and rough waters. Whether it pertains to matters of love and relationships, career and finances, health and well being or personal growth and self discovery, every aspect offers an opportunity for learning and evolution.

The key to making the most out of this year lies in harnessing your strengths as a Gemini. Your intellectual curiosity, communication skills and ability to adapt will be your assets. By staying attuned to cues while remaining true, to your nature you can transform challenges into stepping stones towards success.

Amidst all the whirlwind activities and changes that may come your way this year it is crucial for Geminis to find moments of stillness and grounding. Remember to find time for recovery practices such as spending quality time in nature or pursuing your hobbies. These activities will help you maintain a sense of balance and well being in your paced life throughout the year.

When looking ahead keep in mind that every experience you encounter whether positive or challenging presents an opportunity for growth. The astrological events occurring this year are not cosmic happenings but rather serve as guides pointing you towards a deeper understanding of yourself and your role in the world.

To sum it up, the upcoming year holds a multitude of possibilities for Gemini individuals to explore and embrace through their actions, decisions and attitudes. Embrace your Gemini traits, like enthusiasm and adaptability as you venture forth into this chapter. You'll discover that the year has much to offer in terms of enriching the tapestry of your life. Stay open minded, keep a heart and allow the stars to guide you on a journey of self discovery and fulfillment.

CHAPTER 7:
FAMOUS "GEMINI" PERSONALITIES

This chapter celebrates the lives and accomplishments of famous individuals who were born under the sign of Gemini. From leaders and visionaries, to artists and entertainers we can observe how being a Gemini has influenced their journeys by instilling them with adaptability, eloquence and an insatiable thirst for knowledge. Each person we encounter in this section offers us a fresh perspective into the essence of Gemini. A combination of complexity, creativity and an unwavering pursuit of expression and comprehension.

The individuals featured here have made significant contributions to their respective fields and also embody various aspects of Gemini traits. Whether it's in politics, artistry, science or entertainment their stories serve as evidence to the nature of Gemini. As we explore the lives of these known individuals we gain insights into how their dual nature can lead to remarkable accomplishments. Their stories serve as inspiration showcasing how the traits associated with Gemini can be channeled towards achieving greatness, exerting influence and leaving a legacy. Come along as we pay tribute to these Gemini personalities who have made a lasting impact on our world. They truly embody the essence of the Gemini spirit.

DONALD TRUMP

- Date of Birth: June 14 1946.
- Brief Biography: Donald Trump is a businessman, television personality and politician who served as the President of the United States.
- Gemini Traits: Trump is known for his ability to communicate effectively and sometimes controversially showcasing the persuasive qualities associated with Gemini.
- Impact: As a figure in business and a polarizing political leader he has made an impact on American politics and international relations.
- Personal Life: Trump's personal life, including his marriages and large family has received considerable media attention.

PAUL MCCARTNEY

- Date of Birth: June 18 1942.
- Brief Biography: Sir Paul McCartney is a musician who was part of The Beatles and later achieved great success as a solo artist.
- Gemini Traits: McCartneys versatility in music styles and his engaging communication skills highlight his adaptability as a Gemini.
- Impact: He has had an impact on the music industry influencing generations of musicians and fans alike.
- Personal Life: Besides his career, McCartneys activism and philanthropy have played a role in shaping his public image.

MARILYN MONROE

- Date of Birth: June 1 1926.
- Brief Biography: Marilyn Monroe, the known actress, model and singer gained fame for her portrayal of comedic "blonde bombshell" characters.
- Gemini Traits: Her versatility, as an actress and her charismatic personality are a reflection of the traits often associated with Gemini.
- Impact: Monroe's impact on culture was significant as she became a sex symbol and left an enduring legacy in the entertainment industry. Additionally
- Personal Life: Her personal life and tragic death have captivated interest for years.

QUEEN VICTORIA

- Date of Birth: May 24 1819.
- Brief Biography: Queen Victoria held the title of Queen of the United Kingdom of Great Britain and Ireland. She also served as Empress of India during her reign.
- Gemini Traits: Known for her communication skills and adaptability to changing times she exemplified traits commonly associated with Gemini.
- Impact: Queen Victoria's influence extended beyond her reign; she made a lasting impact on politics, culture. Even shaped the image of the monarchy.
- Personal Life: her marriage to Prince Albert and her extended period of mourning following his passing were aspects of her life.

CLINT EASTWOOD

- Date of Birth: May 31st in 1930.
- Brief Biography: Clint Eastwood is widely recognized for his roles in films that showcase his ability to adapt effortlessly to characters.
- Gemini Traits: As a director he exhibits communication skills that align with the traits frequently attributed to Gemini individuals.
- Impact: Eastwood has made an impact in the film industry both through his acting and directing work.
- Personal Life: His personal life, including his involvement in politics and relationships has garnered attention.

ANNE FRANK

- Date of Birth: June 12, 1929.
- Brief Biography: She was a diarist of Jewish heritage who gained fame for her diary chronicling her experiences during the Holocaust.
- Gemini Traits: In her diary she showcased Gemini qualities through writing and expressive communication.
- Impact: Anne Frank's diary has had an effect on shaping how the world perceives the Holocaust and stands as a piece of historical literature.
- Personal Life: Her life in hiding and tragic death in a concentration camp are central to her story.

TUPAC SHAKUR

- Date of Birth: June 16, 1971.
- Brief Biography: Tupac Shakur was a rapper and actor who gained recognition for addressing contemporary social issues through his music.
- Gemini Traits: Tupac's versatility, as an artist and his eloquent and straightforward communication style reflect Gemini characteristics.
- Impact: Tupac Shakur is widely regarded as one of the rappers of all time with his influence continuing to resonate within the hip hop industry.
- Personal Life: The public is still fascinated by his life, which includes his involvement in the East Coast West Coast hip hop rivalry and his unfortunate death.

JOHNNY DEPP

- Date of Birth: June 9 1963.
- Brief Biography: Johnny Depp is an actor and producer renowned for his diverse film choices.
- Gemini Traits: Depp's ability to effortlessly portray a range of characters throughout his acting career truly showcases the versatility often associated with Geminis.
- Impact: With his acting style he has undoubtedly left a mark on the film industry.
- Personal Life: The media has extensively covered Depp's life, including his relationships and legal battles.

KYLIE MINOGUE

- Date of Birth: May 28 1968.
- Brief Biography: Kylie Minogue is a singer, songwriter and actress known for her pop music career and unforgettable hits like "Can't Get You Out of My Head."
- Gemini Traits: Minogues talent for adapting to music styles and her captivating stage presence perfectly exemplify the qualities typically associated with Gemini individuals.
- Impact: Minogue has undeniably made an impact on the pop music scene. Rightfully earned her status as a pop icon.
- Personal Life: known for keeping her personal life private, despite occasional media spotlight on her relationships and health challenges.

ANGELINA JOLIE

- Date of Birth: June 4 1975.
- Brief Biography: Angelina Jolie is an actress, filmmaker and humanitarian known for her work both on and off the screen.
- Gemini Traits: Jolies talent as an actress and her effective communication skills align with the characteristics often associated with Geminis.
- Impact: She has made an impact in the film industry. Has been highly recognized for her humanitarian endeavors.
- Personal Life: Her marriages, family life and dedication to work have garnered attention from the public.

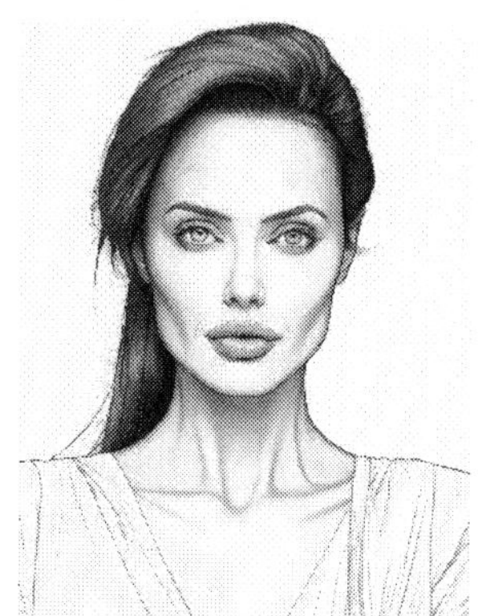

TIM BERNERS LEE

- Date of Birth: June 8 1955.
- Brief Biography: Sir Tim Berners Lee is an engineer and computer scientist who is best known as the creator of the World Wide Web.
- Gemini Traits: Berners Lee's thinking and ability to explain complex ideas in simple terms exemplify qualities often attributed to Geminis.
- Impact: His invention has fundamentally transformed how people access and share information worldwide.
- Personal Life: Although he maintains a low profile in public his contributions to technology and advocacy for an open internet are noteworthy.

ALANIS MORISSETTE

- Date of Birth: June 1 1974.

- Brief Biography: Alanis Nadine Morissette is a Canadian and American singer and songwriter. She is widely recognized for her mezzo soprano vocals and thought provoking lyrics.
- Gemini Traits: Explores various musical styles—a characteristic that resonates with Gemini traits.
- Impact: Alanis Morissette has made an impact on the music industry with her album "Jagged Little Pill" being particularly influential.
- Personal Life: Apart from her achievements she has also been open about her journey, in spirituality and mental health which has become an integral part of her public narrative.

As we come to the end of our exploration into the lives and legacies of these Gemini individuals we are left with a tapestry that beautifully captures the essence of the Gemini spirit. This journey, through Geminis from many walks of life has not only given us a glimpse into their remarkable accomplishments but has also showcased the unique characteristics that define the Gemini zodiac sign.

The stories of these individuals highlight the diversity and adaptability in Geminis. From artists like Marilyn Monroe and Johnny Depp who embody genius to figures like Donald Trump and Queen Victoria, known for their leadership each person exemplifies the dynamic and multifaceted nature of Gemini. Overall they demonstrate how Geminis can channel their curiosity, communication skills and adaptability across fields leaving an indelible impact on the world.

These profiles remind us of the potential that comes with embracing Gemini qualities such as versatility and intellectual agility. They show us that a Geminis ability to perceive things from new perspectives can be a tool for innovation and influence. The lives of these individuals also highlight how important it is to find balance between Gemini's duality of introspection and extroversion.

For those born under the Gemini zodiac sign these stories provide inspiration and a sense of connection. They demonstrate what Geminis can accomplish when they embrace their abilities and approach life with an open mind and adaptable attitude. The achievements of these Geminis can serve as a force encouraging current and future Geminis to pursue their passions and utilize their unique talents to leave a lasting impact. As we conclude this chapter we are reminded that the journey of a Gemini is one defined by exploration, learning and self expression. It is an expedition that encompasses diversity and leaves us in awe of all the personalities we have delved into.

CONCLUSION

Finally we have reached the conclusion of this book. As we conclude our exploration of the world of the Gemini zodiac sign we find ourselves at a moment of introspection and synthesis. This book has taken us through the landscape of Geminis essence from its mythological origins, to its impact on personal and professional aspects. In this conclusion our goal is to bring the diverse facets of the Gemini experience together to provide a cohesive summary and a reflective ending to this enlightening journey. Now let's explore the key points, summarized about Gemini in the previous chapters.

- **Chapter 1. History and Mythology;** Here we delved into how history and mythology have shaped our understanding of Gemini. We explored how ancient stories continue to influence our perception of this zodiac sign. We also highlighted the symbolism of duality and communication skills in Gemini.
- **Chapter 2. Love & Compatibility;** This chapter explored how Geminis approach love and relationships. It revealed their desire for connection with partners who're good communicators and a yearning for a dynamic yet harmonious companionship.
- **Chapter 3. Friends and Family;** In this chapter we examined the dynamics that surround Geminis family and friends. We revealed their adaptability, versatility as well as their emphasis on intellectual bonds, within personal relationships.
- **Chapter 4. Career and Finances;** In this chapter we delved into the career and financial realm of Geminis. This highlighted their inclination towards careers that offer stimulation, creativity and ample opportunities for communication. Additionally we explored their approach to financial matters.
- **Chapter 5. Personal Growth;** In this chapter we extensively discussed the journey of self improvement for Geminis. We emphasized the importance of striking a balance between their ranging interests and personal development. Furthermore we underscored how embracing their versatility and adaptability contributes to their self improvement.
- **Chapter 6. The Year Ahead;** In this chapter we explored astrological forecasts tailored to Geminis. These forecasts provided insights on how they can navigate challenges and seize opportunities across various aspects of life in the year ahead.

- **Chapter 7. Famous Gemini Personalities;** This chapter is dedicated to commemorating individuals who embody the traits associated with the Gemini sign. It serves as a showcase of the impact and diversity displayed by Geminis throughout history.

As we come to the end it's clear that the Gemini zodiac sign is all about duality, curiosity and adaptability. This book has shed light on the diverse nature of those born under this sign. Geminis are encouraged to embrace their unique qualities. Their communication skills, their ability to adapt to new situations and their varied interests. This book serves not just as a wealth of knowledge about Geminis but as a starting point for them to navigate their lives with a deeper understanding of their astrological identity.

In summary this enlightening exploration has taken us through the world that defines what it means to be a Gemini. Throughout the book we have delved into aspects of Gemini individuals ranging from the way they navigate love, friendship, careers and more. Our goal has been to provide readers with an understanding of the complexities and intellectual depth that define a Gemini.

By peeling back the layers of this multifaceted sign we have shed light on their characteristics, challenges and strengths. Through these chapters readers can discover a reflection of themselves. Furthermore they can gain valuable insights on how to embrace their unique qualities. A key takeaway from our exploration is the celebration of Geminis duality as a source of strength. In addition to their ability to adapt and communicate effectively. Forging connections on deep levels is not merely a trait but a remarkable power that aids them in navigating the intricacies of today's world.

Remember that astrology goes beyond uncovering personality traits; it offers us a lens through which we can comprehend our interactions, motivations and life paths. By acknowledging the significance of influences like those observed in Gemini individuals we gain an appreciation for the diversity and richness that characterizes our experiences.

Attention all Gemini individuals; Embrace your energy and intellectual curiosity as they are defining qualities that make you who you are. Your adaptability should not be seen as indecision. Rather, as a testament to your potential. Utilize your communication skills to bridge gaps. Let your curiosity guide you towards new territories and allow your versatility to navigate life's ever changing circumstances.

The world is full of possibilities and Geminis have the abilities to paint their own journeys. One with vibrant colors through innovation, relationships and personal growth. Embrace your duality, cherish your communication skills and thrive in your adaptability. These are the strengths that make you as a Gemini truly remarkable.

Best wishes to you Gemini!

CANCER:

A COMPLETE GUIDE TO THE CANCER ASTROLOGY STAR SIGN

Contents

INTRODUCTION ---------- 1

Cancer Zodiac Sign Overview---------- 2

CHAPTER 1: HISTORY AND MYTHOLOGY ---------- 5

Historical Origins of the Cancer Constellation ---------- 5

CHAPTER 2: LOVE & COMPATIBILITY ---------- 10

Love Approach---------- 10

Compatibility with Other Zodiac Signs ---------- 12

Tips for Dating and Maintaining Relationships with Cancer Individuals----- 15

CHAPTER 3: FRIENDS AND FAMILY ---------- 17

Cancer as a Friend ---------- 17

Family Dynamics---------- 19

CHAPTER 4: CAREER AND AMBITIONS ---------- 23

Cancer Career Preferences and Professional Aspirations---------- 24

Career Challenges and Strategies to Overcome Them ---------- 27

CHAPTER 5: SELF-IMPROVEMENT---------- 30

Personal Growth and Development ---------- 31

Harnessing Strengths and Overcoming Weaknesses:---------- 32

CHAPTER 6: THE YEAR AHEAD ---------- 36

Horoscope Guide for the Year Ahead---------- 36

Key Astrological Events---------- 38

CHAPTER 7: FAMOUS "CANCER" PERSONALITIES ---------- 44

Henry VIII ---------- 44

Diana Spencer (Princess Diana)---------- 44

John D. Rockefeller ---------- 45

Ariana Grande---------- 45

Lionel Messi ---------- 45
Mike Tyson ---------- 46
Elon Musk ---------- 46
Liv Tyler ---------- 47
Malala Yousafzai ---------- 47
50 Cent (Curtis Jackson) ---------- 47
Benazir Bhutto ---------- 47
Selena Gomez ---------- 48

CONCLUSION ---------- 50

INTRODUCTION

Astrology has fascinated humans for centuries. At its core, it is the study of how celestial bodies like the Sun, Moon, planets and stars influence lives and natural events on planet Earth. It takes into account these entities' positions, at someone's birth time to create their natal or birth chart. This chart acts as a snapshot representing an individual's life path personality traits, strengths and challenges.

In this book we embark on a captivating exploration of astrology with a focus on the Cancer zodiac sign. Inside we aim to demystify astrology and provide you with an understanding of the Cancer zodiac sign. Cancer, represented by the crab, holds a key position in the zodiac. People born under this sign are recognized for their emotions, intuition and strong bonds with their homes and loved ones. By exploring the traits and characteristics of individuals with Cancer you will gain insights into your own life as well as those around you. Equipped with this knowledge you can navigate life's trials with enhanced clarity and purpose. Come join us on a journey as we unravel the mysteries of Cancer. A sign that encompasses both the moon's tranquil tides and a crabs protective shell.

CANCER ZODIAC SIGN OVERVIEW

- **Date of Star Sign**: Cancer falls between June 21st and July 22nd, making it the fourth sign of the zodiac in Western astrology.
- **Symbol**; The symbol of Cancer is the Crab. This choice of symbol reflects the nature of Cancer individuals. They often exhibit a protective, resilient and sometimes retreating exterior. Much like a crab's hard shell.
- **Element**; Cancer is associated with the Water element. Water signs are known for their deep emotional capacity and strong intuition.
- **Planet**; The ruling celestial body of Cancer is the Moon. Just as the Moon waxes and wanes, Cancer individuals are known for their fluctuating emotions.
- **Color**; Silver, white and pale shades of blue are often linked to this sign. These colors reflect the connection Cancer has with the Moon and water.

PERSONALITY TRAITS

Cancer is a zodiac sign known for its intricate and diverse personality traits. Here are some essential qualities often associated with individuals born under Cancer.

- **Emotional Sensitivity**; Cancers possess an understanding of their emotions and those of others. They have an empathy towards others feelings.
- **Nurturing**; They have an inclination to care for and support others making them exceptional caregivers and loyal friends.
- **Intuitive**; Cancer individuals possess a strong intuition. Often they pick up on things that might go unnoticed by others. Their instincts are usually spot on.
- **Home and Family Oriented**; They hold their home life and family in high regard considering it as a priority. Building a harmonious, home environment is of great importance to them.
- **Protective**; Similar to the shell of a crab, Cancers fiercely guard their loved ones. They often display remarkable determination when it comes to defending them.

STRENGTHS

- Compassion and empathy.
- Loyalty and devotion to loved ones.
- Strong nurturing instincts.

- Intuitive and perceptive.
- Creative and imaginative.

WEAKNESSES

- Tendency to be moody and emotionally sensitive.
- Can be overly cautious and hesitant to take risks.
- Difficulty letting go of the past.
- May become withdrawn when hurt or feeling vulnerable.
- Prone to mood swings.

COMPATIBILITY

When it comes to compatibility Cancer tends to get along well with Water signs, like Scorpio and Pisces. The emotional, intuitive nature they share makes for excellent connections. Additionally Earth signs such as Taurus and Virgo appreciate Cancer's nurturing qualities. Overall this can also contribute to compatibility. It's worth noting that individual factors beyond zodiac signs can influence compatibility well.

To summarize Cancer is a zodiac sign that is known for its emotions, caring nature and intuitive abilities. Represented by the crab it symbolizes both protection and sensitivity. Understanding the characteristics, strengths and weaknesses of Cancer individuals can provide insights into their compassionate personalities.

As we embark on this voyage this book aims to delve deeper into the qualities, strengths and weaknesses exhibited by Cancer individuals. It serves as a companion for self discovery and personal growth enabling readers to navigate life's challenges, with clarity and purpose. As we progress through the chapters we will explore the qualities of Cancer, its compatibility with other astrological signs and the symbolism behind it. Through this exploration you will acquire a comprehension of the Cancer zodiac sign and how its energies can influence not only your own life but also the lives of those in your vicinity. Come along on this journey as we uncover the nature of Cancer and embrace its energies for a truly meaningful and enriching existence.

CHAPTER 1: HISTORY AND MYTHOLOGY

Welcome to the captivating realm of "Cancer", in History and Mythology a chapter that uncovers the tapestry of stories, legends and ancient wisdom associated with this sign. In this exploration we will embark on a journey through time delving into the observations of the "Cancer" constellation, its representations across different cultures and the lasting impact of this sign in modern astrology.

From the ancient records of Mesopotamia that first documented "Cancer" to the mythological narratives that have shaped its symbolism. This chapter invites you to unravel the enigmatic nature of this celestial sign. We will also examine how it has evolved from its origins into a tool for understanding human emotions in modern astrology.

As we set off on this adventure, get ready to be captivated by tales from eras passed and be enlightened by the significance of "Cancer" in our present lives. Whether you have an interest in astrology or simply hold curiosity about the origins and meaning behind your zodiac sign. Rest assured this chapter promises an enthralling exploration of Cancer.

HISTORICAL ORIGINS OF THE CANCER CONSTELLATION

The constellation known as Cancer, has a history that dates back thousands of years. Different ancient civilizations from around the world documented this group of stars. Each infusing their unique interpretations and meanings into it.

ANCIENT MESOPOTAMIA

The earliest recorded mentions of the Cancer constellation can be traced back to Mesopotamia to the Babylonians. They referred to this grouping as "MUL.AL.LUL," which translates to "the Crayfish" or "the Crab." The Babylonians associated this constellation with the Moon and its cycles symbolizing its connection to tides.

ANCIENT EGYPT

In ancient Egyptian astronomy Cancer was often linked with a scarab beetle. The scarab held significance as a symbol of transformation and rebirth since it was believed to push the Sun across the sky. Much like how dung beetles roll balls of dung. This interpretation emphasizes the relationship between the Cancer constellation and the apparent movement of the Sun in our skies.

ANCIENT GREECE AND ROME

The ancient Greeks and Romans adopted the crab representation for Cancer from their predecessors. According to mythology the constellation known as Cancer is associated with one of Hercules' great challenges, where he encountered a crab sent by the goddess Hera. This intense battle resulted in the crab being immortalized among the stars serving as a lasting tribute to Hercules' heroic feats.

HINDU MYTHOLOGY

In Hindu mythology the constellation known as Cancer holds significance through the story of Daksha. According to legends Daksha created a daughter named Sati who later became Lord Shiva's wife. After Satis self immolation her ashes were scattered in the ocean. In Hindu cosmology it is believed that Cancer represents this aspect.

These historical and mythological connections have resulted in interpretations of the Cancer constellation, across cultures. Whether perceived as a crab scarab beetle or part of a pattern, Cancer's presence in the night sky has sparked awe and has been a source of storytelling throughout human history.

HISTORICAL EVENTS

Throughout history, significant events have taken place during the time period known as the Cancer season, in astrology. While it's important to note that the influence of astrology on events is subjective and open to interpretation there are a few happenings during this timeframe that have captured the attention of astrologers.

- **American Independence**; On July 4th the United States celebrates its independence coinciding with the Cancer season. This momentous occasion is seen by some astrologers as a turning point in history symbolizing the nation's sense of identity and resilience—characteristics often associated with individuals born under the Cancer sign.

- **French Revolution**; The French Revolution, which commenced in the century witnessed significant developments occurring within the Cancer season. The revolution was marked by emotions, passionate ideals and radical transformation. Traits that can be linked to Cancer's emotional depth and transformative nature.

HISTORICAL FIGURES BORN UNDER THE CANCER SIGN

Several influential historical figures who were born under the Cancer sign have left a mark on our world. Here are a few remarkable individuals who exemplify the characteristics of the Cancer zodiac sign.

- **Nelson Mandela** (born on July 18 1918); As a president of South Africa and a prominent anti apartheid activist Mandela showcased the enduring spirit, emotional strength and unwavering commitment to justice. Such traits that are commonly associated with Cancer.
- **Napoleon Bonaparte** (born on July 15 1769); Known for his brilliance and reign. The emperor Napoleon embodied the ambitious nature, resolute determination and exceptional leadership qualities. Such traits are often attributed to those born under the Cancer sign.

EVOLUTION OVER TIME

The understanding and interpretation of the zodiac sign Cancer has undergone significant changes over time. In old times people associated this constellation and sign with tales and celestial symbolism. However as astrology has advanced in the modern era, interpretations have shifted towards a more psychological and personality based approach.

In ancient civilizations like Babylon and Greece, astrology was closely intertwined with religion and mythology. Astrologers primarily studied celestial patterns for their significance and guidance. As the centuries passed astrology underwent a transformation by incorporating advancements ultimately evolving into the astrology we are familiar with today.

Modern astrologers focus on an individual's personality traits and tendencies while exploring how the energies associated with this sign influence one's life, relationships and personal growth. The shift from interpretations to insights reflects a broader trend in astrologys evolution. One from being primarily mystical and predictive to becoming a tool for self exploration and personal growth.

In conclusion the zodiac sign known as Cancer holds an important place in the tapestry of human history. It has been intertwined with legends, cultural interpretations and celestial symbolism. From its early documented observations in Mesopotamia to its multifaceted representations across cultures, Cancer has significantly influenced our collective imagination.

As we have explored this constellation has transformed over time, transitioning from a mythological concept to an astrological tool. A tool that sheds light on psychological tendencies and personality traits. The enduring legacy of Cancer extends beyond its importance. As such it continues to provide insights into our emotions.

For those interested in delving further into the history and mythology surrounding Cancer here is a list of recommended resources for further reading;

FURTHER READING AND REFERENCES

- "The Secret Language of Astrology: The Illustrated Key to Unlocking the Secrets of the Stars" by Roy Gillett.
- "The Oxford Companion to Astrology" by Nicholas Campion.
- "Astrology: History, Symbols, and Signs" by R. A. Waldie.
- "Myths of the Zodiac: A Colorful Illustrated History of the Heavens" by Anna Southgate.
- "The Zodiac and the Salts of Salvation: Homeopathic Remedies for the Sign Types" by George W. Carey.
- "The Living Stars: An Account of the Fixed Stars in Astrology" by Dr. Eric Morse.

CHAPTER 2:
LOVE & COMPATIBILITY

Welcome to the captivating realm of "Cancer" Love and Compatibility. Join us on a journey, through the depths of emotions and harmonious unions experienced by individuals born under the Cancer zodiac sign. In the following pages we will explore the tendencies, desires and dynamics that shape Cancer individuals relationships. From their nurturing and empathetic nature to their search for security we will uncover factors that influence their approach to love and partnerships.

Furthermore this chapter explores how Cancer interacts with each of the other zodiac signs. Whether you are a Cancer or someone with one, we will unveil insights into the dynamics of love between Cancer and each sign. These insights can assist you in navigating the complexities of your relationships. Prepare yourself for a dive into emotions as we explore the bonds forged by Cancer individuals and gain an understanding of their intimate connections.

LOVE APPROACH

Cancer individuals approach love and romance with strong emotions, sensitivity and a desire for intimacy. Those born under the Cancer sign are known for their nurturing nature, which extends to their relationships. Let's take a closer look at how Cancer individuals approach love and romance.

- **Emotional Bond;** Cancer individuals place importance on emotional connection in their romantic relationships. They seek partners who can understand, appreciate and reciprocate their needs. Cancer individuals tend to express their feelings showing how much they care for their loved ones.
- **Nurturing**; Similar to how they're caring and protective within their families Cancer individuals extend this care to their partners as well. They have an inclination towards taking care of the needs of those they love. Maybe it involves simple acts of kindness such as cooking or being a good listener.
- **Focus on Home and Family**; Creating a harmonious home environment with their partners holds value for Cancer individuals. They often envision building a nest while sharing domestic responsibilities. The concept of home and family is deeply cherished by them.

- **Loyalty**; When it comes to loyalty and commitment, in relationships Cancer individuals excel. When they choose someone as their partner they tend to be deeply committed. They highly value long term relationships. As such they are willing to invest the time and effort to nurture them.
- **Empathy**; Cancer individuals possess a nature that allows them to be highly attuned to their partners emotions. They often have a sense of when something's wrong or when their partner needs support. Their empathetic qualities make them exceptional at providing comfort and understanding.
- **Stability**; In relationships Cancer individuals seek security and stability. They are naturally drawn to partners who can offer them safety and a sense of belonging. Financial stability and a solid foundation also hold importance for them.
- **Honesty and openness**; Although Cancer individuals may not always express their feelings verbally they tend to demonstrate their affection through actions and gestures. Open and honest communication is highly valued by them particularly when it comes to addressing concerns.
- **Vulnerability**; Cancer individuals embrace vulnerability within their relationships. They understand that true intimacy requires sharing fears, dreams and insecurities with a partner. This willingness to be authentic strengthens the bonds they develop.
- **Affection**; Romantic gestures and tokens of affection hold significance for Cancer individuals as they appreciate these expressions of love.
- **Experience**; Cancer individuals take pleasure in crafting experiences, for their significant others. Be it through arranging unexpected romantic outings or leaving heartfelt messages.

To summarize, Cancer's perspective on love and romance is characterized by emotions, caring, loyalty and a deep longing, for both security and closeness. They are devoted partners who prioritize the happiness and welfare of their loved ones.

COMPATIBILITY WITH OTHER ZODIAC SIGNS

Cancer is a water sign in astrology, and individuals born under this sign are known for their nurturing and emotional nature. When it comes to love and compatibility with other zodiac signs, Cancer's compatibility can vary depending on the partner's sign. Let's explore how Cancer interacts with each of the other twelve zodiac signs.

CANCER AND ARIES

Cancer and Aries have contrasting personalities. Cancer seeks emotional security and stability. On the other hand Aries is adventurous and impulsive. While there can be initial attraction due to their differences, long-term compatibility may be challenging due to their conflicting needs and communication styles.

CANCER AND TAURUS

Cancer and Taurus are both nurturing signs and share a deep appreciation for stability. They connect on an emotional level and create a loving partnership. These two signs can build a strong and lasting relationship based on mutual support and shared values.

CANCER AND GEMINI

Cancer and Gemini have different approaches to relationships. Cancer is emotional and values commitment. Gemini is more intellectually driven and enjoys variety. Their differences can lead to misunderstandings and challenges in maintaining a long-term connection. However, with effort and compromise, they can make it work.

CANCER AND CANCER

When two Cancer individuals come together, there is a deep understanding of each other's emotions. They share a strong emotional connection and can create a loving and supportive home life. However, they may also struggle with mood swings and emotional sensitivity. This can lead to occasional conflicts.

CANCER AND LEO

Cancer and Leo have contrasting personalities. Cancer is introverted and nurturing. Leo is outgoing and confident. They may initially be drawn to each other's differences. Although long-term compatibility can be challenging due to Leo's need for attention and Cancer's need for emotional security.

CANCER AND VIRGO

Cancer and Virgo can complement each other well. Virgo's practicality balances Cancer's emotional nature. Thus they can work together to create a stable and loving partnership. Their attention to detail and commitment to one another can make for a successful relationship.

CANCER AND LIBRA

Cancer and Libra have different needs in a relationship. Cancer desires emotional connection and security. Libra seeks balance and harmony. They may enjoy each other's company. However, they might struggle to fulfill each other's emotional needs, leading to potential challenges.

CANCER AND SCORPIO

Cancer and Scorpio share a deep emotional connection. They both value intensity and commitment in relationships, making them highly compatible. Their passionate and loyal natures can lead to a strong and lasting bond.

CANCER AND SAGITTARIUS

Cancer and Sagittarius have very different outlooks on life and relationships. Cancer seeks security and stability, while Sagittarius craves adventure and freedom. These differences can lead to misunderstandings and could make long-term compatibility challenging.

CANCER AND CAPRICORN

Cancer and Capricorn can create a harmonious partnership. Capricorn's stability and Cancer's emotional depth complement each other. They share a commitment to building a secure and nurturing home life, making for a strong foundation in their relationship.

CANCER AND AQUARIUS

Cancer and Aquarius have contrasting personalities and communication styles. Cancer is emotional and nurturing. Aquarius is intellectual and independent. These differences can lead to challenges in understanding each other's needs and perspectives.

CANCER AND PISCE

Cancer and Pisces are both water signs. This means they share a deep emotional connection. They understand each other's feelings intuitively and can create a loving and supportive relationship. Their compatibility is often characterized by empathy, romance, and shared dreams.

Remember that in astrology, while compatibility can provide insights into the dynamics of a relationship, it's essential to remember that individual personalities and experiences play a significant role in how two people connect and build a successful partnership. Remember people can overcome differences with effective communication, understanding and mutual respect.

TIPS FOR DATING AND MAINTAINING RELATIONSHIPS WITH CANCER INDIVIDUALS

IF YOU'RE DATING A CANCER WOMAN

- Give her time to open up and share her feelings at her pace. Be patient and understanding.
- Plan dates that create an atmosphere, like cooking dinner or having an intimate picnic in a peaceful location.
- Show genuine empathy and listen attentively when she talks about her emotions. Offer support when she needs to vent or express herself.
- Show interest in her family as they hold importance in her life.
- Be there for her emotionally, during times providing comfort and a shoulder to lean on.

IF YOU'RE DATING A CANCER MAN

- Help him create a home environment as Cancer men value their homes as havens.
- Be patient and reassuring during his moments of sensitivity or insecurity. Let him know your feelings and commitment are steadfast.

- Cancer men have an inclination towards caregiving. Show appreciation for the things he does to take care of you whether it's preparing a meal or offering an embrace.
- Cancer men often have artistic interests. Participate in activities that he enjoys and is passionate about.
- Loyalty holds importance for Cancer men. Show your commitment to the relationship. Assure him of your faithfulness.

GENERAL TIPS FOR DATING AND MAINTAINING RELATIONSHIPS WITH INDIVIDUALS BORN UNDER THE SIGN OF CANCER

- **Respect their need for space**; While Cancer individuals are nurturing, they also value their time. Respect their desire for solitude. Avoid pressuring them to open up when they're not ready.
- **Share your emotions**; Cancer individuals appreciate openness. Be willing to share your feelings and concerns with them as it helps strengthen the bond.
- **Celebrate occasions**; Remember dates such as anniversaries or birthdays. Put thought into meaningful gifts or gestures.
- **Offer support**; Cancer individuals are likely to have dreams and aspirations. Be supportive of their goals and provide encouragement.
- **Establish trust**; Trust forms the foundation of any relationship. Be open and honest, in your communication to establish a foundation of trust.
- **Plan outings**; Cancer individuals enjoy settings. Arrange dinners at home stargazing sessions or peaceful walks in nature.
- **Show gratitude**; Express your appreciation for their care and support. Recognize the efforts they put into nurturing the relationship.

Remember that everyone is unique and these suggestions serve as guidelines. It's crucial to understand the preferences and needs of the Cancer individual you are dating and adapt your approach accordingly. Developing a nurturing and lasting bond requires patience, empathy and genuine affection.

Throughout this chapter we have delved into the realm of Cancer individuals exploring their characteristics, desires and their unique ways of approaching matters of the heart. As we conclude this chapter let us again remember that astrology offers insights into the complexities of relationships. Understand that each person is unique. In the end love is a voyage of exploration, personal development and forming connections. Love indeed resembles a constellation that illuminates our lives, leading us through its transforming and captivating patterns.

CHAPTER 3: FRIENDS AND FAMILY

Welcome to this chapter which delves into the dynamics of friendship and family relationships that define those born under the Cancer zodiac sign. Within these pages we will uncover the essence of Cancer, as friends and family members. Prepare to be moved by the warmth and depth found within Cancers friendships and family connections. If you happen to be a Cancer sign looking to embrace your traits or if you simply want to understand the Cancer individuals, in your life better this chapter guarantees an exploration. One filled with empathy, affection and the lasting connections that characterize the star sign Cancer.

CANCER AS A FRIEND

Being friends with a Cancer individual is like stumbling upon a treasure filled with unwavering support. People born under the Cancer zodiac sign are known for their ability to forge meaningful connections with their friends. They embody the essence of being a "ride or die" friend you can always rely on. Let's take a closer look at what it means to have a Cancer friend.

- **Emotional Support**; Cancer friends serve as your go to support system. They possess an intuition that allows them to sense when something is bothering you even without you having to say a word. Be it celebrating your achievements or when going through tough times they are always there to offer their comforting presence.
- **Nurturing**; Like the crab, their symbol. Cancer friends have an inherent nurturing instinct. They take pleasure in taking care of their friends whether it's by preparing home cooked meals, giving thoughtful gifts or simply checking in on you.
- **Loyalty**; When it comes to loyalty Cancer friends stand unmatched. They remain steadfastly by your side through thick and thin. Their loyalty is unwavering, making them friends you can rely on.
- **Events**; They enjoy planning events such as movie nights celebrating friendship anniversaries and ensuring that every holiday goes well.
- **Like family**; Cancer friends often consider their friends as part of their family. They warmly welcome you into their homes creating a sense of belonging and comfort that's hard to find.
- **Intuitive**; Cancer friends possess strong intuition. They have an ability to perceive your moods and feelings, even when you try to conceal them. This intuitive understanding enables them to provide the kind of support when you need it the most.
- **Patience and forgiveness**; these are virtues cherished by Cancer friends. They know everyone has their own imperfections and they readily overlook them. In case of any misunderstandings they are quick to extend a branch and mend the friendship.
- **Resolution**; Conflict resolution is a priority, for Cancer individuals who prefer peace, within friendships. If conflicts arise they will diligently work towards finding resolutions that preserve the bond between friends. They place a value on their friendships and strive to make sure they endure over time.
- **Empathy and Compassion**; Friends who are Cancer zodiac sign individuals possess a sense of empathy and compassion. They genuinely care about your well being. As such they will go the extra mile to ensure your happiness.

Ultimately when you have a Cancer friend you will discover a companion who nurtures your spirit, supports your aspirations and treasures your friendship. While they may have their shell once you are granted access you will encounter the warmth and unwavering dedication that characterizes Cancer as a friend.

FAMILY DYNAMICS

The Cancer astrological sign represents a connection to family, home and deep emotional bonds. People born under this sign are profoundly influenced by their family dynamics. They are well known for their attachment to their loved ones. Let's explore how Cancer individuals interact within the context of their families.

- **Nurturing**; Those with the Cancer sign naturally take on the role of nurturers within their families. They ensure that everyone is well taken care of, both physically and emotionally.
- **Emotional Pillars**; Cancer individuals serve as support systems within their families. They become the go to person when someone needs a listening ear or advice. Their empathetic nature allows them to connect with family members on a deep level.
- **Home Focused**; Cancer is synonymous with home. Those born under this sign often prioritize creating an inviting environment in their homes. They take pride in their living spaces and place importance on preserving family traditions while also establishing ones.
- **Loyalty**; Loyalty holds value, for Cancer individuals. They wholeheartedly devote themselves to their families. As such they typically go above and beyond to protect and support them. Through thick and thin they remain steadfast by the side of those they love.
- **Family Dynamics and Sensitivity**; People born under the Cancer zodiac sign are highly attuned to the dynamics within their families. They possess an ability to detect tension or underlying emotions. In turn they actively work towards resolving conflicts and restoring harmony.
- **Preserving Traditions**; Cancer individuals place value on tradition and often take on the role of preserving family customs, rituals and celebrations. They ensure that these cherished traditions are passed down from one generation to the next.
- **Addressing Conflict with Care;** Despite their preference for harmony Cancer individuals are not afraid to address family conflicts. With tact and sensitivity they navigate these situations in order to find resolutions.
- **Encouraging Independence**; While deeply connected to their families Cancer individuals also understand the importance of fostering individuality and independence among family members. They encourage their loved ones to pursue their dreams while providing unwavering support along the way.

In conclusion it is evident that cancer's influence on family dynamics is profound.

They are like the backbone of their families offering encouragement, nurturing affection and devotion. Despite their somewhat cold exteriors Cancer individuals willingly expose their feelings and demonstrate an unwavering dedication, towards fostering a loving household.

CHALLENGES IN FRIENDSHIPS AND FAMILY RELATIONS

While people born under the zodiac sign of Cancer are often recognized for their positive impact they also encounter challenges in their relationships with friends and family. Understanding these challenges can assist both Cancer individuals and their loved ones in navigating their relationships. Here are some common obstacles they may face.

- **Emotional Sensitivity**; Cancer individuals possess a sensitivity to the emotions of others which can sometimes become overwhelming for them. They may absorb emotions from family members or friends resulting in strain and exhaustion.
- **Overprotective**; The protective instincts of Cancer individuals can occasionally manifest as overprotectiveness. They may feel compelled to shield their loved ones from difficulty. Ultimately this can lead to feelings of suffocation.
- **Letting Go**; People belonging to the Cancer sign often find it challenging to let go of hurts or conflicts. They may hold onto grudges or dwell on wounds for a long period of time, placing strain on their relationships.
- **Fear of Rejection**; Due to their heightened sensitivity Cancer individuals may experience a fear of rejection or abandonment. This fear can make them hesitant to open up to friends or initiate conversations about topics within their families.
- **Mood Swings**; Cancers, governed by the Moon are known for their mood swings. Navigating through their fluctuations can be challenging for loved ones who may not always comprehend the root cause of these changes.
- **Traditional Values**; Cancer individuals place importance on tradition and family customs. However their strong attachment to these traditions can sometimes make it difficult for them to embrace change or adapt.
- **Emotional Boundaries;** Cancer individuals occasionally face difficulties in establishing boundaries. They often prioritize others' needs above their own which can result in fatigue over time.

Remember that dealing with these challenges, in friendships and family relationships requires communication, patience and understanding from both parties involved. People with Cancer zodiac signs can benefit from learning how to express their emotions and finding ways to handle their sensitivity. Friends and family members can contribute to the success of these relationships by respecting boundaries, offering support and openly addressing any issues in a caring manner.

As we wrap up this chapter lets take a moment to consider how we can enhance, sustain and cultivate these connections, with Cancer individuals;

IMPROVING RELATIONSHIPS

- **Foster Open Communication**; Encourage Cancer individuals to honestly express their feelings. This promotes better understanding.
- **Respect Personal Boundaries;** Recognize and honor their need for time and personal space. Strive for a balance between closeness. Respect boundaries.
- **Conflict Resolution;** Handle conflicts with sensitivity and empathy when they arise. Cancer individuals dislike confrontation. Approach discussions calmly with a focus on finding solutions.

MAINTAINING STRONG RELATIONSHIPS

- **Express Appreciation;** Regularly show gratitude for their nurturing and supportive nature. Small acts of appreciation can make a difference in maintaining a bond.
- **Embrace Traditions;** Participate in family traditions and rituals. These hold meaning for Cancer individuals as they strengthen family ties.
- **Support Them Emotionally;** Be there for them in tough times, just like they are for you. Offer support, lend a listening ear and provide comfort whenever needed.

BUILDING STRONGER RELATIONSHIPS

- **Shared Activities;** Take part together in activities that strengthen the bond between you. Whether it's cooking together, sharing stories or attending family gatherings. Together these experiences can deepen your connection.
- **Create Meaningful Memories;** Put effort into making memories and traditions together. Cancer individuals greatly appreciate such moments. Value the efforts put into building new ones.
- **Encourage Independence;** Support Cancer individuals in pursuing their interests and hobbies. Assure them of your backing. Striking a balance between individuality and togetherness fosters growth. Ultimately it leads to healthier relationships.

In essence nurturing and developing relationships with Cancer individuals requires patience, understanding and embracing their qualities. By fostering communication, respecting boundaries and offering support you can create lasting bonds that reflect Cancers nurturing and loving nature. As you embark on this journey of connection and love, with your Cancer friends and family members may your hearts forever be touched by the warmth and depth of these enduring relationships.

CHAPTER 4: CAREER AND AMBITIONS

Welcome to this chapter dedicated to exploring the relationship between individuals born under the Cancer zodiac sign and their professional lives. Within these pages we aim to uncover the qualities, strengths and challenges that Cancer individuals bring to their careers and financial endeavors. Furthermore we will look into their approach to financial matters.

Throughout this chapter we'll provide strategies for achieving success in the workplace while offering insights into money management. Whether you are a Cancer seeking guidance in your career and financial pursuits. Or if you're someone eager to gain a better understanding of Cancer individuals, rest assured this chapter holds valuable insights.

CANCER CAREER PREFERENCES AND PROFESSIONAL ASPIRATIONS

Individuals, with the Cancer zodiac sign possess a set of qualities and strengths that can greatly benefit their lives. They are driven by their depth, empathy and strong sense of responsibility. This often leads them to find fulfillment in careers where they can make an impact on others. Now let's take a closer look at the career preferences and professional aspirations of those born under the zodiac, Cancer.

- **Nurturing**; Caring for others comes naturally to Cancer individuals making them excel in professions related to healthcare, nursing, counseling, social work and psychology. Their innate empathy and ability to connect with people on a deep level make them exceptional caregivers.
- **Home body**; Due to their attachment to home and family, Cancer individuals often gravitate towards careers that revolve around these themes. They may find fulfillment as stay at home parents. As such they often pursue professions such as designing, real estate or work related to home renovation.
- **Emotionally Intelligent**; With their emotional intelligence, Cancer individuals thrive in careers that require understanding and managing emotions. They shine in roles such as human resources management, conflict resolution specialists or coaching positions where they can assist individuals in navigating their feelings and relationships.
- **Leaders**; Teaching and education naturally align with the interests of Cancer individuals. They derive joy from nurturing minds and guiding students through their journeys. As such they might choose to pursue careers in education. For example, as teachers, professors or counselors.
- **Foodies**; Cancer individuals often find joy in creating a home atmosphere that extends to their love for cooking. Many of them thrive as chefs, bakers or food stylists deriving pleasure from preparing meals and curating a dining experience.
- **Attention to detail**; Entrepreneurship is an area where Cancer individuals excel due to their skills and meticulous attention to detail. Their dedication and unwavering commitment contribute significantly to the triumph of their business ventures.
- **Security;** Cancer individuals are sometimes drawn towards careers in finance because they place a priority on security. They demonstrate proficiency in roles that involve planning and analysis such as financial advisors or investment analysts.

- **Philanthropy**; Driven by a desire to make an impact on society, Cancer individuals often find fulfillment in professions relating to philanthropy. They naturally enjoy charity initiatives and philanthropic endeavors where they can contribute meaningfully towards causes they care about.
- **Creativity**; With their creative inclinations Cancer individuals may explore paths within creative professions such as writing, music or the arts. These outlets enable them to express themselves while tapping into their inner world.
- **Management and Leadership**; Cancer individuals have the potential to excel as managers and leaders in positions that foster a nurturing atmosphere.

To summarize Cancer individuals' career preferences and professional aspirations are deeply influenced by their caring nature, emotional intelligence and desire to establish a comfortable environment. They thrive in roles that allow them to care for others, make an impact and contribute to the well being of their colleagues or clients.

STRENGTHS THAT MAKE CANCER INDIVIDUALS EXCEL IN THE WORKPLACE:

Individuals, with the zodiac sign Cancer, bring a distinguished set of strengths to the workplace. Of course this makes them valuable assets in professional environments. Their innate ability to nurture and empathize, coupled with their emotional intelligence greatly contribute to their success. Here are some notable strengths that distinguish Cancer individuals in the workplace.

- **Empathy and Compassion**; People born under the sign of Cancer possess a large capacity for empathy and compassion. This allows them to deeply understand the emotions and needs of their colleagues and clients. Overall this leads to fostering relationships and teamwork.
- **Strong Emotional Intelligence**; Cancer individuals exhibit a high level of emotional intelligence enabling them to navigate complex dynamics within the workplace with finesse.
- **Loyalty and Dedication**; Known for their loyalty and dedication Cancer individuals take their commitments seriously. They are willing to go above and beyond to achieve their goals and support their teams.
- **Excellent Team Players;** Cancer individuals thrive in team settings as they possess a team nature that promotes collaboration among team members.

Often taking on the role of an anchor within the team they foster unity among colleagues while boosting morale and productivity.

- **Problem Solvers**; When it comes to problem solving, those born under Cancer approach it with creativity and sensitivity in mind. They consider both aspects well, as emotional nuances when seeking innovative solutions that address diverse needs.
- **Organizational Skills**; Their ability to pay attention to detail and stay organized is truly impressive. Cancer individuals shine in roles that involve planning and effectively managing resources, projects or teams.
- **Adaptability**; While they appreciate stability Cancer individuals are also adept, at adapting to circumstances and embracing challenges. Their flexible nature allows them to thrive in dynamic work environments.
- **Dependability**; Colleagues and supervisors often rely on Cancer individuals because of their dependability. They are trusted team members who prioritize meeting deadlines and fulfilling their responsibilities.
- **Strong Work Ethic**; Cancer individuals possess a work and approach their professional duties with utmost seriousness. They are known for their diligence, thoroughness and persistent efforts in achieving their goals.
- **Intuition**; Their intuitive instincts serve as an asset when it comes to decision making. Cancer individuals often have a sense about situations or people which helps them make informed choices.
- **Attention to Well Being**; Prioritizing the well being of both themselves and their colleagues is paramount, for Cancer individuals. They actively promote self care and stress reduction. Maintaining a work life balance is important for them to create a happier and more productive workplace environment.
- **Leadership Potential**; With their nurturing and supportive leadership style Cancer individuals naturally excel as leaders. They inspire trust, loyalty while also serving as mentors and role models.

To summarize individuals born under the Cancer zodiac sign, possess valuable qualities in terms of empathy, emotional intelligence, loyalty and a strong work ethic. They thrive in positions that involve fostering connections, with others promoting teamwork and creating a harmonious atmosphere.

CAREER CHALLENGES AND STRATEGIES TO OVERCOME THEM

While individuals born under the zodiac sign of Cancer bring strengths to the workplace they also face challenges that can impact their professional development. Understanding these challenges and implementing strategies to overcome them can help Cancer individuals thrive in their careers. Let's explore some challenges and corresponding strategies.

Sensitivity to Feedback

- Challenge; Cancer individuals may take criticism personally leading to hurt feelings and a dip in confidence.
- Strategy; Focus on feedback rather than perceiving it as a personal attack. Seek guidance from mentors to gain a perspective on your performance and grow through feedback.

Difficulty Establishing Boundaries

- Challenge; Cancer individuals often struggle with setting boundaries. This can result in taking on much and experiencing burnout.
- Strategy; Practice assertiveness. Learn to say no when necessary. Prioritize self care. Establish limits to avoid overextending yourself.

Fear of Change

- Challenge; Cancer individuals tend to prefer stability and may be resistant to change making it challenging for them to adapt in paced industries.
- Strategy; Embrace change as an opportunity for growth. Stay updated with industry trends. Proactively seek ways to expand your skills ensuring you remain competitive.

Emotional Overwhelm

- Challenge; The emotional demands of the workplace can sometimes overwhelm Cancer individuals impacting their productivity.
- Strategy; Take steps towards managing emotions by seeking outlets outside of work such as meditation or hobbies that provide rejuvenation.

Avoiding conflict

- Challenge; Cancer individuals have a tendency to avoid conflict. This can result in issues in the workplace.
- Strategy; It is important to learn conflict resolution skills and practice clear communication. By addressing conflicts you can prevent them from escalating and find productive resolutions.

Indecisiveness

- Challenge; Cancer individuals can be indecisive when it comes to career choices. This often stems from their desire for security and fear of making the wrong decision.
- Strategy; Seeking guidance from mentors or career counselors can help clarify your career goals. Breaking down decisions into manageable steps can make the process less overwhelming.

Blurred boundaries

- Challenge; Cancer individuals tend to identify with their careers making it difficult for them to separate work from their lives.

- Strategy; Establishing boundaries between work and personal life is crucial. Engaging in activities outside of work that bring joy and fulfillment can help maintain a work life balance.

Procrastination

- Challenge; Procrastination is another obstacle that Cancer individuals commonly face. It often leads to missed deadlines.
- Strategy; Setting goals and prioritizing tasks can help overcome procrastination tendencies. Breaking projects into smaller steps not only reduces overwhelm but also ensures timely completion.

In conclusion we have explored the connection between Cancer individuals and their professional lives as well as their distinct approach to money. Throughout this chapter we have uncovered the strengths, challenges and strategies that define how a Cancer pursues success.

Individuals belonging to the Cancer zodiac sign bring a wealth of intelligence and dedication to their careers due to their nurturing and nature. Their unwavering loyalty, resilience and commitment to creating work environments make them highly valuable in a range of professions. Moreover their focus on home and family extends to their aspirations as they strive to provide security and stability for their loved ones.

However, like individuals from any zodiac sign Cancers also face certain challenges. These challenges include sensitivity towards criticism and a reluctance when it comes to self promotion. Nevertheless these obstacles can be seen as opportunities for growth and development. By embracing change, setting boundaries, improving communication skills and developing conflict resolution abilities; Cancer individuals can overcome these hurdles and achieve their career objectives.

As we wrap up this chapter it's important to remember that the path to success and financial well being is different for everyone. Whether you're a Cancer sign aiming to thrive in your career and finances or someone intrigued by the approach to work and money let the insights we've shared here serve as guidance on your journey towards a prosperous life. Like the phases of the moon your professional growth and financial circumstances may fluctuate. But with patience, determination and the wisdom of the Crab you'll be able to navigate life's ups and downs, with grace and resilience.

CHAPTER 5: SELF-IMPROVEMENT

Welcome to a new chapter where we embark on a journey of growth and development! A journey specifically for those born under the Cancer zodiac sign. Their journey towards self improvement is deeply rooted in their desire to enhance their lives while providing unwavering support to their loved ones. Within these pages we uncover how Cancer individuals can harness their strengths, overcome weaknesses and navigate the path to personal growth.

From embracing change and setting boundaries to nurturing well being and fostering resilience. This chapter offers insights and strategies for Cancer individuals to embark on a journey of self discovery and improvement. Whether you are seeking to enhance your life or someone interested in understanding the unique path of personal growth for Cancer individuals this chapter promises valuable guidance.

PERSONAL GROWTH AND DEVELOPMENT

Personal growth and development deeply resonates with Cancer individuals. Nurtured by their compassionate nature, they have a drive to become the best versions of themselves. Now let's explore some key aspects of growth and development for Cancer individuals.

- **Introspection**; Reflecting on oneself and being aware of emotions. Cancer individuals can greatly benefit from self reflection and emotional awareness. Taking time to understand their feelings and motivations helps them navigate life with clarity and purpose. Practices, like keeping a journal or practicing meditation can support this process.
- **Establishing boundaries;** Cancer individuals often find it challenging to set boundaries since they naturally prioritize taking care of others. However, learning to set and maintain boundaries is crucial for their growth ensuring they balance their own needs with their nurturing instincts.
- **Developing conflict resolution skills**; As individuals who dislike conflict Cancer individuals can enhance their development by acquiring conflict resolution skills. This empowers them to address issues in a manner while maintaining harmony in their relationships.
- **Embracing change**; Cancer individuals tend to prefer stability over change. However personal growth often requires stepping out of one's comfort zone. Learning to embrace change as an opportunity for growth becomes an aspect of their development journey.
- **Practicing self care and stress management**; Considering their inclination, towards caring for others individuals born under the zodiac sign Cancer might sometimes overlook the importance of self care. It becomes crucial for them to prioritize self care routines. Relaxation techniques and strategies to manage stress are a good idea.
- **Communication skills**; Improving communication skills especially when it comes to expressing their needs and desires can empower Cancer individuals in their journey of growth. Effective communication plays an important role in fostering understanding and establishing connections with others.
- **Goal setting**; Setting attainable goals is beneficial for Cancer individuals. Whether these goals pertain to their career, relationships or personal aspirations. Overall having a roadmap helps them stay focused and motivated on their path of growth.
- **Resilience**; Developing resilience is a part of growth for Cancer individuals. Life inevitably presents challenges along the way. However, nurturing resilience allows them to bounce back stronger than before.
- **Independence**; Cultivating independence is an area where Cancer individuals can focus on as they tend to prioritize others needs over their

own. Learning how to stand on one's feet and pursue interests contributes significantly to one's growth and self discovery.

- **Creativity**; Cancer individuals possess creative potential. Exploring outlets such as art, writing or music can provide a fulfilling avenue for them to express themselves artistically and emotionally.
- **Learning**; The love for learning and innate curiosity are deeply ingrained within Cancer individuals. They have an inclination towards learning that serves as a catalyst for continuous personal growth.
- **Seek support;** In the case of Cancer individuals, they should not hesitate in seeking support when needed. Just as they offer support to others. Whether it's through therapy, counseling or mentorship, seeking guidance can greatly contribute to growth.

To summarize, personal growth and development, for Cancer individuals involves deepening awareness, establishing and maintaining boundaries embracing change and fostering resilience. By prioritizing self care, communication and nurturing their creativity Cancer individuals can aspire to become resilient and authentic individuals as they continue to evolve. Lastly, remember that personal development is an individual journey where individuals have the opportunity to continuously expand their knowledge and skills throughout their lives.

HARNESSING STRENGTHS AND OVERCOMING WEAKNESSES:

Those born under Cancer's zodiac possess a unique blend of strengths and weaknesses that shape their character. By embracing their strengths and working on areas for improvement they can embark on a journey of growth and self improvement. Here's a look at how they can achieve that.

Empathy and Compassion (Strength)

- Embrace; Utilize your empathy to foster meaningful connections. Provide support to loved ones. Consider pursuing careers where you can make a positive difference in others lives.
- Overcome; Be mindful not to shoulder the burdens of others. Practice establishing boundaries to prevent burnout.

Strong Emotional Intelligence (Strength)

- Embrace; Utilize your intelligence to navigate social situations effectively. Employ it to build rapport, resolve conflicts and excel in roles that require understanding and managing emotions.
- Overcome; Avoid overanalyzing situations. Avoid being overly sensitive to criticism. Recognize that not everything carries a weight.

Loyalty and Dedication (Strength)

- Embrace; Channel your loyalty and dedication towards achieving your career goals. Commit to your projects, team members and personal endeavors. Your determination can pave the way for long term success.
- Overcome; Exercise caution, in remaining in situations that no longer contribute positively to you.

Security focus Strength)

- Embrace; Embrace your cautious approach. Build a secure future for yourself and your loved ones. Develop budgeting and savings habits. Consider long term investment opportunities for financial stability.
- Overcome; Avoid worrying too much about security. Strike a balance between saving for the future and enjoying the present.

Handling Criticism Sensitively (Weakness)

- Embrace; Transform your sensitivity towards criticism into an opportunity for growth. Use feedback as a tool to enhance your skills and improve yourself.
- Overcome; Develop resilience by focusing on self confidence and self worth. Remember that not all criticism reflects your abilities.

Reluctance to Promote Yourself (Weakness)

- Embrace; Recognize the importance of self promotion in your career. Highlight your accomplishments and skills when appropriate and take credit for your contributions.
- Overcome; Practice self affirmation and build confidence in yourself. Acknowledge your achievements. Remind yourself of your value.

Fear of Change (Weakness)

- Embrace; Embrace change as a chance, for growth and new experiences. Understand that change can lead to both professional development.

- Overcome; Developing adaptability involves taking steps of your comfort zone. Gradually exposing yourself to experiences can help you build confidence, in navigating through changes.

Remember that by capitalizing on your strengths and actively addressing any weaknesses, individuals with the Cancer zodiac sign can embark on a fulfilling journey of self improvement. This balanced approach allows them to continue nurturing and supporting others while also nurturing their own development.

Throughout this chapter we have delved into their strengths, weaknesses and the strategies they can employ to become the versions of themselves. As Cancer individuals embrace growth and development they can look forward to better relationships, increased self assurance and the ability to navigate life's ever changing circumstances, with confidence. Ultimately each step you take brings you closer, to becoming the best version of yourself.

CHAPTER 6: THE YEAR AHEAD

In this chapter we offer individuals born under the Cancer zodiac sign a glimpse into the upcoming year. As celestial bodies align, their influence will shape your life in many ways. This chapter serves as your guiding compass through the events that may impact the many aspects of your life. As we traverse through these events and their implications Cancer individuals will gain valuable insights. These insights will help you to navigate challenges, seize opportunities and make the most of this year. So my dear friend, let's embark on this voyage guided by the stars as we embrace all the possibilities that await us.

HOROSCOPE GUIDE FOR THE YEAR AHEAD

As you begin a journey, around the sun the vast universe has a tale to share with you. Here is your horoscope guide for the year ahead providing insights into the energies that will impact your life.

Aries season (March 21. April 19)

- Relationships; Make harmony a priority in your relationships. Be open to compromise and understanding as this will strengthen the connections you share.
- Career; New opportunities might come your way. Trust your instincts. Embrace challenges to progress in your path.

Taurus season (April 20. May 20)

- Finances; Keep an eye on your financial situation. Budget wisely. Consider long term investments for future stability.
- Health; Prioritize your well being through a healthy lifestyle. Eat clean. Take up regular physical activity.

Gemini season (May 21. June 20)

- Career; Your professional life is poised for growth. Embrace new roles and projects as they will lead you towards advancement.

- Travel; Explore the idea of travel or engaging in pursuits to broaden your horizons and gain fresh perspectives.

Cancer season (June 21. July 22)

- Self Discovery; Focus on growth and self exploration. Be receptive to change and establish boundaries that nurture your well being.
- Family; Strengthen ties, through communication and quality time spent together.

Leo season (July 23. August 22)

- Creativity; Your creative energy will shine as you explore creative pursuits or hobbies that ignite your passion.
- Love; Love and romance may flourish during this time. Cherish these moments. Nurture your relationships.

Virgo season (August 23. September 22)

- Career; You have the potential for career advancements within your reach. Your meticulous approach and dedication will lead to success.
- Health; Take care of yourself by prioritizing a diet and regular exercise.

Libra season (September 23. October 22)

- Love; Foster harmony in your relationships through quality communication and if necessary compromise.
- Money; Ensure stability through long term planning and responsible spending.

Scorpio season (October 23. November 21)

- Self improvement; Embark on a journey of self discovery and personal growth. Explore your potential to evolve as an individual.
- Travel; Consider expanding your horizons through travel or educational opportunities.

Sagittarius season (November 22. December 21)

- Career; Pursue your career ambitions with fresh enthusiasm as new opportunities and challenges will lead to advancement.
- Family; Strengthen family bonds. Create a nurturing home environment.

Capricorn season (December 22. January 19)

- Money; Focus on achieving stability through budgeting and wise long term investments.
- Health; Make sure to take care of both your mental and physical health by finding a balance in your life.

Aquarius season (January 20. February 18)

- Friendships; It's important to nurture your friendships and expand your circle. Collaborative opportunities might lead to lucrative ventures.
- Romance; Be open to new possibilities. Embrace the connections.

Pisces season (February 19. March 20)

- Self Care; Remember to prioritize self care and relaxation. Taking time for rest and rejuvenation is crucial for your overall well being.
- Career; There's potential for career growth. Trust your intuition when making career related decisions.

So as you embark on the journey of the year remember that while the cosmos can offer guidance it is ultimately your choices and actions that will shape your destiny. Embrace the opportunities that come your way, learn from challenges and trust in your wisdom. May this year bring you growth, love and fulfillment in many ways.

KEY ASTROLOGICAL EVENTS

Astrological events play an important role in shaping the experiences and energies that impact individuals born under the Cancer zodiac sign. Here are some important astrological events and how they can potentially affect Cancer individuals.

New Moon in Cancer

- Impact; The New Moon in Cancer brings a surge of fresh energy making it an ideal time for setting intentions related to growth, family matters and emotional healing.
- How it affects Cancer; During this time Cancer individuals may experience heightened intuition and emotional depth. It's an opportunity for self care and nurturing relationships.

Full Moon in Capricorn

- Impact; The Full Moon in Capricorn often highlights career and ambition. It will be shedding light on areas where balancing work and home life is necessary.
- How it affects Cancer; Cancer individuals may find themselves managing dual responsibilities between their personal lives. Remember it's important to maintain harmony while prioritizing self care.

Jupiter Transits

- Impact; When Jupiter, the planet of expansion and growth enters or aligns favorably with the sign of Cancer it can bring many opportunities. Notably for personal development, travel and education.
- How it affects Cancer; During these times Cancer individuals may feel a desire for learning new things and exploring new horizons. Now is the perfect time to expand your knowledge and focus on personal development.

Saturn Transits

- Effects; When Saturn transits it can bring challenges and lessons related to responsibilities. For Cancer individuals it may be an opportunity to evaluate their commitments and make some adjustments.
- How it impacts Cancer; Cancer individuals might feel inclined to bring better organization and discipline into their lives. Although these transits can be demanding they offer chances for growth and maturity.

Mercury Retrograde

- Effects; During Mercury Retrograde there may be disruptions in communication and technology. It's a period for reflection and reevaluation.
- How it impacts Cancer; Cancer individuals should be cautious of miscommunications and delays during this time. Utilize this period for introspection and revisiting decisions.

Eclipses

- Effects; Solar and lunar eclipses have the potential to bring changes in both professional and personal aspects of life. They often signify a shift in focus or the beginning of a new chapter in life.
- How it impacts Cancer; Eclipses can inspire Cancer individuals to reassess their goals, relationships and overall life direction. Embrace these changes as opportunities for growth.

Venus Transits

- Effects; Venus transits highlight matters of love, relationships and beauty. They can create opportunities for romance, as enhanced creativity.
- How Cancer is influenced; They may experience a boost in harmonious energies during Venus transits. It's a period for nurturing relationships and expressing their creativity.

These astrological events bring a backdrop to the lives of Cancer individuals. By understanding the effects of these events they can make better informed choices, embrace opportunities for personal growth and navigate challenges.

Below are some key areas to consider in the year ahead.

LOVE AND RELATIONSHIPS

In the realm of love and relationships, Cancer individuals are deeply influenced by the celestial movements of the year. Let's delve into how astrological events will impact their romantic lives.

New Moon in Cancer

- Impact: The New Moon in Cancer is an emotional powerhouse. It sets the stage for self-discovery and renewed commitment in relationships.
- Advice: Embrace this time to strengthen your emotional bonds with loved ones. Reflect on your desires and communicate openly with your partner.

Venus in Cancer

- Impact: Venus, the planet of love and beauty, graces Cancer with its presence. This period may bring increased romance and sensuality.
- Advice: Nurture your romantic relationships during Venus' stay in your sign. Plan special dates and express your affection openly.

Mars Retrograde

- Impact: Mars Retrograde can create tension and conflicts in relationships. Misunderstandings may arise, leading to introspection.
- Advice: Be patient and avoid unnecessary confrontations. Use this time to reflect on your desires and consider the long-term health of your relationships.

Solar and Lunar Eclipses

- Impact: Eclipses can bring pivotal changes in love and relationships. They may signify new beginnings or the end of certain connections.
- Advice: Embrace change and transformation. Be open to the opportunities that eclipses bring, even if they initially seem challenging.

CAREER AND FINANCES

Astrological events also play a significant role in shaping Cancer individuals' career and financial prospects. Here's how the celestial movements of the year ahead may impact these areas.

Jupiter in Pisces

- Impact: Jupiter's influence in Pisces may bring career growth and expansion. Financial opportunities could well be on the horizon.
- Advice: Seize professional opportunities with enthusiasm. Invest in your skills and knowledge to maximize your career potential.

Saturn in Aquarius

- Impact: Saturn's presence in Aquarius may prompt career reassessment. It encourages a focus on long-term goals and financial stability.
- Advice: Take a disciplined approach to your career and finances. Build a solid foundation for your future and consider necessary changes.

Mercury Retrograde

- Impact: Mercury Retrograde can lead to miscommunications and delays in financial matters. Caution is advised in money-related decisions.
- Advice: Double-check contracts and financial agreements. Use this time for careful financial planning and budgeting.

HEALTH AND WELLNESS

Cancer individuals' well-being is closely tied to key astrological events. Let's explore how these cosmic movements may affect their health and offer guidance for maintaining wellness.

Solar and Lunar Eclipses

- Impact: Eclipses can trigger stress and emotional challenges, potentially affecting physical health.
- Advice: Prioritize self-care during eclipse periods. Maintain a balanced routine, practice relaxation techniques, and seek support when needed.

Venus in Leo

- Impact: Venus in Leo brings a boost of vitality and self-confidence. It's an excellent time for self-care and enhancing overall well-being.
- Advice: Focus on self-care routines that make you feel confident and radiant. Engage in physical activities that bring you joy.

PERSONAL GROWTH AND SELF-DISCOVERY

Astrological events offer opportunities for personal growth and self-discovery. Here's how Cancer individuals can make the most of the year ahead.

New Moon in Cancer

- Impact: The New Moon in Cancer invites self-reflection and the setting of new intentions.
- Advice: Use this time for deep self-discovery. Set intentions for personal growth and emotional healing. Embrace change with an open heart.

Saturn in Aquarius

- Impact: Saturn's presence in Aquarius encourages self-examination and personal growth.

- Advice: Embrace the challenges as opportunities for growth. Focus on long-term goals and cultivate resilience.

Solar and Lunar Eclipses

- Impact: Eclipses mark moments of transformation and new beginnings.
- Advice: Embrace change with an open mind. Use eclipses as catalysts for positive personal growth and self-discovery.

Overall in the year ahead, Cancer individuals can harness the energy of these astrological events to nurture their relationships, advance their careers, enhance their well-being and embark on a journey of self-discovery. By staying attuned to the cosmic currents, they can ultimately navigate the challenges ahead. At the same time they can seize the opportunities that arise.

The vast expanse of the cosmos with its dance of movements and celestial alignments reveals valuable insights into what lies ahead in the coming year. As we say goodbye to this chapter remember that while astrology gives us guidance it's up to you to shape your destiny. Move forward with bravery and determination! May the upcoming year be like a canvas. One where you can create a picture filled with love, success, health and personal growth.

CHAPTER 7:
FAMOUS "CANCER" PERSONALITIES

In this chapter we will embark on a journey through the lives of people who were born under the Cancer zodiac sign. As we delve into the stories of these figures from fields such as entertainment, politics, sports and business we will uncover the distinct qualities that have propelled them towards greatness. Join us as we celebrate their achievements. Let us also navigate through their challenges and explore how these famous Cancer individuals have made an impact. Whether you share a Cancer sign or simply seek inspiration from their journeys this chapter promises to be an exploration. One that explores how stars have influenced some of history's most influential figures.

HENRY VIII

- Date of Birth: June 28, 1491.
- Brief Biography: Henry VIII was the King of England from 1509 to 1547. He is best known for his six marriages and his role in the English Reformation.
- Cancer Traits: Henry displayed traits of sensitivity, loyalty, and a deep emotional nature often associated with Cancer individuals.
- Impact: His reign was marked by significant political and religious changes, including the establishment of the Church of England.
- Personal Life: His marital struggles and quest for a male heir are legendary, leading to his separation from the Catholic Church.

DIANA SPENCER (PRINCESS DIANA)

- Date of Birth: July 1, 1961.
- Brief Biography: Princess Diana was the first wife of Prince Charles and a beloved member of the British royal family. She was known for her philanthropy and humanitarian work.
- Cancer Traits: Diana embodied the nurturing and empathetic qualities of Cancer individuals, making her a compassionate figure.
- Impact: Her charitable endeavors and efforts to destigmatize issues like HIV/AIDS had a lasting impact on global awareness.

- Personal Life: Diana's personal life, including her public struggles and divorce from Prince Charles, garnered significant media attention.

JOHN D. ROCKEFELLER

- Date of Birth: July 8, 1839.
- Brief Biography: John D. Rockefeller was an American business magnate and philanthropist who co-founded the Standard Oil Company.
- Cancer Traits: His strong sense of financial security and dedication to family align with Cancer's traits.
- Impact: Rockefeller's business empire revolutionized the oil industry and made him one of the wealthiest individuals in history.
- Personal Life: His philanthropic endeavors, including the creation of the Rockefeller Foundation, have had a lasting impact on education and public health.

ARIANA GRANDE

- Date of Birth: June 26, 1993.
- Brief Biography: Ariana Grande is a renowned American singer, songwriter, and actress known for her powerful vocal range.
- Cancer Traits: She embodies Cancer's emotional depth and artistic creativity, often infusing her music with personal experiences.
- Impact: Grande's music career has achieved immense success, earning numerous awards and a dedicated fan base.
- Personal Life: She's known for her resilience in the face of personal challenges, including the Manchester Arena bombing during her concert.

LIONEL MESSI

- Date of Birth: June 24, 1987.
- Brief Biography: Lionel Messi is an Argentine professional footballer often regarded as one of the greatest soccer players in history.
- Cancer Traits: Messi exhibits Cancer's dedication, emotional intelligence, and strong work ethic on the field.
- Impact: His exceptional skills have earned him numerous accolades, including multiple FIFA Ballon d'Or awards.
- Personal Life: Messi's commitment to philanthropy is reflected in his work with children's charities and UNICEF.

MIKE TYSON

- Date of Birth: June 30, 1966.
- Brief Biography: Mike Tyson is a former professional boxer known for his ferocious fighting style and being the youngest heavyweight champion.
- Cancer Traits: Despite his tough exterior, Tyson has spoken about his emotional nature, a characteristic of many Cancer individuals.
- Impact: He left a significant mark on the boxing world with his dominance and intense fighting style.
- Personal Life: Tyson's tumultuous personal life and legal issues have been well-documented.

ELON MUSK

- Date of Birth: June 28, 1971.
- Brief Biography: Elon Musk is a tech entrepreneur and CEO known for founding companies like SpaceX and Tesla.
- Cancer Traits: Musk's determination, visionary thinking, and occasional emotional intensity align with Cancer characteristics.
- Impact: His ventures are at the forefront of space exploration and electric vehicles, pushing technological boundaries.
- Personal Life: Musk's public persona often includes candid expressions of his thoughts and feelings on social media.

LIV TYLER

- Date of Birth: July 1, 1977.
- Brief Biography: Liv Tyler is an American actress known for her roles in films like "The Lord of the Rings" trilogy.
- Cancer Traits: Her gentle and empathetic on-screen presence reflects the qualities of Cancer individuals.
- Impact: Tyler's acting career has spanned various genres, earning her acclaim in both film and television.
- Personal Life: She's known for her close-knit family and artistic endeavors.

MALALA YOUSAFZAI

- Date of Birth: July 12, 1997.
- Brief Biography: Malala Yousafzai is a Pakistani education activist and Nobel Prize laureate who advocates for girls' education.
- Cancer Traits: Her unwavering determination, compassion, and commitment to education align with Cancer traits.
- Impact: Malala's advocacy has led to global recognition and support for girls' education worldwide.
- Personal Life: She continues to inspire and promote change through her work.

50 CENT (CURTIS JACKSON)

- Date of Birth: July 6, 1975.
- Brief Biography: 50 Cent is a renowned American rapper, actor, and producer known for his influence on hip-hop.
- Cancer Traits: His emotional depth and determination align with Cancer characteristics, influencing his music and career.
- Impact: 50 Cent has made a significant impact on the music industry and ventured into various business endeavors.
- Personal Life: He has faced personal and legal challenges but continues to thrive in his career.

BENAZIR BHUTTO

- Date of Birth: June 21, 1953.
- Brief Biography: Benazir Bhutto was the first woman to lead a Muslim-majority country, serving as Pakistan's Prime Minister.

- Cancer Traits: Bhutto exhibited Cancer's strong leadership qualities, nurturing spirit, and emotional intelligence.
- Impact: Her political career had a transformative impact on Pakistan's history, emphasizing democracy and women's rights.
- Personal Life: Bhutto's political journey was marked by challenges, including periods of exile and political opposition.

SELENA GOMEZ

- Date of Birth: July 22, 1992.
- Brief Biography: Selena Gomez is an American singer, actress, and producer known for her versatile talents.
- Cancer Traits: She reflects Cancer's emotional depth in her music and her commitment to mental health advocacy.
- Impact: Gomez has achieved fame as both a musician and actress, using her platform to raise awareness about important issues.
- Personal Life: She has been open about her struggles with mental health, contributing to reducing stigma.

As we contemplate the stories of these legends we are reminded that while cosmic alignment at birth plays a role it is only part of the equation. Their unwavering resolve and dedication to their callings have propelled them towards greatness.

Whether you find inspiration in their journeys, relate to their shared characteristics or simply value their contributions. Overall the lives of these Cancer individuals provide us with a glimpse into the diverse tapestry of human existence. They serve as a reminder that while celestial bodies above may guide our paths it's ultimately our efforts, resilience and dedication that truly shape our destinities.

CONCLUSION

As we approach the end of this eye opening journey into the realm of Cancer, the Zodiac Sign it's time to pause and reflect on the array of knowledge we have gathered together. Throughout this book we have delved deeply into the world of Cancer. We have unraveled its essence and its profound impact on individuals' lives. Let us now revisit the main points that have shed light on our understanding of Cancer.

Individuals born under this sign are characterized by their depth, empathy and nurturing nature. Their remarkable intuition and strong connection to family and home define them. The symbol associated with Cancer, the Crab represents their shell and their ability to navigate through a sea of emotions. Being a water sign emphasizes how emotions and intuition hold importance in their lives. The Moon governs Cancer symbolizing change and emotional cycles. Furthermore it amplifies their connection to emotions while reflecting their evolving nature.

People born under the sign of Cancer are well known for their loyalty, sensitivity and commitment. They thrive in roles that require empathy and compassion making them natural caregivers. Their strong intuition, nurturing nature and adaptability are what make them truly shine. They have a knack for creating holistic environments not just for themselves but also for those around them. Though sometimes Cancers can be overly emotional, sensitive to criticism and experience mood swings. Learning to balance their emotions can be an ongoing journey throughout their lives.

In our exploration throughout this book we have delved into the origins of Cancer, its significance in mythologies as well as its evolution within astrology over time. We have witnessed how Cancer has influenced events and notable figures while also playing a role in personality based astrology. From matters of love and relationships to friendships, family dynamics and career aspirations – we have extensively covered the aspects that shape the lives of individuals born under the sign of Cancer. Alongside providing tips and guidance on navigating challenges we have offered insights on nurturing strengths and pursuing growth. Let's now summarize the chapters we have traversed.

- **Chapter 1: History and Mythology**; In Chapter 1, we delved into the historical origins of the Cancer constellation and explored how different cultures perceived and represented it in their star maps. We also journeyed through the rich tapestry of "Cancer" in ancient mythologies, uncovering the stories and symbolism associated with this zodiac sign.

- **Chapter 2: Love & Compatibility**; Chapter 2 illuminated the intricacies of love and relationships for Cancer individuals. We examined their approach to romance and compatibility with other zodiac signs. The chapter also provided valuable tips for dating and maintaining relationships with Cancer partners.
- **Chapter 3: Friends And Family**; Chapter 3 delved into the dynamics of friendships and family relations for Cancer individuals. We explored their nurturing nature and the challenges they may encounter. In addition we looked at how to improve, maintain and grow these essential connections.
- **Chapter 4: Career And Money**; In Chapter 4, we uncovered Cancer individuals' career preferences and professional aspirations. We also discussed their strengths and challenges in the workplace. Inside we provided strategies to overcome obstacles and thrive in their chosen fields.
- **Chapter 5: Self-Improvement**; Chapter 5 offered insights into personal growth and development for Cancer individuals. We explored how they can harness their strengths and overcome weaknesses. Overall it facilitates self-improvement and achieving their potential.
- **Chapter 6: The Year Ahead**; Chapter 6 provided a horoscope guide for Cancer individuals in the year ahead. The chapter provided analysis of astrological events and their influence on their lives. Overall it offered valuable advice on making the most of the year ahead.
- **Chapter 7: Famous "Cancer" Personalities**; In Chapter 7, we celebrated the achievements of famous Cancer personalities. We explored the lives and legacies of individuals born under this zodiac sign. From political leaders to artists, athletes, and business moguls. These profiles illustrated how Cancer traits shaped their journeys to greatness.

Throughout the chapters of this book we have embarked on an exploration of the Cancer zodiac sign. From its ancient origins, to its relevance in aspects of life today we have gained comprehensive insights and a deeper understanding. Whether you're a Cancer individual seeking self discovery or simply intrigued by this sign. You have truly been on a rich and enlightening journey through the world of Cancer.

This book serves as a reminder that astrology, rooted in wisdom yet relevant today, continues to offer guidance on understanding our personalities and navigating our life paths. As we reach the end of this book lets carry with us the knowledge we've gained about Cancer and all the zodiac signs. May it empower us to have a better understanding of ourselves, our loved ones and the world around us. The stars above continue to guide us and through astrologys wisdom we embark on a journey of discovering ourselves and growing as individuals.

Thank you for joining us on this adventure through the realm of Cancer. May the cosmic energies always light up your path towards fulfillment, understanding and harmony with the universe. We committed to unraveling the enigmas surrounding the Cancer zodiac sign. By exploring aspects of life through a Cancer lens we have fulfilled this commitment. Ultimately this book serves as a guide for individuals born under Cancer assisting them in embracing their qualities while navigating lifes ups and downs. Above all else, our goal is for readers to understand that astrology, including the Cancer zodiac sign, provides a framework for self discovery and personal growth. Embracing our qualities, strengths and weaknesses is essential, for leading an harmonious life.

To conclude, astrology serves as a timeless language that resonates with individuals seeking insights into themselves and their life paths. The Cancer zodiac sign offers a perspective on the world characterized by depth nurturing qualities and resilience. For all those who identify as Cancer individuals we encourage you to embrace your qualities with pride. Your intuition, empathy and dedication are your strengths that will guide you towards a life filled with creativity and meaningful connections.

Astrology beckons us to connect with the cosmos and gain a deep understanding of ourselves and the world around us. Like all signs of the zodiac Cancer is a tapestry of potentials waiting to be woven into a fulfilling life. Continue your journey of self discovery while allowing the stars above to illuminate your path. Embrace who you truly are and cultivate your strengths. Allow the guidance of the stars to illuminate a bright pathway to follow. A pathway towards a brighter and more harmonious future.

Best wishes to you

LEO:

A COMPLETE GUIDE TO THE LEO ASTROLOGY STAR SIGN

Contents

INTRODUCTION -- 1
Leo Zodiac Sign Overview and Symbolism -- 2

CHAPTER 1: HISTORY AND MYTHOLOGY ------------------------ 5
Historical Origins -- 5
Notable events during the Leo season--- 7

CHAPTER 2: LOVE & COMPATIBILITY --------------------------10
The Leo approach to love--11
Compatibility With Other Signs --12
Tips for Dating and Relationships with a Leo -------------------------------------15

CHAPTER 3: FRIENDS AND FAMILY ---------------------------18
Leo as a Friend --18
Leo and Family Dynamics ---20
Challenges in Friendships and Family for Leo ----------------------------------21

CHAPTER 4: CAREER AND MONEY -------------------------- 23
Career Preferences and Professional Goals--24
Challenges and Strategies to Overcome Them--------------------------------------26

CHAPTER 5: SELF-IMPROVEMENT -------------------------- 29
Personal Growth and Development --29
Leveraging Strengths and Overcoming Weaknesses------------------------------31

CHAPTER 6: THE YEAR AHEAD------------------------------- 33
Horoscope Guide for the Year Ahead--33
Key Astrological Events and Their Impact on Leo: ------------------------------37

CHAPTER 7: FAMOUS "LEO" PERSONALITIES ---------------- 39

Napoléon Bonaparte ---------- 39

Whitney Houston ---------- 39

Barack Obama ---------- 40

Coco Chanel ---------- 40

Marcus Garvey ---------- 40

Madonna ---------- 41

Arnold Schwarzenegger ---------- 41

Usain Bolt ---------- 41

Dua Lipa ---------- 42

Tom Brady ---------- 42

J.K. Rowling ---------- 42

Kylie Jenner ---------- 42

CONCLUSION ---------- 44

INTRODUCTION

Astrology has fascinated humans for centuries. At its core it revolves around the notion that positions and motions of the planets and stars can influence and mirror our behavior, personality traits and life events. By analyzing the combination of placements at someone's birth moment astrologers, create birth charts (also known as natal charts) which serve as a guide to understanding an individual's character traits and life journey.

The zodiac plays an important role in astrology as it consists of twelve signs. Each sign falls within specific dates of the year. Each with their unique personality traits, strengths, weaknesses and distinct characteristics. In this book we provide an exploration of the Leo zodiac sign. The book has three objectives.

1. **Understanding**; We will delve deeply into the characteristics and traits that define Leos. Readers will gain an understanding of what makes individuals born under Leo unique. This includes exploring their strengths, weaknesses and how they navigate various aspects of life.

2. **Insights**; This book offers insights not only for Leo individuals but also for anyone interested in astrology. Through studying Leo readers can gain an understanding of astrology and how it can be applied to gain insights into oneself as well as others.

3. **Guidance**; This book provides advice and tips on how Leos can leverage their strengths, address their weaknesses and make the most of their attributes.

As you delve into the following pages we invite you on a captivating journey of self discovery and exploration through the lens of a Leo. Whether you're a Leo yourself or simply fascinated by astrology, this book aims to shed light on the path.

LEO ZODIAC SIGN OVERVIEW AND SYMBOLISM

1. **Date**; Leo, the fifth sign of the zodiac, spans from July 23rd to August 22nd.
2. **Symbol**; The symbol for Leo is the Lion. Strength, courage, and nobility represent it. Like the king or queen of the jungle, Leos often exhibit regal qualities and hold a commanding presence.
3. **Element**; Leo is a Fire sign. Fire signs are known for their passion, energy and enthusiasm. Leos are no exception. They bring warmth and vitality to their interactions.
4. **Planet**; The ruling planet of Leo is the Sun. Leos often radiate confidence and seek to shine like the Sun in their lives.
5. **Color**; The vibrant and bold color associated with Leo is gold. This reflects Leo's love for attention and their desire to stand out.

PERSONALITY TRAITS

Leos are known for their charismatic, generous and outgoing nature. They exude a natural magnetism that draws people toward them. Some key personality traits of Leos include.

- **Confidence**: Leos have an innate self-assuredness that helps them tackle challenges head-on.
- **Creativity**: They possess a creative spirit and a flair for the drama, often enjoying the arts and entertainment.
- **Leadership**: Leos are natural leaders who can inspire and motivate others with their enthusiasm.
- **Warmth**: They have a warm and generous heart, making them loyal and protective friends or partners.
- **Optimism**: Leos tend to maintain a positive outlook on life and believe in their ability to achieve their goals.

STRENGTHS

- **Leadership**: Leos have the ability to take charge and lead with charisma.
- **Courage**: They are not afraid to take risks and stand up for what they believe in.
- **Creativity**: Leos have a strong artistic and creative streak.
- **Generosity**: They are generous with their time, affection, and resources, often willing to help those in need.

WEAKNESSES

- **Ego**: Leos can sometimes have a pronounced ego, seeking attention and validation.
- **Stubbornness**: They can be resistant to change and hold onto their viewpoints firmly.
- **Impulsivity**: Leos' fiery nature can lead to impulsive actions and decisions.
- **Dramatic**: They may have a tendency to make a big production out of small issues.

From its representation as the Lion to its association with the radiant sun, Leo holds many captivating secrets. The following chapters will explore the intricacies of Leo's personality that make them such intriguing individuals. You will also learn all about its history through the ages, career prospects, relationships and much more.

Throughout this journey you will gain valuable insights into how Leos navigate their world and understand their compatibility with zodiac signs.

Prepare to encounter stories, anecdotes and practical guidance that will deepen your appreciation for Leos in your life. Be it yourself, a loved one or a friend. This book celebrates the spirit of the leo. So let us now immerse ourselves in the captivating world of Leo where courage, creativity and charisma reign supreme!

CHAPTER 1:
HISTORY AND MYTHOLOGY

The Leo zodiac sign has intrigued humanity for generations. In this chapter we embark on a journey through the tapestry of history and mythology that envelops this sign. A deeper understanding awaits you as you become acquainted with this zodiac lion. From the earliest recorded observations to the enduring legacy of Leo in present day astrology. Here we will uncover the tales, legends and symbolism that have shaped this passionate sign. Join us as we delve into the lion hearted bravery, strength and charm associated with Leo.

HISTORICAL ORIGINS

The Leo constellation, also known as the Lion, has held a position in the night sky for generations. Its origins can be traced back to ancient civilizations, where it was observed, recorded and woven into the mythologies of diverse cultures. Here are some of the most notable accounts.

BABYLONIAN AND SUMERIAN

The ancient Babylonians and Sumerians recognized the lion figure of Leo in the night sky. They documented their observations on clay tablets dating back to the 2nd millennium BCE. Leo was associated with their narratives, often portraying it as a creature with a lion's body and eagle's wings. The Babylonians connected this constellation with the "Great Lion,". This was a being that played a role in their cosmology and religious beliefs. For them the lion has long been regarded as a symbol of protection and guidance.

ANCIENT EGYPTIAN

In Ancient Egypt the constellation Leo was linked to Sekhmet, a goddess associated with war and healing. Sekhmet was known for both destruction and healing. She was believed to have the power to bring plagues and diseases.

Believers erred on the side of caution and appealed to her protective nature. As such the symbol of a lioness represented her protective nature. The Egyptians held lions in high regard. The Sphinx, a statue in Egypt with a lion's body and pharaoh's head is thought to have symbolic connections to Leo.

ANCIENT GREEK MYTHOLOGY

In Ancient Greek mythology Leo was frequently connected to the Nemean Lion. This was a creature with impenetrable skin. Hercules faced it as part of his Twelve Labors. This heroic tale became intertwined with the constellation itself, leading star maps to depict Leo as a lion. This myth highlights themes of courage, strength and heroism.

MODERN ASTROLOGY

In modern astrology there has been a shift, towards a psychological and personality based approach. While Leos still maintain their confidence and charisma, astrologers now explore their characteristics within a context of growth and self awareness. The emphasis lies on how individuals born under Leo can leverage their strengths while addressing any weaknesses. The goal is to direct them towards fulfilling lives. Although we still hold an appreciation for the symbolic aspects of Leo, modern astrology focuses on the interactive relationship between celestial forces and our individual psyches. This approach provides an introspective viewpoint, on the majestic Lion of the Zodiac.

NOTABLE EVENTS DURING THE LEO SEASON

It is important to note that astrology does not establish a cause and effect relationship with events. However certain noteworthy occurrences align with the attributes commonly associated with Leo. For instance periods of creativity, leadership or displays of courage may be more pronounced during this time.

Throughout history many influential figures have been born under the sign of Leo. While astrology does not determine one's destiny outrightly, these notable individuals possessed qualities often linked to Leos. Confidence, charisma and a strong desire to lead.

- **Napoleon Bonaparte**, born on August 15th in 1769. The French military leader and emperor renowned for his leadership and magnetic personality exemplified Leo traits. Those could be seen in his pursuit of power and his ability to inspire his troops.
- **Barack Obama**, born on August 4 1961. Obama served as the President of the United States. He was widely admired for his captivating speeches and ability to inspire millions of people. Such traits are often associated with individuals born under the Leo zodiac sign.
- **The Olympics (Creativity, Enthusiasm)**: The Summer Olympics often occur during Leo season. This global event showcases the creativity in opening ceremonies and the enthusiasm of athletes representing their countries.
- **National Independence Days (Enthusiasm, Generosity)**: Many countries celebrate their independence during this period, such as India and Pakistan. These celebrations are often marked by enthusiastic festivities and a generous spirit of unity and pride.

As we come to the end of this chapter we have delved into the stories and historical background surrounding the Leo zodiac sign. From its roots in ancient civilizations to its significant role in mythologies and beyond. Leo has always represented courage, strength and charismatic leadership.

Throughout history individuals born under the Leo sign have left their mark on the world by showcasing qualities like confidence, creativity and a natural ability to inspire others. From figures such as Napoleon Bonaparte. To transformative leaders like Barack Obama. Those with Leo personalities have truly made a lasting impact on the course of history.

The enduring influence of Leo continues to shine in astrology. While we hold the mythological interpretations, contemporary astrology provides a more comprehensive perspective on how Leo influences our lives. It guides individuals, towards self discovery, personal growth and a deeper understanding of their strengths and challenges. In an evolving world Leo's timeless attributes of self expression, vitality and unwavering determination remain relevant and highly valuable.

If you're interested in delving further into the history and mythology of Leo there are recommended sources worth exploring. These include texts, ancient writings and more contemporary works. All of which offer a wealth of knowledge and insights that will allow you to immerse yourself in the world of Leo and astrology. Whether you're seeking a perspective or a modern take, these resources provide an abundance of information to delve into and appreciate.

- **"The Astrology Encyclopedia"** by James R. Lewis: This comprehensive reference book offers insights into the history of astrology. Including the Leo sign, its symbolism, and historical significance.
- **"The Secret Language of Astrology"** by Roy Gillett: Delve into the symbolism and interpretation of Leo in modern astrology. This has a focus on personality traits and personal development.
- **"Star Myths of the Greeks and Romans"** by Theony Condos: Explore the rich tapestry of Greek and Roman mythology. Includes stories related to the Leo constellation.
- **"The Babylonian World"** edited by Gwendolyn Leick: This book provides a glimpse into the ancient Babylonian civilization. Early observations of celestial bodies and their significance took root.
- **"The Oxford Companion to World Mythology"** by David Leeming: An invaluable resource for understanding mythologies from around the world. Includes those associated with the Leo constellation.

- **"The Only Astrology Book You'll Ever Need"** by Joanna Martine Woolfolk: A modern guide to astrology that covers all aspects of the zodiac signs. Leo is included with insights into compatibility, career, and more.

CHAPTER 2:
LOVE & COMPATIBILITY

This chapter explores how individuals born under Leo can navigate love and relationships with their unique qualities. Leos, the captivating zodiac sign ruled by the Sun and symbolized by the Lion, brings a fiery and passionate approach to matters of the heart. From their pursuit of passion, to their generous nature, Leos leave a lasting impression on the canvas of love. Within this chapter we explore the complexities of Leo's approach to love. We will also delve into how they connect with other zodiac signs.

Join us on a journey through Leo's love life as we examine their vibrant personalities and how they harmonize with other signs in the zodiac. Whether you're a Leo seeking a partner or someone intrigued by their heart, this chapter promises an enthralling exploration of love and compatibility.

THE LEO APPROACH TO LOVE

Leos, ruled by the Sun and symbolized by the Lion, bring their lively and theatrical personalities into their romantic relationships. Overall their approach to love is characterized by warmth and passion. Let's take a closer look at how Leos approach love.

- **Passion and Intensity**; Leo individuals are renowned for their passionate nature. When they fall in love they do so with intensity and wholeheartedness.
- **Generosity and Affection**; Leos are generous lovers who take pleasure in spoiling their partners. They thrive on making their loved ones feel adored and valued. Expect surprises, heartfelt compliments and grand gestures from a Leo partner.
- **Desire for Attention**; Leos have a need for attention and admiration. In love they often seek partners who can provide them with the praise they yearn for. This doesn't imply selfishness. Rather it reflects their longing to feel appreciated.
- **Loyalty and Devotion**; like the unwavering Lion, Leos are devoted companions. They take their commitments seriously. Trustworthiness and loyalty play a central role in Leo's approach to love.
- **Dramatic Flair**; Leos add a captivating touch to their relationships infusing them with drama and style. They take pleasure in crafting memorable moments. Their imaginative nature and love for theatrics bring a sense of thrill to the relationship.
- **Independence and Confidence**; Leos are self confident individuals. This can be both an asset and a challenge in their relationships. They value partners who admire their self assuredness while also respecting their need for space and independence.
- **Challenges**; Leos longing for attention and admiration can sometimes lead to feelings of jealousy or possessiveness if not handled well. Additionally they have a tendency to be stubborn. This might lead to conflicts when their pride is at stake.
- **Compatibility**; Leo often finds compatibility with signs that appreciate their warmth and vitality such as Aries and Sagittarius. Libra and Gemini also make good matches as they offer the communication skills and intellectual stimulation that Leos enjoy.

In summary the Leo approach to love and romance is marked by passion, generosity and a desire to make their partners feel like royalty. They infuse excitement and theatrics into their relationships creating magical experiences.

While it's important to understand their need for attention and admiration, Leo's loyalty and devotion make them exceptional loving partners. Surely for those who appreciate such energy.

COMPATIBILITY WITH OTHER SIGNS

LEO AND ARIES

Leo and Aries are both Fire signs. Their relationship is often characterized by intense passion and enthusiasm. They share a zest for life and thrive on excitement. This dynamic duo can have a vibrant and energetic partnership, with both partners encouraging each other's ambitions. However, their strong personalities may occasionally clash, leading to power struggles. Communication is key to resolving conflicts. Overall when they work together, they can achieve remarkable goals.

LEO AND TAURUS

Leo, a Fire sign and Taurus, an Earth sign, have contrasting approaches to life and love. Leo seeks excitement and attention. Taurus values stability and security. Despite their differences, this combination can work well if they appreciate each other's strengths. Leo's passion can ignite Taurus's sensuality. Taurus can provide Leo with a stable foundation. However, Leo's desire for admiration may clash with Taurus's need for loyalty and commitment.

LEO AND GEMINI

Leo and Gemini share a dynamic and intellectually stimulating partnership. Both signs are social, communicative and love to have fun. Leo's charisma and Gemini's wit make them an engaging couple in social settings. However, Leo's desire for commitment and stability may clash with Gemini's need for variety and freedom. Trust and open communication are essential for this relationship to flourish.

LEO AND CANCER

Leo and Cancer have contrasting elements, with Leo as Fire and Cancer as Water. While this combination can have challenges, it can also be deeply nurturing and passionate. Leo's warmth and protective nature can complement Cancer's emotional depth and sensitivity. However, Leo's desire for attention may inadvertently hurt Cancer's feelings. Building trust and open communication is vital for long-term harmony.

LEO AND LEO

Two Leos in a relationship can create a fiery and intense connection. They share similar values, such as the desire for attention and admiration. However, their shared love for the spotlight can lead to power struggles and occasional clashes of ego. Both partners must be willing to compromise and share the spotlight for the relationship to thrive. When they do, this duo can create a passionate and dynamic partnership.

LEO AND VIRGO

Leo, a Fire sign and Virgo, an Earth sign, have contrasting approaches to life and love. Leo seeks excitement and attention. Virgo values practicality and order. This pairing may require patience and compromise, as Leo's extravagant nature may clash with Virgo's practicality. Virgo's attention to detail can help Leo in achieving their goals. Leo must appreciate Virgo's need for stability and avoid overwhelming them with drama.

LEO AND LIBRA

Leo and Libra share an affinity for beauty, socializing, and harmony. Both signs appreciate the finer things in life and enjoy a sense of style. This combination can create a loving and balanced partnership. Leo's charisma complements Libra's charm. Together they can engage in intellectual and passionate conversations. However, Leo's desire for attention may occasionally compete with Libra's need for balance and fairness. Communication and compromise are essential for a harmonious relationship.

LEO AND SCORPIO

Leo and Scorpio have passionate and intense personalities, making their relationship both magnetic and challenging. Leo's outgoing nature may initially intrigue Scorpio. However their possessiveness and jealousy can trigger Leo's desire for freedom. Trust is a significant issue in this partnership. Both partners must work on open communication and mutual respect to overcome their differences. If they can find common ground, their connection can be deeply transformative.

LEO AND SAGITTARIUS

Leo and Sagittarius share a Fire sign bond characterized by enthusiasm, adventure and a love for freedom. They have a dynamic and passionate connection, enjoying each other's company in social settings and taking on adventurous activities. Both signs value honesty and directness in communication. This can strengthen their bond. However, Leo's desire for attention may occasionally clash with Sagittarius's independent spirit. Trust and mutual respect are key to resolving any conflicts.

LEO AND CAPRICORN

Leo, a Fire sign and Capricorn, an Earth sign, have contrasting approaches to life and love. Leo seeks excitement and attention. Capricorn values structure and ambition. This pairing can be challenging, as Leo's desire for admiration may clash with Capricorn's focus on their goals. However, if they appreciate each other's strengths, Leo's charisma can complement Capricorn's ambition. Meanwhile Capricorn's stability can provide Leo with a solid foundation.

LEO AND AQUARIUS

Leo and Aquarius have a dynamic and intellectually stimulating partnership. They both appreciate creativity and enjoy socializing, making them an engaging couple in various social circles. Leo's charisma and Aquarius's unique perspective complement each other. However, Leo's desire for attention and admiration may occasionally conflict with Aquarius's need for independence and individuality. Trust and open communication are essential for a harmonious relationship.

LEO AND PISCES

Leo and Pisces have contrasting elements, with Leo as Fire and Pisces as Water. This combination can be both passionate and challenging. Leo's charisma and Pisces's sensitivity can create a deeply emotional connection. However, Leo's desire for attention and Pisces's need for emotional security may sometimes clash. Leo must be considerate of Pisces's feelings. Pisces should appreciate Leo's warmth and protectiveness. Building trust and understanding is crucial for their relationship's success.

In a nutshell those are the main compatibilities of Leo and the other Zodiac signs. Overall one must remember in astrology that while compatibility can provide insights, individual personalities, values and communication styles play significant roles in the success of a relationship. Ultimately, every partnership is unique.

TIPS FOR DATING AND RELATIONSHIPS WITH A LEO

Dating and being in a relationship with a Leo can be an exhilarating experience. Known for their fiery, passionate, and confident nature, Leos are often seen as the life of the party and can bring a dynamic energy to any relationship. However, understanding their unique characteristics is key to building a strong, harmonious partnership. Now we'll delve into essential tips for dating and maintaining a thriving relationship with Leo. Overall, these tips will help you navigate the ups and downs of loving a Leo.

FOR MEN DATING LEO WOMEN

- **Show your appreciation**; Leo women thrive on admiration and compliments. Let her know how much you admire her qualities, accomplishments and appearance.
- **Plan exciting dates**; Leos love adventure and grand gestures. Organize thrilling and unforgettable dates that cater to her sense of fun and excitement. Surprise her with a weekend getaway or getting tickets to an exhilarating event.
- **Share the spotlight**; While Leo women enjoy being in the center of attention it's important to give them space to shine too. Show interest in their passions and achievements without overshadowing them in gatherings.

- **Be supportive**; Leo women appreciate partners who believe in their dreams and support their ambitions. Encourage them to pursue their goals while being their cheerleader.
- **Respect their independence**; Leo women value their independence greatly. Give them the freedom they need when they require it, trusting them to handle their affairs. Avoid being overly possessive.

FOR WOMEN DATING LEO MEN

- **Offer admiration**; Leo men have a desire for admiration and recognition. Compliment his accomplishments and express appreciation for his efforts and unique qualities.
- **Engage in his passions;** Leo men often have interests or hobbies that they deeply care about. Show interest by participating in those activities, alongside him or encouraging him to pursue his endeavors.
- **Allow him to shine**; Leo men thrive on being in the spotlight. Support his need for attention. Take pride in his accomplishments. Be a partner when he receives recognition.
- **Maintain communication**; Leo men value honesty and direct communication. If any concerns or issues arise in the relationship, address them openly and respectfully.
- **Respect his pride;** Leo men can be proud individuals and their egos are sensitive. Steer clear of criticizing or belittling them as it can dent their confidence. Instead provide feedback when necessary.

As we wrap up this chapter discussing love and compatibility, for Leo it's important to highlight the valuable role astrology can play in our understanding of relationships. While exploring the characteristics of Leo and how it interacts with zodiac signs can offer insights we must remember that each person is a unique combination of traits and experiences. The dynamics of a relationship are not solely determined by the stars but by the personalities, backgrounds and life stories involved.

Astrology can be a tool for gaining perspective and igniting curiosity about how we connect with others. It encourages us to delve into the details of our personalities as well as those of our partners often leading to deeper understanding and empathy. However it should be seen as a source of inspiration rather than a rulebook.

When it comes to matters of the heart, effective communication, trust and mutual respect are principles that hold significance. These elements form the pillars of healthy relationships; they surpass astrological signs and configurations to create a foundation for enduring love and companionship.

So let astrology serve as your guide while adding an element of fascination to your journey through love and relationships. Always remember to ground your connections in timeless principles such, as understanding, compassion and respect.

By combining the insights gained from guidance with an understanding of behavior and emotional desires one can skillfully navigate the complex journey of relationships experiencing both elegance and personal satisfaction.

CHAPTER 3: FRIENDS AND FAMILY

Leos, symbolized by the Lion and guided by the Sun, bring a unique combination of loyalty, generosity and leadership to both their friendships and families. Whether they take on the role of life's party spark, protective guardian or nurturing presence. Leo individuals play central roles in the lives of those who are most important to them. Join us as we delve into Leo's web of friendships and family where their warmth and charm radiate brightly.

LEO AS A FRIEND

When you become friends with a Leo you welcome a companion who embodies charisma, loyalty and passion into your life. The qualities of a Leo friend often reflect their warm hearted nature associated with this symbol. Here's what you can expect when you have Leo as a friend.

- **Loyalty**; Leos are loyal friends. Once they commit to a friendship they remain steadfast through thick and thin. You can rely on them for unwavering support and trust.
- **Warmth and Generosity**; Leo friends are well known for their warm nature. They enjoy showering their friends with affection, compliments and thoughtful gestures. They will make you feel truly valued and appreciated.
- **Natural Leaders;** Leos have an inclination to take charge in situations. They are often the ones organizing meetups. With a Leo friend you'll never be short of adventures and memorable experiences.
- **Positive Energy**; Leos possess enthusiasm and radiate positivity. They uplift those around them. Being in their company is often uplifting.
- **Supportive**; Leo friends are fiercely protective while also providing support. They will go to lengths to ensure that their friends are safe, happy and successful. You can trust them with your secrets knowing that they will always have your back.
- **Social Butterflies**; Leos enjoy having a big circle of friends. They can introduce you to new people or help you expand your social network. Their outgoing nature adds liveliness and enjoyment.
- **Drama and Entertainment**; Leos have a knack for infusing excitement and entertainment into their friendships. They excel at storytelling, cracking jokes and creating unique moments.
- **Occasional Ego**; While Leo friends are generally generous individuals they may be sensitive about their egos at times. They appreciate recognition for their accomplishments and may occasionally seek validation. It's important to acknowledge their achievements with compliments.
- **Directness**; Leos appreciate friends who are straightforward, genuine and transparent. Hidden agendas or aggressive behavior is not something they prefer.

To put it simply. Having Leo as a friend is akin to having a bright star in your life. Their warmth, generosity and upbeat energy can make your friendship feel like a celebration. With a Leo friend you can anticipate a friendship brimming with laughter, escapades and cherished moments that will stay with you forever.

LEO AND FAMILY DYNAMICS

When it comes to family dynamics, Leos have a way of bringing warmth and charisma to the forefront. Represented by the Lion and ruled by the Sun, Leos are known for their protective nature. They are cherished and distinctive members of the family unit. Let's take a look at how Leo individuals contribute to family dynamics.

- **The Natural Leader**; Leos naturally gravitate towards taking on leadership roles within the family. They are often the ones who organize family gatherings, celebrations and outings.
- **Protector and Provider;** Leos see themselves as protectors and providers for their families. They take these responsibilities seriously, going above and beyond to ensure the well being and happiness of their loved ones.
- **Affection**; Leo individuals are renowned for their warmth and affectionate nature. They express love through hugs, kisses and words of admiration. In the family setting they make sure everyone feels cherished.
- **Generosity and Thoughtfulness**; Leos generously offer their time, attention and resources to those around them. They take pleasure in giving presents and unexpected surprises to their family members. Often they go the extra mile to make their loved ones feel truly special.
- **Entertaining**; As storytellers and entertainers Leos thoroughly enjoy captivating their family. With a Leo present at family gatherings, it becomes an entertaining affair.
- **Peacemakers**; With their innate leadership abilities Leos often assume the role of peacemakers, during family conflicts. Their diplomatic approach helps mediate disputes and fosters harmony within the family.
- **Supportive**; Leo family members are supporters of their loved ones dreams and aspirations. They consistently encourage their siblings, parents and children to pursue their passions in order to achieve success.

Overall Leos play a role in creating an loving atmosphere filled with celebration. Their natural ability to lead, generosity and knack for uplifting the spirits of their loved ones make them cherished members within their family circles.

CHALLENGES IN FRIENDSHIPS AND FAMILY FOR LEO

While individuals born under the Leo zodiac sign bring warmth, charm and generosity to their relationships, with friends and family. They also face challenges. Being aware of these challenges can contribute to fulfilling interactions. Here are some to be aware of.

- **Neediness**; Leos often have a need for attention and admiration. This can sometimes be challenging in friendships and family dynamics. It may lead to conflicts when they feel overlooked or not appreciated enough. It's important for Leos to understand that different people may express love and support in many ways. Open and honest communication about their needs is crucial.
- **Pride and Ego**; Leo's pride is a two edged sword. While it can motivate them to achieve greatness. It can also make them sensitive to criticism or perceived offenses. This sensitivity can result in conflicts when they feel that their pride is being threatened. Learning how to accept feedback without letting ego hinder relationships is vital.

- **Overwhelming Energy**; Leo individuals' boundless energy and enthusiasm may at times overwhelm others. They might come across as dominant or excessively enthusiastic causing others to feel overshadowed or exhausted. Leos should keep in mind the importance of finding a balance between their energy levels and those of their loved ones.
- **Being Considerate;** Leos may come across as self centered or overly focused on their needs and desires. This can pose challenges for others who might feel overlooked or overshadowed. It's important for Leos to actively listen to their friends and family members whilst showing interest in their lives and concerns.
- **Impulsiveness**; Leos passion and spontaneity can occasionally lead them to make impulsive decisions. This may sometimes result in misunderstandings or unintended consequences within their relationships. Taking a moment to pause, reflect and consider the potential impact of their actions can help Leo individuals make the right choices.
- **Sharing the Spotlight**; Multiple strong personalities within family dynamics might make it challenging to strike a balance when it comes to receiving attention or recognition. It's crucial for Leo to acknowledge and appreciate others by sharing the spotlight.
- **Protectiveness**; In family dynamics Leo's protective nature can sometimes lead them towards being overly protective. This might not be well received by family members. Especially if they feel suffocated or controlled. Leo individuals should strive to strike a balance, between nurturing their loved ones and giving them the freedom to make their choices.
- **Conflict Resolution**; Sometimes Leos desire to maintain harmony can lead them to avoid conversations or sweep problems under the rug. However it's important for Leo individuals to learn communication and conflict resolution skills in order to address such issues.

To summarize, Leo individuals are known for their charm, warmth and generosity. However they may also face challenges related to their need for attention, ego and strong personalities. Overcoming these challenges requires self awareness, communication and a willingness to adapt to the needs of others. With patience and understanding Leo individuals can cultivate more fulfilling relationships.

As we wrap up this chapter it's important to acknowledge that like any relationships those involving Leos require nurturing, understanding and effort to thrive. By understanding the significance of balance, humility and effective communication Leos can continue to radiate warmth, love and appreciation.

CHAPTER 4:
CAREER AND MONEY

Leos, governed by the powerful Sun and represented by the majestic Lion are propelled by a deep desire to leave their mark on the world. Within this chapter we delve into the domain of Leo's financial mindset as well as the strategies they employ to achieve success in their careers. Furthermore this chapter also provides insights on how Leo individuals can leverage their strengths along with wisdom. Ultimately this will lead them to flourish in their careers while turning their monetary aspirations into reality.

Join us as we navigate through the maze of Leos career preferences, leadership qualities and creative pursuits. Discover how their natural charm and unwavering determination propel them towards their dreams.

CAREER PREFERENCES AND PROFESSIONAL GOALS

Leo individuals are widely recognized for their charm and self assured nature. These traits greatly influence their career choices and aspirations. Let's delve deeper into an examination of what careers Leos tend to prefer and what they aspire to achieve

- **Leadership**; Leos possess an inclination towards leadership roles. They thrive when entrusted with authority and responsibility. Whether it be managing teams, spearheading projects or taking charge of organizations. Guiding others toward success is a driving force for them.
- **Creativity**; A considerable number of Leos possess a creative streak. They gravitate towards careers in the arts, entertainment and creative industries. Here they can express their talents freely. Acting music, theater, fashion design and visual arts provide platforms for them to showcase their skills while reveling in the limelight.
- **Public Speaking and Communication**; With great communication skills and an eloquent demeanor Leos have a talent for public speaking. They excel in roles that involve addressing audiences. As such they seek to inspire change with their words.

- **Entrepreneurship**; Leos embody an entrepreneurial spirit. They find pleasure in the freedom and creative opportunities that come with being an entrepreneur. As such they often have visions for their own ventures.
- **Education and Training**; Leo individuals are attracted to roles that involve teaching and mentoring. They have a passion for sharing their knowledge

and expertise with others whether it be as educators, coaches or trainers. They take pride in helping others learn and develop.

- **Event Planning and Management**; Leos possess a talent for organizing and hosting events. Careers in event planning and management allow them to utilize their skills while indulging in their love for creating experiences for others.
- **Healthcare and Healing**; Some Leos are drawn to healthcare careers. Particularly those focused on healing and holistic wellness. They may pursue professions as doctors, therapists or counselors where their empathy and compassion can truly shine.
- **Philanthropy**; Leos have caring hearts always aspiring to make a positive impact on the world around them. They may find themselves gravitating towards careers in philanthropy or areas where they can contribute to meaningful causes.

KEY STRENGTHS

Leo individuals possess a charisma and self assurance that sets them apart as leaders. Their natural leadership skills shine through due to their confidence and ability to make choices. This is why they excel when placed in leadership roles.

Here are some more strengths that propel them forwards.

- **Charismatic Personality and Strong Presence**; Leos possess a charm and presence that captivates those around them. In work environments this charisma aids them in building connections, negotiating effectively and leaving a memorable impact.
- **Confidence and Self Assurance**; Leos radiate self confidence, which is an asset in the workplace. Their belief in their abilities encourages them to take on challenges and make good decisions.
- **Communication Skills**; Communication is one of Leo's main strengths. They excel at conveying ideas whether through speaking engagements, presentations or interpersonal interactions. Their eloquence and clarity make them excellent communicators.
- **Motivating Teams;** Leos have a talent for motivating and inspiring their colleagues. They can elevate team morale, encourage productivity and foster a sense of unity among team members leading to performance levels.
- **Creativity and Innovation**; Many Leos possess an inclination towards creativity. They bring perspectives and innovative ideas to the table

contributing to problem solving processes and the development of solutions, within their workplaces.

- **Determination and Perseverance**; Once Leos set their sights on a goal they pursue it with unwavering determination. Their persistence aids them in overcoming obstacles along the way as they strive to achieve their objectives.

In a nutshell people born under the sign of Leo bring a mix of leadership qualities, charm, self assurance and innovation to the workplace. Their talent, for motivating others, communication skills and ability to inspire make them natural leaders and valuable team members. Leo's optimistic outlook, perseverance and flexibility empower them to thrive in positions. Overall this makes them highly valued assets for any organization lucky enough to welcome them.

CHALLENGES AND STRATEGIES TO OVERCOME THEM

As we have seen, Leo individuals possess a set of qualities that contribute to their professional success. Their strong personalities, although beneficial, can sometimes pose challenges. It's crucial for Leos to strike a balance between seeking attention and maintaining humility while also navigating office politics with tact.

While individuals born under the sign of Leo possess strengths that contribute to their lives they may also encounter specific hurdles related to their personalities and career aspirations. By recognizing and addressing these challenges head on, Leo individuals can navigate their career paths effectively. Here are some common obstacles faced by Leo individuals along, with strategies to overcome them;

Desire for Recognition

- Challenge; Leos often crave recognition and appreciation. When they feel undervalued or overlooked it can negatively impact their motivation and job satisfaction.
- Strategy; To combat this challenge Leos should actively seek feedback and acknowledgment for their contributions. They should proactively communicate their achievements to supervisors and colleagues. This will ensure that their accomplishments receive recognition. Additionally focusing on motivation and finding fulfillment in growth can be beneficial.

Managing Ego

- Challenge; Leo individuals may struggle with managing their pride and ego which can lead to conflicts with colleagues or superiors.
- Strategy; To overcome this challenge Leos should practice humility and remain open minded. Actively listen to others perspectives. Being receptive to opinions can help them keep their egos in check. Seeking feedback and constructive criticism will also assist in maintaining a balanced perspective.

Balancing Leadership and Collaboration

- Challenge; Leos thrive in leadership roles. But they may face challenges when required to collaborate or work in team positions.
- Strategy; It's important for them to actively seek opportunities to work in teams. There they can listen to others' ideas and recognize the value of team efforts. Through learning how to be a team player while maintaining their leadership qualities, they can contribute to a harmonious work environment.

Taking things personally

- Challenge; Leo individuals might take criticism personally due to their egos, which can impede their professional growth.
- Strategy; To tackle this challenge Leos can develop resilience by reframing criticism as an opportunity for improvement. They should focus on feedback and leverage it to refine themselves.

Spontaneous

- Challenge; Leo's passion and spontaneity can sometimes lead them towards decisions that may not always be in their interest.
- Strategy; In order to address this challenge Leos should practice calculated decision making. Taking a step back to evaluate options and seeking input from others before making decisions is a wise move. Furthermore, creating a decision making process that includes reflection and analysis will help them avoid wrong choices.

Balance between work and personal life

- Challenge; Sometimes Leo's strong commitment to their careers can lead to an imbalance between their work and personal life. This may impact their well being and relationships.

- Strategy; To maintain a work life balance Leos should prioritize setting boundaries and making time for relaxation. It is important for them to communicate these boundaries with colleagues and supervisors while seeking support from loved ones.

Adaptability

- Challenge; Leos might face difficulties when it comes to adapting to changes or setbacks in their lives.
- Strategy; To overcome this challenge Leos can develop adaptability skills by embracing change as an opportunity for growth. They should focus on problem solving, resilience and learning from challenges rather than perceiving them as failures.

In conclusion individuals with Leo traits possess confident personalities and strong, self assurance that can pave the way for success in their careers. Natural leaders, innovators and valued team members. Indeed they face challenges too. But by being self aware and employing strategies to tackle these challenges they can leverage their strengths, overcome obstacles and make a positive impact in their chosen fields. Always remember that success and financial stability are within your reach when guided by your valiant spirit and unwavering confidence in your abilities.

CHAPTER 5: SELF-IMPROVEMENT

In the world of astrology Leos are known for their confident and charismatic nature. This chapter takes us into the heart of Leo's quest for personal growth and development. We'll delve into how they can nurture their leadership skills, foster their creativity and master the art of self awareness. Inside you will discover insights into Leo individuals unique path as they strive to accomplish their goals cultivate growth and live life with unwavering vitality and purpose.

Represented by the Lion and guided by the Sun, Leos possess an unwavering determination to excel, inspire others and make a lasting impression. This chapter explores the qualities, strengths and areas where Leo individuals can grow to be their best. It delves into how they tap into their potential for self improvement and the strategies they employ to become the best versions of themselves. Join us as we embark on a captivating exploration of Leo's journey towards self improvement.

PERSONAL GROWTH AND DEVELOPMENT

Leos possess personalities filled with confidence which naturally drives them towards personal growth and development. They are motivated to achieve greatness while leaving a lasting impact on the world. Here are some important areas and strategies that can contribute to their overall growth and development.

- **Self Reflection**; Take time to reflect on your goals, values and aspirations. It's essential to understand what truly inspires and motivates you. Developing self awareness is the first step towards growth.
- **Setting Ambitious Goals**; Leos thrive when they set goals for themselves. Define inspiring objectives for both your professional and personal life. Break goals down into manageable steps and milestones.
- **Embracing Challenges**; Don't shy away from challenges or setbacks. See them as opportunities for growth and learning. Your resilience and determination will help you overcome obstacles along the way.

- **Developing Leadership Skills**; Leverage your natural leadership qualities to foster growth. Seek out opportunities to lead whether it be in your workplace, community or personal projects. These experiences will enhance your skills and boost your confidence.
- **Refining Communication Skills**; Continuously work on improving your communication skills. Effective communication is crucial in forming connections with others whether it's in relationships or professional settings.
- **Expanding Knowledge**; Engage in learning by pursuing education, attending workshops or engaging in self study activities. Expanding your knowledge base will significantly enhance your development.
- **Balancing Confidence with Humility**; While confidence is valuable it's equally important to maintain a sense of humility. Be receptive to feedback and be willing to acknowledge when you don't have all the answers.
- **Find mentors**; Seek guidance from individuals you admire and respect. Mentors can offer insights, advice and support as you navigate both your professional and personal journey.
- **Gratitude**; Cultivate a sense of gratitude for the blessings in your life. Appreciate the people, opportunities and experiences that have contributed to your growth and achievements. Gratitude is a solid foundation.
- **Balance ego;** Maintain a level of self esteem and confidence while embracing humility. A balanced ego can motivate you to reach your goals and serve as an inspiration to others.
- **Celebrate**; Take time to celebrate your accomplishments no matter how big or small they may be. Acknowledge your achievements and milestones as you progress on the path of self development.
- **Openness**; Stay open minded towards change, be adaptable to experiences and different perspectives. This openness can lead to growth and a broader understanding of the world around us.
- **Networking**; Continue building connections in social spheres. Networking can provide opportunities for personal development and learning.
- **Wellness**; Make it a priority to take care of your well being. Prioritize activity, a well rounded diet and adequate rest. Ensure you have the energy levels for pursuing your ambitions. For Leos specifically it can be beneficial to explore creative outlets for expression. For example art or music as this can contribute to growth and fulfillment.

In summary the journey of growth and self development for Leo individuals involves leveraging their strengths while remaining open to learning and embracing challenges. By setting goals, honing leadership skills and striking a balance between confidence and humility Leos can continue to evolve.

Ultimately they can leave a lasting legacy of growth and achievement on the world stage.

LEVERAGING STRENGTHS AND OVERCOMING WEAKNESSES

Just like individuals of any zodiac sign Leos possess a unique set of strengths and weaknesses. It is important to understand and make the most of these qualities in order to experience growth and achieve success. Here's a guide that outlines how Leo individuals can effectively utilize their strengths while working on their weaknesses.

STRENGTHS

- **Leadership**; The innate leadership qualities that Leos possess are truly assets. To harness this strength actively seek out leadership roles or projects where you can confidently lead and inspire others.
- **Confidence**; Embrace your confidence. Remember to avoid arrogance. Utilize your confidence to tackle challenges head on and step out of your comfort zone in order to achieve professional growth.
- **Communication Skills**; Your ability to communicate effectively is a tool. Continually work on refining your communication skills by focusing on listening and empathetic communication. This will help you to connect with others on a deeper level.
- **Charisma**; Make use of your charisma to build relationships and social networks. It has the potential to open doors and create opportunities for both personal and professional advancement.
- **Creativity**; Embrace your creative side in all aspects of life. Personal or professional. Seek avenues for expression utilizing your thinking abilities to solve problems creatively and make a positive impact.
- **Determination**; Your determination acts as a driving force behind achieving success. Set goals for yourself while maintaining focus. Also be open to adapting when necessary.

WEAKNESSES

- **Ego**; Keep in mind the importance of staying humble and avoid arrogance. While having self confidence is crucial, too much pride can hinder growth and harm relationships. Practice being humble. Remain open to feedback from others.

- **Impulsivity**; Leo individuals spontaneity may sometimes lead to bad decisions. It's beneficial to establish a decision making process that involves consideration of options, consequences, values and seeking input from others. Overall this will help you avoid bad choices.
- **Desire for Recognition**; While it's natural to desire recognition for your accomplishments it's important not to make it your sole motivation. Find motivation in the work you do. Remember that not all achievements will be immediately acknowledged. Sometimes you have to work diligently in silence.
- **Balancing Leadership and Collaboration**; Learn how to strike a balance between showcasing your leadership skills while also fostering teamwork. Recognize when it's appropriate for you to take the lead and when it's better to empower others so they can shine.
- **Handling Criticism**; Cultivate resilience in the face of criticism. Seek feedback from others and use it as a tool for improvement.
- **Work Life Balance;** Aim for an equilibrium between work commitments and personal life. Don't let your career aspirations overshadow your relationships or well being. Set aside time for relaxation, hobbies and spending quality moments with family.
- **Patience**; Develop patience within yourself by allowing time required to accomplish your goals. Rushing into things can often result in stress or mistakes. Take your time and ensure accuracy, even if it means slowing down.

Remember to lead a fulfilling life it's crucial to embrace your strengths and work on your weaknesses. Utilize your strengths to achieve greatness while dedicating yourself and persevering through addressing your weaknesses. Overall this balance will contribute to a satisfying life.

The potential for growth and self improvement is limitless. In the case of Leos, they possess the potential to become great leaders, innovative creators and empathetic communicators. Their journey towards self improvement is a pursuit of excellence fueled by their enthusiasm for life and unwavering belief in their abilities.

As they navigate the path of self improvement, Leo individuals can leverage their strengths, address their weaknesses and shape a life filled with purpose, vitality and infinite success. The road ahead is illuminated by their ambition. Guided by the sun and lion that constantly propels them towards new realms of personal growth and accomplishment.

CHAPTER 6:
THE YEAR AHEAD

This chapter serves as your guide to navigating the currents that will shape your life over the year ahead. As a Leo your personality and unwavering confidence are beautifully complemented by the energy of the Sun and the Lion, which govern your astrological sign. This chapter warmly invites you to delve into the events that will influence aspects of your life. Love, career, finances, health, personal growth and self discovery in the year ahead.

Throughout this chapter we will explore movements, eclipses and celestial alignments with your Leo spirit on your journey through life. By gaining an understanding of how these cosmic forces interact with you as a Leo individual you will be empowered to make wise decisions, seize exciting opportunities and overcome challenges with grace and determination.

The upcoming year presents itself as a canvas upon which you can paint your ambitions, dreams and aspirations. So come along with us as we embark on this voyage uncovering celestial guidance that will inspire you to radiate brightly while pursuing your passions and charting a fulfilling path, towards a future filled with brilliance.

HOROSCOPE GUIDE FOR THE YEAR AHEAD

Welcome, Leo individuals, to a year brimming with opportunities, challenges and personal growth. As the mighty Lion of the zodiac, you're known for your charisma, leadership and boundless ambition. In the year ahead, your unique qualities will shine brightly as you navigate the cosmic currents. Here's a horoscope guide to help you make the most of the year ahead.

CAREER AND FINANCES

This year, your career ambitions will take center stage. Leverage your leadership skills to seize new opportunities for growth and advancement. Be open to collaboration and teamwork. Partnerships may bring exciting projects your way.

Stay adaptable and embrace change, as it could lead to unexpected career breakthroughs.

Your financial prospects look promising this year. Your determination and creativity can lead to financial gains. Consider long-term financial planning and investments to secure your future. Be cautious about impulsive spending and ensure your financial decisions align with your long term goals.

Leo individuals' career paths and financial situations will be influenced by the celestial movements of the year. Here are some key astrological events to watch for in relation to your professional and financial endeavors.

- **Saturn in Aquarius (All year)**: Saturn's influence in Aquarius encourages discipline and hard work. It may require Leo individuals to establish a solid foundation for their career goals and financial stability.
- **Uranus in Taurus (All year)**: Uranus in Taurus can bring unexpected changes in your financial situation. Be prepared to adapt to new financial opportunities or challenges.
- **Mars in Leo (July 17 to August 31)**: Mars in your sign boosts your career drive. It's a favorable time for taking on leadership roles, pursuing promotions, or launching new projects.
- **Jupiter in Pisces (December 28, 2023 to December 20)**: Jupiter's transit can bring fortunate circumstances in your career and financial pursuits. Be open to new opportunities and partnerships.
- **Mercury Retrogrades (Multiple times throughout the year)**: Be cautious during Mercury retrogrades. They may affect communication in your workplace and financial transactions. Double-check details and avoid signing important contracts during these periods.

LOVE AND RELATIONSHIPS

In your relationships, your natural charm will draw people closer to you. Nurture your relationships by actively listening to your loved ones. Be mindful of your ego. Practice humility to maintain harmonious relationships. In matters of the heart, your charisma will be a magnet for potential partners. Existing relationships may deepen as you invest time and effort into nurturing them. Keep your heart open to new romantic experiences and connections. Family bonds will be essential sources of support and comfort. Consider making improvements to your home environment to enhance your sense of security and well-being.

For Leo individuals, matters of the heart will be significantly influenced by the astrological events of the year. Astrology offers insights into the ebb and flow of relationships and the potential for love to flourish or face challenges. Here are some key astrological aspects to consider.

- **Venus Retrograde (December 19, 2023 to January 29)**: This retrograde period may prompt Leo individuals to reevaluate their values in relationships. It's a time for introspection and refining what they seek in love and partnership.
- **Venus in Leo (June 6 to July 3)**: During this period, Leo's charisma and magnetism will be amplified. It's an excellent time for romance and rekindling the flames of passion in existing relationships.
- **Mars in Leo (July 17 to August 31):** Mars in your sign brings heightened passion and assertiveness. It can fuel both romantic pursuits and conflicts. Use this energy wisely to communicate your desires and needs.
- **Jupiter in Pisces (December 28, 2023, to December 20)**: Jupiter's transit can bring expansion and growth in your relationships. Be open to new experiences and opportunities for personal and romantic growth.
- **Eclipses in Leo-Aquarius Axis (Throughout the year)**: Lunar eclipses in Leo and Aquarius may bring shifts in your love life and partnerships. These eclipses can herald significant changes or revelations in your relationships.

HEALTH AND WELLNESS

Prioritize your physical health with regular exercise and a balanced diet. Practice stress management techniques to maintain your vitality. Pay attention to your mental health and seek support if needed. Remember, seeking help is a sign of strength.

Leo individuals' health and wellness are closely connected to astrological influences. Pay attention to celestial events that may impact your well-being and consider the following advice.

- **Solar Eclipse in Leo (April):** This powerful event can mark a period of personal transformation. Use it as an opportunity to set intentions for improved health and vitality.
- **Lunar Eclipses in Leo-Aquarius Axis (Throughout the year)**: These eclipses may bring emotional intensity. Practice self-care, engage in stress-reduction techniques, and maintain a balanced lifestyle.

- **Jupiter in Pisces (December 28, 2023, to December 20):** Jupiter's transit can enhance your overall well-being. Explore holistic health practices and consider incorporating spirituality into your wellness routine.

PERSONAL GROWTH AND SELF-DISCOVERY

This year offers ample opportunities for personal growth and self-discovery. Set ambitious personal goals and work on developing your self-awareness. Embrace your creative side and seek outlets for artistic expression.

Travel may be on the horizon, offering you fresh perspectives and exciting experiences. Embrace opportunities for adventure and exploration. Whether it's a new destination or a novel endeavor.

Explore your spiritual side and seek inner peace through meditation, mindfulness, or spiritual practices that resonate with you. Trust your intuition and inner guidance to navigate life's challenges.

Astrological events can be powerful catalysts for personal growth and self-discovery. Here's how Leo individuals can make the most of the year ahead.

- **Lunar Eclipses in Leo-Aquarius Axis (Throughout the year)**: These eclipses may prompt self-reflection and transformation. Embrace change and be open to new perspectives.
- **Venus in Leo (June 6 to July 3):** During this period, focus on self-love and self-expression. Explore your creative side and take time for personal passions.
- **Jupiter in Pisces (December)**: This transit offers opportunities for spiritual growth and inner exploration. Consider meditation, mindfulness, or spiritual practices to facilitate self-discovery.
- **Mars in Leo (July 17 to August 31):** Use this period to assert your individuality and take bold steps toward personal goals.
- **Saturn in Aquarius (All year):** Saturn's influence encourages self-discipline and self-improvement. Set clear intentions for personal growth and work diligently toward your aspirations.

By staying aware of these events and considering how they may impact us, Leo individuals can approach the year with purpose, resilience and commitment.

Overall this year offers you the chance to shine brighter than ever before. Embrace your natural strengths, stay open to growth, and take bold steps toward your goals. Your magnetic energy and determination will lead you to success and fulfillment.

As the Sun governs your sign, remember that you carry its radiant energy within you. Embrace the opportunities, face the challenges with confidence and bask in the warmth of your own brilliance throughout the year ahead.

KEY ASTROLOGICAL EVENTS AND THEIR IMPACT ON LEO:

Astrological events play a significant role in shaping the experiences and energies that Leo individuals encounter throughout the year. As a Leo, your Sun sign is ruled by the Sun itself, making you particularly attuned to the celestial movements and their influence on your life. Here are some key astrological events and their potential impact on Leo individuals.

- **Solar Eclipse in Leo;** When a solar eclipse occurs in Leo, it can be an incredibly powerful and transformative time for you. It may usher in new beginnings and opportunities for self-discovery. Use this period to set ambitious goals, as the energy of a solar eclipse can amplify your intentions and desires.
- **Mercury Retrograde;** Mercury retrogrades can affect communication and decision-making, and as a Leo, you might feel the impact in your interactions with others. Be mindful of miscommunications and delays, and use this time to review and reflect on your plans and goals.
- **Venus in Leo;** When Venus, the planet of love and beauty, moves through Leo, it enhances your charisma and attractiveness. This period is favorable for romance and enhancing your personal style and self-expression.
- **Mars in Leo;** When Mars, the planet of action and motivation, transits Leo, your drive and determination are amplified. This can be a time of increased energy and assertiveness, making it an excellent period to pursue your goals with passion and vigor.
- **Full Moon in Leo;** A Full Moon in your sign can bring heightened emotions and a sense of culmination. It's an ideal time to reflect on your achievements, express yourself creatively, and release anything that no longer serves your growth.
- **Jupiter Transits;** Jupiter's transits through various signs can impact your opportunities for expansion and growth. Pay attention to Jupiter's movements, as they can bring fortunate circumstances and new adventures into your life.
- **Saturn Transits;** Saturn's transits may bring challenges and lessons, but they also offer opportunities for discipline and long-term growth. Use Saturn's

influence to work diligently toward your goals and build a strong foundation for your ambitions.

- **Lunar Eclipses;** Lunar eclipses can trigger significant emotional shifts and changes in your personal life. Be prepared for moments of insight and transformation during these celestial events.
- **New Moon in Leo;** New Moons are potent for setting intentions and initiating new projects. Take advantage of the New Moon in Leo to plant the seeds of your dreams and aspirations.
- **Outer Planet Transits;** Pay attention to the movements of outer planets like Uranus, Neptune, and Pluto, as they bring deeper and long-lasting transformations. These transits can impact your generational influences and encourage profound personal growth.

As we wrap up this chapter it's important to keep in mind that cosmic forces serve as guides in our journey. Remember that astrology offers insights and guidance. Ultimately your free will and choices play a significant role in how you navigate these celestial events. Use your Leo strengths of confidence and determination to harness the energies of the cosmos. Adapt to challenges and embrace opportunities for growth and self-expression throughout the year.

Again remember that you are in control of shaping your destiny while considering the celestial bodies as supportive companions, on this journey. As you embark on the journey in the year ahead may your way be illuminated by the brilliance of your aspirations and the warmth of your compassionate nature. May you leave behind a lasting heritage of bravery, originality and unwavering confidence.

CHAPTER 7:
FAMOUS "LEO" PERSONALITIES

Welcome to the captivating realm of "Famous Leo Personalities." In this chapter we embark on an exploration of some famous individuals born under the Zodiac sign of Leo. As we delve into the lives of these personalities you will learn how their nature, ambition and self assurance as Leos have propelled them to achieve greatness in various domains. Be it entertainment, sports, politics or entrepreneurship. Their stories are a testament to the qualities that define Leo individuals and their ability to make an impact on the world.

Join us on this journey as we commemorate the accomplishments, influence and enduring legacies of these Leo personalities whose brilliance continues to shine brightly as the Sun itself.

NAPOLEON BONAPARTE

- Date of Birth: August 15, 1769.
- Brief Biography: Napoléon Bonaparte was a French military leader and emperor. He rose to prominence during the French Revolution. He is famous for his military conquests and the Napoleonic Code. This laid the foundation for modern civil law.
- Leo Traits: Charismatic, ambitious and confident.
- Impact: Napoléon's legacy is marked by his impact on European history through his military campaigns and political reforms.
- Personal Life: He married Josephine de Beauharnais but divorced her to marry Marie Louise of Austria.

WHITNEY HOUSTON

- Date of Birth: August 9, 1963.

- Brief Biography: Whitney Houston was an American singer, actress and model. She is one of the best-selling music artists in history, known for her powerful vocals and iconic songs like "I Will Always Love You."
- Leo Traits: Charismatic, confident and creative.
- Impact: Houston's music and talent left an indelible mark on the music industry and continues to inspire artists worldwide.
- Personal Life: She had a tumultuous personal life and tragically passed away in 2012.

BARACK OBAMA

- Date of Birth: August 4, 1961.
- Brief Biography: Barack Obama is an American politician who served as the 44th President of the United States. He is known for his charismatic leadership and historic presidency.
- Leo Traits: Charismatic, confident and visionary.
- Impact: Obama's presidency marked a significant era in American politics, with accomplishments like the Affordable Care Act and the killing of Osama bin Laden.
- Personal Life: He is married to Michelle Obama. Together they have two daughters.

COCO CHANEL

- Date of Birth: August 19, 1883.
- Brief Biography: Coco Chanel was a French fashion designer and businesswoman. She revolutionized women's fashion with her iconic designs, including the little black dress and Chanel No. 5 perfume.
- Leo Traits: Confident, creative and independent.
- Impact: Chanel's influence on fashion and her enduring brand have made her a fashion icon.
- Personal Life: She had several love affairs but never married.

MARCUS GARVEY

- Date of Birth: August 17, 1887.
- Brief Biography: Marcus Garvey was a Jamaican political activist and leader of the Pan-Africanism movement. He advocated for the unity and empowerment of people of African descent.

- Leo Traits: Charismatic, confident and visionary.
- Impact: Garvey's ideas and activism laid the groundwork for the civil rights and Black liberation movements.
- Personal Life: He was married to Amy Ashwood Garvey.

MADONNA

- Date of Birth: August 16, 1958.
- Brief Biography: Madonna is an American singer, actress, and businesswoman. She is often referred to as the "Queen of Pop" and has had a profound influence on music and culture.
- Leo Traits: Charismatic, confident and creative.
- Impact: Madonna's music, style, and boundary-pushing artistry have made her a pop culture icon.
- Personal Life: She has been married twice and has several children.

ARNOLD SCHWARZENEGGER

- Date of Birth: July 30, 1947.
- Brief Biography: Arnold Schwarzenegger is an Austrian-American actor, bodybuilder, and politician. He is famous for his roles in "The Terminator" series, bodybuilding career and his tenure as Governor of California.
- Leo Traits: Charismatic, confident and ambitious.
- Impact: Schwarzenegger's career in bodybuilding, entertainment and politics has made him a global figure.
- Personal Life: He was married to Maria Shriver and has several children.

USAIN BOLT

- Date of Birth: August 21, 1986.
- Brief Biography: Usain Bolt is a Jamaican sprinter and widely regarded as the fastest man in the world. He holds numerous records in sprinting events.
- Leo Traits: Confident, competitive and energetic.
- Impact: Bolt's dominance in track and field has made him a legendary figure in sports.
- Personal Life: Bolt has a daughter. He has been involved in various charity work.

DUA LIPA

- Date of Birth: August 22, 1995.
- Brief Biography: Dua Lipa is an English singer and songwriter known for hits like "New Rules" and "Levitating." She has won several awards for her music.
- Leo Traits: Charismatic, confident and creative.
- Impact: Dua Lipa has emerged as a prominent pop artist with a global fanbase.
- Personal Life: She is in a relationship with Anwar Hadid.

TOM BRADY

- Date of Birth: August 3, 1977.
- Brief Biography: Tom Brady is an American football quarterback known for his exceptional career with the New England Patriots and later with the Tampa Bay Buccaneers.
- Leo Traits: Charismatic, competitive and determined.
- Impact: Brady is considered one of the greatest quarterbacks in NFL history, with numerous Super Bowl victories.
- Personal Life: He is married to supermodel Gisele Bündchen and has children with her.

J.K. ROWLING

- Date of Birth: July 31, 1965.
- Brief Biography: J.K. Rowling is a British author best known for creating the beloved "Harry Potter" series, which has become a global phenomenon.
- Leo Traits: Creative, imaginative and confident.
- Impact: Rowling's books have inspired a generation of readers and made her one of the world's wealthiest authors.
- Personal Life: She is known for her philanthropic work and advocacy for various causes.

KYLIE JENNER

- Date of Birth: August 10, 1997.

- Brief Biography: Kylie Jenner is an American media personality, businesswoman, and socialite. She is known for her cosmetics company, Kylie Cosmetics.
- Leo Traits: Confident, entrepreneurial and influential.
- Impact: Jenner has built a successful business empire and is one of the youngest billionaires globally.
- Personal Life: She has a daughter and is part of the Kardashian-Jenner family.

In the world of astrology individuals born under the Leo zodiac sign shine like stars captivating others with their charm, ambition and creativity. These extraordinary individuals, such as the commanding presence of Napoléon Bonaparte, the mesmerizing melodies of Whitney Houston and the indomitable spirit of Coco Chanel serve as reminders that Leos are destined for greatness. Their influence spans many fields including entertainment, politics, sports and entrepreneurship. These have left a positive impact on history.

As we celebrate their accomplishments and legacies as Leos it is important to recognize both the effect of their astrological sign and their charismatic nature. Leos possess confidence, in abundance and an unwavering determination that continuously inspires us all. Their stories demonstrate firsthand how self expression, ambition and leadership are qualities deeply rooted in this zodiac sign. They serve as beacons of inspiration urging us to embrace our attributes while allowing our inner light to radiate like the Sun itself.

In the story of existence the captivating presence of Leo personalities remains at the forefront leaving behind a lasting legacy that shines brightly as the stars, in the night sky. As we say goodbye to this chapter, may you find inspiration in the individuals who embody the essence of Leo. Finally may you embrace your Leo characteristics to radiate brilliantly in your own personal journey.

CONCLUSION

Here we stand at the edge of discovery and contemplation. We have reached the conclusion of our journey exploring the Leo, Zodiac sign. Now we aim to distill the essence of the Leo zodiac sign bringing together the threads that have woven a tapestry of insights, revelations and inspirations.

Throughout this book we have delved into the core qualities that make Leo truly remarkable. We have celebrated Leo's charm, boundless confidence and captivating presence. Traits that distinguish Leos as born leaders and show stoppers. The innate creativity and ability to express oneself have been recurring themes in relation to Leo. These remind us of how important it's to embrace our talents and allow our inner artists to shine.

The unwavering determination and ambitious nature of individuals born under Leo have demonstrated the power of setting bold goals and pursuing them with unmatched passion. We explored Leo's passionate approach to love as their ability to create captivating connections, with partners, friends and family members.

Leo's drive for success and commitment to excellence motivates us to utilize our abilities and climb the ladder of accomplishment. We have witnessed how Leos can turn challenges into chances, for growth and self exploration emphasizing the significance of self reflection and understanding. We have explored the vastness of the universe studying how celestial occurrences and planetary forces impact individuals born under the sign of Leo.

In our journey we have covered an exploration of Leo in some enthralling chapters. Here let us summarize them for you in a concise rememender.

- **Chapter 1: History and Mythology**; In this chapter, we embarked on a journey through time to uncover the historical and mythological origins of the Leo constellation. We explored how different civilizations perceived and represented Leo in their star maps. From ancient Egypt's reverence for the lioness-headed goddess Sekhmet to Greek mythology's depiction of the Nemean Lion. Ultimately we learned how Leo has left an indelible mark on human history and imagination.

- **Chapter 2: Love & Compatibility**; Chapter 2 delved into the world of Leo's approach to love and romance. We explored the personality traits, strengths, and weaknesses of Leo individuals in matters of the heart. Compatibility with other zodiac signs was examined. From which valuable insights into potential relationships for Leos were found. From passionate connections with Aries to the harmonious partnership with Libra. Overall we unraveled the complexities of Leo's love life.
- **Chapter 3: Friends and Family**; In Chapter 3, we turned our focus to Leo's interactions with friends and family. We explored the dynamic Leo brings to friendships. Their loyalty and how they navigate relationships within their inner circles was a noticeable tenet. We also delved into Leo's role within the family unit, examining their strengths and potential challenges in maintaining familial bonds.
- **Chapter 4: Career and Money**; Chapter 4 explored Leo's career preferences and professional aspirations. We identified the strengths that make Leo individuals excel in the workplace, as well as the challenges they may face and strategies to overcome them. Leo's approach to financial matters and money management was also analyzed, providing valuable insights for achieving financial success.
- **Chapter 5: Self-Improvement**; Chapter 5 focused on personal growth and development for Leo individuals. We examined how Leos can harness their strengths and overcome weaknesses to facilitate self-improvement. The chapter also featured exercises and strategies for self-reflection, empowerment and embracing their full potential.
- **Chapter 6: The Year Ahead**; In this chapter, we ventured into the astrological realm to explore the impact of celestial events on Leo individuals in the year ahead. From love and relationships to career and wellness, we offered guidance on how Leos can navigate the cosmic energies. In turn to make the most of the opportunities and challenges that arise in the upcoming year.
- **Chapter 7: Famous "Leo" Personalities**; Our final chapter celebrated the legacies of famous individuals born under the Leo sign. We profiled iconic figures such as Napoléon Bonaparte, Whitney Houston, Tom Brady and others. There we highlighted their Leo traits, impact on history and personal lives. These Leo personalities served as inspirational examples of the power and potential of this zodiac sign.

Throughout the course of this book we have embarked on a captivating journey diving into the world of astrology. Our main focus has been, on the charismatic Leo zodiac sign. Not only have we unravel the mysteries surrounding Leo. We have also provided a comprehensive understanding of what it truly means to be an individual born under this sign. Our commitment to shedding light on the nature of Leo has been fulfilled through our exploration. An exploration of many aspects such as Leo's historical background, distinctive personality traits, relationships, career ambitions, self improvement, astrological insights and even how famous individuals embodying this sign have left their mark on the world.

The main idea we hope readers take away from this book is the notion that they are special and extraordinary individuals. The key lies in embracing your Leo essence and harnessing your strengths while confidently navigating any challenges that may arise along your path. We urge you to acknowledge and embrace your Leo traits as these qualities serve as your superpowers that can lead to growth, meaningful connections and success in life.

Astrology goes beyond being a mere belief system; it serves as a tool for self discovery and comprehension. Leo, with its characteristics, epitomizes individuality and self expression. It teaches us that each one of us is like a shining star in our way capable of leaving a lasting legacy.

To all those who fall under the Leo sign we encourage you to let your inner light shine brightly. Your charm, ambition and creativity are your gifts. Embrace your strengths, celebrate your passions and know that you possess the power to accomplish your dreams while inspiring others along the way.

To conclude let us appreciate the fascinating world of Leo and astrology. May the insights we have gained from this exploration inspire you to embark on a journey of self discovery, empowerment and unlocking your potential. Always remember that, like the Sun at the center of our system, you are a radiant force in the universe and your presence brings brightness to the world.

As we say goodbye to this book, about Leo let us carry with us the wisdom gained from embracing their Lions den. Let's embrace our Leo regardless of our zodiac sign and embody their confidence, creativity and determination.

In conclusion, always remember that while the stars above guide us it is ultimately our light that illuminates our path. May your exploration of the Leo constellation bring you inspiration. May your radiance match that of the Sun, for you are also a celestial presence, in the vast fabric of the cosmos.

VIRGO:

A COMPLETE GUIDE TO THE VIRGO ASTROLOGY STAR SIGN

Contents

INTRODUCTION 1
Compatibility 2
Personality Traits 3
Strengths 3
Weaknesses 3

CHAPTER 1: HISTORY AND MYTHOLOGY 5
Notable historical events 7
Historical Figures Born under the Virgo Sign 8

CHAPTER 2: LOVE & COMPATIBILITY 10
Virgo and Aries 12
Virgo and Taurus 12
Virgo and Gemini 12
Virgo and Cancer 13
Virgo and Leo 13
Virgo and Virgo 13
Virgo and Libra 14
Virgo and Scorpio 14
Virgo and Sagittarius 14
Virgo and Capricorn 14
Virgo and Aquarius 14
Virgo and Pisces 15
Tips for Men Dating Virgo Women 15
Tips for Women Dating Virgo Men 15

CHAPTER 3: FRIENDS AND FAMILY 17

CHAPTER 4: CAREER AND MONEY 23

CHAPTER 5: SELF-IMPROVEMENT 30

CHAPTER 6: THE YEAR AHEAD 34
Career and Finances 34
Love and Relationships 35
Health and Well-being 36

Personal Growth and Spirituality 37
Family and Home Life 37
Travel and Adventure... 37
Social Life... 38

CHAPTER 7: FAMOUS "VIRGO" PERSONALITIES --------------- 41

CONCLUSION... 48

INTRODUCTION

Welcome to the realm of astrology, an age old practice that has captivated humanity for generations. At its core it is a belief system that suggests a connection between celestial entities like planets and stars, and human lives. It proposes that these bodies' positions at one's birth can offer insights into their personality traits, strengths, weaknesses and life path. The heavens are divided into twelve sections in astrology called zodiac signs. Each zodiac sign is associated with its own set of personality traits and characteristics.

Within the pages of this book we embark on a journey of one zodiac sign. Virgo, the sixth sign. The objective of this book is to provide readers with an exploration into the world of Virgo. Whether you're someone intrigued by the Virgo sign or a Virgo yourself this book aims to offer you an understanding and appreciation. One that celebrates this fascinating and complex astrological sign.

Within these pages you will discover;

- **Historical Roots;** Embark on a journey through the history of Virgo. Discover its origins and evolution. In addition we will be exploring its impact on cultures and civilizations throughout time.

- **Cosmic Blueprint**; Dive into the core qualities and characteristics associated with Virgo ranging from their ruling planet Mercury, to their connection with Earth.
- **Compatibility**; Understand how Virgo interacts with other zodiac signs. Learn about compatibility and dynamics in relationships.
- **Virgo in Today's World**; Explore how Virgo traits manifest in society including their roles in career paths, family dynamics, personal growth and much more.
- **Practical Guidance**; Discover advice and helpful tips tailored specifically for Virgo individuals. Learn how to harness your strengths and manage weaknesses. In addition, learn how to navigate life's challenges successfully.

If you happen to be a Virgo seeking an understanding of your traits or if you're simply intrigued by the complex network of celestial forces this book warmly welcomes you to embark on a fulfilling journey. One of self discovery and exploration into the realm of Virgo.

VIRGO ZODIAC SIGN OVERVIEW

- **Date of Star Sign**: August 23 - September 22.
- **Symbol**: The symbol for Virgo is the Virgin. It is represented by a young woman holding a sheaf of wheat. This symbolizes purity, fertility and the nurturing qualities associated with the sign.
- **Element**: Earth. As an Earth sign, Virgos are generally characterized by their grounded nature, practicality, and stability.
- **Planet**: Mercury, the planet ruling communication, intellect, and learning, governs Virgo. This planetary influence is reflected in the intellectual and analytical abilities often found in Virgos.
- **Color**: Virgo is often associated with earthy, muted colors. Emphasis is on shades of green and brown.

COMPATIBILITY

Virgos are most compatible with other Earth signs (Taurus and Capricorn) and Water signs (Cancer, Scorpio, and Pisces). They share a practical and grounded approach to life with Earth signs and a strong emotional connection with Water signs. More on this later!

PERSONALITY TRAITS

Virgo is ruled by Mercury, the planet of communication and intellect. This contributes to the sign's analytical and detail-oriented nature. Individuals born under the Virgo sign are known for their practicality, precision and dedication. Here are some key personality traits associated with Virgo:

- **Analytical**: Virgos have a sharp, analytical mind. They excel at analyzing complex situations and solving complex problems.
- **Practical**: They are highly practical and grounded individuals. As such they often focus on the tangible and realistic aspects of life.
- **Organized**: Virgos have a strong sense of order and cleanliness. They appreciate structure and strive for neatness and efficiency.
- **Nurturing**: Virgos have a nurturing side. They often take care of others. As such they are reliable friends and partners.
- **Modest**: Virgos tend to be modest and unassuming. They don't seek the limelight and are content to work behind the scenes.
- **Intellectual**: Mercury's influence grants Virgos a love of knowledge and a strong intellectual curiosity. They enjoy learning and can be excellent problem solvers.

STRENGTHS

- **Attention to Detail**: Virgos excel in tasks that require precision and attention to detail. Thus making them reliable and thorough workers.
- **Analytical Thinking**: Their ability to analyze situations helps them make well-informed decisions.
- **Organization**: Virgos are great at creating order out of chaos and thrive in structured environments.
- **Loyalty**: They are dedicated and loyal friends and partners. As such they can be counted on in times of need.
- **Practicality**: Virgos' down-to-earth nature allows them to navigate real-world challenges effectively.

WEAKNESSES

- **Overcritical**: Virgos can be overly critical, both of themselves and others. This can lead to perfectionist tendencies.
- **Worry-Prone**: They may have a tendency to worry excessively.

- **Shyness**: Some Virgos can be reserved and introverted, making it challenging for them to open up to others.
- **Difficulty Delegating**: Due to their desire for perfection, Virgos may struggle to delegate tasks to others. Sometimes they take on too much themselves.
- **Inflexibility**: Their strong desire for order and routine can make them resistant to change.

Welcome once again to the captivating realm of Virgo! This introductory chapter sets the stage for delving into the intricacies and often misunderstood nature of this personality. We've established that Virgos astrological period spans from August 23 to September 22. We showed how it is symbolized by the Virgin and influenced by the Earth element. This imbues them with a practical disposition. Mercury, as Virgos ruling planet bestows upon them brilliance and acute attention to detail. While Virgos possess strengths like precision and loyalty they are not exempt from weaknesses such as their inclination towards perfectionism and worry.

As we venture deeper into this book you can anticipate uncovering more aspects of Virgo's personality. Along with exploring their compatibility with other signs and receiving practical guidance on navigating life as a Virgo. In the chapters ahead you'll find a thought provoking exploration of the Virgo zodiac sign brimming with valuable insights, practical guidance and a newfound admiration for this captivating and multifaceted sign.

CHAPTER 1:
HISTORY AND MYTHOLOGY

In the tapestry of the zodiac, Virgo is a constellation that holds a wealth of history and mythology. As we dive into this chapter we embark on a journey through time exploring its origins and evolution. We will also discover its impact on modern astrology. Additionally we will meet figures born under the sign of Virgo. Furthermore we will trace how perceptions of Virgo have evolved over time. From its origins to its interpretation in modern astrology. Come along with us as we delve into the history and mythology of Virgo.

THE HISTORY OF VIRGO

The constellation known as Virgo has a history that goes back thousands of years. It originated from early observations and recordings made by ancient civilizations.

- **Babylonians**; The Babylonians were one of the first civilizations in the world to observe Virgo. They associated this constellation with Shala, a goddess symbolizing fertility, abundance and harvest. It held great significance for them.
- **Ancient Egypt;** In Ancient Egypt Virgo was linked to Isis, a goddess representing fertility, motherhood and healing. The appearance of Virgo in the night sky was considered a sign for the flooding of the Nile River. This was and still is a crucial event for agriculture.
- **Ancient Greece**; Renowned for their contributions to astronomy and mythology the ancient Greeks identified Virgo as Demeter. She was a goddess associated with agriculture and harvest. Demeters connection to changes and planting cycles added depth to their perception of this constellation.

- **Roman Mythology;** The Romans adopted much of Greek mythology; thus Virgos association with Demeter continued within culture. However they also connected Virgo with Ceres, the equivalent to Demeter.
- **Ancient Chinese Astronomy**; In Ancient Chinese astronomy the constellation known as Virgo was not considered an entity but rather part of a larger constellation called "the Weaving Girl" or "Zhi Nü." This constellation represented a princess, in weaving, symbolizing craftsmanship and dedication.
- **Islamic Astronomy**; Islamic astronomers had their own interpretations of Virgo. They are often referred to as "the Lady," symbolizing purity and fertility. Some Islamic star maps depicted the constellation holding a sheaf of wheat.
- **Native American Astrology**; Native American tribes had their understandings of celestial patterns and it is possible that elements of Virgo were incorporated into their cosmology. However specific records detailing their interpretations are limited.
- **Other Cultural Perceptions and Representations**; Over the years many other cultures depicted Virgo in their star maps with variations. However they all recognized its association with fertility, agriculture and the natural cycles.

Throughout the course of history the presence of the Virgo constellation has been a source of inspiration. It symbolizes the bond between humanity and the natural cycles that govern our world. Its depiction in mythologies and cultural interpretations reflects how vital agriculture and the changing seasons have been.

The perception and understanding of Virgo has evolved significantly over time. In ancient civilizations, Virgo was primarily associated with fertility, agriculture and mythology. As cultures transitioned into the Middle Ages and the Renaissance, astrologers began to explore the personality traits and astrological attributes associated with Virgo.

In modern astrology, there has been a shift from purely mythological interpretations to psychological and personality-based insights. Modern astrologers analyze Virgo in terms of its personality traits, strengths, weaknesses and compatibility with other signs. This shift reflects a broader movement in astrology towards self-awareness and personal growth.

NOTABLE HISTORICAL EVENTS

Throughout history many significant events have taken place during the Virgo season. While astrology does not necessarily determine or predict events we can analyze some occurrences during this time for their potential astrological significance.

- **Autumnal Equinox;** The Virgo season signifies the arrival of the equinox in the Northern Hemisphere indicating the transition from summer to fall. This shift is associated with themes of balance, introspection and preparation for the months

- **Harvest Festivals**; Many cultures celebrate harvest festivals during the Virgo season. This highlights the importance of harvests and our Earth's abundance. These celebrations align with Virgos qualities. Nurturing nature.
- **Martin Luther King Jr.'s "I Have a Dream" Speech;** One of the most iconic moments of the Civil Rights Movement in the United States occurred during Virgo season. Dr. Martin Luther King Jr. delivered his famous "I Have a Dream" speech during the March on Washington for Jobs and Freedom, a pivotal event in the fight for civil rights.

HISTORICAL FIGURES BORN UNDER THE VIRGO SIGN

Numerous influential historical figures were born under the sign of Virgo each leaving a mark on history;

- **Mother Teresa** (August 26 1910); Mother Teresa symbolized compassion and selflessness as she dedicated her life to aiding India's impoverished individuals. She was a true embodiment of Virgos nurturing and service oriented traits.
- **Leo Tolstoy** (September 9 1828); Leo Tolstoy was an author and philosopher famous for his monumental work "War and Peace." He exemplified Virgos intellectual characteristics through his writings

As we come to the end of this chapter we can't help but be amazed by the stories, legends and historical events that revolve around the Virgo constellation. From Babylonians' deep respect for the goddess Shala. To the Greeks connections with Demeter and the Egyptians association with Isis. Virgo has symbolized fertility, agriculture and the nurturing forces of the universe. Its presence during the transition from summer to fall marked by the equinox further emphasizes its impact on human culture. In modern astrology Virgo continues to hold a radiant place as a sign, with an enduring legacy.

For readers who wish to delve deeper into the history and mythology of Virgo, here are some recommended primary sources, ancient texts, and modern writings:

- **"Star Names: Their Lore and Meaning"** by Richard H. Allen: This classic work provides insights into the origins and symbolism of constellations, including Virgo.
- **"The Secret Teachings of All Ages"** by Manly P. Hall: An esoteric exploration of ancient wisdom, including astrological symbolism and mythology.

- **"Mythology"** by Edith Hamilton: A comprehensive overview of Greek and Roman mythology, which includes the stories of Demeter, Isis, and other deities linked to Virgo.
- **"The Inner Sky"** by Steven Forrest: This modern astrology book explores the psychological dimensions of Virgo and other signs, offering insights into self-discovery and personal growth.
- **Online Resources:** Websites like the American Federation of Astrologers (AFA) and the Astrological Association of Great Britain provide valuable information on astrology's history, symbolism, and contemporary interpretations.

CHAPTER 2:
LOVE & COMPATIBILITY

When it comes to love and relationships Virgo individuals bring a combination of practicality, dedication and attention to detail. In this chapter we will explore how Virgo approaches matters of the heart and their compatibility, with other zodiac signs. This exploration will shed light on both the challenges and harmonious connections that arise when a Virgo meets someone from another star sign.

Whether you're a Virgo seeking insights into your tendencies or simply curious about building a fulfilling relationship with a Virgo, this chapter offers valuable guidance. Join us on this journey as we explore the secrets behind how Virgos approach matters of love.

THE VIRGO APPROACH TO LOVE

Virgo, being an Earth sign governed by Mercury approaches love in a way that combines practicality, analytical thinking and devotion. When Virgos experience love they do so with sincerity. Let's look closer at how Virgos approach love.

- **Analytical and Thoughtful**; Virgos are known for their analytical minds. In matters of the heart they take their time to carefully assess partners and relationships.
- **Attention to Detail**; Virgo's meticulous nature extends to their relationships. They pay close attention to the details, making considerate gestures and remembering important dates. This can make their partners feel cherished.
- **Practicality**; Virgos highly value stability and practicality. In matters of love, they often seek partners who share their life values. Dramatic or tumultuous relationships generally don't pique their interest. Instead they prefer a dependable partnership.
- **Loyalty and Dedication**; Once Virgos commit to a relationship they display loyalty and dedication. They are willing to put in the effort to make the relationship thrive while standing by their partner through thick and thin.
- **Affectionate**; Virgos have an inclination to care for their loved ones. They show their affection by offering help organizing things and providing assistance whenever needed.
- **Sincere**; In matters of love Virgos tend to be humble and unpretentious. While they may not be the most romantic sign their love is genuine and unwavering.
- **Honesty**; Open and honest communication holds importance for Virgos in relationships. They value discussing issues, finding solutions and working together with their partners to establish a healthy connection.
- **Alone time**; Despite being committed partners Virgos also appreciate having space for themselves. They understand the significance of maintaining a sense of independence while nurturing the relationship.
- **Critical**; Due to their analytical nature Virgos can sometimes become excessively critical. Both towards themselves and their partners. Overall it would benefit them to learn how to balance this tendency in order to avoid conflicts.
- **Trust**; Trust is of huge importance for Virgos in a relationship. They need to feel secure and confident about their partners' loyalty.

To sum it up when it comes to love and romance Virgos tend to be practical, loyal and focused on building meaningful relationships. Virgos desire a balanced love life that allows both individuals to grow and flourish together. They may not be extravagant in expressing their love but their commitment to the little things make them dependable partners.

COMPATIBILITY WITH OTHER SIGNS

VIRGO AND ARIES

Virgo and Aries are signs with distinct differences in their personalities and approaches to life. Virgo is practical, detail-oriented and prefers a structured routine. Aries, on the other hand, thrives on spontaneity. While they may be attracted to each other's strengths. For example, Aries' energy and Virgo's attention to detail, their differences can create challenges. Virgo may find Aries too impulsive and impatient. Aries may perceive Virgo as overly critical. For this pairing to work, they need to appreciate each other's unique qualities and find a balance.

VIRGO AND TAURUS

Virgo and Taurus share the Earth element, which grounds them and fosters stability. Both signs appreciate the finer things in life and value security and practicality. This is a highly compatible match. Virgo and Taurus understand each other's need for stability and are both dependable and loyal partners. They share common values. Overall they can build a strong and enduring relationship based on trust and shared goals.

VIRGO AND GEMINI

Virgo is practical and detail-oriented. Gemini is curious and adaptable. Gemini thrives on variety and intellectual stimulation. Both have contrasting approaches to life and may find it challenging to connect deeply. Virgo may see Gemini as flighty. Gemini may view Virgo as too serious. However, if they can communicate openly and appreciate each other's strengths, they can learn from each other. Overall they can then create a balanced relationship.

VIRGO AND CANCER

Both Virgo and Cancer are nurturing signs, albeit in different ways. Virgo nurtures through practical support. Cancer is emotionally nurturing. Together they can create a loving and supportive partnership. They share a deep emotional connection and understand each other's need for security. Virgo's practicality can complement Cancer's emotional sensitivity, creating a harmonious relationship.

VIRGO AND LEO

Virgo and Leo have contrasting personalities. Virgo is modest, detail-oriented and practical. Leo is confident, outgoing and seeks the spotlight. This pairing can be challenging due to their differences. Virgo may find Leo's need for attention overwhelming. Leo may perceive Virgo as overly critical. However, with effort and understanding, they can complement each other. Virgo's attention to detail can help Leo in their endeavors. Meanwhile Leo's charisma can bring excitement to Virgo's life.

VIRGO AND VIRGO

When two Virgos come together, they share a deep understanding of each other's tendencies. Positive and negative. Both value practicality and attention to detail. This can be a harmonious relationship based on shared values and a strong sense of responsibility. However, they may also share the tendency to be overly critical. It's essential for them to focus on mutual support and avoid nitpicking each other.

VIRGO AND LIBRA

Virgo and Libra have different approaches to life. Virgo is practical and detail-oriented. Libra is diplomatic and values harmony. This pairing can be challenging, as their priorities differ. Virgo may find Libra's indecisiveness frustrating. Meanwhile Libra might see Virgo as overly critical. To make it work, they need to appreciate each other's strengths. Together they can find ways to balance their differences.

VIRGO AND SCORPIO

Both Virgo and Scorpio are analytical and value deep emotional connections. They share a mutual dedication to their goals. This pairing can create a strong and passionate bond. They understand each other's intensity and need for privacy. Virgo's practicality can complement Scorpio's emotional depth, making them a well-rounded couple.

VIRGO AND SAGITTARIUS

Virgo is practical and detail-oriented. Sagittarius is adventurous and loves spontaneity and freedom. This pair can face challenges due to their differing priorities. Virgo may feel that Sagittarius is too carefree, while Sagittarius might perceive Virgo as too serious. For this relationship to work, they need to respect each other's need for both structure and spontaneity.

VIRGO AND CAPRICORN

Virgo and Capricorn are both Earth signs. This means they share common values such as stability and practicality. This is a highly compatible match. Virgo and Capricorn understand each other's goals and ambitions. As such they support each other's efforts. Together they can build a stable and prosperous life together. One based on mutual trust and shared values.

VIRGO AND AQUARIUS

Virgo is practical and detail-oriented. Aquarius is independent and values innovation and freedom. This pair may have challenges due to their differing priorities. Virgo may find Aquarius too unpredictable. Aquarius might perceive Virgo as too structured. To make it work, they need to find a balance between Virgo's practicality and Aquarius' need for freedom.

VIRGO AND PISCES

Virgo and Pisces have different approaches to life. Virgo is practical and analytical. Pisces is intuitive and emotionally sensitive. This can be a complementary match, as they balance each other's strengths and weaknesses. Virgo's practicality can provide stability to Pisces. Meanwhile Pisces' emotional depth can help Virgo connect on a more profound level. However, Virgo may need to be careful not to be overly critical of Pisces' sensitive nature.

TIPS FOR RELATIONSHIPS WITH VIRGO INDIVIDUALS

Dating and being in a relationship with a Virgo can be truly fulfilling. They are known for their loyalty and practical nature. To establish a better connection with a Virgo partner here are some tailored tips.

TIPS FOR MEN DATING VIRGO WOMEN

- **Respect Her Independence**; Virgo women highly value their independence and personal space. It's important to respect her need for alone time. In addition, encourage her to pursue her interests and goals.
- **Be Thoughtful**; Pay attention to the details. Virgo women appreciate romantic gestures. Remember important dates. Surprise her with small gifts or lend a hand with practical tasks when needed.
- **Engage in Intellectual Conversations;** Virgo women often have an interest in intellectual topics. Engage in such conversations. Share your ideas and be open to discussing subjects of her interest.
- **Be Patient and Supportive;** Virgo women can be self critical and strive for perfection. Offer support and reassurance when she doubts herself. Be patient as she pursues excellence.
- **Maintain Cleanliness;** Virgo women appreciate cleanliness and organization. By keeping your living spaces neat and tidy she will feel more comfortable and relaxed.

TIPS FOR WOMEN DATING VIRGO MEN

- **Appreciate His Practicality;** Virgo men are known for being individuals who can be relied upon. Express your gratitude, for his problem solving skills and their dedication to making your life easier.

- **Openness**; It's important to be open in your communication with Virgo men. Share your thoughts and feelings honestly so that they can better understand your needs and desires.
- **Support their passions;** Support their hobbies or interests. Whatever it is. Whether it's a passion for fitness, a love for books or a fascination with technology.
- **Patience**; Remember to be patient when faced with criticism from Virgo men. For them they often intend it to be feedback aimed at helping you improve.
- **Problem solving;** When planning dates consider activities that involve problem solving or learning something. For example cooking classes, DIY projects or visits to museums and exhibits.

Overall when dating a Virgo it's important to prioritize loyalty, honesty and reliability. Both partners should also strive for a balance between practicality (a characteristic often associated with Virgos) and the need for spontaneity within the relationship.

In our exploration of love and compatibility, within the Virgo zodiac sign we have delved into the essence of this grounded and practical sign. Virgos possess an approach to love and relationships combining their minds with their nurturing spirits. Throughout this chapter we have revealed the intricacies of Virgos tendencies. We have explored how they connect with each of the twelve zodiac signs. From forming enduring partnerships with Taurus to experiencing synergy with Capricorn. Overall we have uncovered the potential for love and connection that Virgo shares with every star sign.

As we conclude this chapter it is important to understand that while astrology offers insights, it is ultimately the blend of personalities, experiences and choices that shape our romantic connections. The compatibility guidelines presented here serve as a starting point. Ultimately love goes beyond zodiac boundaries. By embracing effective communication we can cultivate lasting and rewarding relationships not only with Virgos but also with people, from all walks of life.

CHAPTER 3:
FRIENDS AND FAMILY

In this chapter we will uncover the subtleties of how Virgos approach family bonds and friendships. We will highlight both the strengths and the potential challenges they may encounter. Whether you're a Virgo seeking an understanding of your role in your loved ones lives, or someone to appreciate the unique qualities that Virgo friends and family members possess. This chapter will provide valuable insights. Join us as we explore the dynamics of familial ties, for Virgos and the enduring connections forged in the realm of friendship.

VIRGO AS A FRIEND

When you have a friend who's a Virgo, you can count on having a reliable companion. One with a unique blend of qualities that enhance your friendship. Let's take a close look at what it's like to have a Virgo friend.

- **Reliability**; Having a Virgo friend means having a reliable person in your life. They are punctually organized and follow through on their commitments.
- **Attention to Detail;** Virgos possess an eye for detail. They have an ability to notice things that others may overlook. This makes them excellent problem solvers and planners.
- **Problem Solvers**; Virgo friends excel at analyzing complex situations and finding practical solutions. When faced with dilemmas they offer valuable insights.
- **Loyalty**; Above all else Virgos are fiercely loyal to their friends. They stand by your side through thick and thin.
- **Practical Support**; Virgo friends are always ready to assist you whether it's helping, with your move, organizing an event or providing advice.
- **Modesty**; Virgo individuals have a modest nature. They prefer to work behind the scenes rather than seeking attention. As such they find joy in supporting their friends' endeavors.
- **Honesty**; Honesty and integrity hold value for Virgo friends. They offer feedback with the intention of aiding your growth and improvement.
- **Analytical Listening**; When you share your thoughts and concerns with a Virgo friend they listen attentively. In turn they excel at providing feedback from perspectives you might have overlooked. They want you to succeed so they provide guidance considerately.
- **Tidiness**; Virgo friends appreciate cleanliness and orderliness. Spending time with them often means enjoying organized spaces and environments. However it's important to note that due to their pursuit of perfection, Virgos may sometimes become overly critical of themselves or others. They might also tend to worry a lot. As a friend it's important to provide reassurance and remind them to take it easy when necessary.

To sum up, having a Virgo friend means having someone who's loyal, practical and pays attention to details. Their distinctive qualities enrich the strength and depth of your friendship making it a bond worth treasuring. Ultimately they will always be there for you.

VIRGO AND FAMILY DYNAMICS

Virgo individuals, bring a combination of practicality skills and dedication to their families. When they actively engage in family life they do so with a sense of responsibility and a genuine desire to nurture and support their loved ones. Now let's take a closer look at how Virgos contribute to the dynamics within the family.

- **Nurturing**; Virgos possess an ability to nurture others. They take their caregiver roles seriously. As such they are always ready to offer support and practical assistance to their family.
- **Attention to Detail**; Known for their meticulousness Virgos excel in organizing and planning. Their attention to detail becomes an asset within the context of family life.
- **Reliability**; If you have a Virgo as a part of your family you can rely on them without hesitation. They are known for being individuals who will go above and beyond to fulfill their responsibilities.
- **Problem Solvers;** Thanks to their analytical nature Virgos make excellent problem solvers within the family. Whenever conflicts or challenges arise they often step up as mediators who propose solutions.
- **Health**; Virgos prioritize healthy living for themselves as well as for those around them. They often show an interest in the well being of their family members. As such they are usually encouraging health habits and providing support during times of illness.
- **Modest**; When it comes to family interactions Virgos tend to be modest and unassuming. They prefer to work behind the scenes rather than seeking the spotlight.
- **Honesty**; Open and honest communication is highly valued by Virgos within their families. They are willing to discuss any issues or conflicts that arise in order to find solutions and promote harmony at home.
- **Routine**; Virgos appreciate having a routine and structure in their lives. They may play a role in establishing and maintaining household schedules. Overall this can bring stability and a sense of security for everyone involved.
- **Mentor**; In the family dynamic Virgo members often take on the role of teacher or mentor. They derive joy from sharing their knowledge and skills with loved ones while taking pride in helping them learn and grow.
- **Listeners**; While they may not always openly express their emotions Virgos excel at listening. Family members can rely on them for providing a space where they can share their feelings and concerns receiving advice along with comfort.

To sum up, Virgos make valuable contributions to family dynamics due to their caring supportive traits. They play key roles in ensuring the well being of the family. In times of conflicts or challenges they are there mediating or offering practical assistance. As a result they are seen as cherished members of the family.

CHALLENGES IN FRIENDSHIPS AND FAMILY RELATIONS FOR VIRGO

While Virgos possess positive qualities in their friendships and family relationships they also face certain unique challenges. It's crucial to acknowledge these pitfalls in order to cultivate harmonious connections with individuals who are Virgos. Let's explore how.

- **Being Overly Critical**; Virgos are renowned for their attention to detail and relentless pursuit of perfection. However this characteristic can sometimes make them excessively critical of themselves as others. Within friendships and family dynamics this tendency to be overly judgmental can become burdensome for those who feel constantly evaluated or scrutinized.
- **Worry**; Virgos have a tendency to be worriers by nature. They may find themselves constantly preoccupied with the well being of their loved ones. If not properly managed this anxiety can introduce tension into relationships.
- **Difficulty Expressing Emotions**; Virgos often feel more at ease expressing gestures or offering solutions than articulating their emotions verbally. This inclination can pose a challenge for friends and family members who strive to comprehend their sentiments or needs accurately.
- **Perfectionism**; The desire for perfection that characterizes Virgos can result in high expectations for both themselves and those around them. Consequently this may create an environment of pressure and stress within relationships where others feel compelled to meet high standards.
- **Self Criticism**; It is worth noting that Virgos tend to be especially hard on themselves when it comes to self evaluation. This tendency to criticize themselves can affect their relationships when they impose their standards on others.
- **Concern for Health**; Virgos are individuals who prioritize health and may sometimes worry excessively about the well being of their loved ones. While it's natural to be concerned, excessive worry can create stress in relationships.

- **Preference for Structure**; Virgos can be inflexible at times preferring routines and structure. This preference for predictability may clash with the spontaneity or adaptability of friends or family members.
- **Introverted Nature;** Some Virgos lean towards introversion which means they may require more time compared to extroverted friends or family members. Also their need for solitude can sometimes be misinterpreted as a lack of interest or emotional distance.
- **Difficulty Seeking Help**; Virgos often prefer being the ones offering assistance and support rather than receiving it. This inclination might make it challenging for friends and family to offer help when it's needed.

As we come to the end of this chapter let's reflect on what we have discovered. Virgos bring a combination of qualities to their relationships with family and friends. They take care in nurturing their families paying attention to the smallest details. They offer solutions when faced with problems and show unwavering loyalty to their companions. Their presence adds depth and richness to our connections, with others making their contributions truly invaluable.

As we conclude this chapter, we celebrate the unique role Virgo individuals play in their families and friendships. Their dedication, practicality and unwavering support are invaluable assets. Ones that enrich the lives of those fortunate enough to have them in their circle. Through open communication, mutual understanding and a willingness to embrace both strengths and weaknesses, the bonds with Virgo friends and family members can flourish. As a result these relationships will continue to be a source of enduring love and support.

CHAPTER 4: CAREER AND MONEY

In this chapter we will delve into the world of how Virgos approach their lives and their relationship with money. When it comes to careers and finances, Virgos bring a powerful combination of practicality, attention to detail and a strong work ethic.

Throughout this chapter we will explore in detail the strengths and challenges that Virgo individuals face in their careers and financial journeys. Whether you're a Virgo seeking insights into your path or someone about how Virgos handle money matters this chapter will provide valuable guidance.

VIRGO CAREER PREFERENCES AND PROFESSIONAL ASPIRATIONS

As mentioned above, Virgos bring a powerful combination of practicality, attention to detail and a strong work ethic to their lives. Their meticulous nature and desire for order make them well suited for certain career paths. Here's an overview of Virgos career preferences and aspirations.

- **Precision and Attention to Detail;** Virgos excel in careers that demand precision and meticulousness. They have a unique ability to identify errors and inconsistencies. This makes them valuable in various fields. For example auditing, quality control, data analysis and accounting.
- **Service Oriented Professions;** Many Virgos are inclined towards careers that involve helping others. They thrive in roles such as healthcare professionals (nurses, doctors, pharmacists) social work, counseling and teaching.
- **Administrative and Organizational Roles;** Virgos are often sought after for positions that require task management, scheduling expertise and resource coordination. These roles can include assistants, project managers, event planners and office managers.
- **Research & Analysis**; Virgos possess analytical skills and a talent for research. They have the potential to thrive in paths, such as those of scientists, researchers, analysts and statisticians. These careers highly appreciate their skills in collecting and analyzing data.
- **Writing and Editing**; Virgos possess a talent for writing, editing and proofreading tasks. Their meticulousness when it comes to language usage and grammar makes them exceptional editors, content creators and technical writers.
- **Wellness**; Due to their healthy nature Virgos are often drawn towards healthcare and wellness professions. They may choose careers as dietitians, nutritionists, physical therapists or alternative healthcare practitioners.
- **Agricultural Fields**; With their connection to the Earth element Virgos find themselves well suited for careers related to the environment and agriculture. They may flourish as scientists, farmers or horticulturists.
- **Consulting**; The analytical abilities of Virgos make them highly valuable in consulting roles where problem solving skills are crucial. They excel at providing solutions and recommendations in areas like management consulting IT consulting or financial advisory services.

- **Entrepreneurship**; Virgos attention to detail and strong work ethic are great traits for entrepreneurs. They might focus on areas such as e-commerce platforms, small scale manufacturing or service oriented startups.
- **Education and Training;** Virgos often derive satisfaction from roles related to education and training. They excel as teachers, mentors and trainers who can patiently and precisely guide others.
- **Philanthropy**; Virgos are frequently driven by a sense of serving others. They may pursue careers in charity organizations where they can have a meaningful impact.
- **Holistic and Wellness Practices**; Virgos naturally have an interest in well being. Some might explore careers in areas such as health, yoga instruction or holistic therapy aligning their work with their values.

STRENGTHS THAT MAKE VIRGO INDIVIDUALS EXCEL IN THE WORKPLACE

Virgo individuals possess a set of qualities that make them exceptional in the workplace. Here are some of the strengths that distinguish Virgo. One should focus on building on these.

- **Attention to Detail;** Virgos possess an ability to observe the smallest details. This keen eye allows them to identify errors, inconsistencies and find opportunities for improvement that others may overlook.
- **Strong Work Ethic;** Virgo individuals are renowned for their diligence. They take their responsibilities seriously. Their dedication makes them reliable and trustworthy members of any team.
- **Organizational Skills;** Virgos flourish in structured environments. They have a talent for organizing tasks, schedules and projects effectively.
- **Analytical Thinking**; Virgos excel at problem solving and analysis. They have a knack for breaking down issues and finding practical solutions. Overall these strengths make Virgo individuals highly effective professionals, across various industries.
- **Flexibility**; Although Virgos are known for their inclination towards structure they also possess the ability to adapt.
- **Effective Communication**; Virgos excel in articulate communication both in written form and verbally. Their attention to detail extends to conveying ideas and information. This skill proves advantageous in professions that prioritize communication, such as teaching, writing or customer service.

- **Dependability**; Virgos strong sense of responsibility and dedication towards their work makes them highly reliable employees. They consistently follow through on their commitments ensuring delivery of results.
- **Team Player Mentality**; Virgo thrive as team players who collaborate effectively with others. They readily embrace collaboration opportunities while often taking on roles within teams. Their positive contribution to group efforts fosters a positive work environment.
- **Excelling in Time Management**; Virgos possess high level skills in managing their time. They prioritize tasks, set deadlines and maintain a professional approach to their work. This ability to manage time effectively greatly contributes to their productivity.
- **Embracing Growth;** Virgos are always on the lookout for ways to improve themselves and their work. They welcome feedback and seek opportunities for learning and development. This helps them stay current and competitive in their careers.

The above strengths collectively make Virgo valuable assets in any workplace. Next let's look at some of the challenges they may face.

CHALLENGES FACED BY VIRGO IN THEIR CAREERS AND STRATEGIES TO OVERCOME THEM

Virgo individuals despite their strengths may face challenges in their professional lives. Being aware of these challenges and implementing strategies to overcome them can help them navigate their careers successfully. Here are some common difficulties that Virgos often encounter in the workplace, along with strategies to overcome them.

Perfectionism

- Challenge; Virgos are known for their pursuit of perfection which can sometimes lead to setting unrealistic expectations for themselves and others.
- Strategy; It is important for Virgos to practice self compassion and understand that perfection is an ideal that may not always be attainable. Setting goals and recognizing that mistakes provide opportunities for growth can be helpful.

Being Overly Critical

- Challenge; Because of their attention to detail Virgos may tend to be overly critical at times. As such it could strain relationships with colleagues.

- Strategy; When providing feedback or constructive criticism it is advisable for Virgos to focus on being constructive. Recognizing the efforts of others and emphasizing solutions of dwelling on problems can foster relationships.

Worry and Anxiety

- Challenge; Virgos sometimes experience worry and anxiety about their performance. Ultimately this can lead to stress and potential burnout.
- Strategy; Developing stress management techniques like mindfulness practices can be beneficial for managing worry and anxiety. Additionally seeking support could also aid in managing these feelings.

Difficulty Delegating

- Challenge; Virgos often find it hard to entrust tasks to others as they strive for excellence. This can result in a heavy workload.
- Strategy; It is important for Virgos to learn the art of delegation. By placing trust in colleagues and subordinates they can lighten their load.

Overload of Details

- Challenge; Virgos may feel overwhelmed, by the abundance of details they need to manage which can impede productivity.
- Strategy; To overcome this challenge Virgos should develop work systems. Utilizing technology tools for task management and prioritizing tasks based on their importance and urgency will help them stay on track.

Self Criticism

- Challenge; Virgos tend to be extremely self critical often struggling with issues related to self esteem.
- Strategy; Cultivating self compassion is crucial for overcoming this challenge. Engaging in positive self talk and taking time to acknowledge achievements are essential steps.

Resistance to Change

- Challenge; Virgos may exhibit resistance towards change.
- Strategy; Embrace change as an avenue for growth and learning. Staying updated on industry trends and technological advancements will allow Virgos to remain competitive and adaptive.

Difficulty Expressing Emotions

- Challenge; Virgos sometimes encounter difficulty in expressing their emotions which can hinder communication.
- Strategy; It's important to engage in honest communication with your colleagues. Express your thoughts and emotions when necessary in team settings or when resolving conflicts.

Reluctance to Seek Help

- Challenge; Virgos often prefer being the ones offering help rather than seeking assistance themselves which can lead to burnout.
- Strategy; Recognize that asking for help is a sign of strength, not weakness. When you need support don't hesitate to seek guidance or delegate tasks as it helps maintain a work life balance.

Balancing Work and Personal Life

- Challenge; Virgos strong work ethic may cause them to prioritize their careers over their personal lives.
- Strategy; Set boundaries between work and personal life. Make self care hobbies and spending time with loved ones a priority in order to maintain a work life balance.

As we wrap up this chapter it is clear that Virgos accomplishments in their careers and financial stability are a testament to their commitment to hard work. Their skill in navigating the complexities of work and wealth management is an asset that enriches not only their own lives but also the lives of those around them.

However, like everyone, Virgos face challenges such as striving for perfectionism and being overly critical of themselves. These challenges can be seen as opportunities for growth when acknowledged and addressed. May these insights give you the strength and clarity to navigate your journey, towards success and financial security while aligning with the order of the universe.

CHAPTER 5: SELF-IMPROVEMENT

In this chapter we set sail on an exploration, through the realm of self improvement. We are about to traverse the cosmos uncovering how Virgo individuals can utilize their qualities to become the versions of themselves. From their mindset and analytical thinking to their inclination towards perfectionism and critical nature. Virgos face unique advantages and challenges that shape their personal growth journey.

Join us as we delve into the choreography of self improvement, where Virgos strive relentlessly to become the best versions of themselves.

PERSONAL GROWTH AND DEVELOPMENT FOR VIRGO

People born under the zodiac sign of Virgo, possess a powerful set of qualities that can contribute to growth and development. That is when nurtured effectively. Here are some important aspects of growth for individuals with a Virgo zodiac sign.

- **Embrace Self Compassion**; Virgos often hold themselves to high standards. This can sometimes lead to self criticism and striving for perfection. Understand that making mistakes is acceptable. Ultimately one's self worth isn't solely determined by their achievements.
- **Find Balance in Attention to Detail;** While being detail oriented is a positive trait it's essential not to become overly consumed by the details. Virgos can experience growth by learning when to focus on specifics and when it's necessary to step back.
- **Explore Emotional Expression**; Virgos tend to approach life from a logical standpoint. They may find it challenging to express their emotions openly. Personal growth involves developing the ability to connect with emotions for improved relationships and self awareness.
- **Manage Worry and Anxiety**; It is common for Virgos to experience worry and anxiety. Practicing mindfulness, meditation or stress reduction techniques can greatly contribute to mental health.
- **Being adaptable**; While Virgos tend to appreciate routine and structure, personal growth often involves embracing change and being adaptable. Learning to be more flexible and open to experiences is key for development.
- **Listen intently**; Virgos are known for their precise communication skills, which's a strength. However personal growth can also involve improving listening skills.
- **Stepping out of the comfort zone;** Virgos have a tendency to avoid taking risks. Personal development however, often requires taking risks and stepping out of comfort zones. Embrace opportunities for growth and learning.
- **Set boundaries**; Virgos strong work ethic may sometimes lead them to overwork or neglecting their personal lives. Set boundaries, prioritize self care and find a work life balance.
- **Education**; Virgos love for knowledge and learning is an asset for growth. Continuously pursuing skills, hobbies or further education can lead to more personal development.
- **Seek Support and Feedback**; Although Virgos tend to prefer handling challenges themselves, seeking support can accelerate growth

To pursue growth and development effectively Virgos can tap into their qualities while embracing flexibility and self compassion. By maintaining a balance between their strengths and areas where they can grow further, Virgo individuals can evolve into more successful individuals.

HARNESSING STRENGTHS AND OVERCOMING WEAKNESSES

To lead fulfilling lives and unleash their fullest potential Virgos can utilize their qualities while also working on overcoming challenges. Here's a helpful guide on how to achieve that.

- **Attention to Detail (Strength);** Utilize your precise nature in roles that demand precision, such as data analysis, quality control or project management. To avoid hindering progress it's important not to get too caught up in details. Learn how to effectively prioritize tasks.

- **Strong Work Ethic (Strength);** Fully commit yourself to tasks and projects with the delivery of high quality results. However it's crucial to also keep an eye on maintaining a work life balance. Never neglect your well being.
- **Practicality (Strength);** Leverage your analytical mindset for solving real world problems and making decisions. At the same time make sure not to let practicality stifle creativity. Allow space for imaginative thinking.
- **Organization Skills (Strength);** Effectively manage schedules, tasks and resources to bring order out of chaos. Nevertheless avoid becoming too rigid in your approach. Embrace adaptability when planning.

- **Communication Skills (Strength);** Embrace the ability to express your thoughts and ideas clearly. This will help you to effectively communicate in many situations. To overcome any challenges, focus on listening to others. Understand other perspectives and build connections.
- **Analytical Thinking (Strength);** Leverage your skills to break down problems and offer practical solutions. Avoid getting caught up in overanalyzing situations as it can lead to indecisiveness. Trust your instincts when necessary.
- **Perfectionism (Weakness);** Striving for perfection is a great attitude. However it can be unrealistic. Recognize that making mistakes is a part of growth and development. Shift your focus from being overly critical, towards embracing criticism. Prioritize finding solutions rather than dwelling on problems.
- **Worry and Anxiety (Weakness);** Develop stress management techniques like mindfulness or meditation to reduce worry and anxiety.
- **Difficulty Expressing Emotions (Weakness);** Work on expressing your feelings particularly within personal relationships. Practice communicating emotions with authenticity.
- **Reluctance to Seek Help (Weakness);** Understand that seeking assistance is a sign of strength rather than weakness. Embrace the opportunity for growth by reaching out for support when needed.
- **Resistance to Change (Weakness);** View change as an avenue, for growth and learning. Embrace new opportunities instead of resisting them.
- **Self Criticism (Weakness);** To overcome self criticism it's essential to cultivate self compassion. Take the time to celebrate your achievements and recognize your worth, beyond accomplishments.
- **Balancing Work and Personal Life (Weakness);** Establishing boundaries between work and personal life is crucial. Prioritize self care. Make sure to spend quality time with loved ones.

By acknowledging strengths and actively addressing weaknesses Virgos can lead successful lives. As Virgos progress, on their journey of self improvement they not only become the finest versions of themselves but also serve as inspiring mentors.

In conclusion, this chapter has shed light on the path that Virgos tread, characterized by a focus on practicality, attention to detail and a constant drive towards reaching their potential. May this understanding ignite a renewed sense of enthusiasm and determination in Virgos. In addition may it also add value to those accompanying them as they embark on their expedition, towards self improvement.

CHAPTER 6:
THE YEAR AHEAD

The stars and planets have long been our celestial guides, providing a roadmap to navigate the intricacies of life. For Virgo individuals, the year ahead holds the promise of growth, transformation and many opportunities. While astrology doesn't dictate destiny, it does offer valuable insights.

Throughout this chapter, we'll delve into the influences of key astrological events, highlighting significant dates and time periods that hold particular importance. From the impact on love and relationships to career prospects, health, the potential for personal growth and much more.

Whether you are a Virgo seeking insights to make the most of the year ahead or someone interested in understanding how the stars align for Virgo. This chapter provides a celestial compass to navigate the cosmic currents that will shape the year ahead. Join us as we explore the cosmic dance of Virgo in the year ahead!

HOROSCOPE GUIDE FOR VIRGO INDIVIDUALS

The year ahead holds promise and opportunities for Virgo individuals. With your innate practicality and attention to detail, you can make significant strides in various areas of your life. Here's a glimpse of what the stars may have in store for you in the coming year.

CAREER AND FINANCES

Your career prospects look positive this year. Your meticulous approach and analytical thinking will help you excel in your current role or to take on new challenges. Be open to innovative solutions. Don't hesitate to share your ideas with colleagues. Financially, your careful budgeting and saving habits will pay off.

Astrological events can provide insights into potential career growth and financial stability. Here's a closer look at how the year's astrological events may impact Virgo individuals' professional lives.

- **Mercury Retrogrades** (Dates: Multiple throughout the year): Mercury, the ruling planet of Virgo, will have its retrograde periods. These can affect communication and decision-making at work. Exercise caution in professional interactions and avoid signing contracts during these times.
- **Saturn Transits** (Throughout the year): Saturn's influence may bring lessons and challenges in your career. Embrace responsibilities and challenges with discipline, as they can lead to long-term growth and success.
- **New Moons in Virgo** (Dates: To be determined): New Moons in Virgo are opportunities for setting practical career goals and initiating projects that align with your ambitions. Use this time to plan and focus on your professional growth.
- **Jupiter Transits** (Throughout the year): Jupiter's presence can expand your career horizons. Be open to new job opportunities, promotions, or collaborations. These may enhance your professional life and financial prospects.

LOVE AND RELATIONSHIPS

In matters of the heart, expect growth and deepening connections. For singles, there are chances to meet someone special through work or mutual interests. For those in relationships, open communication will strengthen your love. Be sure to balance your dedication to work with quality time for your loved ones. The stars favor harmony in your relationships this year.

Virgo individuals can anticipate a year influenced by astrological events that will impact their romantic lives. While the stars do not dictate destiny, they can offer guidance on potential opportunities and challenges. Here's a look at how astrological events in the upcoming year may influence Virgo individuals' love lives.

- **Venus in Virgo** (Date: August 16 to September 10): When Venus, the planet of love and harmony, enters Virgo, it can enhance Virgo individuals' romantic connections. This period offers an opportunity to strengthen existing relationships and express love.
- **New Moons in Virgo** (Dates: To be determined): New Moons signify new beginnings. When they occur in Virgo, they encourage Virgos to set practical relationship goals. It's a time for introspection, self-improvement and initiating positive changes.

- **Jupiter Transits** (Throughout the year): Jupiter's influence can bring expansion and growth to your love life. Be open to new experiences and connections. Jupiter's positive energy may lead to romantic opportunities and personal growth within relationships.
- **Lunar Eclipses** (Dates: To be determined): Lunar eclipses can bring revelations and shifts in your emotional life. Embrace changes in your relationships. Overall they often pave the way for personal growth and positive transformation.

HEALTH AND WELL-BEING

Maintaining good health should always be a priority. Pay attention to your stress levels. Your natural tendency to worry can affect your well-being. Consider incorporating mindfulness practices. For example yoga or meditation. A balanced diet and regular exercise will further contribute to your overall vitality.

Astrological events can offer insights into how you can maintain your well-being. Here's a look at how the year's astrological events may affect Virgo individuals' health and wellness.

- **Lunar Eclipses** (Dates: To be determined): Lunar eclipses may signal the need for change in your daily routines and habits. Embrace these opportunities for self-improvement and prioritize self-care practices.

- **Venus in Virgo** (Date: August 16 to September 10): During this period, focus on self-love and self-care. Pamper yourself and engage in activities that promote emotional and physical well-being.
- **Mindfulness and Stress Management**: Given Virgo's tendency to worry, consider incorporating mindfulness, meditation, or stress-reduction techniques into your daily routine. These practices can help manage anxiety and promote overall health.

PERSONAL GROWTH AND SPIRITUALITY

The year ahead offers numerous opportunities for personal growth and self-discovery. Embrace change and step out of your comfort zone to explore new horizons. Pursue hobbies or interests that ignite your creativity and passion. Engaging in spiritual practices or self-reflection can provide valuable insights into your inner self. Astrological events can guide you on this journey of self-improvement. Here's how you can use these events to facilitate personal growth.

- **New Moons in Virgo** (Dates: To be determined): Utilize New Moons in Virgo as moments of introspection and goal-setting. Set intentions for self-improvement. Take practical steps toward personal growth.
- **Jupiter Transits** (Throughout the year): Embrace new experiences and opportunities for growth. Jupiter's positive influence can expand your horizons and lead to personal development in various aspects of your life.
- **Lunar Eclipses** (Dates: To be determined): Welcome changes and transformations, even if they initially feel challenging. Lunar eclipses often signify moments of growth and self-discovery.

FAMILY AND HOME LIFE

Family relationships will be a source of support and joy this year. Plan quality time with loved ones to nurture these bonds. If you've been considering home-related changes, such as redecorating or moving, this could be a perfect time.

TRAVEL AND ADVENTURE

If travel is on your mind, the stars encourage exploration and adventure. Whether it's a short getaway or a more extended journey. Truly, you'll find inspiration and personal growth through new experiences. Embrace spontaneity and relish the unexpected.

SOCIAL LIFE

Your social circle may expand this year. Networking could lead to exciting opportunities. Attend social events, join clubs, or participate in group activities to broaden your connections. Your practical advice and problem-solving abilities will make you a valuable member of any community.

Ultimately as a Virgo individual, you have the potential to make the most of the year ahead. Do this by being proactive in your love life, career, health and personal growth. The stars offer guidance, but it's your actions and choices that will ultimately shape your journey in the coming year.

KEY ASTROLOGICAL EVENTS AND THEIR IMPACT ON VIRGO:

Astrological events can have a significant influence on the lives and experiences of individuals born under the Virgo sign. These celestial occurrences can shape various aspects of Virgos' lives, including their personal growth, relationships and career. Here are some key astrological events and their potential impact on Virgo individuals.

Mercury Retrogrades

- Impact: Mercury is the ruling planet of Virgo, and its retrogrades may affect communication and decision-making.
- Advice: During Mercury retrogrades, be extra cautious with contracts, communication and travel plans. Take time to review and revise and practice patience in all interactions.

New Moons in Virgo

- Impact: New Moons signify new beginnings, and when they occur in Virgo, it's a time for setting practical goals and initiating projects.
- Advice: Use New Moons in Virgo as opportunities to make plans, set intentions and focus on self-improvement.

Full Moons in Pisces (Opposite Sign)

- Impact: Full Moons in Pisces, the opposite sign of Virgo, can bring emotional intensity and challenges.
- Advice: Be mindful of heightened emotions during these periods. Balance your practicality with empathy and self-care.

Jupiter Transits

- Impact: When Jupiter, the planet of expansion and growth, transits through Virgo or compatible signs, it can bring opportunities. Both for personal and professional development.
- Advice: Embrace new opportunities and take calculated risks. Explore areas of personal growth during Jupiter transits.

Saturn Transits

- Impact: Saturn transits can bring lessons and challenges, pushing Virgos to mature and take on greater responsibilities.
- Advice: Face challenges with determination and discipline. Saturn's influence can lead to long-term growth and success.

Venus in Virgo

- Impact: When Venus, the planet of love and harmony, enters Virgo, it can enhance Virgo individuals' relationships.

- Advice: Use this time to nurture existing relationships and engage in acts of self-love and self-care.

Solar Eclipses

- Impact: Solar eclipses can bring significant changes and new beginnings. Their influence varies depending on the eclipse's position in the zodiac.
- Advice: Pay attention to eclipses in compatible signs, as they may signal opportunities for growth and transformation.

Lunar Eclipses

- Impact: Lunar eclipses can signal the culmination of projects or relationships, bringing closure and revelations.
- Advice: Embrace the changes that lunar eclipses bring, even if they initially feel challenging. They often pave the way for positive transformations.

Ultimately it's important to remember that astrological events provide a framework for understanding cosmic energies. However individual experiences may vary. While astrology provides a compass it is ultimately the choices we make as Virgos that shape our destiny. Virgo individuals can use astrology as a tool for self-awareness and personal growth. They can make the most of favorable influences and navigate challenges with wisdom.

Reflecting upon these insights we can gather guidance for Virgo individuals as they navigate the year ahead. The alignment of stars and planets has created a tapestry of influences that bring forth both opportunities and challenges in love, relationships, career, finances, health, wellness, personal growth and self discovery. Throughout this year's journey it is important for Virgo individuals to embrace change willingly while nurturing their relationships. Prioritizing self care and actively pursuing growth with determination will also prove to be beneficial.

The celestial events highlighted in this chapter provide moments for reflection, setting goals and experiencing transformation. May the year ahead be filled with love, success, good health and personal growth. The universe provides its guidance. In the end it's up to you to navigate your journey. Take the opportunity for a rewarding and purposeful year. A great one is within your reach!

CHAPTER 7: FAMOUS "VIRGO" PERSONALITIES

Virgos are widely recognized for their attention to detail, unwavering work ethic and their relentless pursuit of perfection. In this chapter we embark on a journey exploring the lives and accomplishments of famous people born under the zodiac of Virgo. As we delve into these profiles you will discover the Virgo qualities and traits that define them. From musicians and legendary actors, to leaders and celebrated authors, Virgos have made lasting impressions in many domains.

Join us on this tour as we delve into their lives, careers and contributions. Lets celebrate their dedication, precision driven approach and tireless pursuit of excellence. Their stories stand as a testament to the potential possessed by those born under the sign of Virgo. Furthermore they provide inspiration for all who aspire to excel in their chosen paths.

MICHAEL JACKSON

- Date of Birth: August 29, 1958.
- Brief Biography: Michael Jackson, often referred to as the "King of Pop," was a legendary American singer, songwriter and dancer. He rose to fame as a member of the Jackson 5. Later he enjoyed a highly successful solo career. His groundbreaking albums, including "Thriller," remain some of the best-selling in music history.
- Virgo Traits: Meticulous attention to detail, strong work ethic and dedication to his craft.
- Impact: Michael Jackson's influence on the music industry is immeasurable. He revolutionized pop music, set new standards for music videos and left an enduring legacy. His philanthropic efforts also left a significant impact on humanitarian causes.

- Personal Life: Despite his worldwide fame, Jackson was known for his private and enigmatic persona. He faced numerous controversies and legal challenges throughout his life. Jackson's untimely death in 2009 marked the end of an era in music. He left behind a legacy that continues to inspire and entertain.

BARBARA BACH

- Date of Birth: August 27, 1947.
- Brief Biography: Barbara Bach is an American actress and model best known for her roles in the James Bond film "The Spy Who Loved Me" and the fantasy film "Caveman." She gained international recognition for her beauty and acting talent during the 1970s and 1980s.
- Virgo Traits: Attention to detail, strong work ethic and commitment to her career.
- Impact: Barbara Bach's presence in Hollywood during her prime left an indelible mark on the film industry. Her performances and beauty made her a prominent figure in the entertainment world.
- Personal Life: Barbara Bach's personal life includes her marriage to Ringo Starr, the drummer of The Beatles. She has also been involved in various

charitable endeavors and continues to be a beloved figure in the entertainment industry.

KOBE BRYANT

- Date of Birth: August 23, 1978.
- Brief Biography: Kobe Bryant was an iconic American professional basketball player who spent his entire 20-year career with the Los Angeles Lakers in the NBA. He is regarded as one of the greatest basketball players of all time, winning numerous championships and accolades.
- Virgo Traits: Exceptional work ethic and dedication to his sport.
- Impact: Kobe Bryant's impact on the game of basketball and sports culture as a whole is immense. He inspired countless athletes with his competitive spirit, leadership and commitment to excellence.
- Personal Life: In addition to his basketball career, Kobe Bryant was a loving husband and father. His tragic death in a helicopter crash in 2020 was a profound loss for the sports world and beyond, leaving a lasting legacy of determination and passion.

MOTHER TERESA

- Date of Birth: August 26, 1910.
- Brief Biography: Mother Teresa, known as Saint Teresa of Calcutta, was an Albanian-Indian Roman Catholic nun and missionary. She devoted her life to helping the poor, sick and needy in the slums of India. She also founded the Missionaries of Charity, a religious congregation.

- Virgo Traits: Compassionate and devoted to serving others.
- Impact: Mother Teresa's selfless work and dedication to the poor earned her worldwide recognition. She was awarded the Nobel Peace Prize in 1979 for her humanitarian efforts.
- Personal Life: Mother Teresa's life was dedicated to her religious calling and her mission to help those in need. Her work continues to inspire people around the world to selflessly serve others.

LYNDON B. JOHNSON

- Date of Birth: August 27, 1908.
- Brief Biography: Lyndon B. Johnson, often referred to as LBJ, was the 36th President of the United States, serving from 1963 to 1969. He played a pivotal role in advancing civil rights legislation and implementing his "Great Society" programs during his presidency.
- Virgo Traits: Strong work ethic and commitment to public service.
- Impact: Lyndon B. Johnson's presidency left a lasting impact on civil rights, education and healthcare.
- Personal Life: LBJ's personal life was marked by his dedication to public service. His presidency, while tumultuous, was defined by his commitment to social reform and the betterment of American society.

BEYONCE

- Date of Birth: September 4, 1981.
- Brief Biography: Beyoncé Knowles-Carter is an American singer, songwriter, actress and businesswoman. She rose to fame as a member of Destiny's Child and later pursued a highly successful solo career. Beyoncé is renowned for her powerful voice, dynamic performances and influence in the music industry.
- Virgo Traits: Strong work ethic, dedication to her craft and attention to detail.
- Impact: Beyoncé's impact on music and popular culture is immeasurable. She is celebrated for her vocal talent, stage presence and contributions to social justice through her art.
- Personal Life: Beyoncé is known for her privacy. She has been involved in various charitable endeavors and advocacy work. Her marriage to Jay-Z and their family life have garnered significant media attention.

CHARLIE SHEEN

- Date of Birth: September 3, 1965.
- Brief Biography: Charlie Sheen is an American actor known for his roles in films such as "Platoon" and the television series "Two and a Half Men." He has been a prominent figure in both film and television throughout his career.
- Virgo Traits: Strong work ethic, particularly in his acting career.
- Impact: Charlie Sheen's career has had its share of highs and lows. His talent and charisma have made him a recognizable and influential figure in the entertainment industry.
- Personal Life: Sheen's personal life has been marked by controversies and public struggles, including issues with substance abuse. Despite these challenges, he remains a figure of interest in the world of entertainment.

COLONEL SANDERS

- Date of Birth: September 9, 1890.
- Brief Biography: Colonel Harland Sanders was an American businessman and the founder of Kentucky Fried Chicken (KFC). His famous recipe for fried chicken and his franchise system revolutionized the fast-food industry.
- Virgo Traits: Strong work ethic, particularly in building his business empire.
- Impact: Colonel Sanders' entrepreneurial spirit and dedication to his fried chicken recipe led to the worldwide success of KFC. His legacy endures through the global popularity of the brand.
- Personal Life: Sanders' life was centered around his business endeavors, and his dedication to KFC made him an iconic figure in the fast-food industry.

AMY WINEHOUSE

- Date of Birth: September 14, 1983.
- Brief Biography: Amy Winehouse was an English singer and songwriter known for her distinctive voice. She achieved critical acclaim and commercial success during her brief career.
- Virgo Traits: Strong dedication to her music and songwriting. Attention to detail in her vocal delivery and compositions.
- Impact: Amy Winehouse's music left a lasting impact on the music industry. Her album "Back to Black" received widespread acclaim and recognition, earning her multiple Grammy Awards.

- Personal Life: Winehouse's personal life was marked by struggles with addiction and mental health issues. Her tragic death in 2011 at a young age was a profound loss to the music world.

AGATHA CHRISTIE

- Date of Birth: September 15, 1890.
- Brief Biography: Agatha Christie was an English writer known as the "Queen of Mystery." She authored numerous detective novels, short stories and plays. These include iconic works like "Murder on the Orient Express" and "Death on the Nile."
- Virgo Traits: Attention to detail in crafting intricate mysteries. Strong work ethic in producing a vast body of work.
- Impact: Agatha Christie's detective novels have captivated readers for generations. Her characters Hercule Poirot and Miss Marple have become iconic figures in the mystery genre.
- Personal Life: Christie's personal life was marked by her love of writing and her prolific output as an author. Her works continue to be celebrated in literature and adapted into various forms of media.

LARRY NELSON

- Date of Birth: August 10, 1947.
- Brief Biography: Larry Nelson is a retired American professional golfer known for his achievements in the sport. He won three major championships and had a successful career on the PGA Tour.
- Virgo Traits: Strong work ethic and dedication to golf.
- Impact: Larry Nelson's impact on professional golf is evident through his major championship victories and successful career. He is respected for his golfing abilities and contributions to the sport.
- Personal Life: Nelson's personal life revolves around his passion for golf. He continues to be involved in the sport as a course designer and commentator, sharing his expertise with the golfing community.

CAMERON DIAZ

- Date of Birth: August 30, 1972.

- Brief Biography: Cameron Diaz is an American actress, producer and author. She is well known for her roles in films such as "There's Something About Mary" and "Charlie's Angels."
- Virgo Traits: Strong work ethic and commitment to her acting career.
- Impact: Cameron Diaz's talent and charisma have made her a prominent figure in Hollywood. Her contributions to film and her versatile acting roles have garnered her wide spread recognition and acclaim.
- Personal Life: While Diaz has kept a relatively private personal life. She has been involved in various philanthropic endeavors and continues to be a beloved figure in the entertainment world.

These profiles offer a glimpse into the lives and traits of famous individuals born under the Virgo sign. They showcase their unique talents and contributions to various fields. While their journeys differ, they all exemplify the diligence, attention to detail and pursuit of excellence often associated with Virgo individuals.

From the glitz and glamor of Hollywood to the world's heights. From sports arenas, green fields to the enchanting melodies of music. Virgos have engraved their names in history. Their impact resonates not only in their fields but also in the hearts and minds of countless admirers worldwide.

As we celebrate the Virgo personalities showcased in this chapter we encourage you to draw inspiration from their journeys. Whether you share their birthdate or simply share a desire for excellence. Always remember that while stars may guide us it is your determination, work and attention to detail that will ultimately shape your path towards greatness.

Let the tales of these Virgo's serve as a reminder that striving for excellence and dedicating oneself to their chosen path with unwavering pursuit are qualities that lead to success. Embrace these attributes and may your own journey be just as extraordinary and motivating

CONCLUSION

As we draw the celestial curtain on this book dedicated to the Virgo star sign, we invite you to embark on one final exploration. One that summarizes the intricate tapestry that weaves through the lives of those born between August 23 and September 22. This concluding chapter serves as a celestial compass, guiding us through the key points and insights shared throughout the book.

In our journey through the world of Virgo, we've uncovered a rich tapestry of traits, influences and insights that define this zodiac sign. Let's now take a moment to revisit the key points and discoveries that have illuminated the Virgo personality.

- **The Pragmatic Perfectionist**: Virgos are known for their meticulous attention to detail and their relentless pursuit of perfection in all aspects of life, making them excellent problem-solvers and organizers.
- **The Earth Element:** As an Earth sign, Virgos are grounded, practical and deeply connected to the physical world. They find comfort in the tangible and often excel in hands-on tasks.
- **Mercury's Influence**: Mercury, the ruling planet of Virgo, bestows intellectual acumen, effective communication skills and a love for learning upon Virgo individuals.
- **Symbolism**: The symbol of the Virgin represents purity, virtue and a desire for order. Virgos seek to harmonize their inner and outer worlds.
- **Virgo in Love**: Virgo individuals approach love and relationships with thoughtfulness and care. They seek partners who appreciate their attention to detail and appreciate practical gestures of love.
- **Compatibility**: Virgos often find compatibility with Taurus, Capricorn and other Earth signs. Water signs like Cancer and Scorpio also connect well with them, balancing their practicality with emotional depth.
- **Challenges**: Virgos' pursuit of perfection can lead to self-criticism and anxiety. Learning to balance their high standards with self-compassion is essential for their well-being.

- **Friends and Family**: Virgos are loyal and dependable friends and family members. They value close relationships and often serve as anchors in their social circles.
- **Career and Money**: Virgos excel in careers that require attention to detail, problem-solving, and organization. Their strong work ethic often leads to financial stability and success.
- **Personal Growth**: Virgos can harness their analytical skills and practicality to achieve personal growth and self-improvement. Setting realistic goals and focusing on self-care are key to their development.

Throughout this book we've taken a journey to uncover what makes the Virgo zodiac sign unique. We've explored its history, delved into its personality traits and examined how Virgos handle various aspects of life. Including love and relationships, career choices, personal development and much more.

Our main goal has been to provide understanding and a roadmap for both Virgos themselves and those interested in this sign. We aim to highlight the nature of Virgo by emphasizing their strengths while addressing challenges they may face. Additionally we offer advice to help individuals close with the Virgo sign, thrive.

The core message of this book is crystal clear; Virgos stand out with their attention to detail, unwavering pursuit of excellence in all they do well. This in addition to their dedication, towards self improvement and caring for others. We encourage readers to embrace these qualities recognizing that they are not simply characteristics but powerful tools, for growth and fulfillment.

Ultimately this book showcases astrology as a perspective that helps us better understand ourselves and the world around us. It provides insights into the forces that shape our lives and promotes self awareness, self acceptance and personal development.

In conclusion we urge individuals born under the sign of Virgo to wholeheartedly embrace their qualities. Your dedication, practicality and attention to detail are attributes that can lead to great accomplishments and meaningful connections. By aligning your traits with your aspirations you can confidently navigate life's dance with purpose.

As we conclude this voyage remember that you are not confined by the stars; rather you are in control of your destiny. You are the captain steering your ship through the celestial seas. May the insights of Virgo and the influence of astrology inspire you to navigate a path of deep fulfillment and joy.

As we wrap up this exploration of the Virgo zodiac sign we find ourselves immersed in a realm of wisdom, groundedness and commitment. The sharp intellect and compassionate hearts of Virgos remind us that striving for perfection is not a fixed destination. Rathermore it is an ongoing journey towards self growth and self discovery.

In conclusion let us honor the presence of Virgo individuals in our lives and acknowledge the contributions they make to our world. Their unwavering dedication to excellence, meticulous attention to detail and boundless capacity for compassion are blessings that enrich our existence.

May this book serve as a guiding light, for both Virgos themselves and those seeking an understanding of them. As we bid farewell to this book may the wisdom associated with the Virgo sign continue to illuminate your path. May it lead you towards a life brimming with purpose, personal development and your own pursuit of excellence.

LIBRA:

A COMPLETE GUIDE TO THE LIBRA ASTROLOGY STAR SIGN

Contents

INTRODUCTION 1

Libra Zodiac Sign Overview 2

CHAPTER 1: HISTORY AND MYTHOLOGY 5

Historical Origins of the Libra Constellation 5

Historical Events Under the Libra Season 7

CHAPTER 2: LOVE & COMPATIBILITY 10

The Libra Love approach 11

Compatibility with Other Zodiac Signs 12

Tips for Dating and Maintaining Relationships with Libra 15

CHAPTER 3: FRIENDS AND FAMILY 17

Libra as a Friend 18

Libra and Family Dynamics 19

Challenges in Friendships and Family Relations for Libra 20

CHAPTER 4: CAREER AND MONEY 23

Career Preferences and Professional Aspirations 24

Strengths in the Workplace 25

Challenges Faced by Libra and Strategies to Overcome Them 27

CHAPTER 5: SELF-IMPROVEMENT 30

Personal Growth and Development 31

Harnessing Libra Strengths and Overcoming Weaknesses 32

CHAPTER 6: THE YEAR AHEAD 35

Horoscope Guide 35

Key Astrological Events and Their Impact on Libra 37

Key Life Areas 38

CHAPTER 7: FAMOUS LIBRA PERSONALITIES 42
Mahatma Gandhi 42
Serena Williams 43
John Lennon 43
Brigitte Bardot 44
Eminem 44
Margaret Thatcher 45
Dwight D. Eisenhower 45
Elisabeth Shue 45
Cardi B 46
Vladimir Putin 46
Alfred Nobel 47
Barbara Walters 47
CONCLUSION -- 49

INTRODUCTION

Welcome to the captivating world of astrology, where the movements of entities hold significance for our lives on Earth. At its core, astrology is an intricate belief system. One that examines the relationship between the positions and motions of bodies like planets and stars and their impact on human existence and personality traits. It is a field with roots that trace back thousands of years, across cultures worldwide.

Astrology operates under the principle that the positions of objects at the time of an individual's birth can provide insights into their character, behaviors and potential life paths. The positions of these bodies within the twelve zodiac signs form unique cosmic blueprints for each person known as birth charts. Astrologers interpret these charts to offer guidance, self awareness and a deeper understanding of oneself as well as their interactions with others.

In this book we embark on a journey to explore one of the signs of astrology. The Libra zodiac sign. The main objective of this book is to shed light on the mysterious Libra zodiac sign. If you happen to be a Libra or have someone close to you who is, then this book can serve as your window into unraveling the enigmatic traits of this air sign.

Our journey into Libra's world will include:

- **Understanding Libra:** We will explore the core traits, strengths and weaknesses of Libra individuals. Overall you will gain a comprehensive understanding of their unique character.
- **Love and Relationships**: Libras are renowned for their romantic and partnership-oriented nature. We will delve into how Libras approach love and relationships. Furthermore we will explore their compatibility with other zodiac signs.
- **Career and Ambitions**: Libras have a knack for diplomacy and collaboration. We will explore how these traits influence their career choices, work style and professional success.
- **Self-Discovery**: This book will serve as a tool for Libras and anyone interested in astrology to embark on a journey of self-discovery. We'll provide insights into personal growth and harnessing Libra's innate qualities for personal development.
- **Astrological Guidance**: You'll find guidance on harnessing Libra's strengths, managing challenges and aligning with the cosmic energies to lead a fulfilling life.

Throughout this book, we'll draw on the wisdom of astrology, drawing connections between the celestial world and your personal experiences. Whether you're a Libra seeking to deepen your self-awareness or simply curious about astrology and its influence on your life. This promises to be an enlightening journey into the world of astrology and the captivating Libra star sign.

LIBRA ZODIAC SIGN OVERVIEW

- **Date of Star Sign**: Libra falls between September 23rd and October 22nd, making it the seventh sign of the zodiac.
- **Symbol**: The symbol of Libra is the Scales, representing balance, harmony and justice. The scales are an emblem of the Libra's quest for equilibrium and fairness in all aspects of life.
- **Element**: Libra belongs to the Air element, along with Gemini and Aquarius. Air signs are associated with intellect, communication and social interaction. Libras are skilled at using their mental faculties to navigate the complexities of relationships and society.
- **Planet**: Venus, the planet of love and beauty, is the ruling planet of Libra. Venus brings a sense of refinement, charm and aesthetic appreciation to Libra's personality and pursuits.

- **Color**: Libra's primary color is typically considered to be blue. Particularly shades that evoke peace and tranquility. Blue reflects their desire for balance and serenity in life.
- **Personality Traits**: Libras are known for their charming and diplomatic nature. They possess a strong sense of fairness. Their desire for harmony often leads them to seek compromise and avoid conflict.

COMPATIBILITY

Libras are most compatible with fellow Air signs like Gemini and Aquarius. They share similar intellectual and communicative qualities. They also tend to get along well with Fire signs, such as Aries, Leo and Sagittarius. These bring passion and energy to the relationship. However, their diplomatic nature means that Libras can also establish harmonious connections with individuals of various zodiac signs.

STRENGTHS

- **Charm and Grace:** Libras have an innate ability to put people at ease with their charm and social skills.
- **Diplomacy**: They excel at mediating conflicts and finding common ground in disputes.
- **Artistic Sensibility**: With Venus as their ruling planet, Libras often have a strong appreciation for art, beauty and aesthetics.
- **Fairness**: Libras have a strong sense of justice and fairness and are often advocates for equality.

WEAKNESSES

- **Indecisiveness:** Libras' desire for balance and harmony can sometimes lead to indecisiveness, as they weigh all options carefully.
- **Avoidance of Conflict**: They may avoid confrontations to maintain peace, even when addressing issues is necessary.
- **Dependency**: Libras may struggle with a tendency to seek validation and approval from others, which can lead to dependency.
- **Superficiality**: Their focus on aesthetics and surface harmony may sometimes make them appear superficial.

Welcome once again to our exploration of Libra! Symbolized by the scales representing balance, harmony and justice, Libra stands as the seventh sign in the zodiac. Governed by Venus and classified as an Air sign individuals with a Libra Sun are renowned for their charm, impartiality and artistic sensibilities. However, like all signs in astrology, they possess both strengths and weaknesses.

Subsequent chapters will take us on a journey into all aspects of Libras realm. We will unravel intricacies surrounding Libra's personality traits while delving into their perspectives on love and relationships. Furthermore we will uncover how their innate qualities influence their paths and personal development. Expect insights into compatibility, between Libra individuals and other zodiac signs while receiving guidance on embracing their strengths and overcoming challenges along the way.

Get ready to embark on an adventure of self exploration and growth! Whether you're a Libra searching for self awareness or simply curious about the world of astrology this guarantees to be an enriching and fulfilling exploration. Come along with us as we unravel the secrets of Libra and unlock its full power.

CHAPTER 1:
HISTORY AND MYTHOLOGY

In this chapter we embark on an exploration of history and mythology. A journey to uncover the significance of the Libra star sign. Its roots extend far back into the fabric of civilization. As we delve into this chapter's pages we will journey back to ancient civilizations to explore some of the first observations and interpretations of Libra. From ancient stargazers to mythological tales we will discover how different cultures perceived and depicted Libra.

Our exploration doesn't end with history and astronomy alone. We will also meet Libra individuals who have shaped history and truly left a mark on our world. Furthermore we will examine the evolution of how Libra has been perceived and understood from ancient times up until today.

Now let us embark on a voyage through history and mythology influenced by the Libra zodiac sign. Together we will unveil the timeless wisdom and lasting impact of Libra!

HISTORICAL ORIGINS OF THE LIBRA CONSTELLATION

The constellation Libra, has a rich history dating back to ancient civilizations. Over the centuries, its symbolism has continued to evolve and influence culture. Here's a glimpse into some of its earliest history.

BABYLONIAN ASTRONOMY

The earliest known observations of Libra can be traced back to ancient Mesopotamia, particularly Babylon. The Babylonians recognized the stars within the constellation as early as 2000 BCE. They associated Libra with the concept of justice and balance. This was reflected in their legal and societal systems.

ANCIENT GREEK INFLUENCE

The Ancient Greeks adopted the Babylonian constellation system, incorporating Libra into their own celestial maps. However, in Greek mythology, Libra is often linked to the scales held by Astraea. She is the goddess of justice and is believed to have lived among humans during the Golden Age. She symbolizes the harmony and balance that humanity once enjoyed.

Themis, another Greek goddess of justice, is often associated with the scales. Her daughter, Dike, represents the concept of moral justice. The presence of these deities in Greek mythology underscores the idea of balance and fairness associated with Libra.

ROMAN INTERPRETATION

The Romans, influenced by Greek astronomy and mythology, adopted the concept of Libra as the Scales of Justice. The Roman association with this constellation further solidified its significance in matters of law and fairness.

CHINESE AND ARABIC VIEWS

In Chinese astronomy, the stars of Libra are often incorporated into other constellations, such as the adjacent Scorpius. Arabic astronomers, too, didn't have a distinct constellation corresponding to Libra. However they recognized the stars within it.

HINDU PERSPECTIVE

In Hindu astrology, the concept of Libra is not tied to a specific constellation. Instead it is represented through the zodiac sign of Tula. Tula is associated with balance and fairness. It is represented by a scale or a balance.

EGYPTIAN MYTHOLOGY

In Egyptian mythology the representation of Libra as we know it in contemporary astrology did not exist. However the core idea of balance and order which Libra represents in astrology held importance in their cosmology and religious beliefs.

Although there was no equivalent to the zodiac sign of Libra in Egypt the concept of balance and justice embodied by Libra found personification in the goddess Ma'at. Ma'at played a role in religion symbolizing truth, equilibrium order, harmony, lawfulness, morality and justice. Depictions often portrayed her with a feather adorning her hair. A feather that symbolizes truth itself.

HISTORICAL EVENTS UNDER THE LIBRA SEASON

Throughout history, many important events have occurred during the "Libra" season. Some astrologers believe these events may carry astrological significance. Here are some notable events which have occurred during the Libra season.

- **The Signing of the United Nations Charter** (June 26, 1945): The establishment of the United Nations, an organization aimed at promoting peace and cooperation among nations, occurred during the Libra season. This event aligns with Libra's association with diplomacy and balance.
- **The Start of the French Revolution** (September 17, 1789): The French Revolution began during the Libra season. This was a period marked by calls for equality, justice and social harmony.

- **The Fall of the Berlin Wall** (November 9, 1989): The collapse of the Berlin Wall symbolized the reunification of East and West Germany. It occurred during the Scorpio-Libra cusp. This event represented a dramatic shift toward balance and reconciliation in a divided world.

HISTORICAL FIGURES BORN UNDER THE LIBRA SIGN

Several historical figures born under the Libra sign have made significant impacts on history.

- **Mahatma Gandhi** (October 2, 1869): Gandhi, born under the Libra sign, was a symbol of peace and nonviolent resistance. His leadership played a pivotal role in India's struggle for independence. He inspired movements for civil rights and freedom worldwide.
- **Eleanor Roosevelt** (October 11, 1884): As an American diplomat, humanitarian, and former First Lady, Eleanor Roosevelt advocated for civil rights, women's rights and social justice during her time. Her Libra traits of diplomacy and advocacy for fairness are evident in her legacy.

As we come to the end of this chapter we look back on the stories and historical significance associated with the Libra zodiac sign. From its early observations to modern astronomy, Libra has consistently represented values like balance, justice and harmony. The enduring legacy of Libra continues to have an impact today. Ultimately the teachings of Libra inspire all of us to seek equilibrium in our lives, fairness in our interactions and to appreciate beauty in life.

FURTHER READING AND REFERENCES

For readers eager to delve deeper into the history and mythology of Libra, as well as astrology in general, here is a list of primary sources, ancient texts and modern writings:

- **"Babylonian Star Catalogs"** - Explore ancient Babylonian records to uncover the earliest references to Libra in astronomy and astrology.
- **"The Works of Ptolemy"** - Ptolemy's "Tetrabiblos" is a classic text that delves into the principles of Western astrology.
- **"The Greek Myths"** by Robert Graves - This comprehensive work delves into Greek mythology, shedding light on the stories and deities associated with Libra's symbolism.
- **"Astrology: A Guide to Understanding Your Birth Chart" by Kevin Burk** - This modern guide offers a practical approach to understanding astrology, including insights into Libra's personality traits and influences.
- **"The Secret Language of Birthdays"** by Gary Goldschneider and Joost Elffers - This book provides detailed personality profiles for each day of the year, including those born under the Libra sign.
- **Online Resources**: Explore astrology websites, forums, and academic journals to keep up with the latest research and interpretations related to Libra and astrology in general.

CHAPTER 2: LOVE & COMPATIBILITY

Few topics in the realm of astrology generate as much intrigue and curiosity as love and compatibility. In this chapter we embark on an exploration of how the Libra star sign approaches love and its compatibility with zodiac signs. We explore their qualities, desires and tendencies when it comes to love. From their pursuit of balance and partnership to their diplomatic disposition. In the following pages we uncover what makes Libra individuals such captivating companions in relationships.

However our exploration doesn't end with Libra. We will also examine how Libra's compatibility plays out with each of the twelve zodiac signs. If you're a Libra looking for insights into your love life or if you're fascinated by how astrology influences relationships this chapter will provide guidance.

THE LIBRA LOVE APPROACH

People born under the sign of Libra are seen as romantic and inclined towards building long term relationships. Let's take a closer look at how Libras approach love and romance.

- **Striving for Balance**; Libras are ruled by Venus, the planet of love and beauty. This greatly influences their perspective on romance. They aim to create equilibrium and harmony in all aspects of their lives including their relationships.
- **Focusing on Partnership**; Libras value the concept of partnership and companionship. They thrive when they are in a loving relationship. For them connection and shared experiences are musts. Being single for long periods does not typically satisfy a Libra. Ultimately they yearn to share their life with another.
- **Exuding Charm and Grace;** Libras are renowned for their charm, grace and impeccable manners. Overall this makes them especially appealing in matters of love. Furthermore they utilize their skills to create an inviting ambiance filled with romance.
- **Loyalty**; Once Libras are committed to a relationship they display unwavering loyalty and take their commitments seriously. They are willing to work through any challenges that arise to ensure harmony in their partnership. As such they expect their partners to reciprocate the same level of trust.
- **Conflict Avoidance**; Libras have an aversion to conflicts and confrontations. They prioritize maintaining peace and avoiding arguments within their relationships. While this trait can be considered positive it can also result in issues that require attention.
- **Appreciation for Aesthetics**; Libras possess an admiration for beauty and aesthetics. Art, music and the finer aspects of life hold beauty for them which they eagerly share with their partners.
- **Emphasis on Communication**; Effective communication holds importance for Libras when it comes to love. They value honest conversations with their partners as these conversations foster better harmony within the relationship. Libras excel at listening to others perspectives while empathizing with their loved ones emotions.

To sum it up when it comes to love and romance, Libras strive for equilibrium, charm and dedication. They have an inclination towards romantic gestures and place great importance on maintaining harmony in their relationships. While their desire for balance can be advantageous it is crucial for Libras to find ways to address conflicts in their pursuit of long lasting love.

COMPATIBILITY WITH OTHER ZODIAC SIGNS

LIBRA AND ARIES

Libra and Aries are both cardinal signs, which means they share a strong desire for leadership and action. While they have different approaches (Libra seeks balance, Aries seeks assertiveness), their dynamic can be invigorating and passionate. Libra can help Aries refine their impulsive nature. Aries can encourage Libra to be more decisive. With effort and understanding, this pairing can find a harmonious balance between Libra's diplomacy and Aries' enthusiasm.

LIBRA AND TAURUS

Libra and Taurus are both ruled by Venus. This connects them through a shared appreciation for beauty and sensuality. Taurus' stability and Libra's charm can create a secure and enjoyable partnership. Libra may introduce Taurus to more social experiences. Taurus can ground Libra in practicality. Their shared love of the finer things in life can make them compatible. However they may need to navigate Taurus' stubbornness and Libra's indecisiveness.

LIBRA AND GEMINI

Libra and Gemini are both air signs, fostering excellent communication and intellectual connection. They share a love for socializing, learning and exploration. This makes for a lively and engaging partnership. Libra's diplomacy can help ease Gemini's tendency to be indecisive. Gemini can stimulate Libra's curiosity. Their mental connection and shared interests often lead to a harmonious relationship.

LIBRA AND CANCER

Libra and Cancer have contrasting emotional needs and communication styles. Libra values harmony and intellectual connection. Cancer seeks emotional security and nurturing. Their differences may lead to misunderstandings. However, with effort, they can learn from each other. Libra can help Cancer express emotions more openly. Cancer can teach Libra the importance of emotional depth and security.

LIBRA AND LEO

Libra and Leo both appreciate socializing, beauty, and aesthetics, creating a vibrant and affectionate bond. Leo's warmth and generosity align well with Libra's charm and diplomacy. Both signs enjoy the finer things in life and can create an elegant and stylish partnership. Libra's willingness to compromise can help mitigate Leo's occasional need for attention.

LIBRA AND VIRGO

Libra and Virgo have significant differences in their approaches to life. Libra's focus is on balance. Virgo's is on details and practicality. Their connection may require effort. Libra may find Virgo too critical. Virgo may see Libra as indecisive. However, with patience and understanding, they can learn from each other. Overall they can create a complementary partnership.

LIBRA AND LIBRA

Two Libras share a strong intellectual connection and an appreciation for beauty and harmony. They value balance in their relationship and are skilled at resolving conflicts diplomatically. However, they may struggle with decision-making, as both tend to weigh options extensively. Overall, their shared values and social compatibility can create a harmonious partnership.

LIBRA AND SCORPIO

Libra and Scorpio are neighboring signs. They can either create a strong bond or lead to conflicts. Libra is diplomatic and seeks harmony. Scorpio is intense and desires depth in relationships. If they learn to appreciate each other's strengths and find a middle ground, their connection can be passionate and transformative. Trust and open communication are essential for this pairing to thrive.

LIBRA AND SAGITTARIUS

Libra and Sagittarius both enjoy socializing and exploring the world, creating a lively and adventurous partnership. They value freedom and independence. This they grant each other willingly. Libra's diplomacy can balance Sagittarius' bluntness. Sagittarius can inspire Libra to be more spontaneous. Their shared love for intellectual pursuits and optimism often leads to a harmonious and exciting relationship.

LIBRA AND CAPRICORN

Libra and Capricorn have differing approaches to life. Libra's focus is on relationships and aesthetics. This contrasts with Capricorn's practicality and ambition. While they may appear to be opposites, they can complement each other effectively. Libra can introduce Capricorn to the value of social connections and diplomacy. Capricorn can provide stability and security. With effort, they can create a partnership that combines beauty and practicality.

LIBRA AND AQUARIUS

Libra and Aquarius are both air signs, fostering excellent communication and intellectual connection. They share progressive and humanitarian values, creating a forward-thinking and innovative partnership. Both signs appreciate individuality and freedom, which they respect in each other. Their mental connection and shared ideals can often lead to a harmonious relationship.

LIBRA AND PISCES

Libra and Pisces have a natural affinity for each other, often forming a romantic and empathetic bond. Libra appreciates Pisces' sensitivity and creativity. Pisces admires Libra's charm and diplomacy. They share a love for art, beauty and romance. This leads to creating a dreamy and affectionate partnership. However, Libra's need for balance may clash with Pisces' occasional emotional turbulence, requiring understanding and patience to overcome.

TIPS FOR DATING AND MAINTAINING RELATIONSHIPS WITH LIBRA

DATING A LIBRA MAN

- **Engage in Intellectual Conversations**; Libra men enjoy stimulating discussions. Talk about topics like art, culture and current events to connect with them on a deeper level.
- **Set an Ambience**; Libra men have a soft side. Pay attention to creating a beautiful and unforgettable experience.
- **Respect Their Need for Personal Space**; While Libra men value relationships they also require some time and space. Allow them to pursue their interests and maintain connections with their circles.
- **Be Patient with Decision Making;** Libra men can be indecisive as they carefully consider options. Practice patience. Avoid pressuring them when it comes to making choices whether decisions like dinner plans or more significant ones.

DATING A LIBRA WOMAN

- **Appreciate Their Social Nature**; Many Libra women are outgoing and enjoy socializing. Support their desire for a group of friends. Be open to attending social events together.
- **Compliment Their Sense of Style;** Libra women often have fashion sense. Compliment their style choices. Show appreciation for the effort they put into looking good.

- **Share Your Thoughts and Emotions**; Open communication is important to Libra women. Feel free to share your thoughts, emotions and any concerns you may have with them. This will help trust and a deeper understanding, between you both.
- **Balance**; Striving for balance is crucial when it comes to relationships with Libras. Aim for a partnership that's harmonious by being open to compromise and working together to find solutions that satisfy both of your needs.

Remember these tips can be helpful when dating or maintaining a relationship with a Libra individual. However it's essential to recognize that everyone is unique. Building a long lasting connection requires understanding and appreciating each other's individuality and respecting each other's needs. Effective communication, trust and mutual respect form the foundation of any relationship.

As we wrap up our exploration of "Libra Love and Compatibility " we gain an understanding of how Libra's nature interacts with other zodiac signs. Throughout this journey we've discovered insights into how Libra approaches love and partnership. These insights serve as guidance for those navigating the tapestry of love and connection in their lives.

In conclusion we've learned that while astrology provides insights into relationship dynamics it is just one aspect of the complex dance known as love. Every person regardless of whether they're a Libra or have another zodiac sign brings their own uniqueness to any relationship. Ultimately the success of a relationship relies on communication, mutual respect and a shared commitment.

As you continue on your path may the wisdom and understanding gained from this chapter guide you towards embracing the beauty and equilibrium that Libra seeks in love. May it also help you build connections with those you encounter along the way. Love is a language that transcends signs. Ultimately it is within our power to shape heartwarming tales filled with beauty and serenity.

CHAPTER 3:
FRIENDS AND FAMILY

In the tapestry of connections few signs shine as brightly as Libra. In this chapter we embark on a journey into the realm of how Libra interacts with friends and family. Here we will be exploring the roles they assume and the dynamics they bring to these vital aspects of life.

Throughout this chapter's pages we will delve into the qualities that make Libra individuals such cherished friends and family members. However like any sign Libra also encounters challenges, within their friendships and familial relationships. These challenges will also be explored. As we delve into the realm of Libra's connections may you develop a better understanding of the roles they fulfill and the profound impact they have on the lives of those close to them.

LIBRA AS A FRIEND

Libra brings a delightful dynamic to friendship. With their ability to create harmony and balance in relationships Libras are often cherished companions. Here's a glimpse into what you can expect when you have a Libra as your friend.

- **Natural Mediators**; Libras act as peacemakers within their circles. They possess a talent for resolving conflicts and soothing tensions. If you find yourself in disagreement with someone, having a Libra friend by your side increases the likelihood of finding compromise and achieving resolutions.
- **Social**; Libras are like social butterflies. They effortlessly attract people with their charm and grace. As your friend they will introduce you to new people and make gatherings more enjoyable.
- **Engaging Conversationalists**; Libras genuinely care about others thoughts and emotions making them excellent conversationalists. They listen attentively to your ideas and feelings engaging you in discussions. Whether you need someone to bounce ideas off or simply share a chat with a Libra friend will be there for you.
- **Appreciation of Beauty**; Libras possess an admiration for art, culture and aesthetics. Expect them to introduce you to the wonders of beauty, in many forms. Whether it's through captivating art exhibitions or their impeccable fashion choices. They'll inspire you to see and embrace the beauty that surrounds us.
- **Dependable and Trustworthy**; Libras highly value trust in their relationships. As friends they are incredibly reliable and loyal. You can always rely on them to keep your secrets safe. They will stand by your side when you're in need of support.
- **Empathy**; Libras possess a strong sense of empathy and understanding. They genuinely strive to empathize with your perspective and offer advice. During times they will be there as a listening ear providing comfort with their words.
- **Love for Adventure**; Libras are always up for new experiences and exciting adventures. They'll be the ones to suggest road trips or weekend getaways. With a Libra friend you can anticipate a blend of planned activities along with escapades.
- **Fairness**; Fairness holds great importance for Libras when it comes to friendships. They make sure that your needs and opinions are respected and taken into consideration seriously. If any conflicts arise they approach them with grace while striving for a resolution.
- **Supportive and Encouraging**; When it comes to cheering others on Libras excel at being cheerleaders. They will wholeheartedly support your goals and

aspirations providing you with encouragement and motivation every step of the way. When you have a friend who's a Libra they empower you to chase after your dreams.

In essence having a Libra as a friend means being in the company of someone who deeply values friendship. They constantly strive for harmony and fairness bringing an air of elegance to your interactions. Having them as part of your circle of friends is truly delightful.

LIBRA AND FAMILY DYNAMICS

Within the interplay of family dynamics, the seventh sign of the zodiac, Libra brings forth a unique set of qualities and influences. Libras, renowned for their skills, charm and commitment to maintaining balance hold a key role in shaping familial dynamics. Let's delve deeper into how individuals with a Libra nature contribute to the tapestry of family life.

- **The Peacemaker**; Libras often find themselves assuming the role of peacemakers within their families. Their diplomatic approach and tact allow them to defuse tensions and resolve conflicts effectively. Whenever disagreements arise among family members you can count on a Libra to create an atmosphere of harmony.
- **Cultivating Family Bonds and Togetherness**; Family connections hold tremendous value for Libras. They consistently prioritize spending quality time with their loved ones. Initiating family gatherings, outings or special celebrations is something they actively engage in. Overall their aim is to strengthen bonds while nurturing a sense of unity.
- **The Fair minded Parent**; When it comes to parenting roles, Libra parents strive for fairness and justice. Their mission is to ensure that every decision is equitable, by considering each child's needs.
- **The Creative and Homemaker**; Libras have an eye for beauty. Frequently they contribute to enhancing the family's living space making it visually welcoming. They enjoy decorating their homes, organizing family gatherings and creating a harmonious environment for their loved ones.
- **Striving for Equilibrium**; Libras bring a sense of balance to family dynamics encouraging compromise and fairness in decision making processes. They may act as the voice of reason during family discussions urging all members to express their viewpoints.
- **Conflict Avoidance**; Libras often go to great lengths to sidestep conflicts within the family unit in order to maintain harmony. While this trait can be

advantageous it can also pose challenges when important matters are left unresolved. Remember it is crucial for Libras to strike a balance between preserving peace and addressing issues.

- **The Social Connectors**; Libras have a knack for introducing their family members to other people, expanding the network and connections within the family. They truly enjoy hosting get-togethers bringing together friends and family in an atmosphere of harmony.

In summary Libras play a role in shaping family dynamics by promoting fairness, balance and harmony. They excel in their abilities as peacemakers, diplomats and creators of a visually appealing family environment. While their inclination to avoid conflict can be advantageous it's important for Libras to address and resolve family matters to maintain a balanced dynamic within the family.

CHALLENGES IN FRIENDSHIPS AND FAMILY RELATIONS FOR LIBRA

While individuals born under the zodiac sign Libra possess qualities that contribute to their friendships and family relationships they also encounter specific hurdles. Being aware of these challenges can assist Libras in navigating their interactions effectively. Here are some common obstacles that Libras may come across.

- **Difficulty Making Decisions**; One of the challenges faced by Libras is their inclination, towards indecisiveness. They tend to weigh the pros and cons of choices which can result in frustration for friends and family.
- **Avoidance of Confrontation;** Libras possess an aversion to conflict. Often they will go to great lengths to evade it. While this may foster a tranquil atmosphere it can also lead to issues.
- **Trouble Saying "No"**; The desire to maintain harmony can make it arduous for Libras to say no. Consequently they may find themselves overcommitted and stressed out as they take on more than they can manage.
- **Seeking Validation from Others**; Libras frequently seek validation and approval from others. This makes them susceptible to peer pressure or the influence of people's opinions. Which can result in decisions that do not align with their desires.
- **Struggles, with Confrontation**; When it comes to facing confrontation or receiving criticism Libras often find it difficult to assert themselves. They tend to shy away from addressing issues. Overall it can hinder conflict resolution and impede personal growth.
- **Balancing Relationships**; One of the challenges that Libras encounter is finding a balance in their relationships. Especially when conflicts or tensions arise. Ultimately they may feel torn between their loyalty to individuals.
- **Overemphasis on Aesthetics**; Libra's deep appreciation for beauty and aesthetics sometimes leads them to place importance on appearance. This can cause them to prioritize surface level aspects of relationships over fostering deeper connections.
- **Difficulty in Letting Go**; Libras have a tendency to hold onto relationships even when they have run their course hoping to restore harmony. Consequently they may struggle with letting go of friendships or family connections that're no longer healthy or beneficial.
- **Striving for Perfection**; Setting high standards for themselves and others is something Libras often do. This can result in disappointment when reality falls short of their expectations.

To overcome the obstacles they face and strengthen their relationships, individuals born under the zodiac sign of Libra can focus on developing assertiveness, making decisions and addressing conflicts in a manner. It is crucial for them to strike a balance between their desire for harmony and the need for communication. By engaging in these practices Libras have the opportunity to enhance and fortify their relationships.

In this chapter we have explored how Libras influence their friends and family members. Their ability to create harmony reflects their dedication to the well being of those they cherish. However we have also discussed some challenges that Libras may encounter, such as indecisiveness or avoidance of conflicts. It is important to note that despite these traits causing obstacles in relationships, Libras possess the capacity for growth and improvement. This enables them to navigate these challenges effectively.

By embracing their strengths facing challenges head on and consistently nurturing connections, with others Libras can cultivate relationships.

CHAPTER 4: CAREER AND MONEY

In this chapter we will delve into the workplace preferences, career goals, strengths and challenges that shape individuals born under the zodiac sign of Libra. Known for their ability to maintain balance and harmony, Libras often find themselves drawn towards roles that allow them to utilize their diplomatic skills. They have a talent for mediation. They are skilled negotiators who prioritize fairness in all their interactions. This quality makes them highly valued in professions where a strong sense of justice and the ability to see things from perspectives crucial.

Libras also possess a sense and a deep appreciation for beauty, which often leads them to excel in fields related to art, design and creative industries. Their keen eye for detail combined with their understanding of harmony makes them well suited for careers that require both creativity and practicality. In this chapter we will explore how these unique qualities influence their career choices and professional growth.

However just like every other sign has its challenges Libras are not exempted. We will also examine the difficulties they may encounter in the workplace. Their aversion to conflict and constant desire for consensus can sometimes result in indecisiveness or hesitancy to take a stance on matters. Understanding these challenges is crucial, in harnessing their potential.

Furthermore we will explore how Libras manage their finances. Libras are known for their balanced approach to decisions but they also have a penchant for luxury and aesthetics which can sometimes lead to indulgent spending. In this guide we will explore strategies that can help Libras maintain stability while satisfying their tastes.

So dear reader, get ready for a journey into the realm of career and finances from a Libras perspective. This chapter aims to provide an understanding and practical tips on how to harness the talents and inclinations of Libras in their professional lives.

CAREER PREFERENCES AND PROFESSIONAL ASPIRATIONS

Individuals born under the sign of Libra bring a unique set of qualities to the workplace. Here are some key aspects regarding Libras inclinations when it comes to careers.

- **Diplomats**; Libras excel in positions that necessitate mediation and diplomacy. They possess a talent for resolving conflicts. Naturally this makes them valuable team members and leaders in workplaces that prioritize collaboration and cooperation. Professions such as law, negotiation, counseling or human resources are well suited for their skill set.
- **Advocates for Justice;** Libras are inclined towards professions that involve advocating for fairness and justice. They are often motivated by the desire to make a positive impact on society. This can lead them towards careers in law, social work, advocacy or nonprofit organizations dedicated to social justice causes.
- **Creativity and Aesthetics**; Libras have an appreciation for beauty and aesthetics. This makes them well suited for careers in the arts or design fields such as fashion or interior decoration.
- **Social Butterflies;** Libras thrive in social situations. As such they are often attracted to careers, in fields like relations, marketing, event planning and customer service. Here their people skills and charisma can really shine.
- **Intellectual Pursuits;** Libras have a curiosity and a passion for challenges. They may be inclined towards careers in academia, research, journalism or any field that allows them to engage in thought provoking conversations and explore ideas.

- **Teamwork**; Libras excel as both leaders and team players. They strive to create a work environment that encourages open communication.
- **Entrepreneurship**; Some Libras are drawn to entrepreneurship as it allows them to utilize their creativity, diplomacy and sense of balance.

STRENGTHS IN THE WORKPLACE

Libra individuals bring a powerful set of strengths to the workplace making them highly valuable there. Their natural charm and diplomatic abilities, coupled with a commitment to balance and harmony contribute significantly to their success in professional settings. Here are the key strengths that distinguish Libra individuals.

- **Diplomacy**; Libras excel in resolving conflicts and finding common ground in disputes. Overall they contribute to fostering a productive atmosphere.
- **Charisma and Approachability**; Libra's charming and sociable nature makes them incredibly easy to work with. They effortlessly build relationships with colleagues creating a sense of camaraderie and cooperation.
- **Communication**; Libras are communicators who can express themselves clearly and persuasively both in written form or when speaking. This valuable skill greatly enhances team collaboration efforts as well as interactions with clients.

- **Commitment to Fairness and Justice;** Libras have a strong sense of ethics and fairness. They passionately advocate for fair treatment of their colleagues making them reliable champions for equality and justice.
- **Team Player Mentality;** Libras thrive within team environments where they positively contribute to group dynamics by encouraging teamwork. They ensure that every voice is heard and foster collaboration within teams.
- **Expertise in Negotiation**; Libras possess excellent negotiation skills that enable them to navigate situations, with finesse. Whether they involve business deals, contracts or workplace conflicts is crucial for achieving successful outcomes.
- **Detail oriented**; Paying attention to the details in their work is a strength of Libras. This trait proves valuable in roles that demand precision, such as project management, quality control and design.
- **Aesthetic appreciation;** Libra's sense of style and appreciation for aesthetics can be advantageous in fields and industries where visual presentation holds importance. They possess an eye for design and can positively contribute to projects that require an element of beauty.
- **Flexibility**; Libras can handle changing circumstances and unexpected challenges with grace. Overall this makes them valuable assets in dynamic work environments.
- **Leaders**; When it comes to leadership potential Libras shine brightly. They prioritize fairness and teamwork while leading by example. Their leadership style fosters a work culture that inspires others to excel and collaborate.
- **Balanced perspective;** Libras approach problem solving with a balanced perspective by considering alternative viewpoints. Their ability to see the bigger picture and explore diverse solutions proves highly beneficial, in decision making processes.
- **Connector**; Building networks is something that Libras truly enjoy. They have a talent for forming connections. Furthermore they know how to use these relationships to advance their careers and benefit their organizations.

Overall Libras are highly committed to professional growth. They are always striving to improve themselves. Whether it's to seek out opportunities for learning and development or staying informed about the industry trends and best practices. In the workplace Libras excel as team players, effective communicators and advocates for fairness and harmony. Their unique strengths contribute to creating a productive work environment making them an invaluable asset to any organization.

CHALLENGES FACED BY LIBRA AND STRATEGIES TO OVERCOME THEM

While individuals born under the zodiac sign Libra possess a range of strengths that greatly contribute to their professional lives they also encounter challenges that may impede their career growth. By recognizing and addressing these challenges head on Libras can thrive in any workplace setting. Here are some common career hurdles faced by Libras and effective strategies to overcome them.

Difficulty in Decision Making

- Challenge; Libras often find it challenging to make decisions as they meticulously analyze all options.
- Strategy; To overcome this challenge Libras can set deadlines for decision making. Learn to trust their instincts. Seeking advice from trusted colleagues can provide insights and clarity.

Conflict Avoidance

- Challenge; Libras tend to shy away from conflicts. This can result in long term unresolved issues.
- Strategy; Developing assertiveness skills is crucial for Libras to address conflicts constructively. By learning how to diplomatically communicate concerns and resolving conflicts directly they can foster better relationships within the workplace.

External Validation Dependency

- Challenge; Libras commonly seek approval and validation from others. This leads to self doubt and excessive reliance on feedback.
- Strategy; It is important for Libras to build self confidence and prioritize self validation. Acknowledging achievements and placing trust in their judgment will reduce dependency on external opinions.

Overcommitment

- Challenge; Libras often fall into the trap of overcommitting themselves due to their desire for balance.
- Strategy; To avoid this challenge it's essential for Libras to prioritize tasks effectively by setting boundaries. Furthermore, learning when it's necessary to say no is key.

Burn out

- Challenge; Libras often find themselves overwhelmed and burdened by their desire to please others resulting in taking on responsibilities.
- Strategy; To avoid burnout Libras should prioritize their tasks. It's crucial for them to effectively manage their workload to maintain a work life balance.

Procrastination

- Challenge; Due to their inclination towards balance Libras may tend to procrastinate when faced with challenging tasks.
- Strategy; To overcome this challenge Libras can break down tasks into manageable steps and assign deadlines for each step. Creating a structured to do list can greatly assist in staying organized and motivated.

Self Criticism

- Challenge; Libra's tendency towards high standards often leads them down a path of self criticism and perfectionism. This ultimately results in overload and stress.
- Strategy; To combat this challenge Libras need to cultivate self compassion and recognize their achievements even if they fall short of perfection. Setting goals and focusing on progress rather than striving for flawlessness can help alleviate this internal struggle.

Taking Initiative

- Challenge; Libras tend to wait for others to take charge in projects or decision making processes.
- Strategy; Libras can boost their confidence by seizing the initiative and actively seeking opportunities to lead or contribute their ideas. Ultimately stepping out of their comfort zone can facilitate growth.

Conflict Resolution Skills

- Challenge; While Libras prefer avoiding conflicts they may lack the skills needed to address them effectively when necessary.
- Strategy; Libras can invest in conflict resolution training. Develop assertiveness skills. Learning how to deal with conflicts and engage in conversations can enhance their professional relationships.

By acknowledging the obstacles they face and adopting strategies to overcome them Libras can utilize their strengths in the workplace while still upholding their commitment to maintaining harmony.

Throughout this chapter we have explored the qualities and characteristics that define Libras in their financial lives. With their charm, diplomacy and dedication to fairness and equilibrium Libras are well equipped to excel in fields.

When it comes to financial matters Libras strike a balance between their love for elegance and a practical approach to managing money. They appreciate the finer things in life. Also they understand the importance of responsible financial planning. This combination of valuing luxury while being financially prudent is evident in how they handle budgeting, investing and saving.

Whether you're a Libra seeking guidance on your career and financial journey or simply intrigued by the traits associated with this zodiac sign, let the insights from this chapter be your guiding light. Allow it to illuminate your path as you navigate through the realms of work and finance, with grace and equilibrium.

CHAPTER 5:
SELF-IMPROVEMENT

In the adventure of life, the pursuit of personal growth is a universal theme that resonates with everyone. For those born under the sign of Libra, this journey takes on a fascinating dimension. In this chapter we delve into the art of self improvement through the lens of Libra's qualities and characteristics. We will see how they can navigate their personal growth journey by leveraging their strengths while addressing areas for improvement.

Whether you're a Libra looking for insights into your journey or someone fascinated by the traits of this zodiac sign this chapter guarantees to provide helpful guidance. Furthermore it will give you a deeper comprehension of how Libra approaches the timeless quest of self improvement.

PERSONAL GROWTH AND DEVELOPMENT

Personal growth is a journey that lasts a lifetime. For a Libra it presents an opportunity to refine their qualities, build upon their strengths and tackle their challenges. Here are some important areas where Libra individuals can experience growth and development.

- **Embracing Decisiveness**; Making decisions can be a challenge for Libras since they tend to consider all options. Remember that personal growth entails becoming more decisive. Practice making choices without overthinking. Trust your intuition.
- **Assertiveness Training**; To overcome their inclination to avoid conflict and seek validation Libras can focus on developing assertiveness skills. Learning how to express their needs, opinions and boundaries is an asset.
- **Self Validation**; Building self confidence and self validation should be emphasized by Libras. They can remind themselves that their worth isn't solely dependent on the approval of others.
- **Establishing Boundaries**; Personal growth involves setting boundaries in relationships and commitments. Learning to say "no" when necessary while prioritizing self care contributes to a fulfilling life.
- **Overcoming Perfectionism**; Libras should strive to overcome their inclination towards perfectionism. It's important for them to embrace progress, rather than obsessing over flawlessness. By setting goals and celebrating their achievements even if they're not flawless Libras can foster growth.
- **Communication**; Personal development for Libras involves refining their communication skills. They can work on expressing themselves, handling conflicts constructively and actively listening to others.
- **Taking Initiative**; Libras should challenge themselves by stepping out of their comfort zones and taking initiative in their lives. This may involve seeking leadership roles pursuing opportunities or actively participating in decision making processes.
- **Conflict Resolution Skills**; Developing conflict resolution skills is vital for growth among Libras. They can learn to approach conflicts with an open mind seeking beneficial solutions and addressing issues promptly and constructively.
- **Embracing Self Care**; Prioritizing self care is crucial for the growth of Libra individuals. By establishing routines that nurture their emotional and mental well being they can maintain a sense of harmony in their lives.
- **Exploring Individuality**; Alongside enjoying interactions Libras can foster growth by exploring their own uniqueness and interests. It's important for

them to dedicate time to cultivate their hobbies, passions and talents while maintaining a rounded social life.

- **Goal Setting**; Setting attainable goals plays a role in personal growth, for everyone, including Libras. Libra individuals have the ability to create a roadmap, for their professional goals, which helps them maintain focus and motivation.

By embracing these areas of growth Libras can enhance their well being, relationships and career success. By doing so they can stay true to their commitment to balance and harmony, in all aspects of life.

HARNESSING LIBRA STRENGTHS AND OVERCOMING WEAKNESSES

Libra individuals have a set of strengths and weaknesses. Just like anyone else with a zodiac sign. Thus it's important for them to understand how to utilize their strengths while also addressing their areas for improvement. Ultimately it will help them to grow personally and achieve success. Here are some ways Libras can do that.

HARNESSING STRENGTHS

- **Diplomacy and Mediation**; Libras excel at resolving conflicts and facilitating harmonious communication. This makes them exceptional at mediating disputes in professional settings. Overall they have the ability to promote harmony and understanding.

- **Communication Skills**; Libras possess communication skills that can be utilized in leadership roles, public speaking engagements and effective collaboration within teams. Their ability to express ideas often inspires others.
- **Fairness and Justice**; Libra's commitment to fairness can drive them to advocate for fair causes. Volunteer work or actively participate in organizations focused on promoting equality and justice.
- **Charm and Likeability**; Libras charm and likability make them natural networkers who can build connections that help advance their careers.
- **Creativity and Aesthetics**; Libra's appreciation for aesthetics can be channeled into careers within design, art or other creative fields. Here their keen eye for detail and style leads to innovative and visually appealing work.

OVERCOMING WEAKNESSES

- **Dealing with Indecisiveness**; To tackle indecisiveness Libras can set concrete deadlines for making decisions. Trust their instincts. Seeking advice from trusted individuals can also help them feel more confident in their choices.
- **Addressing Conflict Avoidance**; Libras can overcome their tendency to avoid conflict by learning diplomatic ways to resolve conflicts. It's important for them to directly and assertively address issues with clear communication.
- **Reducing Dependency on External Validation;** To become less reliant on external validation Libras should focus on building self acceptance. Recognizing their worth and acknowledging their achievements is crucial.
- **Managing Overcommitment**; Libras can handle overcommitment by setting boundaries and learning to say "no" when necessary. Prioritizing self care and striving for balance is vital in order to avoid burnout.
- **Overcoming Procrastination;** To combat procrastination Libras can break tasks into small steps. Furthermore they can set deadlines for themselves and establish structured routines. It's important for them to focus on progress rather than seeking perfection.
- **Balancing Multiple Relationships;** For managing many relationships Libras can organize their commitments carefully, maintain open communication with loved ones and prioritize their own well being.
- **Overcoming perfectionism;** Libras can combat their perfectionism tendencies by setting goals and acknowledging their accomplishments even if they aren't flawless. Embracing progress, then striving for perfection is crucial.

For Libra individuals the process of harnessing their strengths and addressing their weaknesses is continuous. By focusing on growth they can lead balanced and fulfilling lives.

In this chapter we have deeply explored the art of self improvement guided by the principles that Libras hold dear; balance, harmony and fairness. We have discovered how Libras wholeheartedly embrace the journey of self improvement, with a sense of equilibrium and justice.

Libras understand that personal growth is a process that requires self awareness and a commitment to better oneself. They recognize the value of nurturing their strengths while addressing their weaknesses striving for a character. This journey exemplifies the power of self awareness and personal growth as Libras continuously evolve themselves. They seek harmony not only within themselves but in all aspects of life from personal relationships to professional pursuits.

As Libras embark on this path of self improvement they demonstrate how maintaining balance in one's character and actions can lead to development. Their dedication to finding equilibrium in emotions, thoughts and behaviors serves as an inspiration for others. Their journey motivates those around them to also strive for balance and harmony in their lives.

To summarize, this chapter not only showcases the qualities of Libras in their pursuit of self improvement but also emphasizes the broader impact of their journey. It is a journey that resonates with themes like growth, balance and the unwavering pursuit of becoming oneself. All while embracing life's challenges and opportunities, with a harmonious and balanced approach.

CHAPTER 6: THE YEAR AHEAD

Dear Libra, we are delighted to invite you to a chapter that focuses on exploring the influences that will shape your life in the year ahead. As the stars gracefully move and align in their dance they offer insights into various aspects of your life. This celestial journey will shed light on areas, including love and relationships, career aspirations, financial stability, health and more.

Our goal, as we embark on this voyage together is to provide you with an understanding of how these celestial bodies may impact your experiences. Whether its Venus gently influencing your encounters or Mars fueling ambition within your pursuits or even the introspective effect of Mercury during retrograde periods – each astrological event carries significance.

That's not all. This chapter goes beyond predictions; it serves as a tool to help you harness the energies of the universe in your favor. We will navigate through times predicted by the stars while offering insights into making the most of moments and gracefully maneuvering through difficult periods with resilience.

Libra let us embark together on this captivating journey, with minds and hopeful hearts. As we move forward in the year, allow the stars to serve as beacons lighting your way and helping you synchronize your actions with the flow of life. Embrace this journey through the year filled with opportunities for growth and exciting discoveries.

HOROSCOPE GUIDE

As a Libra, you are known for your diplomacy, charm and commitment to harmony. Remember that you possess the qualities needed to navigate any challenges and embrace opportunities with grace. Trust in your innate ability to find equilibrium and harmony in all aspects of life. May the stars guide you on your journey, Libra, as you continue to shine with your unique blend of charm, diplomacy and elegance.

- **Aries (March 21 - April 19);** This year, Aries individuals may enter your life. They will be bringing a dynamic energy that can inspire your own pursuits. Embrace their adventurous spirit and consider taking calculated risks in your career or personal life.
- **Taurus (April 20 - May 20);** Taurus energies encourage you to focus on financial stability and personal values. This is an excellent time to reassess your budget. Make wise investments and prioritize your long-term financial goals.
- **Gemini (May 21 - June 20);** Gemini influences may spark your curiosity and desire for intellectual growth. Engage in learning opportunities. Take short trips. Foster open communication in your relationships.
- **Cancer (June 21 - July 22);** Cancer energies inspire emotional depth and connection in your relationships. Focus on nurturing your closest bonds. Both romantic and familial. Remember to also strengthen your emotional well-being.
- **Leo (July 23 - August 22);** Leo influences may encourage you to shine in your career and take on leadership roles. Embrace your natural charisma and seize opportunities for professional growth.
- **Virgo (August 23 - September 22);** Virgo energies encourage you to pay attention to your health and well-being. Prioritize self-care routines, dietary habits. Exercise to maintain balance and vitality.
- **Libra (September 23 - October 22);** This year, focus on your personal growth journey. Embrace your diplomatic nature to resolve any conflicts in your life. Harness your charm to build positive relationships.
- **Scorpio (October 23 - November 21);** Scorpio influences may bring transformative experiences. Embrace change, let go of what no longer serves you. Trust in your ability to rise from any challenges.
- **Sagittarius (November 22 - December 21);** Sagittarius energies inspire adventure and exploration. Plan a trip or embark on a new educational journey to broaden your horizons.
- **Capricorn (December 22 - January 19);** Capricorn influences encourage you to focus on your finances. Set clear financial goals, manage your resources wisely. Invest in long-term stability.
- **Aquarius (January 20 - February 18);** Aquarius energies may bring new friendships and opportunities for collaboration. Embrace your social side and join group activities. Contribute to causes that matter to you.

- **Pisces (February 19 - March 20);** Pisces influences inspire your spiritual growth. Explore mindfulness practices, meditation, or yoga to connect with your inner self. Strive to find peace and balance.

KEY ASTROLOGICAL EVENTS AND THEIR IMPACT ON LIBRA

Astrological events can have a significant influence on Libra individuals, guiding their experiences and personal growth throughout the year. Here are some key astrological events and their potential impact on Libra.

- **New Moon in Libra (Date Varies Each Year);** The New Moon in Libra marks a powerful time for self-reflection and setting intentions. Libras can use this period to focus on personal goals. Especially those related to balance, harmony and relationships.
- **Mercury Retrograde (Multiple Times a Year)**; Mercury Retrograde periods may bring communication challenges and misunderstandings. Libras should be cautious in their interactions and use these times for reflection. Work on resolving any lingering issues in their relationships.
- **Venus Retrograde (Happens Approximately Every 18 Months);** Venus, Libra's ruling planet, occasionally goes into retrograde. During this time, Libras may reevaluate their values and relationships. Ultimately it's a period for introspection and possibly making changes in these areas.
- **Full Moon in Libra (Date Varies Each Year);** The Full Moon in Libra illuminates the need for balance and fairness in your life. It may bring clarity to your relationships and help you make decisions regarding partnerships and commitments.
- **Jupiter in Air Signs (Approximately Every 12 Years);** When Jupiter, the planet of expansion and growth, transits through air signs like Gemini or Aquarius, it can bring opportunities for intellectual growth, travel. It's about expanding our horizons. Libras may find themselves drawn to higher education, travel adventures, or broadening their knowledge during these periods.
- **Saturn in Air Signs (Approximately Every 28-29 Years);** Saturn's transit through air signs can lead to significant life changes and personal growth. It may challenge Libras to redefine their goals and ambitions. This can lead to fostering a more structured and disciplined approach to their lives.
- **Lunar and Solar Eclipses (Multiple Times a Year);** Eclipses often signify endings and beginnings. Libras should pay attention to eclipses in their birth chart. They can herald shifts in relationships, career, or personal identity. These times may prompt transformative experiences.

- **Venus in Libra (Periodic Transit);** When Venus, your ruling planet, transits through Libra, it enhances your natural charm and appeal. It's a favorable time for love, romance and enhancing your personal style.
- **Mars Retrograde (Happens Approximately Every 2 Years)**; Mars Retrograde can bring a slowdown in energy and motivation. Libras may need to be patient and avoid impulsive actions during this time. Reassess and refine your goals and actions.
- **Sun Entering Libra (Around September 23);** As the Sun enters Libra, it marks the start of Libra season. This is a time when your strengths and qualities shine brightly. It's an excellent period for setting intentions and strengthening relationships.

The above astrological events can serve as guides for Libra individuals. Knowledge of them will help to navigate life's twists and turns while staying true to their commitment to harmony and fairness. Embrace these celestial influences and use them as opportunities for personal growth throughout the year.

KEY LIFE AREAS

The year ahead promises a journey of self-discovery, personal growth and transformation for Libra individuals. By navigating the celestial influences wisely and with intention, you can enhance your life in many ways. Now let's take a look at some key areas.

LOVE AND RELATIONSHIPS

The year ahead brings a transformative wave in the romantic life of Libra individuals. Venus, your ruling planet, embarks on a journey that amplifies your charm and enhances your relationships.

Key Periods:

- February to April: A time of renewed passion and deeper connections. Venus aligns with Jupiter. Now is a chance for new love or the rekindling of old flames.
- Mid-July: A potential period of turbulence. Mars's influence may bring challenges that test the strength of your relationships.
- Advice: Embrace honesty and open communication. This year is an excellent opportunity to build stronger, more meaningful bonds.

CAREER AND FINANCES

Jupiter's transit through your career house heralds a period of expansion and growth in your professional life. However, be wary of Saturn's retrograde phase. It may bring about unexpected challenges.

Key Periods:

- Late March to June: Career growth is accelerated. Opportunities for promotion or new ventures are likely.
- September to November: Caution advised in financial matters. Saturn's influence may lead to delays or setbacks.
- Advice: Stay adaptable and open to new opportunities. Careful financial planning is essential during the latter half of the year.

HEALTH AND WELLNESS

Neptune's presence in your health sector suggests a need for balance in physical and mental wellness. It's a year to focus on holistic health.

Key Periods:

- April to May: Ideal for starting new health regimes or diets.
- August: Potential for stress-related issues. Prioritize mental health and relaxation.
- Advice: Regular exercise, balanced nutrition and mindfulness practices will be crucial in maintaining your health throughout the year.

PERSONAL GROWTH AND SELF-DISCOVERY

The year's planetary alignment encourages introspection and self-improvement for Libra individuals. Pluto's transformative energy is particularly influential, fostering deep personal changes.

Key Periods:

- January to March: Reflection and setting personal goals.
- October to December: A powerful period for self-discovery and implementing life changes.
- Advice: Utilize this year for self-reflection. Engage in activities that nurture your soul and help you connect with your true self. Be open to change and personal evolution.

Throughout this chapter we have discussed the significance of events in various aspects of life. These celestial happenings act as guiding stars that provide insights and opportunities to align yourself with your path. Always remember that you possess qualities like diplomacy, charm and an unwavering commitment to maintaining balance and harmony. With these traits combined with the guidance from the cosmos you are empowered to navigate both challenges and triumphs that lie ahead.

As you move forward into this year, embrace each astrological event as an opportunity for self discovery, progress and renewal. Seize these chances with grace and intention. May the upcoming year provide you with a canvas to create a beautiful and balanced masterpiece of your life.

CHAPTER 7: FAMOUS LIBRA PERSONALITIES

In the celestial tapestry of the zodiac, Libra emerges as a constellation marked by its charm, diplomacy and commitment to balance. As we delve into this chapter, we embark on a captivating exploration of the lives and achievements of famous Libra individuals who have left an indelible mark on the world.

Libras are known for their elegance, artistic inclinations and the ability to bring equilibrium to any situation. They possess an innate sense of justice and a desire to foster peaceful coexistence. It is no wonder that many of history's most influential figures have been born under the Libra sign.

Within these pages, you will encounter an array of remarkable Libra personalities from diverse fields. Including politics, sports, music, film and more. Each of them embodies the unique qualities of Libra in their own exceptional way, leaving an enduring legacy for generations to come.

Join us as we celebrate the enchanting charm and profound impact of these famous Libra individuals. Through their stories and contributions, we gain a deeper understanding of the celestial gifts bestowed upon this remarkable sign.

MAHATMA GANDHI

- Date of Birth: October 2, 1869.
- Brief Biography: Mahatma Gandhi was a renowned Indian leader who played a pivotal role in the country's struggle for independence from British rule. He is known for his philosophy of nonviolent resistance and civil disobedience.
- Libra Traits: As a Libra, Gandhi embodied qualities of diplomacy, fairness, and a strong sense of justice. His commitment to nonviolence and peace aligns with Libra's desire for harmony.

- Impact: Gandhi's leadership and nonviolent approach to resistance inspired movements for civil rights and freedom around the world. He is remembered as a symbol of peace and is often referred to as the "Father of the Nation" in India.
- Personal Life: Gandhi lived a simple and ascetic life, dedicated to his principles. He was married to Kasturba Gandhi and had four children.

SERENA WILLIAMS

- Date of Birth: September 26, 1981.
- Brief Biography: Serena Williams is one of the greatest tennis players of all time. She has won numerous Grand Slam titles and is known for her powerful and dynamic playing style.
- Libra Traits: Serena's determination, sense of balance on the court, and ability to maintain composure under pressure reflect Libra's qualities of grace, poise, and competitiveness.
- Impact: Serena Williams has left an indelible mark on the world of tennis. Her accomplishments and advocacy for gender equality have made her an iconic figure in sports.
- Personal Life: Serena is the sister of Venus Williams, also a tennis champion. She is married to Alexis Ohanian, with whom she has a daughter.

JOHN LENNON

- Date of Birth: October 9, 1940.

- Brief Biography: John Lennon was a legendary musician and member of the iconic band The Beatles. He was a prolific songwriter and advocate for peace.
- Libra Traits: Lennon's artistic creativity, desire for harmony in his music and commitment to peace resonate with Libra's artistic and diplomatic qualities.
- Impact: His music with The Beatles and as a solo artist has left an enduring legacy in the music industry. Lennon's activism and calls for peace made him a symbol of hope during turbulent times.
- Personal Life: Lennon was married to Yoko Ono. They were known for their activism and artistic collaborations.

BRIGITTE BARDOT

- Date of Birth: September 28, 1934.
- Brief Biography: Brigitte Bardot is a French actress, singer and fashion model. She became an international sex symbol during the 1950s and 1960s.
- Libra Traits: Bardot's beauty, elegance and allure on screen epitomize Libra's sense of aesthetics and charm.
- Impact: She was a cultural icon and influenced fashion and film during her era. Bardot's career and style have left a lasting mark on the entertainment industry.
- Personal Life: Bardot was married multiple times and later became an animal rights activist.

EMINEM

- Date of Birth: October 17, 1972.
- Brief Biography: Eminem, born Marshall Mathers, is a highly influential American rapper, songwriter and record producer.
- Libra Traits: Eminem's lyrical talent, storytelling abilities and his pursuit of balance in his personal life are in line with Libra's artistic and harmonious inclinations.
- Impact: He is one of the best-selling music artists globally and has received numerous awards for his contributions to hip-hop and music in general.
- Personal Life: Eminem has faced personal struggles and addiction but has also championed self-improvement and sobriety.

MARGARET THATCHER

- Date of Birth: October 13, 1925.
- Brief Biography: Margaret Thatcher, also known as the "Iron Lady," was the first female Prime Minister of the United Kingdom. She held office from 1979 to 1990.
- Libra Traits: Thatcher's strong leadership, diplomacy in international relations, and her determination to restore economic balance in the UK resonate with Libra's qualities.
- Impact: She was a polarizing figure but left an indelible mark on British politics. Her conservative policies and strong leadership style defined an era.
- Personal Life: Thatcher was married to Denis Thatcher and had two children.

DWIGHT D. EISENHOWER

- Date of Birth: October 14, 1890.
- Brief Biography: Dwight D. Eisenhower, often called "Ike," was a five-star general during World War II and the 34th President of the United States, serving from 1953 to 1961.
- Libra Traits: Eisenhower's diplomatic skills, sense of justice, and efforts to maintain international peace align with Libra's characteristics.
- Impact: As a military leader, he played a crucial role in the Allied victory in WWII. His presidency marked a period of relative stability in the United States during the 1950s.
- Personal Life: Eisenhower was married to Mamie Eisenhower. Together they had two children.

ELISABETH SHUE

- Date of Birth: October 6, 1963.
- Brief Biography: Elisabeth Shue is an American actress known for her roles in films like "The Karate Kid," "Back to the Future Part II," and "Leaving Las Vegas."
- Libra Traits: Shue's talent in the arts, her graceful presence on screen, and her ability to strike a balance in her diverse roles resonate with Libra's artistic and harmonious qualities.
- Impact: She has had a successful career in Hollywood and received critical acclaim for her performances, including an Academy Award nomination for "Leaving Las Vegas."

- Personal Life: Shue is married to film director Davis Guggenheim. Together they have three children.

CARDI B

- Date of Birth: October 11, 1992.
- Brief Biography: Cardi B, born Belcalis Marlenis Almánzar, is a Grammy-winning rapper, songwriter and actress. She is known for her chart-topping hits and outspoken personality.
- Libra Traits: Cardi B's artistic expression, charm, and ability to balance her career with her personal life align with Libra's creative and harmonious qualities.
- Impact: She has become a prominent figure in the music industry and a voice for female empowerment. Her music and outspoken nature have garnered a massive following.
- Personal Life: Cardi B is married to rapper Offset. Together they have a daughter.

VLADIMIR PUTIN

- Date of Birth: October 7, 1952.
- Brief Biography: Vladimir Putin is a Russian politician who served as the President of Russia and the Prime Minister at different times. He has been a prominent figure in Russian politics since the late 1990s.
- Libra Traits: Putin's diplomatic and strategic approach to international relations, as well as his ability to maintain balance in Russian politics, align with Libra's qualities.
- Impact: He has been a central figure in Russian politics, overseeing significant changes in the country's political landscape and international relations.
- Personal Life: Putin has kept his personal life relatively private. He was married to Lyudmila Shkrebneva and has two daughters.

ALFRED NOBEL

- Date of Birth: October 21, 1833.
- Brief Biography: Alfred Nobel was a Swedish chemist, engineer, and inventor known for inventing dynamite. He is also the founder of the Nobel Prizes, awarded for significant contributions to humanity.
- Libra Traits: Nobel's innovative spirit, his commitment to promoting peace and progress, and his desire to balance the destructive potential of explosives resonate with Libra's qualities.
- Impact: His invention of dynamite revolutionized construction and mining but also led to his concern about its potential misuse. He left his fortune to establish the Nobel Prizes. This recognizes outstanding achievements in various fields.
- Personal Life: Nobel never married and had no children.

BARBARA WALTERS

- Date of Birth: September 25, 1929.
- Brief Biography: Barbara Walters is an American television journalist, known for her pioneering work in broadcast journalism and her interviews with prominent figures.
- Libra Traits: Walters' ability to mediate interviews, her sense of diplomacy in her reporting, and her knack for striking a balance between hard news and human interest stories align with Libra's qualities.
- Impact: She broke barriers for women in journalism and became one of the most respected figures in the industry. Her interviews with world leaders and celebrities have been iconic.

- Personal Life: Walters has been married four times and has one daughter.

As we conclude this chapter dedicated to the personalities of Libra we have embarked on a journey exploring the lives and achievements of these individuals who have graced our world with their unique talents.

From Mahatma Gandhi's philosophies to Serena Williams dynamic athleticism from Brigitte Bardot's captivating performances to Eminem's brilliance. Each of these individuals showcases their own distinctive interpretation of what it means to be a Libra. They have left a mark on the tapestry of history shaping realms such as politics, sports, music, film and beyond.

As we reflect on the contributions of Libra individuals let us keep in mind the qualities associated with this zodiac sign. Charisma, fairness and a strong sense of justice. Like these known personalities have gracefully and profoundly impacted the world stage, every Libra has the potential to utilize their celestial gifts. With those gifts they also can make a positive impact.

CONCLUSION

Finally we have arrived at the culmination of our journey exploring the fascinating realm of the Libra zodiac sign. It has been a voyage filled with exploration, enlightenment and a deeper understanding of individuals born under Libra. Now as we prepare to say goodbye to the balancing scales of Libra let's take a moment to ponder on the insights and revelations we have discovered. From delving into the historical origins and mythologies surrounding Libra to unraveling the intricacies of love, family connections and friendships. In the lives of those influenced by this sign we have embarked on an extensive expedition through a diverse landscape of knowledge and understanding. Here is a summary of the chapters we have traversed.

- **Chapter 1: History and Mythology** - In this chapter, we delved into the earliest observations of the Libra constellation in ancient civilizations. We explored how different cultures perceived and represented Libra in their star maps. We also uncovered the intriguing role of Libra in ancient mythologies, connecting the celestial scales to captivating tales of balance and justice.
- **Chapter 2: Love & Compatibility** - Here, we ventured into the realms of love and relationships. There we explored the personality traits, strengths, weaknesses and compatibility of Libra individuals with other zodiac signs. We unveiled the unique approach Libras bring to love and romance, shedding light on their quest for balance and harmony.
- **Chapter 3: Friends And Family** - This chapter delved into the dynamics of Libra individuals in their friendships and family relationships. Here we highlighted their charming and diplomatic qualities. We also examined the challenges that Libras may face in maintaining these essential connections.
- **Chapter 4: Career And Money** - In the world of career and finances, we explored the preferences, strengths and potential challenges faced by Libra individuals. We uncovered their abilities to excel in the workplace. From there we offered insights into their diplomatic and balanced approach to professional aspirations.
- **Chapter 5: Self-Improvement** - This chapter guided us through the journey of personal growth and self-improvement for Libra individuals. We

explored how Libras can harness their strengths and overcome weaknesses, fostering a deeper sense of self-awareness and development.

- **Chapter 6: The Year Ahead** - Here, we examined how astrological events impact the lives of Libra individuals in various aspects, including love, career, health and personal growth. We offered insights into the opportunities and challenges that may arise in the year ahead.
- **Chapter 7: Famous "Libra" Personalities** - Finally, we celebrated the extraordinary accomplishments and enduring legacies of famous Libra personalities who have left an indelible mark on the world. From Mahatma Gandhi to Serena Williams, these individuals exemplify the grace, charm and impactful nature of Libra.

As we near the conclusion of our journey let us bid farewell to Libra. A sign that brings harmony and elegance to the universe. May the knowledge and wisdom acquired from our exploration of the Libra zodiac sign continue to light up your path and inspire you on your adventure.

As we draw near to wrapping up our journey our intention has been to celebrate and encourage Libra individuals to embrace their qualities and provide valuable insights for their future paths. Our exploration of what lies ahead for Libra has equipped readers with valuable knowledge while featuring profiles of notable personalities born under this zodiac sign that illustrate real life examples of its impact.

The important lesson from this book is to appreciate and celebrate the unique qualities of Libras. Libras you are known for being diplomatic, seeking balance and promoting harmony. Embrace your charm, artistic sensibilities and commitment to justice. The scales of Libra represent more than a symbol. They signify the gift you bring to the world. Embrace them as they hold the key to establishing connections, personal growth and creating a harmonious world.

To all those born under the Libra sign remember that you possess an ability for balance like no other. Utilize it to create beauty, foster understanding and bring harmony not into your life but also into the lives of those around you. Your natural charm, diplomacy skills and artistic sensibilities are your superpowers. Allow them to shine brightly.

As we conclude this book we encourage you to embrace the wisdom of Libra. Embody your qualities and seek balance in all aspects of life. Finally, allow the celestial bodies to serve as your guiding light on the path towards becoming the best version of yourself. In the tapestry of the Zodiac, you as a Libra shine brightly with beauty and harmony.

SCORPIO:

A COMPLETE GUIDE TO THE SCORPIO ASTROLOGY STAR SIGN

Contents

INTRODUCTION -- 1
Compatibility 2
Personality Traits.......... 2
Strengths.......... 3
Weaknesses 3

CHAPTER 1: HISTORY AND MYTHOLOGY 5
Babylon.......... 5
Ancient Egypt.......... 6
Ancient Greek 6
Chinese 6
Indian.......... 6
Mayan.......... 6
Historical Events Under the Scorpio Sign.......... 7
Historical Figures Born Under Scorpio.......... 8
Further Reading and References 8

CHAPTER 2: LOVE & COMPATIBILITY.......... 10
Scorpio and Aries.......... 12
Scorpio and Taurus.......... 12
Scorpio and Gemini.......... 12
Scorpio and Cancer.......... 13
Scorpio and Leo 13
Scorpio and Virgo 13
Scorpio and Libra.......... 13
Scorpio and Scorpio 13
Scorpio and Sagittarius.......... 13
Scorpio and Capricorn 14
Scorpio and Aquarius 14
Scorpio and Pisces 14
Tips for Men Dating Scorpio Women 15
Tips for Women Dating Scorpio Men 16

CHAPTER 3: FRIENDS AND FAMILY 17

CHAPTER 4: CAREER AND MONEY 23

Intensity and Emotional Expression 27
Tendency to Hold Grudges 27
Desire for Control 27
Resistance to Change 28
Tendency Toward Secrecy 28
Difficulty in Accepting Constructive Criticism 28
Overwhelm from High Expectations 28

CHAPTER 5: SELF-IMPROVEMENT 30

Utilizing Strengths 32
Overcoming Weaknesses 32
Seeking Support 34

CHAPTER 6: THE YEAR AHEAD 35

Love and Relationships 36
Solar and Lunar Eclipses 39
Mercury Retrograde 39
Jupiter Transits 40
Saturn Transits 40
Venus Retrograde 40
Mars Transits 40
New Moon and Full Moon Phases 40

CHAPTER 7: FAMOUS SCORPIO PERSONALITIES 42

CONCLUSION ---------- 49

INTRODUCTION

Throughout history humans have yearned to find significance and direction through the bodies that grace our night sky. This timeless practice, known as astrology, weaves together elements of science, symbolism and spirituality. At its core, astrology is a belief system centered around the idea that the positions and movements of objects like stars and planets can influence our lives here on Earth. It rests upon the belief that the alignment of these bodies at the moment of an individual's birth can provide insights into their personality traits, destiny and life experiences. Various systems and traditions fall under astrologys umbrella. Western astrology stands as its most widely recognized form. This system revolves around twelve zodiac signs, each linked to characteristics and personality traits.

In this book we embark on a journey to explore one of the signs, in the zodiac. Scorpio. Represented by the scorpion, it is known for its intense emotions, passion and transformative nature. In this book's pages we will explore the essence of Scorpio in depth. We'll delve into its symbolism, personality traits, strengths, weaknesses and compatibility with other signs. Our goal is to unravel the mysteries surrounding Scorpio and reveal its hidden aspects. In turn you can gain an understanding of either yourself or the Scorpios in your life.

OVERVIEW OF SCORPIO ZODIAC SIGN

- **Date of Star Sign**: October 23 - November 21.
- **Symbol**: Scorpion. The scorpion symbolizes the sign's intensity, determination and capability for transformation.
- **Element**: Water. Scorpio is associated with the water element. This element signifies Scorpio's emotional depth and sensitivity.
- **Planet**: Pluto (Traditional ruler: Mars). Pluto symbolizes transformation, power and rebirth. Mars, the ancient ruler, adds an element of action, assertiveness and energy.
- **Color**: Deep and intense shades such as dark red, maroon and black. These colors reflect Scorpio's passion, mystery and depth.

COMPATIBILITY

Scorpios compatibility can vary depending on the zodiac sign of the person. Scorpios tend to build strong connections, with signs like Cancer, Pisces and other Scorpios because they share emotional depth and intuition. They may have passionate relationships with Taurus and Leo. However it's important to remember that compatibility also relies on personalities and how well they complement each other's strengths and weaknesses.

PERSONALITY TRAITS

Scorpio individuals are known for their intense and complex personalities. Here are some key personality traits associated with Scorpio.

- **Passionate**: Scorpios are incredibly passionate and driven. They approach life with intensity and commitment. Energy is poured into their pursuits and relationships.
- **Determined**: Scorpios are highly determined and persistent. Once they set their sights on a goal, they will stop at nothing to achieve it. Their strong willpower often leads them to success.
- **Mysterious**: Scorpios have a mysterious aura about them. They tend to keep their true feelings and thoughts guarded. Only revealing what they choose to share. This enigmatic quality adds to their allure.
- **Resilient**: Scorpios possess remarkable resilience. They have the ability to bounce back from adversity and transform challenges into opportunities.

- **Resourceful**: Scorpios are resourceful problem solvers. They have a knack for finding creative solutions to complex problems. As such they are not easily deterred by obstacles.

STRENGTHS

- **Loyal**: Scorpios are fiercely loyal to their friends and loved ones. They will stand by your side through thick and thin.
- **Brave**: They have a fearless nature and are unafraid to confront difficult situations or truths.
- **Determined**: Scorpios have an unwavering determination to succeed in their endeavors.
- **Intuitive**: Their strong intuition allows them to read people and situations well, making them excellent judges of character.
- **Passionate**: Scorpios bring an intense passion to everything they do. This makes them magnetic and captivating individuals.

WEAKNESSES

- **Jealous**: Scorpios can be prone to jealousy and possessiveness. This sometimes leads to conflicts.
- **Secretive**: They tend to keep their emotions and thoughts hidden. Overall this can make things challenging for others to truly understand them.

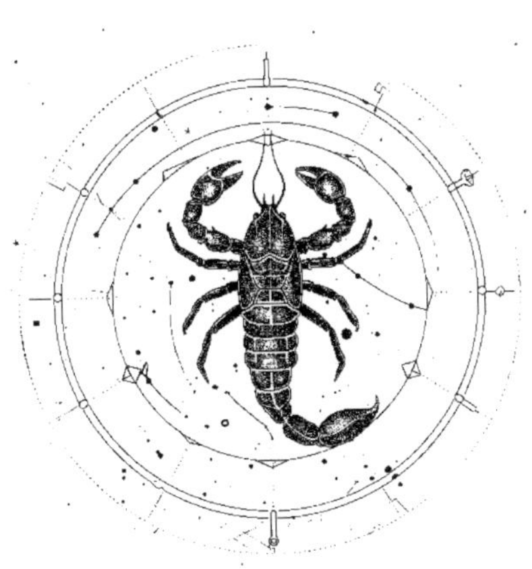

- **Stubborn**: Scorpios can be incredibly stubborn. Once they make up their minds, it's challenging to change their course.

- **Vindictive**: When wronged, Scorpios can hold grudges and seek revenge.
- **Intense**: Their intensity can be overwhelming for some. Clashes may occur in personal and professional relationships.

As we journey through the pages of this book you can anticipate discovering the many aspects of Scorpios energy, strengths and weaknesses. Furthermore we will provide insights to help you navigate relationships with Scorpios or gain a deeper understanding of yourself if you were born under this sign. This exploration will take us on a voyage as we unlock the mysteries of Scorpio. One that will tap into its power for personal growth, meaningful connections with others and a greater appreciation for how the universe subtly influences our lives. So go ahead and turn the page. It's time to embark on this captivating journey into the enigmatic realm of Scorpio.

CHAPTER 1:
HISTORY AND MYTHOLOGY

The Scorpio constellation, a prominent and distinctive figure in the night sky, has captured the imagination of humans for millennia. Its historical and mythological origins vary across different ancient civilizations. Each offers unique insights into how Scorpio was observed and represented in their star maps. Let's take a closer look.

EARLIEST OBSERVATIONS IN ANCIENT CIVILIZATIONS

BABYLON

The origins of Scorpio can be traced back to ancient Babylon, where it was known as "MUL.GIR.TAB," meaning "the scorpion." The Babylonians were meticulous astronomers who associated this constellation with the goddess Ishtar. They believed Scorpio's appearance in the sky was significant for predicting weather patterns and agricultural cycles.

ANCIENT EGYPT

In ancient Egypt, Scorpio held great significance. The constellation was closely linked to the goddess Serqet, often depicted with a scorpion's head. Serqet was a protective deity associated with medicine and healing. Scorpio's appearance in the night sky was considered a symbol of transformation, renewal and protection.

ANCIENT GREEK

In Greek mythology, Scorpio is associated with the story of Orion. A giant scorpion sent by Gaia to defeat him. This battle resulted in Orion's demise and the scorpion was placed in the heavens as a constellation. Scorpio symbolizes the consequences of hubris and revenge.

CHINESE

In Chinese astronomy, Scorpio is not an independent constellation but is part of the Azure Dragon of the East. It represents autumn and the metal element. This plays a key role in Chinese astrology and cosmology.

INDIAN

In Hindu astrology, Scorpio corresponds to the nakshatra (lunar mansion) called Anuradha. Anuradha represents success through determination, devotion and friendship. It is associated with the Hindu god Mitra. She is a deity of contracts and friendship.

MAYAN

The ancient Maya had their own interpretations of celestial objects, including Scorpio. They likely incorporated into their complex calendar systems and mythologies.

The above are all diverse cultural perceptions and representations of Scorpio. All highlight the multifaceted nature of human understanding of the night sky. Scorpio's enduring presence in mythology and astronomy serves as a testament to humanity's timeless fascination with the cosmos.

Throughout ancient civilizations, Scorpio held an important place. As time progressed astrology transformed to introspective and personality focused perspectives. Nowadays Scorpio is associated with depth, passion and personal transformation. Those born under this sign are believed to possess qualities such as intensity, resourcefulness and a sincere desire for authenticity.

HISTORICAL EVENTS UNDER THE SCORPIO SIGN

The Scorpio season has witnessed significant historical events. While it's important to note that astrology doesn't provide explanations for these events, some intriguing occurrences have taken place during this period.

- **The Russian Revolution (October 1917)**: This pivotal event in world history, began in October 1917. Scorpio's association with transformation and upheaval aligns with the radical changes that occurred during this time. Ultimately it led to the establishment of the Soviet Union.
- **The Cuban Missile Crisis (October 1962):** Scorpio's intensity and potential for power struggles were evident during this tense confrontation between the United States and the Soviet Union. It almost brought the world to the brink of nuclear war.
- **The Fall of the Berlin Wall (November 1989)**: Scorpio's theme of rebirth and transformation resonates with the fall of the Berlin Wall. This event symbolized the end of the Cold War era and the reunification of Germany.

HISTORICAL FIGURES BORN UNDER SCORPIO

Several influential historical figures were born under the Scorpio sign. They showcase the diversity of impact and personality traits associated with this sign.

- **Marie Curie (November 7, 1867)**: The pioneering physicist and chemist who conducted groundbreaking research on radioactivity. Her relentless determination and transformative discoveries align with Scorpio traits.
- **Martin Luther (November 10, 1483):** The leader of the Protestant Reformation who challenged established norms and ignited religious and social change. His personality resonates with Scorpio's propensity for transformation.
- **Indira Gandhi (November 19, 1917)**: India's first female Prime Minister who exhibited Scorpio's determination, leadership, and intense commitment to her political ideals.

As we conclude this chapter with contemplation we acknowledge the tapestry of stories and historical significance surrounding the constellation of Scorpio. From its early observations by ancient civilizations to its diverse mythological interpretations over time. Scorpio has consistently captivated human imagination. Its influence transcends time leaving a lasting impact, on both the past and present. In today's astrology Scorpio holds a key position. One for providing understanding into the intricate aspects of human behavior. Whether delving into one's mind or deciphering the complexities of relationships. Scorpio remains meaningful and relatable in our lives.

FURTHER READING AND REFERENCES

For those who wish to delve deeper into the history and mythology of Scorpio, here is a list of primary sources, ancient texts and modern writings.

Primary Sources and Ancient Texts:

- "Enuma Anu Enlil" - An ancient Babylonian cuneiform text that contains references to Scorpio and its astrological significance.
- "Book of the Dead" - Egyptian funerary texts that mention the protective deity Serqet, associated with the Scorpio constellation.
- Classical Greek and Roman mythology texts, including the works of Hesiod, Ovid, and Homer, which feature stories related to Scorpio.

Modern Writings

- "The Only Astrology Book You'll Ever Need" by Joanna Martine Woolfolk - A comprehensive guide to astrology that includes insights into Scorpio and its characteristics.
- "The Secret Language of Birthdays" by Gary Goldschneider and Joost Elffers - This book explores the personality traits associated with each day of the year, offering insights into Scorpio birthdays.
- "Astrology: The Twelve Zodiac Signs" by Judy Hall - A book that provides a detailed overview of each zodiac sign, including Scorpio, with a focus on personality traits and compatibility.
- "The Inner Sky: How to Make Wiser Choices for a More Fulfilling Life" by Steven Forrest - This book delves into the psychological and spiritual dimensions of astrology, including Scorpio's transformative potential.

CHAPTER 2: LOVE & COMPATIBILITY

In this chapter we embark on a journey into the world of love and relationships focusing on the perspective of individuals born under the Scorpio zodiac sign. Scorpios are known for their aura and deep emotional nature, which provides a viewpoint on romantic connections. This chapter will guide you in understanding the intricacies and subtleties of Scorpios language of love. From their needs to their unwavering loyalty we will dissect what makes love such an all encompassing experience for Scorpios.

We will also delve into the dynamics of communication and trust within Scorpio relationships illuminating how these crucial aspects foster connections for them. Additionally we'll explore the compatibility between Scorpios and other zodiac signs shedding light on both the synergies and challenges that may arise in these unions.

Lastly this chapter aims to dispel misconceptions about Scorpios in matters of love by providing an understanding of their true romantic nature. Throughout this journey you will acquire understanding of the realm of love and relationships as experienced by Scorpio individuals. Brace yourself to explore the depths of Scorpio, where intensity and passion intertwine with vulnerability and profoundness.

LOVE APPROACH

Scorpio is often associated with a sense of intensity, passion and a strong desire for connection. Individuals born under this water sign, tend to approach matters of the heart with a blend of intrigue and fervor. Let's take a closer look at how Scorpios approach love and romance.

- **Intense Passion**; Scorpios are renowned for their intense nature. When they fall in love they do so with their whole being. They crave deep connections and are willing to invest into nurturing their relationships. This intensity can create a whirlwind of emotions in their love lives which can be both exhilarating and challenging.
- **Emotional Depth**; Scorpios have mastered the art of delving into the depths of their emotions. They fearlessly confront not only their feelings but also those of their partners. This emotional honesty often leads to close intimacy and strong bonds.
- **Loyalty**; Once committed to a relationship Scorpios display unwavering loyalty. As such they expect the level of commitment from their partners. Meanwhile they occasionally exhibit possessiveness.
- **Unforgiving**; Scorpios are known for their unforgiving nature, driven by their need to safeguard what they hold dear. Betrayal can have a negative impact on them making it difficult for them to forgive and forget.
- **Mysterious**; Scorpios tend to have a mysterious aura. They tend to keep some secrets and emotions hidden. This can be both captivating and alluring to partners. Mystery adds excitement to relationships keeping their partners guessing and intrigued.
- **Overprotective**; Scorpios should be aware that they can sometimes experience feelings of jealousy and possessiveness. As such they may find themselves becoming overly protective of their partners or struggling with trust issues. It is important for them to strike a balance in order to maintain a relationship.
- **Controlling**; Scorpios are naturally drawn towards power and control in their relationships. Typically they seek partners who complement this desire.

However it is crucial for them to manage this need for control carefully. Sometimes it can lead to power struggles within the relationship.

- **Sensuality**; Scorpios take pleasure in exploring their sensuality. They are often regarded as sexual individuals who deeply appreciate physical intimacy.
- **Transformative**; When it comes to love Scorpios have a passionate and all encompassing approach. They are known for their ability to bring about transformation and healing in their partners through profound experiences.

In summary Scorpios approach love with passion, emotional depth, loyalty and an air of mystery. While they possess a charm they also face challenges, like jealousy and possessiveness. Overall this requires collaboration and navigation in their relationships.

SCORPIO LOVE AND COMPATIBILITY WITH OTHER ZODIAC SIGNS

SCORPIO AND ARIES

Scorpio and Aries share a powerful and passionate connection. Both signs are intense and strong-willed. They are drawn to each other's energy and love challenges. This can lead to fiery clashes or incredible chemistry. Communication and compromise are essential for this relationship to thrive.

SCORPIO AND TAURUS

Scorpio and Taurus are opposites in the zodiac. This can create a magnetic attraction. Scorpio's intensity may initially intrigue Taurus. However their stubbornness can lead to conflicts. Shared desire for loyalty and commitment can make this relationship work with effort and patience.

SCORPIO AND GEMINI

Scorpio and Gemini have different approaches to life and love. Scorpio values depth and emotional connection. Gemini seeks variety and mental stimulation. These differences can create misunderstandings. Although with open communication and compromise, they can learn from each other and grow.

SCORPIO AND CANCER

Scorpio and Cancer are a natural match in the zodiac. Both signs prioritize emotional connection and nurturing. Their shared empathy and intuition create a strong bond. They easily understand each other's needs. This relationship is often characterized by deep intimacy and loyalty.

SCORPIO AND LEO

Scorpio and Leo are both strong-willed signs, which can lead to power struggles. However, their intense personalities can also fuel a passionate connection. With respect for each other's need for recognition and control, they can build a dynamic and exciting relationship.

SCORPIO AND VIRGO

Scorpio and Virgo share a deep appreciation for detail and a desire for perfection. While they have different ways of expressing it, their mutual dedication and work ethic can create a harmonious partnership. Overall they can complement each other well if they focus on their strengths.

SCORPIO AND LIBRA

Scorpio and Libra have contrasting approaches to relationships. Scorpio seeks depth and intensity. Libra values balance and harmony. This can lead to conflicts. However if they can find common ground and compromise, their differences can create a well-rounded partnership.

SCORPIO AND SCORPIO

Two Scorpios together can be a passionate and intense combination. They understand each other's emotional depth and need for loyalty. However, their possessiveness and jealousy can lead to power struggles. Trust is key for this relationship to work.

SCORPIO AND SAGITTARIUS

Scorpio and Sagittarius have different outlooks on life and love. Scorpio seeks depth and commitment. Sagittarius values freedom and adventure. These differences can create challenges. Although if they can find a balance, they can make it work.

SCORPIO AND CAPRICORN

Scorpio and Capricorn share a practical and goal-oriented approach to life. They both value commitment and loyalty. This can create a stable and enduring partnership. Their shared determination can help them overcome obstacles together.

SCORPIO AND AQUARIUS

Scorpio and Aquarius have very different personalities and values. Scorpio values emotional depth. Aquarius is more detached and intellectual. Building trust and understanding can be a challenge. However, if they can appreciate each other's uniqueness, they can find common ground.

SCORPIO AND PISCES

Scorpio and Pisces are both water signs, making for a deep and emotionally intuitive connection. They share a profound understanding of each other's feelings and desires. This relationship is often marked by empathy, creativity and a strong spiritual connection.

In astrology, while compatibility can be influenced by sun signs, it's essential to consider the entire birth chart for a more accurate assessment of a relationship's dynamics. Many other factors, such as moon signs, rising signs, and planetary placements, play a significant role in compatibility.

DATING AND RELATIONSHIPS

When it comes to dating and relationships with Scorpio individuals it can be thrilling and intense. Scorpios are famous for their passionate, loyal and intense disposition. Whether you're a man or woman looking to date or maintain a relationship with a Scorpio partner, here are some pointers to guide you.

TIPS FOR MEN DATING SCORPIO WOMEN

- **Honesty**: Scorpio women value honesty and authenticity above all else. Don't try to hide your feelings or intentions. They can easily detect deception. Be open about your emotions and thoughts.
- **Show Loyalty:** Loyalty is a crucial aspect of any relationship with a Scorpio woman. Once she commits to you, she expects the same level of commitment in return. Flirting with others or showing signs of disloyalty can lead to trust issues.
- **Respect Her Independence**: Scorpio women are strong and independent individuals. Respect her need for personal space. Don't try to control or possess her. Encourage her to pursue her passions and interests.
- Embrace Her Intensity: Scorpio women are known for their intense emotions. Be prepared to handle their deep feelings. Don't shy away from discussing emotional topics. Show empathy and understanding when she's going through challenging times.
- **Surprise Her**: Scorpio women appreciate thoughtfulness and surprises. Plan special and meaningful gestures to keep the relationship exciting and show your commitment.
- **Communicate Openly**: Effective communication is essential in any relationship. Particularly with Scorpio women. They value deep conversations. They want to know your thoughts and feelings. Avoid being evasive or non-committal.

TIPS FOR WOMEN DATING SCORPIO MEN

- **Respect His Privacy**: Scorpio men can be quite secretive. They value their privacy. Avoid prying too much into their personal affairs. Allow them space to open up at their own pace.
- **Show Trust**: Trust is vital for Scorpio men. If you want to maintain a relationship with them. Trust them and do not engage in unnecessary jealousy or possessiveness.
- **Be Independent**: Scorpio men are attracted to strong, independent women. Women who have their own goals and passions. Maintain your individuality and encourage him to do the same.
- **Enjoy Intimacy:** Scorpio men are known for their passion and sensuality. Embrace this aspect of your relationship and explore your physical connection together.
- **Handle Conflicts Maturely**: Scorpio men can be intense and argumentative. Maintain your composure. Try to resolve issues through calm and rational discussions. Avoid escalating arguments.
- **Share Your Thoughts**: Scorpio men appreciate partners who can engage in deep and meaningful conversations. Share your thoughts, ideas and feelings openly. This will help you connect on a more profound level.

Regardless of whether you're a man or a woman it's important to keep in mind that every Scorpio individual is unique. As such their compatibility and preferences may differ. Ultimately a relationship with a Scorpio requires patience, understanding and an openness to embrace their passionate nature. By respecting their boundaries, being honest and nurturing the connection you can create a fulfilling and long lasting partnership with a Scorpio.

As we wrap up this chapter one thing is abundantly clear. Scorpio individuals aren't just searching for love. They yearn for connections that touch the depths of their soul. They're willing to put their heart and soul into love. For them it's a profound experience that requires openness, trust and a willingness to delve into the depths of the human heart. While there might be challenges arising from their possessiveness or occasional bouts of jealousy. Scorpios have the ability to bring about healing and personal growth in their partners.

As we continue our exploration of Scorpio's personality we invite you to carry these insights with you. Whether you are a Scorpio seeking love or someone lucky to have encountered the magnetic allure of this zodiac sign. May you embrace the intensity, value the depth and relish in the power that Scorpio love brings into your life.

CHAPTER 3:
FRIENDS AND FAMILY

In this chapter we are about to embark on a journey into the world of Scorpio individuals and their relationships with friends and family. Scorpios have a reputation for being intense, passionate and complex. These unique qualities shape the dynamics within their friendships and families. By reading this chapter you'll gain insight into the intricacies as strengths and challenges of being in a Scorpios inner circle. Whether you're a Scorpio seeking understanding of your place in friendship or family dynamics. Or simply curious about how Scorpios approach these relationships from others. Together let's uncover the depths of Scorpios relationships and witness the transformative power they hold.

FRIENDSHIPS

Having a friend who's a Scorpio is like having a devoted companion who will support you unconditionally. Scorpios possess qualities that make them fascinating and dependable as friends. Here's what it's like to have a Scorpio as your friend.

- **Loyalty**; Scorpios are loyal friends. Once they commit to a friendship they stand by it for the long run. Trust is of great importance to them. As such they will go above and beyond to protect their friends.
- **Intensity and Passion;** Scorpio friends are renowned for their intensity and passion. They approach their friendships with fervent energy and invest deeply. They aim to ensure that their friends feel loved and supported.
- **Depth**; Scorpios dive into the depths of emotions encouraging their friends to do the same. They are the kind of companions with whom you can share feelings without fear of judgment or criticism.
- **Honesty**; Honesty holds important value for Scorpios. Both in themselves and in those they befriend. They will always be honest with you even if the truth is hard to hear. Although they can sometimes come across as blunt. Rest assured that they genuinely care about you.
- **Protective**; Scorpios are incredibly loyal and protective of their friends. They will go to great lengths to support and defend you. Their strong sense of camaraderie ensures they stand by friends during tough times.
- **Empathy and Intuition;** Scorpios possess strong intuition. They are often able to discern their friends' emotions and needs even before they are expressed. Such deep empathy enables them to be there when friends require support.
- **Mystery and Intrigue**; Scorpio friends exude an aura of mystery that's both intriguing and captivating. They willingly discuss topics that others may shy away from. This intellectual stimulation makes their friendships compelling and thought provoking.
- **Challenges**; While Scorpios make great friends it's important to acknowledge that there may be challenges. Dealing with their intensity or occasional possessiveness can prove challenging. In some instances they might hold onto grudges longer than individuals belonging to zodiac signs. In the end their determination to resolve problems and dedication to friendship usually comes out on top.

To sum it up, having a Scorpio as a friend means having a devoted, intense and emotionally profound companion. They bring excitement and intrigue to your life. They are consistently supportive during life's highs and lows. If you appreciate honesty, loyalty and emotional depth, a Scorpio friend in your life is truly valuable.

FAMILY

Family holds great importance for Scorpios. They bring an intense nature into the dynamics of their family life. Overall they approach their family roles with a strong sense of loyalty, protection and emotional depth. Let's take a close look at how Scorpios contribute to the dynamics within their families.

- **Committed**; Scorpios are incredibly loyal to their family. They remain committed to supporting and protecting their loved ones through thick and thin. During challenging times they are often the ones who can be relied upon.
- **Emotional Depth**; Scorpios infuse family relationships with emotional depth. They are often the family members who encourage open and honest communication. As such they create an environment where everyone feels free to express their emotions.
- **Protective**; Scorpios have a protective instinct when it comes to their family. They will go above and beyond to ensure the well being and safety of their loved ones.
- **Empathy and Intuition;** Scorpios possess a strong sense of empathy and intuition. One that allows them to be attuned to the needs of their family. They often have a sense of when something's wrong and are quick to offer support and comfort.
- **Strong Family Bonds**; Scorpios have an ability to form unbreakable bonds within their families. These bonds are built on trust, loyalty and shared experiences. Scorpio family members often confide in each other and provide strength to one another.
- **Resilience and Determination**; Scorpios are renowned for their resilience and determination. As parents or elders, they pass on these qualities, teaching youngsters the importance of perseverance and facing life's challenges head on.
- **Power Struggles;** There can be instances where Scorpios engage in power struggles within the family. Their strong will and desire for control may lead to conflicts with dominant family members. It's important for Scorpios to learn when it is necessary to compromise or let go.
- **Healing and Transformation**; Scorpios possess a transformative quality. They often playing a role in helping their family members grow emotionally and heal from experiences. During times of crisis or personal growth they offer support and guidance.
- **Independence**; Scorpios highly value their independence. This can sometimes cause conflicts within the family during adolescence or early

adulthood. They may assert their need for autonomy, challenging controlling family members' acceptance.

In summary Scorpio's contribution to family dynamics is characterized by their loyalty, emotions and a strong protective instinct. They form deep connections and often serve as the emotional pillars within their families. While their intense nature may occasionally lead to conflicts, their unwavering commitment to their loved ones make them invaluable members of any family.

CHALLENGES IN FRIENDSHIPS AND FAMILY RELATIONS

Scorpios are well known for their loyalty, intense emotions and strong connections with others. However they do face challenges when it comes to their friendships and family relationships due to their personality traits. Here are some of the difficulties Scorpios may encounter in these connections.

- **Intensity and Jealousy**; Scorpio's intense passion can sometimes be overwhelming for those to them. Their occasional jealousy and possessiveness may lead to conflicts especially when they feel threatened or insecure in their relationships.
- **Stubbornness**; Scorpio's determination and stubbornness can be both a strength and a hindrance. While it helps them stay focused in situations it may also make it hard for them to compromise.
- **Secretive**; Scorpios tend to be individuals who cherish secrecy. While this adds an element of mystery around them it can also create trust issues. Others might feel left out or uncertain about what Scorpio feels or intends.
- **Depth**; Scorpios possess emotional depth. This is a quality that can both empower and challenge them in relationships. As such they might find it difficult to navigate through emotions at times. They might expect others to match their level of emotional intensity, which could prove unrealistic for some people.
- **Unforgiving**; It can be challenging for Scorpios to forgive easily. They tend to hold onto grudges and struggle to let go of grievances. This can lead to standing conflicts and strained relationships.
- **Controlling**; Scorpios often have a desire for control. This desire for dominance can create tension and conflicts.
- **Closed off;** Scorpios tend to fear vulnerability. They may find it difficult to open up about their emotions and insecurities. Overall it can hinder emotional connections and prevent them from fully expressing themselves.
- **High expectations**; Scorpios have high expectations for their relationships. They place a burden on their friends and family expecting unwavering loyalty. When these expectations are not met they may feel disappointed or hurt.
- **Emotional intensity**; Scorpios emotional intensity can be overwhelming for some people. Friends and family members may occasionally need breaks from the rollercoaster that comes with being in a relationship with a Scorpio.

Despite these challenges it's important to acknowledge that Scorpios bring excellent qualities to their friendships and families. By acknowledging and addressing their challenges Scorpios can cultivate relationships with their loved ones that're more balanced and satisfying. Effective communication, empathy and self awareness serve as tools in overcoming these challenges. Overall working on these challenges can lead to fostering connections that're healthier and more fulfilling.

Throughout this chapter we have embarked on an exploration of Scorpio individuals within the context of their friendships and family dynamics. With their loyalty, passion and intricate emotional nature Scorpios establish connections that are both captivating and transformative. As we wrap up this chapter lets take a moment to think about the Scorpio people in our lives. They are the friends who always have our backs and the family members who support us no matter what. Let's embrace their intensity, value their loyalty and approach the challenges that come with Scorpio connections, with empathy and understanding. These relationships are intricate and meaningful showcasing how Scorpios influence can truly transform the lives of those they care about.

CHAPTER 4: CAREER AND MONEY

In this chapter we delve into the realm of Scorpio individuals and their connections to their careers and finances. Within this chapter we explore how Scorpios approach their careers with determination, resourcefulness and a yearning for depth. We investigate their leadership qualities, financial expertise and ability to thrive under pressure. From entrepreneurship to healing professions Scorpios exhibit a range of career preferences. Additionally this chapter addresses the obstacles that Scorpios may encounter in their careers and offers strategies to overcome them. By doing so we aim to assist Scorpio individuals in leveraging their strengths while navigating challenges.

Join us as we uncover the secrets behind Scorpios success in the world of work and finance. Whether you are a Scorpio seeking guidance on your career journey or simply intrigued by the approach that Scorpios take towards wealth and work this chapter serves as an invaluable resource.

CAREER ASPIRATIONS

Scorpios approach their career aspirations with the level of intensity and passion that they bring to other aspects of their lives. They are recognized for their determination, resourcefulness and ability to excel in a range of fields. Let's take a look at the career preferences and professional aspirations commonly associated with Scorpios.

- **Craving for Depth**; Scorpios thrive in careers that allow them to dive deep into their work. They are naturally drawn to professions where they can uncover truths, solve problems and explore the underlying motivations behind people or systems. This makes them well suited for careers in fields such as psychology, criminology, research and investigative journalism.
- **Leadership Skills;** Scorpios possess leadership qualities. They have a knack for taking charge and propelling projects forward. Due to this talent they often find themselves attracted to positions of authority. For example in management roles where they can effectively lead and influence others.
- **Financial Acumen**; Many Scorpios have an interest in finance. They possess sharp money management skills. As such they tend to excel in careers related to investments, banking services, financial analysis or accounting. Their natural shrewdness combined with their shrewd attitude equips them well for navigating the complexities of the financial world.
- **Entrepreneurial Drive**; The independent spirit and ambition inherent within Scorpios often lead them down the path of entrepreneurship. They are willing to take calculated risks and work tirelessly to transform their ideas into profitable ventures. Their passion and determination drive them to overcome obstacles and achieve their goals.

- **Healing Professions**; Scorpios naturally possess empathy and are drawn towards professions that involve assisting others. They may choose careers in medicine, psychology, counseling or therapy. Here they can make an impact on people's lives through healing and personal growth.
- **Creative Fields**; Scorpios often have a creative spirit that they express through careers in the arts, music, writing or acting. They approach their pursuits with a sense of passion and emotion creating work that deeply resonates with others.
- **Scientific Research**; Scorpios possess an analytical nature. This makes them well suited for research and exploration. Fields such as biology, chemistry, astronomy and forensics might captivate their interest. Overall they enjoy unraveling the mysteries of the universe.
- **Tech and IT;** With their problem solving skills, Scorpios can excel in the technology and information technology (IT) sectors. They are drawn towards careers, in software development, cybersecurity, data analysis and other tech related domains.
- **Occult and Metaphysical Interests**; Some Scorpios find themselves intrigued by occultism or metaphysical subjects. Careers such as astrology, tarot card reading, spiritual counseling or metaphysical healing.

To summarize Scorpios approach their careers with a sense of purpose, passion and determination. They thrive in roles that allow them to delve into their chosen field, showcase their leadership skills and have an impact on others. Whether they pursue professions, start ventures or engage in creative pursuits. Scorpio's unwavering commitment to excellence and drive for success make them highly accomplished professionals.

CAREER STRENGTHS

Scorpio individuals have a set of unique strengths that often contribute to their success in the workplace. Their intense determination and innate abilities make them highly valued assets in various settings. Let's explore some of the strengths that make Scorpio individuals excel in their careers.

- **Determination and Perseverance**; Scorpios are known for their resolve and persistence. Once they set their sights on a goal or project they pursue it relentlessly. This determination enables them to overcome obstacles and stay focused on achieving their objectives. In conclusion it makes them exceptionally effective in their roles.

- **Resourcefulness**; Scorpios possess a talent for finding solutions to problems. They can think outside the box, which proves invaluable in the workplace. They also excel at discovering unique approaches to tackle challenges and enhance processes.
- **Intuition**; Scorpios have a strong sense of intuition, which allows them to make great decisions. They often trust their gut instincts enabling them to make tough choices in situations such as negotiations, problem solving or decision making.
- **Strong Leadership Skills**; Scorpios inherently possess leadership qualities. They exude confidence, assertiveness and fearlessness when it comes to taking charge when necessary.
- **Emotional Intelligence**; Scorpio individuals possess an understanding of emotions both their own and those of others. This emotional intelligence aids them in building relationships, resolving conflicts and navigating interpersonal dynamics.
- **Attention to Detail**; Scorpios pay attention to the smallest details. They are thorough in their work and often catch errors that others might overlook. This meticulousness ensures that their projects and tasks are executed with precision.
- **Passion and Commitment;** Scorpios bring a passion to their work. They are also fully committed to their responsibilities.
- **Ability to Thrive Under Pressure**; Scorpios excel under pressure. They are known for remaining calm and composed in high stress situations. This resilience enables them to perform well when faced with deadlines or challenging circumstances.
- **Problem Solving Skills**; Scorpios possess an aptitude for problem solving. They enjoy tackling issues and finding solutions. Their analytical mindset coupled with unwavering determination makes them highly adept at resolving challenges.
- **Strategic Thinking Abilities;** Scorpios exhibit strategic thinking skills. They anticipate trends and make decisions that align with long term objectives. This makes them valuable assets, in strategic planning and decision making positions.
- **Dedication to Achieving Excellence**; Scorpios exhibit a dedication to achieving excellence. They set high standards for themselves and take pride in producing quality work. This commitment often leads to recognition and career growth.

To summarize Scorpio individuals thrive in the workplace due to their perseverance, emotional intelligence and exceptional leadership qualities. Their ability to handle pressure, attention to detail and unwavering commitment, to achieving excellence make them valued team members and leaders.

CHALLENGES IN THE WORKPLACE

Scorpio individuals, while possessing many strengths, also face certain challenges that can impact their professional growth. Recognizing these challenges and implementing strategies to overcome them is crucial for Scorpios to thrive in the workplace. Here are some common challenges faced by Scorpio individuals in their careers and strategies to address them.

INTENSITY AND EMOTIONAL EXPRESSION

- Challenge: Scorpios' intense emotions can sometimes be overwhelming in professional settings. Their passion can come across as intimidating or overly dramatic.
- Strategy: Scorpios can work on managing their emotional intensity by practicing mindfulness. Take deep breaths before responding. Find emotional relief through exercise or creative pursuits.

TENDENCY TO HOLD GRUDGES

- Challenge: Scorpios may have difficulty letting go of past conflicts or grievances. This can hinder collaboration and team dynamics.
- Strategy: Scorpios can benefit from practicing forgiveness. Addressing conflicts directly and seeking resolution is also essential.

DESIRE FOR CONTROL

- Challenge: Scorpios' strong desire for control can lead to micromanagement or reluctance to delegate tasks. This can impede team efficiency and collaboration.
- Strategy: Scorpios can develop trust in their colleagues' abilities and focus on delegating tasks according to their team members' strengths. Learning to let go of control and empowering others can lead to more productive teamwork.

RESISTANCE TO CHANGE

- Challenge: Scorpios may be resistant to change, preferring stability and familiarity in their work environment.
- Strategy: Scorpios can cultivate adaptability by embracing change as an opportunity for growth and learning. They can seek out new challenges and view change as a chance to excel rather than as a threat.

TENDENCY TOWARD SECRECY

- Challenge: Scorpios' secretive nature can lead to a lack of transparency in their professional relationships, potentially eroding trust.
- Strategy: Scorpios can practice open communication and transparency with colleagues and superiors. Sharing information and being open about their intentions can foster trust and strengthen workplace relationships.

DIFFICULTY IN ACCEPTING CONSTRUCTIVE CRITICISM

- Challenge: Scorpios may struggle with receiving constructive criticism, interpreting it as a personal attack rather than an opportunity for improvement.
- Strategy: Scorpios can work on developing a growth mindset, understanding that feedback is essential for development. They can learn to separate their self-worth from criticism and focus on using feedback to enhance their skills.

OVERWHELM FROM HIGH EXPECTATIONS

- Challenge: Scorpios' high expectations for themselves and others can lead to feelings of overwhelm and burnout.
- Strategy: Scorpios can set realistic goals and prioritize self-care. Learning to balance their drive for excellence with self-compassion and acknowledging their limits is essential for long-term success.

In summary individuals born under the Scorpio zodiac sign can overcome these obstacles by developing self awareness, practicing adaptability and improving their communication and conflict resolution skills. By acknowledging their tendencies and implementing these strategies Scorpios can navigate their lives effectively and continue to thrive in their chosen fields.

Throughout this chapter we have explored the world of Scorpio individuals and their unique approach to careers and finances. The unwavering determination, resourcefulness and intense passion that drive Scorpios serve as guiding principles on their journey towards success in the workplace and financial mastery.

Their innate leadership qualities, ability to handle pressure with grace and relentless pursuit of excellence distinguish them in any setting. However we have also examined the challenges that may arise for Scorpios such, as intensity and resistance to change. By acknowledging these challenges head on and implementing strategies to overcome them Scorpios can fully unleash their potential within the realm.

As we bring this chapter to a close we encourage you to embrace the Scorpio approach when shaping your career path and financial journey. If you happen to be a Scorpio looking to enhance your abilities or if you are simply fascinated by their characteristics. Allow yourself to be inspired by the drive, persistence and strength that Scorpio individuals exhibit. By staying committed and employing strategic thought processes Scorpios can emerge as successful architects of their financial futures.

CHAPTER 5:
SELF-IMPROVEMENT

In this chapter we will dive into the journey of self discovery for Scorpios. We will explore how they harness their strengths, confront their weaknesses head on and navigate the path towards self improvement. Come along with us as we uncover the secrets behind Scorpios unwavering dedication to growth. We will also provide strategies and insights that can inspire anyone. Regardless of whether they're a Scorpio or not. So whether you are a Scorpio seeking excellence or someone intrigued by the approach that Scorpios take in bettering themselves this chapter will serve as your guide.

PERSONAL GROWTH AND SELF DEVELOPMENT

Personal growth and self development hold significance for individuals born under the zodiac sign of Scorpio. Here are some essential elements pertaining to growth and development specific to Scorpio individuals.

- **Embracing Vulnerability**; Scorpios are renowned for their depth and intensity. A significant aspect of growth for a Scorpio involves embracing vulnerability allowing oneself to express emotions openly. This process fosters connections with others. Ultimately it cultivates a deeper understanding of oneself.
- **Self Reflection**; Self reflection is highly beneficial for Scorpios. Their introspective nature empowers them to delve into their psyche exploring their motivations, desires and fears in detail. Activities such as journaling, meditation or therapy serve as tools for Scorpios to gain insights into their worlds.
- **Life Altering Experiences**; Scorpios often seek experiences that push them beyond their comfort zones. These experiences can take the form of challenges, travel adventures or even spiritual journeys.
- **Embracing Change;** Due to their desire for control Scorpios tend to be resistant, towards change. However personal growth requires embracing

change as a part of life's progression. Scorpios can enhance their adaptability by embracing change by seeing it as an opportunity for growth rather than a threat.

- **Letting go**; This is essential for Scorpios to grow personally as they have a tendency to hold onto grudges and past hurts. By practicing forgiveness and releasing resentments they can embark on a journey of healing and liberation. It's important for Scorpios to find a balance between control and surrender since they may sometimes become controlling both with themselves and their surroundings. By trusting the process and letting go of tension they can develop personally.
- **Compassion**; The innate empathy of Scorpios allows them to deeply connect with others emotions. As part of their growth they can refine their abilities and use them to foster understanding and compassion in their relationships.
- **Confidence**; Scorpios often second guess themselves due to their personality tendencies. Personal growth involves building self trust, embracing instincts and making confident decisions.
- **Seek help**; Seeking guidance from mentors, therapists or spiritual advisors can be beneficial for Scorpios on their growth journey as these individuals provide insights and support. Many Scorpios are naturally drawn to metaphysical topics which offer an avenue for purposeful exploration and connection with the universe
- **Constant learning**; Scorpios are naturally curious with a desire for knowledge. They believe that personal growth is achieved through learning and self improvement. Scorpios can satisfy their curiosity by exploring interests and acquiring new skills.

To sum up personal growth and development for Scorpio individuals involve embracing vulnerability reflecting on oneself engaging in experiences and being open to change. As they navigate these aspects of growth Scorpios can unlock their potential, build deeper connections with others and embark on a journey of self discovery and transformation that leads to a more fulfilling and meaningful life.

HARNESSING SCORPIO STRENGTHS AND OVERCOMING WEAKNESSES

Harnessing the strengths of Scorpio and overcoming their weaknesses is a life changing journey that involves self awareness, personal growth and a commitment to embracing their qualities. Here's how they can effectively utilize their strengths while addressing any areas for improvement.

UTILIZING STRENGTHS

- **Determination**; Scorpios are determined individuals. To harness this strength they can set concrete goals. Break them down into achievable steps. Their unwavering determination will drive them to accomplish the ambitious objectives.
- **Emotional Depth**; Scorpios profound emotional depth can be an asset in relationships and creativity. They can leverage this strength to establish connections with others and channel their emotions into empathetic endeavors.
- **Leadership Qualities**; Scorpios naturally possess leadership abilities that can propel them into roles. To make the most of this strength they should actively seek out leadership positions where their assertiveness and passion can inspire and motivate others.
- **Resourcefulness**; The resourcefulness of Scorpios is invaluable when it comes to problem solving. They should apply this strength to find solutions in their personal lives.
- **Empathy**; The empathetic nature of Scorpios enables them to deeply understand others.They can utilize this strength to foster connections, resolve disagreements and provide support for those who require it.

OVERCOMING WEAKNESSES

- **Jealousy**; Scorpios have the ability to address their emotions and feelings of jealousy by practicing techniques like mindfulness, meditation and open communication with their loved ones. These strategies can assist them in managing these emotions

- **Stubbornness**; It is beneficial for Scorpios to cultivate flexibility and adaptability. They can achieve this by learning to compromise and considering perspectives in both professional settings.
- **Secrecy**; Scorpios can enhance transparency within their relationships by opening up and sharing their thoughts and emotions with trusted individuals. Building trust takes time. It can result in connections.
- **Resistance to Change**; To overcome their resistance towards change Scorpios can gradually expose themselves to experiences. They can start with changes before moving on to significant transitions.
- **Difficulty Accepting Criticism**; Scorpios should view criticism as an opportunity for growth than a personal attack. Reminding themselves that feedback helps them improve and evolve will aid in accepting criticism
- **Excessive Expectations**; Managing expectations is important, for Scorpios. Setting goals that're attainable is crucial; it is essential for them to understand that perfection is not always achievable. Celebrating successes along the way is equally important.

SEEKING SUPPORT

Scorpios can benefit from seeking support in their journey of harnessing strengths and overcoming weaknesses. This support can come from various sources, including:

- **Therapy**: Professional counseling or therapy can help Scorpios address deep-seated emotional issues and develop healthier coping mechanisms.
- **Mentorship**: Seeking guidance from mentors or role models who have successfully navigated similar challenges can be highly beneficial.
- **Peer Support**: Sharing experiences and insights with peers who understand their struggles can provide Scorpios with valuable perspectives and encouragement.
- **Self-Help Resources:** Scorpios can explore self-help books, workshops, and online resources that offer practical strategies for personal growth and development.

In conclusion Scorpios possess a set of strengths and weaknesses that shape their lives. By utilizing their strengths, addressing their areas for improvement and seeking support when necessary, Scorpios can embark on a journey of self improvement. Ultimately this will lead to a fulfilling and harmonious life.

Throughout this chapter we have delved deeply into the commitment of Scorpio individuals, towards self improvement. With their determination and emotional depth Scorpios naturally seek self awareness and transformation. As we wrap up this chapter lets take a moment to reflect on the aspects of the Scorpio journey and the positive outlook for their potential.

Scorpio individuals have potential for growth and self improvement. With unwavering determination, depth and innate strengths they are capable of achieving milestones in both their personal and professional lives. As Scorpios continue to embrace their vulnerability, let go of the past and build trust in themselves they will find themselves following a path of self discovery that is constantly evolving. Their strong passion and unwavering determination will drive them forward allowing them to create an impact not, in their own lives but also in the lives of those around them. May the Scorpios journey towards self improvement serve as an inspiration for all of us to embark on our paths of growth and transformation!

CHAPTER 6:
THE YEAR AHEAD

In this chapter we'll be shedding light on the challenges and opportunities that are waiting for Scorprios in the year ahead. As we navigate through the events and planetary influences shaping the year we'll delve into how these cosmic forces impact Scorpios love life, career, finances, health and much more. From enlightening eclipses that reveal truths to empowering transits fueling Scorpios ambitions each astrological event plays a vital role in shaping the path forward.

Join us as we unravel the mysteries of the universe and offer guidance on how Scorpio individuals can maximize opportunities while navigating challenges throughout the year. Whether you're a Scorpio seeking to understand the energies at play or someone captivated by Scorpios journey in the year ahead, this chapter provides an enthralling exploration of celestial forces shaping destinies. So come along on a captivating journey into what the upcoming year has, in store for Scorpio individuals.

SCORPIO HOROSCOPE GUIDE FOR THE YEAR AHEAD

This year Scorpio you can look forward to a journey of growth and self discovery. The universe is aligning to help you unveil truths, make life changes and tap into your inner strength. While there may be obstacles, along the way your determination and enthusiasm will steer you towards success.

CAREER AND FINANCES

Your professional life will experience advancements this year. Exciting opportunities and challenges will arise, providing a chance for you to showcase your leadership abilities. You might find yourself in a position of authority where your skills are highly valued. When it comes to finances, focus on making wise investments and financial diligence.

Scorpio individuals can anticipate a dynamic year in their careers and finances, influenced by celestial events. Here's a glimpse of what to expect:

- **Saturn Transits:** Saturn's presence may bring responsibilities and challenges in your career. Embrace these as opportunities for growth and consider long-term goals.
- **Mars Transits:** Mars will energize Scorpio's career sector. This is an excellent time for taking bold actions, launching projects and asserting your leadership in the workplace.
- **Jupiter Transits:** The influence of Jupiter can expand your financial horizons. Be open to new opportunities, investments, or financial growth during this time.

LOVE AND RELATIONSHIPS

In matters of the heart anticipate a year brimming with emotions and transformative encounters. If you're currently in a relationship it will deepen further and strengthen over time. Single Scorpios may cross paths with someone who deeply resonates with their soul. Be aware of feelings like jealousy or possessiveness that can strain relationships. Open communication and trust are pillars for nurturing connections.

In the realm of love and relationships, Scorpio individuals will find the astrological events of the year bringing both challenges and opportunities.

Here's a closer look at how these celestial occurrences may influence Scorpio's love life:

- **Solar and Lunar Eclipses**: Eclipses can shake up Scorpio's relationships by bringing hidden issues to the surface. Pay close attention to the Solar Eclipse and the Lunar Eclipse. These dates may prompt important conversations and decisions about your romantic partnerships.
- **Venus Retrograde:** Venus retrogrades can affect Scorpios emotional landscape. During this period be prepared for relationship reassessments. Past romantic patterns may resurface, allowing you to make necessary changes for more meaningful connections.
- **Jupiter Transits:** Jupiter's positive influence can bring growth and optimism to Scorpio's love life. When Jupiter transits you may experience expanded horizons and the opportunity to meet someone who ignites your passions.

HEALTH AND WELLNESS

Taking care of your emotional well being should take precedence this year. Prioritize stress management techniques along with exercise routines and maintaining a healthy diet. Take part in relaxation techniques such as meditation or yoga to keep your mind and emotions balanced. Prioritize self care to maintain your energy and resilience.

Scorpio individuals should pay close attention to their health and wellness in light of the year's astrological events. Here are some insights:

- **Mercury Retrograde:** During Mercury retrogrades your stress levels may increase. Practice stress management techniques, maintain a balanced diet, and prioritize self-care to ensure emotional and physical well-being.
- **Jupiter Transits:** Jupiter's positive influence can enhance your overall vitality. Use this time to focus on fitness, well-balanced nutrition, and relaxation practices for optimal health.

PERSONAL GROWTH AND SELF-DISCOVERY

The year ahead offers abundant opportunities for personal growth and self-discovery for Scorpio individuals. Here's how to make the most of it:

- **Solar and Lunar Eclipses:** Eclipses, especially the Solar Eclipse encourage Scorpios to dive deep into self-discovery. Embrace introspection and explore your passions, desires, and hidden potentials.
- **Mars Transits:** Mars' dynamic influence empowers Scorpio to take action. Channel this energy into self-improvement, goals and exploring your passions.
- **Jupiter Transits:** Jupiter's positive energy supports your personal growth journey. Embrace new experiences, engage in spiritual practices and seek wisdom to enhance your self-discovery.

Self Development and Spirituality

This year presents a chance for growth. Embrace introspection and self discovery. Explore your spirituality. Engage in practices that deepen your connection with yourself. Trusting your instincts will provide guidance during times.

Travel and Excitement

Consider embarking on adventures and exploring different places this year. Venturing into new territories will broaden your horizons and offer fresh perspectives. Stay open to spontaneity as some magical moments may arise from unexpected journeys.

Potential Challenges to Be Cautious About

Be mindful of becoming overly controlling or possessive in your relationships as this can lead to conflicts. Your intense nature might also make it challenging for you to embrace change. Remember that growth often requires stepping outside of your comfort zone. It's important to maintain a work life balance to avoid burnout.

Overall the upcoming year holds promise for individuals born under the sign of Scorpio. Embrace the transformative energies, trust your wisdom and remain receptive to both opportunities and challenges that come along the way.

With your resolve and enthusiastic nature you have the ability to turn this year into a satisfying phase, in your life's adventure.

By approaching the happenings with mindfulness and self awareness Scorpio individuals can tap into their potential for professional development, nurture their relationships and prioritize their health and well being in the coming year. Stay tuned for the upcoming year promises a voyage of self discovery, growth and transformation.

KEY ASTROLOGICAL EVENTS

Key astrological events can significantly impact Scorpio individuals. They influence various aspects of their lives, including relationships, career and much more. Here are some notable astrological events and their potential impact on Scorpio individuals:

SOLAR AND LUNAR ECLIPSES

- Impact: Eclipses often bring about significant life changes and transformations. They may prompt Scorpios to reevaluate their goals, make important decisions, or address unresolved issues.
- Advice: Use eclipse periods for self-reflection and setting new intentions. Embrace change and be open to opportunities for personal growth.

MERCURY RETROGRADE

- Impact: Mercury retrogrades can disrupt communication and travel plans. Scorpios may experience misunderstandings or delays in their work and personal relationships.
- Advice: Practice patience and double-check details during retrograde periods. Use this time for introspection and revisiting past projects.

JUPITER TRANSITS

- Impact: When Jupiter transits Scorpio or favorable areas of their chart, it can bring luck, expansion and personal growth. This influence may lead to new opportunities and increased optimism.
- Advice: Embrace Jupiter's positive energy by being open to new experiences, taking calculated risks and pursuing goals.

SATURN TRANSITS

- Impact: Saturn transits can bring challenges and lessons, often in the form of responsibilities or limitations. Scorpios may face obstacles that test their patience and determination.
- Advice: Approach Saturn transits with discipline and resilience. Focus on long-term goals and the lessons that come with adversity, knowing that they contribute to personal growth.

VENUS RETROGRADE

- Impact: Venus retrogrades can affect Scorpio's romantic and social life. Relationships may undergo reassessment and unresolved issues may resurface.
- Advice: Use this period for introspection in relationships. Reevaluate what truly matters in your connections, and address any unresolved issues with empathy and communication.

MARS TRANSITS

- Impact: Mars transits can boost Scorpio's energy and drive. These periods are excellent for taking action, pursuing goals and initiating new projects.
- Advice: Make the most of Mars' dynamic energy by channeling it into your ambitions and physical activities. Be mindful of not becoming overly aggressive in your pursuits.

NEW MOON AND FULL MOON PHASES

- Impact: New Moon phases are ideal for setting intentions and initiating projects, while Full Moons bring culmination and closure. Scorpios may find these phases emotionally charged.

- Advice: Align your intentions with New Moons and use Full Moons for reflection and release. Harness lunar energies for personal growth and manifestation.

Through astrologys lens we have uncovered the challenges and opportunities that Scorpios may encounter in their lives. The celestial events, from revealing eclipses that bring truths to empowering transits act as guides on this captivating journey. Individual birth charts, which consider the time and place of birth also play a significant role in how these astrological events impact Scorpio individuals. Additionally, consulting with an astrologer can provide personalized insights into how these events affect specific aspects of their lives. Overall, Scorpios can navigate these astrological events with mindfulness, adaptability and a focus on personal growth.

Dear Scorpio, your unwavering determination, intensity and emotional depth will serve as your allies as you navigate through the currents. Embrace challenges as chances for growth. Seize moments of alignment to propel yourself forward. Trust your instincts wholeheartedly while allowing your passion to guide you like a star. May this chapter be a source of insight and inspiration as you embark on your voyage among the stars. No matter the challenges or ease you encounter in life, always remember that you have the strength to overcome and the ability to thrive.

As individuals born under the zodiac sign Scorpio move forward into the year they understand that both themselves and the universe are constantly evolving. Embrace this journey. Embrace the influence of the stars and embrace your limitless potential. The celestial tapestry above illuminates your destiny eagerly waiting for you to weave a tale of growth, exploration and fulfillment.

CHAPTER 7:
FAMOUS SCORPIO PERSONALITIES

In the tapestry of astrology Scorpio stands out as a sign known for its intensity, determination and irresistible charm. People born under this sign are recognized for their dedication and the ability to make a lasting impact on the world. Within this chapter we embark on a journey through the lives of some famous Scorpio individuals who have made their mark in the realms of art, entertainment, politics and more. These Scorpios have not only shaped their respective fields but have also captured the admiration of people worldwide.

As we delve into their captivating stories we will explore the traits and characteristics that have propelled these individuals to greatness. From the realm of music where Scorpio's intensity shines brightly to the world of art where their deep emotions find expression. These remarkable personalities exemplify the potential that comes with being born under the constellation of Scorpio. Join us on this journey as we celebrate the achievements, legacies and enduring allure of Scorpio personalities. Their stories stand as a testament to the power of passion, resilience and mysterious charm that define this sign.

CIARA

- Date of Birth: October 25, 1985.
- Brief Biography: Ciara is a Grammy Award-winning singer, songwriter and dancer known for her chart-topping hits like "Goodies" and "1, 2 Step." She has had a successful career in the music industry.
- Scorpio Traits: Ciara exhibits Scorpio traits such as intensity, determination and charisma.
- Impact: Ciara's music has made a significant impact in the world of R&B and pop music, earning her numerous awards and a dedicated fan base.
- Personal Life: She is married to NFL quarterback Russell Wilson. Together they are known for their philanthropic efforts.

WILL DURANT

- Date of Birth: November 5, 1885.
- Brief Biography: Will Durant was an American historian and philosopher. He is best known for co-authoring "The Story of Civilization" with his wife, Ariel Durant. Their work on history and philosophy is highly regarded.
- Scorpio Traits: Will Durant exhibited Scorpio traits such as deep thinking, analytical skills and dedication to intellectual pursuits.
- Impact: Durant's work left a lasting legacy, influencing generations of scholars and readers interested in history and philosophy.
- Personal Life: Will Durant had a lifelong intellectual partnership with his wife, Ariel Durant. Their collaborative efforts are celebrated in the world of literature.

JOE BIDEN

- Date of Birth: November 20, 1942.
- Brief Biography: Joe Biden is the 46th President of the United States. He also served as Vice President under President Barack Obama from 2009 to 2017. His political career spans several decades.

- Scorpio Traits: Joe Biden embodies Scorpio traits like determination, resilience and a strong commitment to public service.

- Impact: His election as President marked a significant moment in U.S. history. Furthermore his long political career has had a substantial impact on American politics.
- Personal Life: Joe Biden has faced personal tragedies, including the loss of his wife and daughter. These have shaped his empathy and leadership style.

CHARLES III (KING CHARLES)

- Date of Birth: November 14, 1948.
- Brief Biography: Charles III, also known as King Charles, is king of the British throne. He has been a prominent figure in the British royal family and has focused on various charitable and environmental causes.
- Scorpio Traits: King Charles exhibits Scorpio traits such as strong leadership qualities and a dedication to social and environmental issues.
- Impact: His role within the British monarchy and his commitment to charitable work have made a lasting impact on the United Kingdom and beyond.
- Personal Life: He has been married to Diana, Princess of Wales, and Camilla, Duchess of Cornwall. He is a father to Prince William and Prince Harry.

JULIA ROBERTS

- Date of Birth: October 28, 1967.
- Brief Biography: Julia Roberts is an Academy Award-winning actress. She is known for her iconic roles in films such as "Pretty Woman," "Erin Brockovich," and "My Best Friend's Wedding."
- Scorpio Traits: Julia Roberts possesses Scorpio traits like charisma, intensity and emotional expressiveness.
- Impact: She has had a profound influence on Hollywood. She remains one of the most beloved actresses of her generation.
- Personal Life: Julia Roberts has been in the spotlight for her relationships and family life.

TONYA HARDING

- Date of Birth: November 12, 1970.
- Brief Biography: Tonya Harding is a former professional figure skater. She gained notoriety for her involvement in the attack on fellow skater Nancy Kerrigan. Her career was marked by both success and controversy.

- Scorpio Traits: Tonya Harding displayed Scorpio traits such as competitiveness, determination and intensity.
- Impact: Her career and her role in the Kerrigan incident garnered significant media attention and controversy.
- Personal Life: She has faced legal issues and challenges in her personal life.

BILL GATES

- Date of Birth: October 28, 1955.
- Brief Biography: Bill Gates is a co-founder of Microsoft Corporation. He is one of the world's wealthiest individuals. He is also a prominent philanthropist and has had a significant impact on the technology industry.
- Scorpio Traits: Bill Gates exemplifies Scorpio traits such as determination, strategic thinking and a focus on innovation.
- Impact: His contributions to the technology sector and his philanthropic work through the Bill and Melinda Gates Foundation.
- Personal Life: Bill Gates is known for his philanthropic efforts. He was married to Melinda Gates for many years before their divorce.

DRAKE

- Date of Birth: October 24, 1986.

- Brief Biography: Drake is a Canadian rapper, singer and actor known for his chart-topping music career. He has won multiple Grammy Awards and is one of the most influential artists in hip-hop.
- Scorpio Traits: Drake embodies Scorpio traits such as emotional depth, charisma and creativity.
- Impact: His music has had a significant impact on the hip-hop and R&B genres. He has a massive global fan base.
- Personal Life: Drake is known for keeping his personal life relatively private. He has been involved in various philanthropic endeavors.

GRACE KELLY

- Date of Birth: November 12, 1929.
- Brief Biography: Grace Kelly was an American actress who later became Princess Grace of Monaco after marrying Prince Rainier III. She was known for her elegance and acting talent.
- Scorpio Traits: Grace Kelly exhibited Scorpio traits such as grace, allure and emotional depth.
- Impact: Her career in Hollywood and her role as Princess Grace of Monaco made her an iconic figure known for her beauty and philanthropic efforts.
- Personal Life: She married Prince Rainier III of Monaco. She became known for her humanitarian work and dedication to the principality.

KATY PERRY

- Date of Birth: October 25, 1984.
- Brief Biography: Katy Perry is a multi-platinum-selling singer, songwriter and television judge. She is also well known for hits like "Firework" and "Roar."
- Scorpio Traits: Katy Perry exhibits Scorpio traits such as intensity, creativity and a magnetic stage presence.
- Impact: Her music has had a significant influence in the pop music industry. She is celebrated for her empowering anthems and unique style.
- Personal Life: Katy Perry has been involved in various charitable causes.

PABLO PICASSO

- Date of Birth: October 25, 1881.

- Brief Biography: Pablo Picasso was one of the most influential artists of the 20th century. He was known for pioneering the Cubist movement and creating iconic works such as "Guernica."
- Scorpio Traits: Picasso embodied Scorpio traits such as intense creativity, a profound sense of emotion. He had a penchant for pushing artistic boundaries.
- Impact: His contributions to art redefined the possibilities of visual expression and continue to inspire artists worldwide.
- Personal Life: Picasso's personal life was as dynamic as his art. He had multiple relationships and a complex family history.

GEORGIA O'KEEFFE

- Date of Birth: November 15, 1887.
- Brief Biography: Georgia O'Keeffe was an American modernist artist. She was known for her iconic paintings of flowers, landscapes and abstract forms.
- Scorpio Traits: O'Keeffe exhibited Scorpio traits such as passion, a deep connection to nature and a unique perspective on art.
- Impact: Her pioneering work in American modernism. Her contribution to the art world continues to be celebrated and studied.
- Personal Life: She was known for her close relationship with photographer Alfred Stieglitz and her solitary life in New Mexico.

These remarkable individuals who were born under the Scorpio zodiac sign have made a lasting impact on art, entertainment, technology and more. Their unique talents and personalities reflect the depth and complexity often associated with Scorpio individuals.

As our exploration of Scorpio personalities comes to a close we are left with an admiration for the intricate nature that characterizes this mysterious astrological sign. From the realms of entertainment, art, politics and beyond these Scorpio individuals have displayed unwavering determination, intensity and passion. What brings together these renowned Scorpio personalities is their ability to transcend boundaries, challenge conventions and leave a mark in their fields. As we honor their achievements and legacies we also celebrate the potential that lies within each individual born under the sign of Scorpio. Their stories stand as proof of the strength of passion, resilience and the mysterious allure that characterizes this zodiac sign.

As we conclude this chapter let us draw inspiration from the lasting impact Scorpio individuals have left behind. Let them remind us that embracing our emotions and pursuing our desires can guide us towards remarkable achievements.

CONCLUSION

As we near the end of our exploration into the Scorpio zodiac sign we arrive at this conclusion. Here we bring together the range of information we've acquired to shed light on the true essence of Scorpio. Now let us present a comprehensive understanding of this mysterious astrological sign. Firstly we will summarize the key points from the chapters.

- **Chapter 1 History and Mythology;** In this chapter, we delved into the historical and mythological roots of Scorpio. We discovered how ancient civilizations, from Babylon to Greece, revered the scorpion as a symbol of transformation and regeneration. The myth of Scorpio's association with Orion and the scorpion's sting as a means of protection provided insights into Scorpio's protective and transformative nature.
- **Chapter 2 Love and Compatibility;** In this chapter we explored Scorpio's approach to love and compatibility. We saw their intense and passionate nature influence romance. Understanding Scorpio's love traits, preferences and compatibility can lead to more fulfilling relationships. In turn we saw how Scorpios are most compatible with water signs like Cancer and Pisces. Together they often share profound emotional connections.
- **Chapter 3 Friends and Family;** In the realm of friendships and family dynamics, we uncovered how Scorpios value loyalty, trust and emotional depth. Their protective nature extends to their loved ones. Overall it makes them fiercely loyal and supportive. Both as a friend and in the family dynamic. We also explored the challenges Scorpios may encounter in these relationships.
- **Chapter 4 Finance and Career**; In this chapter we explored Scorpio's career preferences and strengths. Notable was their determination, focus and ambition in the workplace. They thrive in roles that require research, problem-solving and transformation. We also discussed the challenges they might face and strategies to overcome them, along with their financial attitudes and aspirations.
- **Chapter 5 - Self-Improvement;** This chapter delved into personal growth and development for Scorpios. We discussed harnessing their strengths, overcoming weaknesses and provided guidance on self-improvement.

Scorpios were encouraged to embrace introspection, set goals and pursue their passions for transformative growth.

- **Chapter 6 - Scorpio in the Year Ahead:** In this chapter, we explored how astrological events would influence Scorpio individuals' lives in areas. Special attention was given to significant dates and time periods that hold particular significance for Scorpios throughout the year.
- **Chapter 7 - Famous Scorpio Personalities:** In this chapter we celebrated the achievements and legacies of famous Scorpio personalities from various fields. These individuals, including artists, leaders, and innovators, showcased the intensity, determination, and magnetic allure that define Scorpios. Their stories serve as inspiration for all Scorpio individuals to harness their unique qualities for greatness.

As we wrap up our exploration of the essence of Scorpio, take a moment to reflect on the facets of this passionate and transformative zodiac sign. Whether you identify as a Scorpio on a journey of self discovery or simply find yourself intrigued by the spirit of Scorpio. The knowledge shared in this book may empower you to embrace your emotions, harness your determination and appreciate the allure that comes with being a Scorpio.

Throughout this book our focus has been, on shedding light on the nature of Scorpio celebrating its intensity, unwavering determination and irresistible charm. We have delved into historical accounts, mythology and practical insights to provide you with an understanding of what it means to be a Scorpio. Our aim is to offer guidance and inspiration not for individuals who identify as Scorpios but for those fascinated by their distinctive qualities.

Ultimately our main goal is for readers to grasp that being a Scorpio is an empowering experience. By embracing their intensity, determination and magnetic allure individuals born under this sign can embark on a path of personal growth and achieve extraordinary feats.

In conclusion astrology provides us with a lens through which we can gain insights into ourselves as well as others. The zodiac sign of Scorpio serves as a reminder that embracing change and personal growth is crucial in life. Those who possess the qualities of Scorpios have the opportunity to unlock their potential making a lasting impact on the world.

To all Scorpios out we encourage you to display your intensity, draw strength from your determination and share your magnetic charm as a precious gift. Your presence enriches our world and your journey, as a Scorpio is a tapestry woven with threads of passion, resilience and limitless possibilities.

As we conclude this exploration of Scorpio may you continue to shine as beings. Embrace your strengths and let them empower you as you leave your mark on the universe with each step you take on your journey.

SAGITTARIUS:

A COMPLETE GUIDE TO THE SAGITTARIUS ASTROLOGY STAR SIGN

Contents

INTRODUCTION -- 1

Sagittarius Zodiac Sign Overview and Symbolism ---------------------------------- 2

CHAPTER 1: HISTORY AND MYTHOLOGY ------------------------ 5

Historical & Mythological Origins-- 5

CHAPTER 2: LOVE & COMPATIBILITY -------------------------- 10

Sagittarius' Approach to Love and Romance------------------------------------- 10

Sagittarius Compatibility with Other Zodiac Signs-------------------------------- 12

Tips for Dating and Maintaining Relationships with Sagittarius Individuals-- 15

CHAPTER 3: FRIENDS AND FAMILY -------------------------- 18

Sagittarius as a Friend -- 19

Sagittarius and Family Dynamics -- 20

Challenges in Friendships and Family Relations-------------------------------- 22

CHAPTER 4: CAREER AND MONEY ------------------------- 24

Career Preferences and Professional Aspirations------------------------------- 25

Strengths that Make Sagittarius Individuals Excel in the Workplace ---------- 26

Challenges Faced by Sagittarius Individuals in Their Careers and Strategies to Overcome Them-- 28

CHAPTER 5: SELF-IMPROVEMENT --------------------------- 31

Personal Growth and Development for Sagittarius------------------------------ 32

Harnessing Sagittarius Strengths and Overcoming Weaknesses---------------- 34

CHAPTER 6: THE YEAR AHEAD ------------------------------ 37

Horoscope Guide for the Year Ahead-- 37

Key Astrological Events and Their Impact on Sagittarius---------------------- 42

CHAPTER 7: FAMOUS "SAGITTARIUS" PERSONALITIES --------- 44

Winston Churchill -- 44

Cathy Moriarty --- 45

Bruce Lee-- 45

Taylor Swift-- 46

Nicki Minaj --- 46

Franz Ferdinand --- 46

Emmanuel Macron--- 47

Ian Botham --- 47

Sinead O'Connor -- 48

Scarlett Johansson -- 48

Larry Bird --- 48

Karen Gillan--- 49

CONCLUSION -- 50

INTRODUCTION

Astrology has intrigued humans for centuries. It is a practice that involves interpreting the positions and movements of bodies like planets and stars to gain understanding about human experiences. Astrologers analyze the positions of the sun, moon, planets and other celestial bodies within a belt in the sky known as the zodiac. This belt is divided into twelve signs that are associated with human characteristics and qualities. In this book we embark on a journey to explore the world of astrology in depth with a focus on the Sagittarius zodiac sign.

The main goal of this book is to provide an exploration of the Sagittarius zodiac sign. Sagittarius, symbolized by the archer, is renowned for its curiosity and optimistic outlook. However there's more to this sign than meets the eye. We'll delve into the history and mythology surrounding Sagittarius to uncover tales and symbolic representations that have shaped its character. Throughout the book readers will come across insights and practical advice on how to harness Sagittarius strengths effectively while navigating any challenges.

Come along on a journey that unravels the secrets of Sagittarius and reveals the insights that astrology holds.

SAGITTARIUS ZODIAC SIGN OVERVIEW AND SYMBOLISM

- **Date of Star Sign**: Sagittarius falls between November 22nd and December 21st. It is the ninth sign of the zodiac.
- **Symbol**: The symbol of Sagittarius is the Archer. This is often depicted as a centaur (half-human, half-horse) drawing a bow and arrow. This symbol embodies the adventurous and dynamic nature of this sign.
- **Element**: Sagittarius belongs to the Fire element. Fire signs are known for their passion, energy and enthusiasm. Sagittarians are no exception. They exhibit fiery qualities in various aspects of their lives.
- **Planet**: The ruling planet of Sagittarius is Jupiter which is the largest planet in our solar system. Jupiter represents expansion, growth and the search for knowledge. It amplifies the Sagittarian traits of optimism and exploration.
- **Color**: The color associated with Sagittarius is deep blue or purple. These symbolize wisdom, depth and spirituality. Such colors resonate with the philosophical and adventurous nature of Sagittarius.

COMPATIBILITY

Sagittarius tends to have high compatibility, with Fire signs like Aries and Leo. They also connect well with Air signs such as Gemini, Libra and Aquarius. These signs share a zest for life and intellectual pursuits. However they might face challenges in their relationships with Earth signs like Taurus, Virgo and Capricorn. In addition, Water signs like Cancer, Scorpio and Pisces may clash due to differences in temperament and priorities. Nonetheless with patience and understanding Sagittarius can connect meaningfully with any sign.

PERSONALITY TRAITS

Sagittarius individuals are characterized by a range of distinctive personality traits.

- **Optimistic**: Sagittarians are eternal optimists. They are always looking on the bright side of life. As such they have an infectious enthusiasm that uplifts those around them.
- **Adventurous**: They have an insatiable desire for adventure and exploration. They love to travel, learn about different cultures and embrace new experiences.
- **Independent**: Independence is highly valued by Sagittarius. They are self-reliant. Freedom and autonomy is valuable to them.

- **Philosophical**: Sagittarians are often drawn to philosophy, spirituality and higher learning. They seek meaning in life and are on a constant quest for knowledge.
- **Honest**: Honesty is a key trait of Sagittarius individuals. They value truthfulness and speak their minds. Sometimes bluntly.
- **Generous**: Sagittarians are generous by nature, always willing to lend a helping hand or share with others.

STRENGTHS

Sagittarius individuals possess several strengths, including:

- **Open-Mindedness**: They are open to new ideas and perspectives.
- **Problem solvers;** Overall they are excellent problem solvers.
- **Courage**: Sagittarians have the bravery to pursue their goals and take on challenges.
- **Sense of Humor**: They have a great sense of humor and can find laughter even in difficult situations.
- **Intelligence**: Sagittarius individuals are often highly intelligent and quick learners.
- **Adaptability**: They are adaptable and can thrive in various environments.

WEAKNESSES

While Sagittarius has many positive traits, they also have some weaknesses:

- **Impulsivity**: Their adventurous spirit can lead to impulsive decisions and actions.
- **Restlessness**: Sagittarius may struggle with commitment and become restless if they feel tied down.
- **Bluntness**: Their honesty can sometimes come across as tactlessness or insensitivity.
- **Overconfidence**: Their optimism can lead to overconfidence and taking on too much.

In the opening chapter of our exploration into the Sagittarius zodiac sign we have set forth on a journey into astrology. We have introduced you to the qualities and symbols that define Sagittarius. From its Archer symbol to its association with the fiery element of Fire and its governance by Jupiter.

Moreover we delved into the influence of blue and purple, the colors that resonate with Sagittarius' adventurous spirit and philosophical nature.

As you delve deeper into the pages of this book you can expect an exploration of Sagittarius history and mythology. We will uncover tales and symbols that have influenced Sagittariuss character over time. Our journey will take us through the tapestry of Sagittarius personality providing insights and practical advice on how to embrace their strengths and navigate potential challenges. You'll also gain an understanding of how Sagittarius individuals approach love, career and much more. Furthermore we will offer an overview of astrological concepts and terminology to ensure that you can fully grasp the complexities of the zodiac.

Whether you're new to astrology or an experienced enthusiast, this book is designed to be a resource for self discovery, personal development and forging a connection with the celestial forces that shape our lives. So as we embark on this journey together by turning the page, prepare yourself to unravel the mysteries surrounding Sagittarius and tap into the wisdom bestowed upon us by astrology. Prepare yourself to delve into the realm of the Archer with an open mind and a sense of adventure as we embark on a journey to uncover the cosmos of the Sagittarius zodiac sign.

CHAPTER 1:
HISTORY AND MYTHOLOGY

Welcome to a captivating journey, into the history and mythology of the Sagittarius zodiac sign. In this chapter we will uncover tales, cultural interpretations and enduring legacies that have shaped the archer we recognize today. From the earliest observations of the Sagittarius constellation to its modern significance in astrology. Here we will traverse through time exploring how this symbol has captivated human imagination. As we unveil narratives and historical events that unfolded during Sagittarius season we'll gain insights into how this sign has profoundly influenced history and our understanding of cosmic forces that shape our existence. So come along as we step into the realm of Sagittarius, a place where myths intertwine with history.

HISTORICAL & MYTHOLOGICAL ORIGINS

The constellation Sagittarius, often referred to as "The Archer" or "The Centaur," has a rich history that spans numerous ancient civilizations. In the night sky it has been a prominent feature for thousands of years. Its interpretations and representations have varied among different cultures.

BABYLONIAN AND SUMERIAN CIVILIZATIONS

The earliest known observations and records of the Sagittarius constellation can be traced back to the ancient Babylonians and Sumerians. They associated this constellation with the god Nergal. This deity was often depicted as a centaur-like figure holding a bow and arrow. Nergal was linked to war and the scorching heat of the sun. Such traits align with the symbolism of the Archer.

GREEK AND ROMAN MYTHOLOGY

In Greek mythology, Sagittarius is associated with the centaur, Chiron. A wise healer and mentor to various heroes, including Achilles and Hercules.

Chiron was accidentally wounded by a poisoned arrow. This led to his transformation into the constellation. The Greeks and Romans adapted this mythological figure into the centaur archer, depicted with a bow and arrow.

INDIAN ASTRONOMY (VEDIC ASTROLOGY)

In Indian astronomy, Sagittarius is associated with the nakshatra (lunar mansion) called Mula, which means "The Root." It is symbolized by a bunch of roots or a tied bunch of roots. These represent the origins and foundational aspects of life. This cultural interpretation ties into the Archer's role as a seeker of deeper truths and wisdom.

ARABIAN AND ISLAMIC ASTRONOMY

In medieval Islamic astronomy, Sagittarius was known as "Qaws al-Sa'd," which translates to "The Arrow of the Archer." Islamic scholars preserved and expanded upon the knowledge of the Greek and Roman constellations, including Sagittarius, during the Middle Ages.

CHINESE CONSTELLATIONS

Chinese astronomy had its own constellations and celestial maps, separate from the Western zodiac. The concept of Sagittarius does not have a direct equivalent in traditional Chinese astronomy. However, some Chinese star maps and cosmological texts mention Western constellations like Sagittarius due to cultural exchanges over the centuries.

Overall, the Sagittarius constellation has played a significant role in the mythologies and early astronomical observations of diverse ancient civilizations. Its representation as an archer or centaur has been a recurring theme, reflecting humanity's fascination with the celestial wonders above and the stories we tell to make sense of them. These historical and mythological origins have left an indelible mark on our understanding of the Sagittarius zodiac sign and continue to shape our appreciation of this constellation today.

With advancements in astronomy and astrology there has been a refinement in our understanding of the zodiac. New Age concepts have gained popularity in astrology. These explore metaphysical aspects of the zodiac. Astrology is now viewed as a tool for self awareness, personal growth and spiritual development.

HISTORICAL EVENTS UNDER THE SAGITTARIUS SEASON

Throughout history, the astrological season of Sagittarius, has witnessed numerous important events with potential astrological significance. These events often reflect the characteristics and themes associated with the Sagittarius zodiac sign. Namely, exploration, adventure, and philosophical pursuits. Below are some notable historical events that have taken place during the Sagittarius season.

- Ferdinand Magellan's circumnavigation of the globe (1519-1522) and the Apollo 17 moon landing (1972) occurred during this time. Both reflect Sagittarius' adventurous spirit.
- Philosophical and Ideological Shifts: The publication of Charles Darwin's "On the Origin of Species" (1859) and the Wright brothers' first powered flight (1903) marked significant moments of intellectual and technological advancement. Both align with Sagittarius' quest for knowledge and progress.
- Historical Declarations: The United Nations Universal Declaration of Human Rights was adopted on December 10, 1948. Both emphasize ideals of justice, equality and global cooperation associated with this sign.

HISTORICAL FIGURES BORN UNDER THE SAGITTARIUS SIGN

Several influential historical figures have been born under the Sagittarius sign. They embody its traits and have left a lasting impact on history. Notable Sagittarius-born figures include:

- **Winston Churchill:** Born on November 30, 1874, Churchill's leadership during World War II and his gift for oratory align with Sagittarius' characteristics of courage, optimism and communication.
- **Mark Twain:** Samuel Clemens, known as Mark Twain, born on November 30, 1835, epitomized Sagittarius' humor, wit and adventurous storytelling through his classic works like "The Adventures of Tom Sawyer" and "The Adventures of Huckleberry Finn."
- **Frank Sinatra:** The legendary singer and entertainer, born on December 12, 1915, showcased Sagittarius' love for music, performance, and a larger-than-life persona.

From its earliest origins to its modern significance in astrology, Sagittarius has remained a captivating emblem of exploration, adventure and the pursuit of deeper understanding. As we navigate through the changing realm of astrology, Sagittarius serves as a timeless reminder of the fundamental attributes that define our human essence. It urges us to embrace our adventurous side, to seek answers, beyond knowledge and to continuously explore the depths of our own inner selves.

FURTHER READING AND REFERENCES

For readers who wish to delve deeper into the history and mythology of Sagittarius, here is a list of primary sources, ancient texts and modern writings that provide valuable insights into this captivating sign.

- "Enuma Anu Enlil" - An ancient Babylonian cuneiform tablet containing references to Nergal, associated with Sagittarius.
- "Metamorphoses" by Ovid - A classical Roman poem that features the story of Chiron, the centaur associated with Sagittarius.
- "The Mahabharata" - An ancient Indian epic that explores philosophical and mythological themes, relevant to Sagittarius' symbolism.
- "The Only Astrology Book You'll Ever Need" by Joanna Martine Woolfolk - A comprehensive guide to astrology that includes insights on Sagittarius and other zodiac signs.
- "The Secret Language of Birthdays" by Gary Goldschneider and Joost Elffers - Provides personality profiles for each day of the year, offering a unique perspective on Sagittarius individuals.
- "Astrology for the Soul" by Jan Spiller - Focuses on the soul's evolutionary journey through the zodiac signs, including Sagittarius.

CHAPTER 2:
LOVE & COMPATIBILITY

Step into the enchanting world of love and compatibility where we explore the realm of Sagittarius. In this section we will dive into the realm of romance and relationships through the unique perspective of Sagittarius. Sagittarius is renowned for its love, for freedom, exploration and boundless enthusiasm infusing an energy into matters of the heart. Within these pages we will uncover the approach that Sagittarius takes towards love and how it harmonizes with zodiac signs. Whether you are a Sagittarius seeking insights into your love life or simply curious about this sign this chapter guarantees to illuminate the intricacies of a Sagittarians journey.

SAGITTARIUS' APPROACH TO LOVE AND ROMANCE

Sagittarius individuals bring their unique blend of enthusiasm, optimism and adventure into their romantic lives. They are known for their free-spirited nature and love of exploration. Naturally this extends to their relationships. Here's a closer look at Sagittarius' approach to love:

- **Freedom and Independence**: Sagittarians value their freedom and independence highly. They are not ones to be tied down or constrained by possessiveness. In relationships, they seek partners who understand and respect their need for personal space and autonomy.
- **Optimism and Positivity**: Sagittarius individuals radiate positivity. This makes them attractive and enjoyable to be around. They approach love with a hopeful and open heart. Always believing in the best outcomes.
- **Adventurous Spirit**: Just as in other aspects of life, Sagittarians bring their adventurous spirit into their romantic relationships. They love trying new things. For example going on spontaneous trips and exploring together. They thrive on the excitement of shared experiences.
- **Honesty and Bluntness**: Sagittarians are known for their honesty. Sometimes to the point of bluntness. They appreciate partners who can handle their directness. In return they value straightforward communication.
- **Commitment-Phobia**: While Sagittarius individuals may appear commitment-phobic due to their love of freedom. They are not incapable of forming deep and committed relationships. When they do commit, it's because they genuinely value and love their partner. They simply need a partner who understands their need for occasional space and adventure.
- **Intellectual Stimulation**: Sagittarius individuals are intellectually curious. As such they appreciate partners who can engage them in meaningful conversations. Ones who share their love for learning and exploring new ideas.
- **Challenges of Routine**: The routine and predictability of day-to-day life can sometimes become a challenge for Sagittarius in a long-term relationship. They need partners who can inject spontaneity and excitement into their lives to keep the spark alive.
- **Generosity**: Sagittarians are generous by nature. They often go out of their way to make their partners feel loved and cherished. As such they may surprise their loved ones with thoughtful gestures and gifts.
- **Non-Judgmental**: Sagittarius individuals are open-minded and non-judgmental when it comes to love. They are accepting of different backgrounds, cultures and lifestyles. Overall this makes it easier for them to connect with a diverse range of people.

In summary, Sagittarius' approach to love and romance is characterized by their love of freedom, optimism and adventurous spirit. While they may seem commitment-averse at times. They are fully capable of forming deep, meaningful relationships with partners who understand and appreciate their need for independence and exploration.

SAGITTARIUS COMPATIBILITY WITH OTHER ZODIAC SIGNS

Sagittarius, the adventurous and optimistic Archer of the zodiac, approaches love with an open heart and a sense of excitement. They are enthusiastic, independent and always up for new experiences. Let's explore how Sagittarius' love and compatibility play out with each of the other zodiac signs.

SAGITTARIUS AND ARIES

Aries and Sagittarius share a strong connection due to their shared element, Fire. They both crave adventure, spontaneity and a lively relationship. Their shared enthusiasm and love for action creates a passionate and fun-loving bond. However both can be impulsive and headstrong. This may lead to occasional conflicts. However, their shared zest for life usually helps them to overcome disagreements.

SAGITTARIUS AND TAURUS

Taurus' practicality and stability may clash with Sagittarius' love for freedom and adventure. These differences can create challenges in the relationship. Meanwhile Sagittarius can add excitement to Taurus' life. Sagittarius may find Taurus too possessive. Taurus may see Sagittarius as unreliable or restless. If they can find common ground, Taurus can provide a sense of security to Sagittarius.

SAGITTARIUS AND GEMINI

This is a harmonious pairing. Both signs are curious, adaptable and love communication. Commitment may be an issue for Sagittarius, who can be seen as commitment-phobic by Gemini, who values consistency in a relationship. However, their shared love for exploration and learning creates a dynamic and playful relationship.

SAGITTARIUS AND CANCER

Cancer's emotional depth can clash with Sagittarius' need for independence and adventure, creating potential conflicts. Cancer's desire for stability may seem stifling to Sagittarius, while Sagittarius' restlessness may cause insecurity in Cancer. If both partners are willing to compromise, Cancer can provide emotional support. Sagittarius can introduce Cancer to exciting experiences.

SAGITTARIUS AND LEO

This is a dynamic and passionate match, as both signs share the Fire element. They admire each other's confidence and love for excitement. Their shared enthusiasm and adventurous spirit create a strong and passionate connection. Both can be stubborn and desire to be the leader, leading to power struggles. However, their mutual respect usually helps resolve conflicts.

SAGITTARIUS AND VIRGO

Virgo's practicality and attention to detail may clash with Sagittarius' free-spirited nature, creating challenges in the relationship. Virgo's need for routine may frustrate Sagittarius, who values freedom and adventure. If they can appreciate each other's differences, Virgo can provide stability and structures. Sagittarius can introduce excitement and spontaneity.

SAGITTARIUS AND LIBRA

Libra's social nature and Sagittarius' love for exploration create a harmonious and intellectually stimulating partnership. Although Sagittarius' bluntness and directness may occasionally hurt Libra's sensitive feelings.

Ultimately they share a passion for culture, travel, and socializing, making for a vibrant and lively relationship.

SAGITTARIUS AND SCORPIO

This pairing may face challenges due to their differing emotional needs and communication styles. Sagittarius' need for freedom may trigger Scorpio's jealousy and possessiveness. If they can build trust and open up to each other, Scorpio can offer emotional depth and intensity. Sagittarius can bring excitement and optimism.

SAGITTARIUS AND SAGITTARIUS

When two Sagittarians come together, they share a mutual love for adventure, travel and exploration. Their shared interests and enthusiasm create a dynamic, fun-loving relationship full of exciting experiences. Both may struggle with commitment and routine, as they value their independence. However, they understand each other's need for freedom.

SAGITTARIUS AND CAPRICORN

This pairing may face challenges due to their differing priorities and approaches to life. Capricorn can provide stability and structure to Sagittarius, while Sagittarius can introduce Capricorn to spontaneity and fun. Sagittarius may see Capricorn as too serious and traditional, while Capricorn may find Sagittarius unreliable.

SAGITTARIUS AND AQUARIUS

Both signs value independence, freedom and open-mindedness. This makes for a harmonious and intellectually stimulating partnership. They share a passion for social causes, innovative ideas and a sense of adventure. Overall creating a strong intellectual and emotional connection. Note that Sagittarius' bluntness may occasionally clash with Aquarius' desire for harmony and diplomacy.

SAGITTARIUS AND PISCES

Pisces' emotional depth and Sagittarius' optimism can create a unique and complementary connection. Pisces can provide emotional support and creativity. Sagittarius can bring excitement and new experiences into Pisces' life. Note that Sagittarius' need for independence may occasionally trigger Pisces' insecurities. With their positive traits and acknowledgement of challenges they can create harmony.

In conclusion, Sagittarius' love compatibility varies with each zodiac sign. Some signs offer a harmonious partnership based on shared values. Whilst others present challenges due to differing priorities. While compatibility is influenced by astrological factors, individual personalities and communication play a significant role in the success of a relationship. Ultimately, understanding and respecting each other's needs and differences are key to building a lasting and fulfilling connection for Sagittarius individuals.

TIPS FOR DATING AND MAINTAINING RELATIONSHIPS WITH SAGITTARIUS INDIVIDUALS

FOR MEN DATING SAGITTARIUS WOMEN

- **Embrace Adventure**: Sagittarius women are adventurous spirits. Plan exciting and spontaneous dates. Be open to trying new activities and exploring together.
- **Honesty is Key:** Sagittarius women appreciate honesty and direct communication. Be truthful and straightforward in your conversations.
- **Respect Independence**: Allow her the freedom she values. Don't try to restrict her or limit her personal space.
- **Share in Her Interests**: Show genuine interest in her passions and hobbies. Engage in conversations about travel, philosophy and intellectual topics.
- **Keep Things Fun**: Maintain a sense of humor and playfulness in your relationship. Make her laugh and enjoy lighthearted moments together.
- **Be Adventurous**: Surprise her with spontaneous getaways or outdoor adventures. She loves to explore new places and experiences.
- **Give Her Space**: Understand that Sagittarius women need independence and may sometimes require time alone. Respect her need for solitude without taking it personally.
- **Stay Positive:** Maintain a positive outlook on life, as Sagittarius women are attracted to optimism and enthusiasm.

FOR WOMEN DATING SAGITTARIUS MEN

- **Be Open-Minded**: Sagittarius men value intellectual curiosity and open-mindedness. Engage in stimulating conversations and explore new ideas together.
- **Join in the Adventure:** Embrace his love for adventure by participating in outdoor activities and spontaneous trips. Show that you can keep up with his zest for life.
- **Encourage Independence**: Allow him the freedom to pursue his interests and maintain his independence. Avoid being possessive or controlling.
- **Appreciate His Honesty**: Sagittarius men are known for their honesty. Value his candidness and be honest with him in return.
- **Laugh Together**: A sense of humor is essential in a relationship with a Sagittarius man. Share jokes and enjoy the lighter side of life.
- **Respect His Philosophical Side**: Sagittarius men often have a deep interest in philosophy and spirituality. Show respect for his beliefs and engage in meaningful conversations.
- **Support His Goals:** Encourage his ambitions and dreams. Be a supportive partner who helps him achieve his aspirations.
- **Give Him Space**: Understand that Sagittarius men need moments of solitude to recharge. Allow him the freedom to explore his interests independently.

Overall it's important to remember that astrological signs can give us some insights into people's personalities and preferences. However every individual is unique. No matter how compatible you may be astrologically, communication, respect and understanding are key in any relationship.

As we wrap up this chapter, it becomes apparent that Sagittarius' love life is an exhilarating journey filled with deep experiences. It's a realm where fiery passions, intellectual connections and deep emotions intertwine. Whether they're seeking love or already in a relationship, Sagittarius individuals can draw inspiration from their optimism and open heartedness.

Through their compatibility, with signs Sagittarius teaches us the value of embracing differences while still respecting each other's independence. They show us how to find joy in the journey of love. Although challenges may arise along the way these fiery archers possess the resilience and adaptability needed to navigate through the ups and downs of relationships.

As we come to the end of this chapter I hope you take with you the understanding of love and compatibility that Sagittarius represents. Lets celebrate the range of connections and embrace the endless possibilities, for exciting adventures in matters of the heart. Whether you're a Sagittarius looking for a partner or simply someone interested in astrology, may the stars always guide you on your journey to find love and happiness.

CHAPTER 3:
FRIENDS AND FAMILY

Welcome to the exciting world of Sagittarius when it comes to friendships and family relationships! Sagittarians are known for their enthusiasm, open mindedness and love for adventure. In this chapter we will take a journey through the qualities and dynamics that Sagittarius individuals bring to their friends and families. You're about to discover the challenges they face in relationships, the qualities that make them cherished friends and the dynamic interactions within their families. All of this and much more.

As we delve deeper into the world of Sagittarius you'll gain an understanding of how their adventurous spirit and zest for life shape their bonds with those they hold dear. Whether you're a Sagittarius seeking insight into your family connections or simply curious about astrology this chapter provides a comprehensive exploration of how Sagittarius functions as a friend, sibling, parent or child.

SAGITTARIUS AS A FRIEND

Having a friend who was born under the Sagittarius sign is like a breath of air in your life. They bring a combination of enthusiasm, spontaneity and optimism that can brighten the most mundane days. Let's take a closer look at what it's like to have a Sagittarius friend.

- **Adventurous**; Sagittarians are adventurers who are always up for trying new things and exploring different places. When you have a Sagittarius friend you can expect adventures and impromptu trips that will create happy memories.
- **Positive Vibes**; Sagittarius friends radiate positivity. Their infectious optimism can lift your spirits when you're feeling down. Their "glass half full" outlook on life is refreshing and comforting.
- **Open Mindedness**; Sagittarians are non judgmental individuals. They embrace people from all walks of life and are always eager to learn about other cultures or fresh perspectives. This makes them great friends for promoting inclusivity and diversity.
- **Honesty with Kindness**; Your Sagittarius friend will always tell you the truth as it is. They value honesty and direct communication, which means they'll give you their opinion and advice with your interests, at heart.
- **Sense of Humor**; Sagittarians have a great sense of humor. They love to make others laugh. Having them around guarantees a fun filled time with plenty of moments and clever banter.
- **Independence**; Sagittarius friends highly value their independence much as they respect yours. They won't suffocate you with attention. Rest assured they'll be there for you whenever you need them.
- **Intellectual Stimulation**; Engaging in philosophical conversations is a delight for Sagittarians. They thrive on exploring ideas and sharing their perspectives on a range of topics. This makes them excellent companions for stimulating discussions.
- **Generosity**; Sagittarians are naturally generous. They are often the ones to extend a helping hand or offer support. They go out of their way to ensure that you feel valued and appreciated.
- **Restless Spirit**; While their adventurous nature is certainly appealing, Sagittarians may occasionally struggle with restlessness. They might alter plans. Make spur of the moment decisions, which can be both thrilling and challenging for their friends.
- **Unfiltered Honesty**; When it comes to honesty Sagittarius friends don't hold back. While this admirable quality should be appreciated it's important to brace yourself for their straightforwardness. Remember that they mean well.

In conclusion, having a Sagittarius friend translates into having an inspirational companion by your side, in life. Being around them is always enjoyable. Their adventurous nature guarantees that your friendship will be full of thrilling experiences. So cherish your Sagittarius friend because they bring a kind of enchantment into your life that cannot be replicated.

SAGITTARIUS AND FAMILY DYNAMICS

Sagittarius individuals bring a combination of optimism, enthusiasm and a spirit of adventure, to their families. Their approach to family life is characterized by a love for exploration, a thirst for knowledge and a strong sense of independence. Here's a close look at how Sagittarius interacts within the family;

- **The Adventurous Parent**; If you have a Sagittarius parent you're likely to experience someone who encourages exploration and adventure. They enjoy planning family vacations exposing you to cultures and instilling a love for learning and discovery.
- **The Optimistic Sibling**; Sagittarius siblings are known for their optimistic outlook on life. They bring joy and enthusiasm to family gatherings often becoming the life of the party. They are the ones who suggest road trips or outdoor adventures.
- **Independent Nature**; Sagittarius individuals value their independence within the context of family life. As such they may seek space and freedom to pursue their interests. This can sometimes lead them to be seen as the " spirit" in the family.
- **Honesty and Straightforwardness;** Sagittarians are recognized for being honest even, in a straightforward manner. During family discussions or conflicts they often express their opinions candidly while offering solutions.
- **Intellectual Stimulation**; Members of Sagittarius families thrive on intellectual stimulation. They delight in engaging in conversations, about philosophy and sharing their knowledge with others. When families come together it's not uncommon for debates and the exchange of ideas to take place.
- **Supportive**; Sagittarius individuals have a kind and caring nature. As such they are always there to support their family members. They willingly go the extra mile to lend a helping hand when loved ones are in need. They also are there to provide encouragement for them to pursue their dreams.
- **Respect for Differences**; Sagittarians are known for being open minded and accepting of others. They actively promote tolerance and inclusivity

within their families. Often they take on the role of mediators during conflicts or disagreements.

- **Restlessness**; Every now and then Sagittarius family members may exhibit restlessness. They might seek out new experiences or crave change. This can bring excitement but it may also introduce some instability into the family dynamic.
- **Celebrating Traditions**; Despite their love for adventure Sagittarius individuals also value family traditions and gatherings. They understand the significance of connecting with loved ones during holidays and special occasions.
- **Role as Family Explorers**; It's quite common for Sagittarians to assume the role of being the family explorer. They often suggest trips or new hobbies to other family members. Furthermore they are likely to help with educational opportunities for younger siblings.

In conclusion, Sagittarius family members bring an element of adventure, optimism and intellectual curiosity into their households. They highly appreciate their freedom and the opportunity to explore. They also inspire their loved ones to embark on their quests of exploration. Although they can be straightforward and occasionally restless, their kindness, optimistic attitude and appreciation for diversity enhances the family dynamic.

CHALLENGES IN FRIENDSHIPS AND FAMILY RELATIONS

While Sagittarius individuals are widely recognized for their positive traits such as optimism, enthusiasm and a love for adventure they also encounter challenges. Being aware of these challenges can assist Sagittarians in navigating their relationships. Here are some things to be aware of.

- **Restlessness**; Sagittarians possess a desire for exploration and excitement. However this restlessness can occasionally result in a lack of commitment towards friendships or the tendency to constantly seek out experiences. It is crucial for Sagittarians to find a balance between their thirst for adventure and their responsibilities towards loved ones.
- **Bluntness and Honesty**; Known for their straightforwardness, this can inadvertently come across tactless or hurtful at times. Learning how to provide feedback with sensitivity is a challenge that they might need to overcome.
- **Independence**; Independence is highly cherished by Sagittarians. Although this may occasionally create the perception of distance or unavailability within relationships. Striking a balance between the need for space and nurturing intimate connections can prove challenging.
- **Commitment Issues;** It is not uncommon for Sagittarius individuals to be viewed as hesitant when it comes to commitments. Take time to reflect.
- **Hesitant**; One aspect of their nature is that they may jump into adventures without considering how it affects their loved ones leading to strain and misunderstandings. Additionally Sagittarians tend to resist routine and predictability which can pose challenges, in family life where routines often contribute to maintaining harmony.
- **Adventurous**; Another characteristic is their love for adventure, which could lead them to take risks that others perceive as irresponsible or dangerous. Striking a balance between their adventurous spirit and safety concerns becomes crucial in maintaining relationships.
- **Easily bored**; Sagittarians have a tendency to get easily bored which can affect their interactions with friends and family over time. Making an effort to stay engaged and committed in long term relationships is important.
- **Carefree**; When it comes to Sagittarians their carefree nature sometimes leads them to forget or overlook their responsibilities and commitments. This can be frustrating, for their friends and family members. Additionally Sagittarians often have a range of interests and hobbies which can make it difficult for them to effectively manage their time and energy.

To maintain fulfilling friendships and family relationships it's important for Sagittarius individuals to recognize and address these challenges. By embracing their qualities while also working on the pitfalls mentioned above Sagittarians can build strong and long lasting connections with their loved ones.

In the captivating realm of Sagittarius friendships and family dynamics we have uncovered a tapestry of qualities that make these individuals stand out. From their enthusiasm, to their love for adventure, Sagittarians bring a whirlwind of energy into the lives of those around them. Throughout this chapter we explored the challenges they face. Such as restlessness and straightforwardness. Along, with ways in which they can enhance and enrich their relationships. Within families Sagittarius members infuse curiosity and independence into the household dynamic. Among friends they light up circles with optimism and a great sense of humor.

As we bid farewell to this chapter I hope you carry with you an understanding of how Sagittarius fits within the context of friendships and family. If you're a Sagittarius looking to navigate the scene or someone trying to understand these individuals keep in mind that Sagittarius always seeks new adventures, connections and endless possibilities. May the essence of Sagittarius motivate you to embrace the world with open arms, cherish your loved ones and embark on thrilling journeys of exploration together. Life becomes an exhilarating voyage when you're surrounded by these archers.

CHAPTER 4: CAREER AND MONEY

In this chapter we will embark on a journey through the ambitions, finances and unique qualities that define Sagittarius individuals as they strive for professional success. Sagittarians are known for their optimism, spirit and insatiable curiosity. As we delve deeper into the world of Sagittarius you will gain insights into how their adventurous nature and passion for learning shape their careers and finances.

Get ready to discover the Sagittarius perspective on career and money. Where optimism blends with exploration. Whether you are a Sagittarius looking to enhance your knowledge or someone interested in understanding the mindset of this vibrant sign this chapter will reveal the various aspects of how Sagittarius approaches wealth work and achieving goals.

CAREER PREFERENCES AND PROFESSIONAL ASPIRATIONS

Those born under the Sagittarius zodiac sign are widely recognized for their adventurous nature and enthusiastic demeanor. These characteristics significantly influence their career choices and professional aspirations. Let's dive deeper into the areas that Sagittarius individuals are naturally drawn to in their careers.

- **Travel and Adventure**; Sagittarians possess an affinity towards careers involving travel and adventure. Professions such as writers, photographers, tour guides or jobs within the travel and tourism industry. These vocations allow them to satiate their craving for exploring places and cultures.
- **Education and Intellectual Growth;** Sagittarius have an appreciation for knowledge acquisition and continuous learning. Many of them find fulfillment in roles as teachers or researchers. They derive satisfaction from sharing insights while inspiring others to broaden their perspectives through education.
- **Philosophy and Spiritual Exploration**; A number of Sagittarians display an interest in philosophical contemplation and spiritual pursuits. Some may pursue careers such as philosophers delving into life's questions or theologians studying faith based beliefs systems. Others may engage in practices related to astrology or metaphysics as they seek answers about life's purpose.
- **Media**; With natural communication skills, Sagittarius individuals often thrive in careers associated with media engagement. For example in journalism. Here they can share stories with a captivated audience.
- **Storytellers**; Sagittarius possesses a talent for storytelling. They captivate audiences with their infectious enthusiasm and natural charm.
- **Philanthropy**; Sagittarians often choose careers in charitable organizations, international aid agencies or fields that revolve around justice and humanitarian efforts.
- **Entrepreneurship;** Entrepreneurship appeals to Sagittarius individuals due to their adventurous side and love for freedom. Many of them embark on the journey of starting their own businesses in industries that align with their passions such as travel, education or adventure.
- **Competitive**; Sagittarians find fulfillment in sports and fitness due to their competitive spirits. They often excel as athletes, coaches or fitness trainers. Their unwavering dedication to challenges and personal growth propels them towards these pursuits.
- **Ethics**; Fields involving law and ethics hold an allure for Sagittarius individuals. They are naturally drawn to careers that involve fighting for

justice and upholding principles. With a sense of justice they are willing to stand up for what they believe in.

- **Sales and marketing**; Sales and marketing roles suit Sagittarians thanks to their exceptional communication skills and persuasive abilities.
- **Healers**; Many Sagittarians have an interest in health, wellness and personal growth. They may choose to pursue careers as life coaches, therapists or healers helping others in their quest for self discovery.

Overall, Sagittarius individuals have diverse career interests due to a love for exploration and thirst for intellectual stimulation. They thrive in environments that allow them to be free spirited individuals who are always eager to learn. With their enthusiasm and optimism, Sagittarians ultimately bring a sense of adventure and positivity to any career path they embark on.

STRENGTHS THAT MAKE SAGITTARIUS INDIVIDUALS EXCEL IN THE WORKPLACE

Sagittarius individuals possess a unique set of strengths that leads to success in various professional settings. Their optimistic and adventurous nature, coupled with their passion for learning and exploration, make them valuable assets in the workplace. Here are some of the key strengths that help Sagittarius individuals to excel.

- **Optimism**: Sagittarians are natural optimists. Their positive outlook on life can inspire and motivate colleagues, even during challenging times. They tend to see opportunities in obstacles and approach problems with a "can-do" attitude, which can be infectious in the workplace.
- **Adaptability**: Sagittarius individuals thrive in dynamic environments. They easily adapt to change and are open to new ideas. This flexibility enables them to navigate shifting work landscapes and remain productive in ever-evolving industries.
- **Intellectual Depth**: Sagittarians have a profound thirst for knowledge and a love for intellectual exploration. They are constantly seeking to expand their horizons and delve into new subjects. This intellectual depth can lead to innovative solutions and fresh perspectives in the workplace.
- **Communication Skills**: Sagittarians are excellent communicators. They have a natural gift for storytelling and can convey ideas and information with enthusiasm and clarity. Their ability to articulate complex concepts makes them effective team members and leaders.

- **Team Player**: Despite their independent nature, Sagittarians work well within teams. They respect diverse perspectives and can foster collaboration by promoting an inclusive and open-minded work environment. Overall their optimism can also boost team morale.
- **Leadership Qualities:** Sagittarius individuals can make effective leaders due to their natural charisma and ability to inspire others. They are willing to take calculated risks and lead by example. Their passion and vision can motivate teams to achieve ambitious goals.
- **Global Perspective**: Sagittarians often have a global perspective and a deep appreciation for different cultures. This can be an asset in today's interconnected world, especially in industries with international reach or diverse clientele.
- **Problem-Solving Skills**: Their analytical thinking and problem-solving skills are enhanced by their love for intellectual challenges. Sagittarius individuals are resourceful and can find creative solutions to complex problems.
- **Resilience**: Sagittarians have a strong inner resilience that helps them bounce back from setbacks and failures. They don't dwell on past mistakes but view them as learning experiences, making them more resilient in the face of adversity.
- **Entrepreneurial Spirit:** Many Sagittarius individuals possess an entrepreneurial spirit. They thrive in roles that allow them to take risks and pursue their passions. Their independence and willingness to explore new opportunities make them well-suited for entrepreneurial endeavors.
- **Enthusiasm for Growth:** Sagittarians are constantly seeking personal and professional growth. They are proactive in pursuing opportunities for advancement and self-improvement, which can lead to career success.

In conclusion, Sagittarius individuals bring a unique blend of optimism, adaptability, intellectual curiosity and a global perspective to the workplace. Overall their strengths contribute to a positive work environment and often lead to success in a wide range of careers. From education and media to entrepreneurship and beyond.

CHALLENGES FACED BY SAGITTARIUS INDIVIDUALS IN THEIR CAREERS AND STRATEGIES TO OVERCOME THEM

While Sagittarius individuals possess numerous strengths that benefit them in the workplace, they also encounter certain challenges. Understanding these challenges and implementing effective strategies can help them navigate their careers more successfully. Here are some common career challenges faced by Sagittarius individuals and strategies to overcome them.

RESTLESSNESS AND IMPULSIVITY

- Challenge: Sagittarians can be restless and may struggle with the routine and stability that some careers demand. In addition their impulsivity can lead to hasty decisions.
- Strategy: Cultivate patience and discipline. Before making major career moves, thoroughly research and consider the potential consequences. Create a structured plan for achieving long-term goals.

COMMITMENT ISSUES

- Challenge: Sagittarius individuals may find it challenging to commit to long-term projects or roles. This can hinder career progression.
- Strategy: Focus on building skills and expertise in areas of genuine interest. Seek careers that allow for variety and exploration within a stable framework. Set achievable milestones to stay engaged.

TACTLESSNESS IN COMMUNICATION

- Challenge: Sagittarians' blunt and direct communication style may lead to misunderstandings or conflicts in the workplace.
- Strategy: Develop effective communication skills, including active listening and empathy. Learn to deliver feedback with sensitivity. Consider the perspectives of others before responding.

IMPATIENCE WITH HIERARCHIES

- Challenge: Sagittarians may become frustrated with hierarchical structures and rules in traditional workplaces.
- Strategy: Focus on the bigger picture and the opportunities for growth within the organization. Seek positions that allow for more autonomy and responsibility. Furthermore consider entrepreneurial ventures.

OVERCOMMITMENT AND BURNOUT

- Challenge: Sagittarius individuals' enthusiasm can lead them to overcommit to multiple projects, risking burnout.
- Strategy: Practice time management and prioritize tasks. Learn to say "no" when necessary and delegate responsibilities. Maintain a work-life balance to prevent exhaustion.

RESISTANCE TO ROUTINE

- Challenge: Sagittarians may struggle with repetitive tasks and routines.
- Strategy: Look for roles that offer a degree of variety and challenge. Seek positions that require problem-solving and creativity. Consider freelance or consulting work that allows for flexibility.

LACK OF ATTENTION TO DETAIL

- Challenge: Sagittarius individuals may overlook details while focusing on the big picture.
- Strategy: Develop organizational skills and use tools like checklists and calendars. Collaborate with colleagues who excel in attention to detail to complement your strengths.

IMPULSIVITY IN DECISION-MAKING

- Challenge: Sagittarians may make impulsive career decisions without fully considering the consequences.
- Strategy: Consult with trusted mentors or colleagues before making significant career choices. Take time to weigh pros and cons and assess potential risks.

SEEKING CONSTANT CHANGE

- Challenge: The desire for new experiences may lead to frequent job changes. This can hinder the development of long-term expertise.
- Strategy: Balance exploration with a commitment to mastery in chosen fields. Seek positions that encourage continuous learning and growth.

BALANCING INDEPENDENCE AND COLLABORATION

- Challenge: Sagittarians value independence but must also work effectively within teams.
- Strategy: Cultivate teamwork skills and find roles that allow for both independence and collaboration. Recognize that team efforts can lead to even more significant achievements.

By recognizing and addressing these obstacles, individuals born under the Sagittarius zodiac sign can make the most of their strengths while overcoming challenges in their lives. By employing strategies and being open to adaptation they can pursue successful career paths that align with their adventurous and optimistic nature.

In the captivating realm of Sagittarius professional and financial pursuits we have uncovered a tapestry woven with optimism, exploration and an insatiable thirst for knowledge. This chapter has taken us on a voyage through the strengths, obstacles and approaches that define Sagittarians as they strive for success and financial stability. As we bring this chapter to a close it becomes evident that Sagittarius individuals approach their careers and financial aspirations with a positive spirit and mindset. Their ability to embrace change along with their curiosity often leads them to diverse and fulfilling journeys. As they navigate the ups and downs of life they do so with resilience and optimism perceiving challenges as opportunities for growth.

May the insights gleaned from this chapter serve as a guiding light for Sagittarians who seek to accomplish their career goals. May it also provide understanding, for those who wish to appreciate the mindset of this zodiac sign. Best of luck to you all.

CHAPTER 5: SELF-IMPROVEMENT

Welcome to this chapter that delves into the world of self improvement as viewed through the lens of Sagittarius. Within these pages we will embark on a journey of growth, exploration and the pursuit of knowledge that is synonymous with Sagittarius individuals. Sagittarians possess a thirst for learning, a zest for life and an unwavering belief in the power of positivity. Throughout this chapter we will delve into how these remarkable qualities can be harnessed to cultivate self improvement and empower Sagittarians to realize their fullest potential.

Whether you are a Sagittarius seeking guidance on your path of growth or simply captivated by the distinctive mindset of this vibrant sign this chapter offers valuable insights, practical strategies and inspiration for embracing self improvement. So prepare to embark on a voyage of self discovery where each day presents an opportunity for learning and every challenge becomes a catalyst for growth. Let us follow the arrow of Archer as it guides us in our quest for self improvement.

PERSONAL GROWTH AND DEVELOPMENT FOR SAGITTARIUS

Sagittarius individuals are characterized by their adventurous spirit, optimism and love for exploration. They have a natural zest for life and a curiosity that drives them to seek new experiences and expand their horizons. While these qualities are their strengths, personal growth for Sagittarius often involves honing their boundless energy and enthusiasm into more focused and purposeful endeavors. Here are some key aspects of personal growth and development for Sagittarius individuals:

- **Embrace Commitment**: One of the key challenges for Sagittarians is their resistance to long-term commitments. Personal growth involves learning to commit to goals, relationships and projects that matter most. By cultivating commitment, they can see through their dreams to fruition and build lasting relationships.
- **Balance Freedom and Responsibility**: Sagittarius individuals treasure their independence. But personal growth requires finding a balance between the freedom they cherish and the responsibilities they must fulfill. Learning to navigate obligations without feeling confined is essential for their development.
- **Cultivate Patience**: Sagittarians can be impulsive and eager for instant results. Developing patience allows them to persevere through challenges and stay committed to long-term goals. Patience also helps them appreciate the journey as much as the destination.
- **Focus and Direction**: Their love for exploration can sometimes scatter their energy across various interests. Personal growth entails defining clear goals and channeling their enthusiasm into focused pursuits. Setting priorities and following through with dedication is key.
- **Embrace Routine**: Sagittarians often resist routine, but incorporating structure into their lives can help them achieve consistency and stability. Finding a healthy balance between spontaneity and routine is essential for personal growth.
- **Enhance Empathy**: Sagittarius individuals can be straightforward and blunt in their communication. Developing empathy and emotional intelligence allows them to connect more deeply with others. With this they can navigate relationships with greater sensitivity.

- **Harness Optimism**: While their optimism is a strength, personal growth involves using it to overcome challenges and setbacks. Sagittarians can learn to maintain their positivity while also being prepared for realistic assessments of situations.
- **Nurture Inner Wisdom**: Their love for knowledge often leads to a quest for wisdom. Personal growth entails not only acquiring knowledge but also cultivating inner wisdom through introspection, meditation and self-reflection.
- **Expand Cultural Awareness**: Sagittarius individuals' interest in different cultures and perspectives can be a source of personal growth. Engaging with diverse viewpoints and experiences enriches their understanding of the world . Ultimately it deepens their empathy.
- **Develop Financial Savvy**: Given their love for adventure, Sagittarians may benefit from enhancing their financial management skills. Learning about budgeting, saving and investing can provide them with the stability to pursue their passions.
- **Stay Grounded**: Personal growth involves finding ways to stay grounded amidst their adventurous pursuits. Practices like yoga, mindfulness, or spending time in nature can help Sagittarians maintain inner balance.
- **Seek Continuous Learning**: Sagittarius individuals thrive on learning. Personal growth involves a lifelong commitment to education and personal development. Pursuing new skills and knowledge keeps their curiosity alive.

In conclusion, personal growth and development for Sagittarius individuals involve striking a balance between their adventurous spirit and the need for focus. By harnessing their optimism, embracing responsibility and cultivating empathy, Sagittarians can continue their journey of self-discovery. A successful journey of exploration.

HARNESSING SAGITTARIUS STRENGTHS AND OVERCOMING WEAKNESSES

Sagittarius individuals possess a unique set of strengths and weaknesses, like every other zodiac sign. To maximize their potential and lead their best lives, Sagittarians can harness their strengths while actively working on overcoming their weaknesses. Here's how they can do that.

Strength: Optimism

- Harness: Embrace your natural optimism to inspire and uplift others. Your positivity can be a powerful force for motivation and resilience.
- Overcome: Be mindful of being overly optimistic in situations that require a more realistic assessment. Sometimes, acknowledging challenges is the first step in addressing them.

Strength: Curiosity and Learning

- Harness: Continue to explore new subjects and ideas. Your love for learning can lead to personal growth and career advancement.
- Overcome: Avoid spreading yourself too thin across multiple interests. Focus on mastering a few subjects or skills that align with your long-term goals.

Strength: Adventure and Exploration

- Harness: Embrace your adventurous spirit by seeking out new experiences and cultures. This can broaden your horizons and provide valuable life lessons.
- Overcome: Maintain a balance between adventure and stability. Recognize that some level of routine and commitment is necessary for personal and professional growth.

Strength: Honesty and Directness

- Harness: Use your honesty to build trust in your relationships. Your candidness can lead to open and transparent communication.
- Overcome: Practice delivering feedback with sensitivity, especially in delicate situations. Consider the impact of your words on others' feelings.

Strength: Adaptability

- Harness: Leverage your adaptability to thrive in changing environments. Your ability to embrace new challenges can lead to career success.
- Overcome: Ensure that your adaptability doesn't result in a lack of commitment or follow-through. Set clear goals and stick to them.

Weakness: Impulsivity

Overcome: Pause and reflect before making major decisions. Develop a habit of considering the consequences of your actions to avoid hasty choices.

Weakness: Resistance to Routine

Overcome: Introduce structured routines into your life, especially in areas that require consistency. For example, health and finance. Balance spontaneity with stability.

Weakness: Commitment Issues

Overcome: Recognize the value of commitment in achieving long-term goals. Set achievable milestones and focus on building lasting relationships.

Weakness: Tactlessness

Overcome: Practice empathy and active listening to understand others' perspectives. Think before speaking, especially in sensitive or emotional situations.

Weakness: Restlessness

Overcome: Channel your restlessness into productive outlets. Set clear goals and create a structured plan to avoid constant changes and distractions.

Weakness: Lack of Attention to Detail

Overcome: Use organizational tools and techniques to help you stay on top of details. Collaborate with detail-oriented individuals in projects where precision is crucial.

Weakness: Overcommitment

Overcome: Learn to say "no" when necessary and prioritize your commitments. Focus on quality rather than quantity in your projects and relationships.

By acknowledging their strengths and actively addressing their weaknesses, individuals born under the Sagittarius zodiac sign can lead more well rounded and satisfying lives. Embracing their love for adventure while cultivating discipline and dedication will enable them to harness their qualities and overcome obstacles effectively.

As we wrap up this chapter on self improvement in relation to Sagittarius where we have explored the characteristics and qualities that define this sign known for its nature and optimistic outlook. Overall Sagittarians possess the tools to make significant progress in their pursuit of self improvement. By embracing their strengths while addressing challenges head on they can soar to new heights in many areas of life.

May the essence of Sagittarius ignite your drive to forge your journey, towards personal growth. A journey where passion and knowledge intertwine. Let every obstacle become a milestone on the path to a richer and more satisfying existence.

CHAPTER 6: THE YEAR AHEAD

Welcome to this chapter that delves into the outlook for Sagittarius in the year ahead. In this chapter we will explore how celestial events and astrological alignments might shape the lives of individuals born under the sign of Sagittarius.

As a Sagittarian you possess a sense of optimism, curiosity and a thirst for adventure on your life's journey. Over the upcoming year the movements of stars and planets will impact your professional experiences. This chapter aims to provide insights into what lies ahead and how you can make the most of opportunities while navigating any challenges that may arise.

So get ready, Sagittarian! Prepare to embark on a voyage where optimism intertwines with introspection. Let the Archers arrow guide you towards a year of growth, adventure and self discovery.

HOROSCOPE GUIDE FOR THE YEAR AHEAD

CAREER AND FINANCES

This year promises shifts in your career. Your limitless enthusiasm and adaptability will help you overcome obstacles while seizing opportunities. Keep an eye out for advancement opportunities. Remember the importance of balancing your adventurous spirit with financial stability. It would be wise to make well informed investment decisions that will secure your future.

Sagittarius individuals have a lot of potential in their careers and financial situations this year. Here are some astrological events that will play a role in shaping these aspects of your life.

- **Jupiter in Pisces (May. October);** During Jupiter's transit through Pisces you may experience a sense of creativity and intuition when it comes to your career. It's a time to explore new opportunities or projects that align with your passions. Financially this period is favorable for investments and expanding your sources of income.

- **Saturn in Aquarius (Throughout the Year)**; Saturn's influence continues to impact your career sector as it moves through Aquarius. This urges you to establish long term goals and pursue them diligently. You might find yourself taking on new responsibilities at work which can lead to career advancement and financial stability.
- **Solar and Lunar Eclipses;** Keep an eye out for changes in your situation during the eclipse in Taurus (April 30) and lunar eclipse, in Taurus (November 8). These celestial events could bring about shifts or developments. Please exercise caution when making investments and financial decisions during these periods and take the time to reassess your budget.
- **Mars in Aries; Between January 6th and March 3rd Mars**, Mars in Aries can provide a boost of energy and motivation to propel your career forward. Utilize this time to take initiative and pursue your goals with enthusiasm.

Overall to maximize your career and financial prospects, Sagittarius it is important to set goals, maintain discipline in your pursuits and explore new opportunities. Be mindful of choices during eclipse periods. Lastly, consider seeking professional advice when needed.

LOVE AND RELATIONSHIPS

Sagittarians can expect love to be in the air this year. If you're already in a relationship your bond will deepen as you continue to communicate honestly with your partner. For those who're single, keep an open heart for new connections as someone special may unexpectedly enter your life.

Your relationships will flourish throughout the year Sagittarius. Your honesty and direct communication will strengthen your connections with loved ones. Be open to forming friendships and deepening existing ones. Singles might find new love so again it's important to keep an open heart.

In the year ahead, Sagittarius individuals should anticipate their love lives and relationships being influenced by significant astrological events. These celestial movements may bring both challenges and chances for matters of the heart.

- **Jupiter transits through Pisces;** During the period from May to October with Jupiter transiting through Pisces, which happens to be your ruling planet. You can expect enhancements in your emotional world. You might experience a connection to your instincts and emotions which can deepen your relationships. It's a time to nurture the bonds you already have and explore the depths of your emotions.
- **Saturn in Aquarius (Throughout the Year);** With Saturn remaining in Aquarius it encourages you to assess the dynamics of your connections, including friendships and romantic relationships. You may find yourself desiring genuine connections in your love life. It's a period of growth and maturity within your relationships.
- **Solar and Lunar Eclipses;** The solar eclipse in Taurus (April 30) and lunar eclipse in Taurus (November 8) could bring about changes and revelations in your partnerships. These eclipses might lead you to reevaluate what you value in relationships and let go of any attachments that no longer contribute positively to your well being.
- **Venus in Sagittarius (December 30. January 23 2024);** When Venus graces Sagittarius it enhances your charisma and attractiveness. This is a time for Sagittarians to shine when it comes to love and romance. Embrace this opportunity to openly express your feelings and attract attention.

Overall focus on strengthening connections, nurturing existing relationships and seeking authenticity, within all of your interactions. Stay receptive to the changes that eclipses may bring. Remember they often lead to growth and development in your emotional world.

PERSONAL GROWTH

Sagittarius this year beckons you to tap into your wisdom, explore your passions and seize opportunities for growth. Harness the energies of astrology to embark on a journey of self discovery and improvement. With your optimism and adventurous spirit you hold massive potential for profound personal development throughout this year. Here are some key astrological events of the year that present you with opportunities for growth and self discovery.

- **Jupiters journey through Pisces (May. October);** During this period take the time to delve into your world and embrace your intuition. Engaging in spiritual practices, creative endeavors or deep introspection can help foster growth.
- **Saturn's presence in Aquarius (Throughout the Year);** Saturn's influence encourages self reflection and personal development. Utilize this time to identify areas for improvement and focus on nurturing yourself.
- **Solar and Lunar Eclipses;** Eclipses have the potential to spark revelations. Embrace the changes and insights they bring as they often pave the way for growth and self discovery.

HEALTH AND WELLBEING

Sagittarius folks should focus on their health and overall well being in the year as astrological happenings can have an impact on your energy levels.

- **Jupiter in Pisces (May. October);** When Jupiter moves through Pisces it can enhance your creative endeavors. However it's important to maintain an approach to your well being. Embrace mindfulness practices to nurture your emotional fitness.
- **Saturn in Aquarius (Throughout the Year);** With Saturn in Aquarius you may find yourself inclined towards health routines. Consider incorporating exercise into your routine and prioritize your well being.
- **Solar and Lunar Eclipses;** Eclipses tend to heighten sensitivity. During these times pay attention to your health. Seek support from friends or professionals if needed.

Overall to ensure a healthy body and mind Sagittarius individuals should give importance to exercise, mental wellness practices and emotional balance. Balancing with self care routines will help you maintain vitality throughout the year.

TRAVEL AND ADVENTURE

As an adventurer at heart within the zodiac realm this year presents perfect opportunities to explore new horizons. Plan trips ahead of time while also embracing spontaneous adventures along the way.

FAMILY RELATIONSHIPS

This year your bond with family members will be strong. Make sure to spend quality time and engage in deep conversations. Your positive outlook can uplift your loved ones when they face challenges.

CREATIVITY AND HOBBIES

Get ready for a surge of creativity in the year ahead. Pursue projects that ignite your passions. Your enthusiasm and inspiration will lead to creating something magnificent.

SOCIAL LIFE

Your social calendar is going to be quite busy, Sagittarius! Embrace opportunities to meet people and expand your network. Your charm and charisma will make you a popular figure in diverse social circles.

SPIRITUALITY AND INNER HARMONY

Consider nurturing your spiritual side this year. Explore spiritual practices such as in meditation or taking time for self reflection. Connecting with your inner self will bring you a sense of peace and purpose.

CHALLENGES

While the year ahead holds promise for you it's important to be mindful of impulsiveness and impatience. Avoid making hasty decisions especially when it comes to financial matters. Remember to strike a balance between your thirst for adventure and your responsibilities.

Overall the year ahead is full of potential, for growth both personally and professionally. Embrace the chances that come your path, remain faithful to your outlook. Utilize your limitless passion to craft a life brimming with excitement and satisfaction. Revel in the voyage!

KEY ASTROLOGICAL EVENTS AND THEIR IMPACT ON SAGITTARIUS

Astrological events play a significant role in influencing the lives of individuals, and Sagittarius is no exception. As a Sagittarius, you are ruled by Jupiter, the planet of expansion and optimism. Here are some key astrological events to watch out for in the coming year and their potential impact on your life:

- **Jupiter Transits;** Jupiter in Pisces (May - October): During this period, Jupiter, your ruling planet, moves through the compassionate and intuitive sign of Pisces. This alignment can enhance your spiritual and creative pursuits. You may feel a stronger urge to explore your inner world, engage in artistic endeavors, or deepen your spiritual practices. It's a time for personal growth and introspection.
- **Saturn Transits;** Saturn in Aquarius (Throughout the Year): Saturn continues its transit through Aquarius, which can bring a sense of responsibility and discipline to your social life and friendships. You may find yourself reevaluating your social circles and focusing on building more meaningful connections. It's a time for aligning your personal values with your social interactions.
- **Lunar and Solar Eclipses**; Solar Eclipse in Taurus (April 30): This eclipse may highlight financial matters for you, Sagittarius. It's a good time to review your financial goals, investments, and budgeting habits.
- **Lunar Eclipse in Taurus (November 8):** Another eclipse in Taurus emphasizes your values and possessions. It's an opportunity to let go of what no longer serves you and make changes in your material life.
- **Mercury Retrogrades;** Mercury Retrograde in Air Signs (January 14 - February 3, May 10 - June 3, and September 9 - October 2): During these

retrogrades, communication may become more challenging. Be cautious with contracts and agreements. It's a time for reevaluating your communication style and ensuring clarity in important conversations.

- **Mars Transits;** Mars in Aries (January 6 - March 3): Mars in Aries can bring an extra boost of energy and motivation. You may feel more assertive in pursuing your goals and ambitions. Use this period to initiate projects and take calculated risks.
- **Venus Transits;** Venus in Sagittarius (December 30 - January 23, 2024): When Venus enters your sign, it brings a harmonious and social energy. It's a great time to enhance your personal charm and enjoy social interactions. Your optimism and charisma will shine.

Remember that while astrological events can provide insights into potential themes and energies, how they manifest in your life depends on your individual birth chart. Use these influences as opportunities for personal growth, self-reflection, and positive change. Embrace the adventurous and optimistic spirit of Sagittarius as you navigate the celestial events in the year ahead.

As we wrap up this chapter we've explored the path that awaits individuals born under the sign of Sagittarius, in the year. From matters of the heart to ambitions. From health and wellness to personal development. The stars and planets have revealed a tapestry of opportunities and challenges.

Sagittarius, your natural optimism, endless curiosity and adventurous nature will serve as your guiding principles as you navigate the influences of the year ahead. Embrace the lessons that come your way remembering that every challenge presents an opportunity for growth and every adventure offers a chance for self discovery.

As you traverse through the year, always keep in mind that an archer's arrow points towards a future filled with promise and excitement. Whether you're exploring new horizons or delving into the depths of your soul may this upcoming year be a time of personal growth, fulfillment and realization of your most ambitious aspirations.

CHAPTER 7:
FAMOUS "SAGITTARIUS" PERSONALITIES

In this chapter we'll take a dive into the lives of some known individuals who were born under the Sagittarius zodiac sign. These remarkable people have left an impact in various fields of human achievement. Sagittarius folks are renowned for their nature, inquisitive minds and boundless curiosity. It comes as no surprise that many accomplished individuals share this sign.

As we explore the journeys and achievements of these Sagittarians we'll discover a tapestry of talent spanning politics, entertainment, sports and much more. Each profile will unveil the qualities that make Sagittarius individuals stand out from the crowd – from their pursuit of goals to their charismatic and outspoken personalities.

Embark on this journey, through the lives of Sagittarius personalities as we delve into the driving forces that have propelled them towards greatness. Their stories serve as a source of inspiration. Their legacies continue to shape our world in ways.

WINSTON CHURCHILL

- Date of Birth: November 30, 1874.
- Brief Biography: Sir Winston Churchill was a British statesman, army officer, and writer. He is best known for his leadership as Prime Minister of the United Kingdom during World War II. Churchill's speeches and determination inspired the British people during the darkest hours of the war.
- Sagittarius Traits: Adventurous, optimistic, charismatic, direct and outspoken.
- Impact: Churchill's leadership and unwavering resolve played a pivotal role in the Allied victory in World War II. His speeches, such as the famous "We shall fight on the beaches", continue to be celebrated for their inspiration.

- Personal Life: Churchill was a prolific writer, earning the Nobel Prize in Literature in 1953. He had a lifelong love of adventure, painting and travel.

CATHY MORIARTY

- Date of Birth: November 29, 1960.
- Brief Biography: Cathy Moriarty is an American actress best known for her role as Vicki LaMotta in the film "Raging Bull" (1980), for which she received an Academy Award nomination.
- Sagittarius Traits: Energetic, optimistic, outgoing and adventurous.
- Impact: Moriarty's performance in "Raging Bull" earned her critical acclaim and recognition in the film industry. She has continued to work in film and television, showcasing her versatile talent.
- Personal Life: Moriarty's career has spanned several decades. She remains an influential figure in Hollywood.

BRUCE LEE

- Date of Birth: November 27, 1940.
- Brief Biography: Bruce Lee was a martial artist, actor and filmmaker known for his groundbreaking contributions to martial arts and action cinema. He is considered one of the most influential martial artists of all time.
- Sagittarius Traits: Determined, adventurous, focused and enthusiastic.

- Impact: Bruce Lee's martial arts philosophy and innovative techniques revolutionized martial arts and popularized it worldwide. His films, such as "Enter the Dragon," left an indelible mark on cinema.
- Personal Life: Beyond his martial arts prowess, Lee was a philosopher and author. His legacy continues to inspire generations of martial artists and actors.

TAYLOR SWIFT

- Date of Birth: December 13, 1989.
- Brief Biography: Taylor Swift is an American singer-songwriter and actress. She is known for her narrative songwriting and has won numerous awards, including multiple Grammy Awards.
- Sagittarius Traits: Creative, optimistic, independent and charismatic.
- Impact: Swift's music has resonated with millions worldwide, making her one of the most successful and influential contemporary artists. Her albums have topped charts and earned critical acclaim.
- Personal Life: Swift is also known for her philanthropic efforts and advocacy on various social and political issues.

NICKI MINAJ

- Date of Birth: December 8, 1982.
- Brief Biography: Nicki Minaj is a Trinidadian-American rapper, singer, and songwriter. She is known for her bold and theatrical persona and has achieved significant success in the music industry.
- Sagittarius Traits: Outspoken, confident, ambitious and adventurous.
- Impact: Minaj's music has garnered millions of fans worldwide. Also she has been recognized for her contributions to hip-hop and pop culture.
- Personal Life: Beyond her music career, Minaj has ventured into acting and philanthropy. She is recognized as a multifaceted and influential artist.

FRANZ FERDINAND

- Date of Birth: December 18, 1863.
- Brief Biography: Archduke Franz Ferdinand of Austria was a royal figure whose assassination in 1914 triggered the events leading to World War I.
- Sagittarius Traits: Adventurous, determined and driven by principles.

- Impact: The assassination of Franz Ferdinand set in motion a series of events that ultimately led to World War I, reshaping the course of history.
- Personal Life: Beyond his historical role, Franz Ferdinand was known for his love of hunting and his progressive ideas. This included advocating for greater autonomy within the Austro-Hungarian Empire.

EMMANUEL MACRON

- Date of Birth: December 21, 1977.
- Brief Biography: Emmanuel Macron is a French politician who became the President of France in 2017. He is known for his centrist policies and youthful approach to governance.
- Sagittarius Traits: Charismatic, visionary and open-minded.
- Impact: Macron's election as President marked a significant shift in French politics. He has been a prominent figure in European and international politics.
- Personal Life: Macron's rise to power at a relatively young age reflects his ambitious and adventurous spirit.

IAN BOTHAM

- Date of Birth: November 24, 1955.
- Brief Biography: Sir Ian Botham is a former English cricketer and one of the greatest all-rounders in the history of cricket. He achieved numerous records during his career.

- Sagittarius Traits: Competitive, energetic, adventurous and determined.
- Impact: Botham's cricketing prowess made him a legendary figure in the sport. He contributed significantly to England's cricket success during his era.
- Personal Life: Botham's love for adventure extended beyond the cricket field, as he embarked on charity walks and humanitarian efforts.

SINEAD O'CONNOR

- Date of Birth: December 8, 1966.
- Brief Biography: Sinead O'Connor was an Irish singer-songwriter known for her distinctive voice and socially conscious lyrics. She gained international fame with her hit song "Nothing Compares 2 U."
- Sagittarius Traits: Bold, outspoken and driven by principles.
- Impact: O'Connor's music and activism have resonated with audiences worldwide. She was celebrated for her fearless approach to art and social justice.
- Personal Life: O'Connor's career has been marked by both artistic achievements and personal challenges. She was a complex and influential figure.

SCARLETT JOHANSSON

- Date of Birth: November 22, 1984.
- Brief Biography: Scarlett Johansson is an American actress and singer known for her versatile roles in film. She has received critical acclaim and numerous awards throughout her career.
- Sagittarius Traits: Adventurous, confident and charismatic.
- Impact: Johansson's acting talent has made her one of the most sought-after and highest-paid actresses in Hollywood. Her performances have left a lasting impact on cinema.
- Personal Life: Beyond her acting career, Johansson has ventured into music and has been an advocate for various social and humanitarian causes.

LARRY BIRD

- Date of Birth: December 7, 1956.

- Brief Biography: Larry Bird is a former American professional basketball player and coach. He is widely regarded as one of the greatest basketball players in history.
- Sagittarius Traits: Competitive, determined and driven by a love for the game.
- Impact: Bird's contributions to basketball include multiple NBA championships and MVP awards. He has left an indelible mark on the sport.
- Personal Life: Bird's dedication to basketball extended beyond his playing career. He went on to become a successful coach and executive in the NBA.

KAREN GILLAN

- Date of Birth: November 28, 1987.
- Brief Biography: Karen Gillan is a Scottish actress known for her roles in television and film. She gained prominence for her role as Amy Pond in the TV series "Doctor Who."
- Sagittarius Traits: Energetic, outgoing and adventurous.
- Impact: Gillan's talent and versatility as an actress have earned her acclaim in both British and international entertainment. She has continued to excel in her career.
- Personal Life: Gillan's journey in the entertainment industry reflects her adventurous and determined spirit, as she has transitioned from acting to directing.

These profiles showcase the talents and achievements of known individuals who were born under the Sagittarius sign. Whether in politics, entertainment, sports or art Sagittarius individuals have made a significant impact on the world.

As we conclude this chapter dedicated to Sagittarius personalities we have embarked on a captivating journey through the lives and accomplishments of those who share this zodiac sign. Their stories span domains like politics, entertainment, sports and beyond. Their journeys serve as evidence of the potential and determination that define Sagittarius. Their fearlessness, in pursuing dreams, eagerness to explore territories and commitment to their beliefs are just a few of the qualities that have propelled them towards greatness.

Let us celebrate these Sagittarius personalities' legacies and allow their stories to inspire us on our paths. Whether you belong to this zodiac sign or simply admire the attributes it embodies, always remember that the essence of Sagittarius lives on in the souls of those who dare to dream, discover and leave a lasting imprint on the world.

CONCLUSION

As we approach the culmination of our journey through the world of Sagittarius, it's time to reflect on the key insights and wisdom we've gained about this dynamic zodiac sign. In this concluding chapter, we'll summarize the essential points we've explored in each of the preceding chapters.

Summarization of Key Points about Sagittarius:

- **Chapter 1 - History and Mythology**: In this chapter we explored the historical and mythological origins of Sagittarius. We discovered how different cultures perceived and represented the Archer in their star maps. Furthermore we traced the evolution of Sagittarius from mythological interpretations to modern astrology.
- **Chapter 2 - Love & Compatibility**: In this chapter we delved into Sagittarius' approach to love and romance. Inside we analyzed Sagittarius' compatibility with other zodiac signs. Lastly we offered tips for dating and maintaining relationships with Sagittarius individuals.
- **Chapter 3 - Friends And Family**: Here we explored Sagittarius' role as a friend and family member. Inside we discussed the dynamics and challenges in friendships and family relations for Sagittarius.
- **Chapter 4 - Career And Money**: This chapter explored Sagittarius' career preferences and professional aspirations. It highlighted the strengths that make Sagittarius individuals excel in the workplace. It also addressed the challenges Sagittarius individuals may face in their careers and provided strategies to overcome them.
- **Chapter 5 - Self-Improvement**: In this chapter we explored personal growth and development for Sagittarius. We discussed how to harness Sagittarius' strengths and overcome weaknesses. Furthermore we offered exercises and outlooks for potential self-improvement.
- **Chapter 6 - The Year Ahead**: In this chapter we Analyzed how astrological events of the year influence Sagittarius individuals. We looked in detail at the way it influenced love, career, health, personal growth and much more.

- **Chapter 7 - Famous "Sagittarius" Personalities:** Here we were introduced to profiles of famous individuals born under the Sagittarius sign. Inside we explored their impact and the traits that define them.

As we near the conclusion of our exploration of Sagittarius it's crucial to bear in mind that the essence of the Archer is characterized by a nature unwavering positivity and an insatiable search for truth and adventure. These qualities do not only define individuals born under Sagittarius. They also have a profound impact on the world. May the wisdom and understanding you have acquired about Sagittarius inspire you to embrace these attributes throughout your journey and appreciate the spirit embodied by this zodiac sign.

Throughout this book we embarked on a captivating voyage to unravel the nature of Sagittarius. Our objective was to offer insights, guidance and a deeper understanding of what it means to be a Sagittarius. We explored many aspects such as its history, mythical origins and astrological significance. We delved into topics like love, relationships, friendships, family dynamics, career aspirations, personal growth and more. Cosmic influences will influence Sagittarius individuals in the upcoming year. Furthermore we celebrated personalities who share this zodiac sign while aiming to empower all Sagittarius individuals to embrace their qualities fully.

Our mission in this book was centered around helping a Sagittarius unlock their full potential while navigating life's adventures, with confidence and authenticity. We have fulfilled our promise by providing an exploration of Sagittarius offering insights and unveiling the dynamic characteristics that define this zodiac sign. From delving into the ancient origins to offering guidance on matters of love, career and personal development our aim was to equip Sagittarius individuals with the knowledge and resources they need to flourish.

If there's one major lesson to be gleaned from this book it is the celebration of Sagittarius' distinct qualities; their curiosity, unwavering optimism, adventurous spirit and fearless pursuit of truth and excitement. These qualities are not only attributes; they epitomize what it means to be a Sagittarius. Our hope is that every Sagittarius reader who engages with this book will develop an appreciation for their strengths and experience a renewed sense of purpose in embracing life's adventures.

In conclusion astrology serves as a tool for self discovery and personal growth due to its insights into human nature and cosmic influences. The representation of the Archer as the symbol for the Sagittarius zodiac sign reminds us of the power of optimism, the thrill of exploration and the significance of embracing our qualities.

As we navigate through the changing universe we want to inspire all Sagittarius individuals to embrace their strengths, overcome challenges and keep aiming for a better future. Dear Sagittarius you embody endless possibilities and boundless optimism. Your adventurous nature knows no limits and your unwavering quest for truth and purpose is truly inspiring. Embrace your qualities with pride as they serve as your guiding compass on this journey. As you explore the horizons of life remember that even the stars themselves celebrate your spirit.

This book has been a tribute to the nature and celebration of everything that makes Sagittarius special. As we bring this journey to an end our hope is that you will carry a better understanding of your sign, an increased appreciation for your strengths and be inspired to face life's adventures with unwavering optimism. Whether you are a Sagittarius or someone seeking insight into this sign may the wisdom within these pages light up your path and lead you towards a future filled with exploration, discovery and limitless enthusiasm. Best wishes!

CAPRICORN:

A COMPLETE GUIDE TO THE CAPRICORN ASTROLOGY STAR SIGN

Contents

INTRODUCTION ---------- 1

Overview of the Capricorn Zodiac Sign ---------- 2

CHAPTER 1: HISTORY AND MYTHOLOGY ---------- 5

Historical and Mythological Origins ---------- 5

Historical Figures Born Under the Capricorn Sign ---------- 8

CHAPTER 2: LOVE & COMPATIBILITY ---------- 10

Capricorn's Approach to Love and Romance ---------- 10

Capricorn's Compatibility with Other Zodiac Signs ---------- 12

Dating and Relationships with Capricorn Individuals ---------- 16

CHAPTER 3: FRIENDS AND FAMILY ---------- 19

Capricorn as a Friend ---------- 19

Capricorn and Family Dynamics ---------- 21

Challenges in Friendships and Family Relationships ---------- 22

CHAPTER 4: CAREER AND MONEY ---------- 25

Capricorn Career Preferences and Professional Aspirations ---------- 25

Strengths of Capricorn Individuals in the Workplace ---------- 27

Challenges Capricorns May Face in Their Careers and Strategies to Overcome Them ---------- 29

CHAPTER 5: SELF-IMPROVEMENT ---------- 31

Personal growth and development ---------- 32

Harnessing Capricorn Strengths and Overcoming Weaknesses ---------- 34

CHAPTER 6: THE YEAR AHEAD ---------- 36

Horoscope Guide for Capricorn Individuals ---------- 37

Key Astrological Events and Their Impact on Capricorn---------------------- 38

CHAPTER 7: FAMOUS "CAPRICORN" PERSONALITIES ---------- 44

Elvis Presley -- 44

Richard Nixon-- 45

Betsy Ross--- 45

Greta Thunberg--- 46

Marlene Dietrich--- 46

David Bowie-- 46

Kim Jong-un-- 47

Joan of Arc-- 47

Dolly Parton--- 47

Rowan Atkinson --- 47

Mary Tyler Moore -- 48

Faye Dunaway--- 48

CONCLUSION -- 50

INTRODUCTION

Astrology, with a history spanning thousands of years, goes beyond being a mysticaln art form. This practice is based on the belief that the arrangement of stars and planets has an impact on lives by shaping our characters, influencing our emotions and potentially guiding our paths. It connects the positions of bodies at the time of our birth to different aspects of our personality, life experiences and even our destiny. At its core astrology aims to comprehend the relationships between the universe and our earthly existence. By studying how celestial bodies move, astrologers interpret meanings. From this they can gain insights into various facets of life including personal relationships, career decisions and much more.

Each astrological sign within the Zodiac represents a collection of traits and tendencies that influences individuals born under that sign. This book focuses on exploring the zodiac sign, Capricorn. Our goal is to provide a deep dive into Capricorn. By merging ancient knowledge with contemporary perspectives this book will explore the ways in which Capricorns interact with the world, their strengths, challenges, how they can utilize their traits, compatibility and much more. Whether you happen to be a Capricorn seeking self discovery, someone close to a Capricorn or simply an astrology enthusiast this book guarantees fresh insights and a profound comprehension.

OVERVIEW OF THE CAPRICORN ZODIAC SIGN

- **Date of Star Sign:** Capricorn, the tenth sign in the Zodiac, encompasses those born between December 22nd and January 19th. This period marks the transition from the end of one year to the beginning of the next. It symbolizes a time of reflection and resolution.
- **Symbol**: The symbol of Capricorn is the Sea-Goat. It is a mythical creature with the body of a goat and the tail of a fish. This symbol represents Capricorn's ability to thrive both in the material world (the goat, climbing to the highest mountains) and in the emotional realm (the fish, swimming in the deepest waters), showcasing their versatility and resilience.
- **Element**: Earth is the element associated with Capricorn. Capricorns are known for their pragmatic approach to life. Earth elements ground them, endowing them with a sense of stability, practicality and realism.
- **Planet**: Saturn, the planet of discipline and responsibility, rules Capricorn. This association highlights their structured, ambitious and persevering nature. Saturn's influence is seen in the Capricorn's penchant for setting long-term goals and their determination in achieving them.
- **Color**: The color most often linked with Capricorn is dark brown or gray, reflecting their serious, earthbound and resilient nature.
- **Personality Traits**: Capricorns are known for their discipline, ambition and hardworking nature. They also hold a strong sense of duty and responsibility. While sometimes seen as reserved or cautious, they also possess a dry wit and understated charm.
- **Strengths**: Among their strengths are determination, strong will and the ability to plan and execute long-term projects. Their practicality and reliability make them excellent leaders and trusted advisors. Loyalty and a deep sense of commitment are also hallmark strengths of a Capricorn.
- **Weaknesses**: Their weaknesses might include a tendency towards pessimism or cynicism, being overly reserved or distant and sometimes struggling with stubbornness. Capricorns tend to also be overly concerned with their public image. As such they may fear failure or ridicule.
- **Compatibility**: Capricorns often find the most harmony in relationships with Taurus and Virgo, earth signs that share their practical outlook on life. They also can have strong connections with water signs like Scorpio and Pisces. These can bring emotional depth and balance to the practicality of Capricorn.

In the introduction of this book we have embarked on a captivating journey into the realm of astrology with a focus on the intriguing and ambitious nature of Capricorn individuals. The introduction sets the stage for an exploration of this star sign renowned for its practicality, discipline and strong sense of responsibility. As readers progress through this book they can expect an exploration of many aspects that contribute to the Capricorn personality.

- **In Depth Character Analysis**; A close examination, into typical behavioral patterns, emotional landscape and intellectual traits that shape Capricorns.
- **Historical and Cultural Perspectives**; Delve into the cultural interpretations of Capricorn. Gain an understanding of this astrological sign through diverse perspectives across time.
- **Understanding Capricorn in Relationships;** Discover the dynamics of relationships involving Capricorns. Plus insights into their compatibility with other zodiac signs and tips for fostering harmonious connections.
- **Career and Ambitions;** Explore how Capricorns unique traits shape their lives and aspirations. Discover strategies for maximizing their strengths in the workplace.
- **Overcoming Challenges and Personal Growth;** Uncover the challenges faced by Capricorns. Learn strategies for personal growth, overcoming obstacles and tapping into their full potential.
- **Real life Stories and Experiences;** Hear narratives from individuals who were born under the Capricorn sign. Gain practical insights that resonate with real world experiences.
- **Practical Tips for a Balanced Life;** Discover life advice catered to Capricorns on achieving balance, wellness and fulfillment in various aspects of life.
- All of this and much, much more.

Overall this comprehensive guide is designed to provide an in-depth understanding of the Capricorn sign. Whether you are a Capricorn yourself or one who has connections with one. Or if you're simply having an interest in astrology. This journey of exploration promises wisdom, self reflection and a greater appreciation for this remarkable star sign.

CHAPTER 1: HISTORY AND MYTHOLOGY

In this chapter we embark on a captivating journey, through the ages to explore the history and mythology surrounding the Capricorn zodiac sign. With its representation as the sea goat Capricorn, has captivated people's imaginations across numerous cultures and time periods. Here we unveil the tapestry of stories, beliefs and historical events that have shaped how we understand and appreciate Capricorn throughout history.

We begin our exploration by delving into the ancient origins of the Capricorn constellation. Let us trace its observations and recordings in ancient civilizations such as Babylon, Greece and Rome. These initial discoveries lay the foundation for comprehending how diverse cultures worldwide have perceived, represented and integrated Capricorn into their mythological frameworks.

As we delve deeper into mythology we encounter enchanting tales associated with Capricorn that offer fresh insights into nature and cosmic order. From captivating stories about the Greek god Pan's adventures, to nurturing accounts featuring Amalthea the goat associated with Zeus. These mythological narratives provide a glimpse into attempts to comprehend and personify forces and destiny.

Advancing through time we highlight events and noteworthy individuals born under this sign who have influenced history. Additionally we take a moment to contemplate the changing perception of Capricorn over time. This part offers an overview of how our understanding of Capricorn has evolved from celestial interpretations to a more contemporary approach that focuses on psychology and individual personality traits. Let's begin our journey through time.

HISTORICAL AND MYTHOLOGICAL ORIGINS

The constellation of Capricorn, known for its distinctive sea-goat symbol, holds a rich history that dates back to some of the earliest civilizations. The story of Capricorn begins with ancient sky-watchers who first observed this constellation in the night sky.

BABYLONIAN ASTRONOMY

One of the earliest known records of the Capricorn constellation comes from the Babylonians. They observed it as early as the 2nd millennium BC and named it "Suhur-mash-ha," the "Goat-Fish," due to its symbolic representation of a creature that was half goat and half fish. This depiction was likely influenced by the ancient god Enki, a deity associated with water, knowledge and creation. It was often depicted with a goat-like upper body and a fish-like lower body.

ANCIENT GREECE

In ancient Greek mythology, Capricorn is often linked to the story of the god Pan, who transformed into a half-goat, half-fish creature to escape the monster Typhon. Another Greek myth connects Capricorn to Amalthea, the goat who nursed the infant Zeus, and whose horn was transformed into the "Cornucopia" or "horn of plenty."

ROMAN INFLUENCE

The Romans adopted this constellation into their astrology and integrated it into their mythological tapestry. Capricornus, as it was known in Latin, maintained its significance as a symbol of duality and resourcefulness.

ANCIENT CHINA

In Chinese astronomy, the stars of Capricorn were associated with the water element. These were a part of different constellations that depicted mythical creatures and important figures in Chinese mythology.

INDIAN ASTRONOMY

In Indian astrology, which predates Western astrology, the region of the sky corresponding to Capricorn is known as "Makara." This is a term that also refers to a mythical sea creature. One that is similar to the sea-goat of Western astrology.

ARABIAN ASTRONOMY

In Arabian astronomy, the constellation was seen as a part of larger figures or stories, often blending with their rich tradition of storytelling and sky interpretation.

INDIGENOUS CULTURES

Various indigenous cultures around the world had their interpretations and stories related to the stars of Capricorn, often reflecting their environment, traditions and beliefs.

Throughout history and across cultures the constellation of Capricorn has held an important place in our collective imagination. It has been depicted in stories and symbols that transcend time and geographic boundaries. Each culture's interpretation of Capricorn reflects its values, mythology and understanding of the universe contributing to the diverse history of this celestial formation.

In ancient times Capricorn was often associated with gods and mythical creatures reflecting the beliefs and knowledge about the cosmos prevalent during those eras. In modern astrology there has been a shift from mythological interpretations to psychological insights. Astrology is now commonly used as a tool for self reflection and a way of understanding one's personality traits. We now explore the traits of Capricorns in terms of how they influence our choices, relationships and life journeys.

HISTORICAL EVENTS UNDER THE CAPRICORN SEASON

The Capricorn season, spanning from December 22nd to January 19th, has been a period marked by several significant historical events.

- **Historical Events:** Throughout history, many pivotal events have occurred during the Capricorn season. The signing of important treaties and declarations and significant scientific breakthroughs have often coincided with this period. These events, in astrological terms, could be seen as reflections of Capricorn's traits of determination and groundbreaking ambition.
- **Global Celebrations and Shifts:** Many global celebrations and shifts, including the start of a new year, occur during the Capricorn season. These transitions and celebrations might be viewed as symbolic of the Capricorn's affinity for reflection, planning and setting ambitious goals for the future.

HISTORICAL FIGURES BORN UNDER THE CAPRICORN SIGN

- **Leaders and States Persons**: Many influential leaders and states persons were born under the Capricorn sign. They are known for their strategic thinking and leadership qualities. Figures such as Martin Luther King Jr, Benjamin Franklin, and Muhammad Ali exemplify Capricorn traits. That is through their impactful contributions to society in their respective fields.
- **Scientists and Innovators**: The discipline and dedication of Capricorns have been embodied in several renowned scientists and innovators like Isaac

Newton, whose birthday falls under this sign. Their contributions have significantly advanced human knowledge and understanding.

As we come to the end of this chapter, let us take a moment to reflect on the stories, significant events and influential individuals linked to this enduring zodiac sign. From its ancient origins to its relevance in modern astrology Capricorn has consistently represented ambition, discipline and a practical approach to life's obstacles. In a world that is constantly changing the traits associated with Capricorn, determination, responsibility and practical wisdom remain as relevant as ever.

FURTHER READING AND REFERENCES

For readers interested in delving deeper into the history, mythology and contemporary understanding of Capricorn, the following list of primary sources, ancient texts, and modern writings is recommended:

- **"Hamlet's Mill: An Essay Investigating the Origins of Human Knowledge and Its Transmission Through Myth " by** Giorgio de Santillana and Hertha von Dechend: This work explores the connections between ancient myths and the astronomical knowledge of the time. Context on mythological origins of constellations, such as Capricorn are included.
- **"The Fables of Hyginus"** translated by Mary Grant: This classical text includes stories from Greek and Roman mythology. Insights into the mythological background of the Capricorn constellation are included.
- **"Capricorn": The Art of Living Well and Finding Happiness According to Your Star Sign"** by Sally Kirkman: This contemporary book offers a focused look at the Capricorn sign. Inside it discusses how its traits can be harnessed for personal growth and happiness.
- **"Saturn: A New Look at an Old Devil"** by Liz Greene: This book delves into the influence of Saturn, the ruling planet of Capricorn, in astrology. Insights into how its positioning can affect personality and life events are included.
- **"Astrology, History, and Apocalypse"** by Nicholas Campion: This text provides a historical overview of astrology. It includes the evolution of the interpretation of zodiac signs like Capricorn.
- **Online resources such as The Astrological Association and The American Federation of Astrologers** - These offer a wealth of articles, research papers, and historical texts related to astrology and specific zodiac signs.

CHAPTER 2:
LOVE & COMPATIBILITY

Capricorn is commonly associated with a calm demeanor, unwavering focus on goals and a practical outlook on life. However beneath their reserved exterior lies an realm characterized by profound loyalty, unwavering commitment and an aspiration for long lasting connections. This chapter seeks to illuminate the nuances of Capricorns love life. From their approach to dating and courtship to their compatibility with each zodiac sign.

Firstly we will examine the traits that define Capricorn's experience in love. From how they express affection. To what they seek in a partner and the nuanced ways in which they navigate relationships. Understanding all of this is vital, for appreciating the profoundness of their bonds. Subsequently we will explore the compatibility between Capricorn and the other zodiac signs. We'll delve into the dynamics of each pairing highlighting their strengths and challenges. From the passion of Aries to the depths of Pisces these combinations offer a unique mix of energies, lessons and experiences.

This in depth exploration isn't just for Capricorns and their potential partners. It's also for anyone interested in astrology and the enigmatic world of love. And of course, whether you're a Capricorn looking to understand your nature or a partner seeking to deepen your bond with a Capricorn this chapter will provide guidance and insight. So let's embark on this journey of discovery together as we uncover the secrets of Capricorn's heart and unravel the dance that defines their relationships.

CAPRICORN'S APPROACH TO LOVE AND ROMANCE

When it comes to love and romance, individuals born under the Capricorn sign often exhibit a unique blend of traits that shape their approach to relationships. As an earth sign ruled by Saturn, Capricorns are known for their pragmatic, disciplined, and patient nature. Such traits are reflected in their romantic lives.

- **Slow and Steady**: Capricorns tend to take a cautious and slow approach to romance. They are not known for diving headfirst into relationships. No, instead, they prefer to take their time. They value getting to know their partner and building a foundation of trust and respect before fully committing. This gradual progression ensures that when a Capricorn commits, they are in it for the long haul.

- **Seeking Stability**: Stability and security are paramount to Capricorns in love. They are drawn to partners who are reliable, responsible and have their lives in order. For Capricorns, a stable and predictable relationship is often more appealing. Rather than a whirlwind romance filled with uncertainties.

- **Practical Expressions of Love**: Capricorns express their love in practical ways. Rather than grand gestures or overly sentimental expressions, they show their affection through acts of service, support and loyalty. They are the ones who will remember to do the little things. Things that make their partner's life easier and more comfortable.
- **Ambition and Partnership**: Capricorns are ambitious. As such they appreciate a partner who shares their drive and work ethic. They respect independence and ambition in a partner. They often seek relationships where both individuals can support and motivate each other to achieve their goals.
- **Deep Emotional Reserve**: While they may appear reserved or stoic, Capricorns possess a deep well of emotion. However, they often keep their feelings guarded until they feel completely secure in a relationship. Although once committed, they are deeply loyal and make for a dependable partner.
- **Traditional Values**: Many Capricorns lean towards traditional values when it comes to love and relationships. They appreciate the rituals of dating and courtship. As such they often adhere to conventional relationship milestones.
- **Long-Term Perspective**: Capricorns think long-term and are often planning for the future. In relationships, this means they are always considering how their partner fits into their long-term life plan. This makes them more selective about entering into a romantic commitment.

In summary, Capricorns approach love and romance with the same seriousness and dedication that they apply to other areas of their life. They value stability, practicality and loyalty. Once they find the right partner, they are committed and dependable lovers. While they may take their time to open up emotionally, their deep commitment and steady approach make them reliable and devoted partners.

CAPRICORN'S COMPATIBILITY WITH OTHER ZODIAC SIGNS

Capricorns, known for their discipline and ambition, approach relationships with seriousness and a focus on long-term goals. Let's explore how Capricorn pairs with each zodiac sign.

CAPRICORN AND ARIES

- Compatibility: Moderate to Challenging.
- Dynamics: Aries' impulsiveness clashes with Capricorn's cautious approach. However, both share a drive for success and can motivate each other.
- Challenges: Aries may find Capricorn too reserved. Capricorn might view Aries as too reckless.
- Strengths: If they can balance each other out, they can make a powerful team. Aries brings enthusiasm and Capricorn brings structure.

CAPRICORN AND TAURUS

- Compatibility: High.
- Dynamics: Both are earth signs, valuing security and stability. They share a practical approach to life and love.
- Strengths: Their shared values and goals can create a strong foundation for a lasting relationship.
- Challenges: They need to be wary of becoming too comfortable and avoid a lack of dynamism in the relationship.

CAPRICORN AND GEMINI

- Compatibility: Moderate.
- Dynamics: Gemini's social and adaptable nature can clash with Capricorn's more introverted and structured approach.
- Strengths: Gemini can introduce variety and excitement to Capricorn's life. Capricorn can offer Gemini stability.
- Challenges: Remember their different approaches to life can lead to misunderstandings. Communication is key.

CAPRICORN AND CANCER

- Compatibility: High.
- Dynamics: Opposites in the zodiac, they attract each other with their different yet complementary qualities.
- Strengths: Capricorn provides security that Cancer craves. Cancer brings emotional depth to the relationship.
- Challenges: They need to understand and respect their differing emotional needs and communication styles.

CAPRICORN AND LEO

- Compatibility: Moderate.
- Dynamics: Leo's flamboyance can clash with Capricorn's understated approach. Both are leaders, which can lead to power struggles.
- Strengths: If they align their goals, they can be a dynamic and successful pair.
- Challenges: They must learn to share the spotlight and respect each other's different styles.

CAPRICORN AND VIRGO

- Compatibility: Very High.
- Dynamics: Both are earth signs. Both share a practical approach to life and a strong work ethic.
- Strengths: They understand each other's needs for stability. As such they can build a harmonious and efficient life together.
- Challenges: They need to ensure their shared life doesn't become too routine and devoid of spontaneity.

CAPRICORN AND LIBRA

- Compatibility: Moderate.
- Dynamics: Libra's love for harmony and social interaction might conflict with Capricorn's more solitary and pragmatic nature.
- Strengths: They can complement each other well. Libra brings a sense of balance and Capricorn provides stability.
- Challenges: They need to work on understanding and valuing their different approaches to life and relationships.

CAPRICORN AND SCORPIO

- Compatibility: High.
- Dynamics: Both signs are known for their intensity and depth. They share a strong determination and commitment.
- Strengths: A deep, often unspoken understanding can develop, leading to a powerful emotional and practical bond.
- Challenges: Both need to be mindful of their tendencies towards control and stubbornness.

CAPRICORN AND SAGITTARIUS

- Compatibility: Moderate.
- Dynamics: Sagittarius' love for adventure may seem frivolous to a practical Capricorn. Conversely, Capricorn's seriousness can dampen Sagittarius's spirit.
- Strengths: They can learn a lot from each other. Sagittarius adds fun. Capricorn adds structure.
- Challenges: Finding a balance between freedom and responsibility is key to this pairing.

CAPRICORN AND CAPRICORN

- Compatibility: High.
- Dynamics: They share similar values, goals and approaches to life.
- Strengths: This pair can build a successful, stable life, by understanding each other's ambitions and work ethic.
- Challenges: They need to avoid becoming too focused on work and material success. Remember to not neglect emotional and romantic needs.

CAPRICORN AND AQUARIUS

- Compatibility: Moderate.
- Dynamics: Aquarius' unconventional nature can be intriguing yet baffling to traditional Capricorn.
- Strengths: They can both offer a different perspective. Aquarius brings innovation. Capricorn provides practicality.

- Challenges: They must learn to appreciate their differing approaches to life and freedom.

CAPRICORN AND PISCES

- Compatibility: High.
- Dynamics: Pisces' emotional depth and intuition complement Capricorn's practicality and stability.
- Strengths: Pisces can help Capricorn to relax and open up emotionally. Capricorn can provide Pisces with stability and direction.
- Challenges: They need to balance Capricorn's need for structure with Pisces' need for emotional and creative space.

In summary, Capricorn's approach to love and compatibility varies significantly across the zodiac. While they tend to form the strongest connections with earth and water signs, the potential for a fulfilling relationship exists with any sign. Ultimately, that is provided there is mutual understanding and respect.

DATING AND RELATIONSHIPS WITH CAPRICORN INDIVIDUALS

Capricorns, known for their pragmatic and disciplined approach to life, can be deeply rewarding partners. However, understanding and respecting their unique traits is key to building a strong and lasting relationship. Here are some tips tailored for both men and women when dating and having relationships with Capricorn individuals.

FOR DATING CAPRICORN MEN

- **Appreciate His Ambitions:** Capricorn men are often career-oriented and ambitious. Show interest in his goals and support his aspirations.
- **Be Patient**: He may take time to open up emotionally. Patience is crucial in allowing the relationship to develop at a pace comfortable for him.
- **Respect His Space:** Capricorn men value their personal space and time. Respecting this need can help build trust and understanding.
- **Embrace Traditional Courtship:** Many Capricorn men appreciate traditional dating rituals. Planning thoughtful dates and respecting courtship norms can be appealing to them.

- **Be Honest and Direct:** They prefer straightforward communication. Be open and honest about your feelings and intentions.
- **Show Your Practical Side:** Demonstrating your practical and sensible side can be attractive, as they value responsibility and reliability.
- **Understand His Reserved Nature**: He may not be the most outwardly expressive partner. Understanding and respecting his more reserved nature is key.

FOR DATING CAPRICORN WOMEN

- **Respect Her Independence:** Capricorn women are often independent and self-reliant. Showing respect for her autonomy is important.
- **Be Genuine**: Authenticity is important to Capricorn women. Be yourself and be genuine.
- **Stability is Key**: They are attracted to stability and security. Being reliable and stable in your actions and emotions can go a long way.
- **Appreciate Her Traditional Values:** Many Capricorn women value tradition and may appreciate conventional gestures of romance.
- **Support Her Career Goals**: Capricorn women are often career-driven. Supporting her ambitions and understanding her work commitments is crucial.
- **Patience with Emotional Openness**: She may take time to show her emotional side. Be patient and give her space to open up at her own pace.
- **Quality Time Matters**: Quality over quantity is important. Plan meaningful dates or activities that align with her interests.

Overall building and maintaining relationships with Capricorn partners require being mindful of key elements. Whether you are dating a man or woman born under the sign of Capricorn, understanding their personality traits while respecting their approach to life can foster a fulfilling and enduring relationship. Patience, supportiveness and reliability are just some of the key elements in building a bond with a Capricorn partner.

As we near the end of this chapter where we have gained a deep understanding of the romantic world experienced by those who are born under the Capricorn sign. Throughout this exploration we have delved into the depths of Capricorn's heart exploring their approach to love, how they express affection uniquely and how they find harmony with zodiac signs.

We have observed that Capricorns, with their disciplined demeanor and ambitious nature, bring a sense of seriousness and depth to their endeavors.

Love for them is a process of trust building and respect forming a foundation upon which any committed relationship can thrive. In their quest for love Capricorns seek not a partner but a teammate. Someone who shares their values and comprehends their aspirations. Someone who stands unwaveringly beside them.

As we wrap up it becomes evident that comprehending and valuing the Capricorn approach to love and compatibility necessitates patience and understanding. For those romantically involved with a Capricorn, acknowledging their need for both emotional depth and practical stability can deepen the connection. For Capricorns themselves, this chapter acts as a reflection of their workings in matters of love. Lastly, we want to encourage them to embrace both their strengths and vulnerabilities in order to cultivate fulfilling relationships.

CHAPTER 3:
FRIENDS AND FAMILY

Capricorns are renowned for their positive approach to life, their sense of responsibility and an enduring loyalty. These qualities form the foundation of steady relationships. However they can also present distinctive challenges as Capricorns navigate their social and familial spheres. This chapter delves into the dynamics of how individuals born under the Capricorn sign interact, engage with others and nurture their connections. It goes beyond surface level interactions to explore the underlying currents that influence Capricorn's bonds with those closest to them. So join us as we uncover the intricacies of Capricorn's interactions within this chapter.

CAPRICORN AS A FRIEND

When it comes to friendships, individuals born under the Capricorn sign are known for their reliability, depth and loyalty. Understanding the friendship style of a Capricorn can offer insights into how they build and maintain their social connections.

- **Loyal and Trustworthy:** One of the most defining traits of a Capricorn friend is their unwavering loyalty. Once they consider someone a friend, they are often committed for life. They take their friendships seriously and are incredibly trustworthy.
- **Practical and Helpful**: Capricorns are the friends who offer practical advice and help. They are often the ones you turn to when you need a problem solved or a task accomplished. Their pragmatic approach to life makes them invaluable when it comes to giving realistic and straightforward advice.
- **Reserved but Deep:** Initially, Capricorns might come across as reserved or even aloof. However, once they open up and trust someone, they reveal a depth of character that can be both surprising and refreshing.
- **Selective with Friendships**: Capricorns tend to be selective about who they spend their time with. They prefer a small circle of close friends over a large group of acquaintances. Quality over quantity is their motto.
- **Ambitious and Motivating**: Being ambitious themselves, Capricorns are great at motivating and pushing their friends towards their goals. They are supportive and encouraging. However they also don't shy away from giving a needed reality check.
- **Appreciates Tradition**: Capricorns often have a fondness for traditions and may enjoy celebrating special occasions, anniversaries and milestones in meaningful ways with their friends.
- **Not the Most Spontaneous**: Capricorns are planners and are not known for their spontaneity. They appreciate structured activities and well-planned outings more than impromptu adventures.
- **Dependable and Consistent**: In friendships, Capricorns are incredibly dependable. You can count on them to keep their promises and be there when they say they will.
- **Values Personal Space**: They respect and value personal space. Both theirs and others. They understand and appreciate the need for alone time.
- **Long-Term Friends**: When a Capricorn invests in a friendship, it's often with a long-term view. They value and work hard to maintain lasting relationships.

In essence, a friendship with a Capricorn might take time to develop, but once it does, it often turns into a bond for life. Their loyalty, practicality and depth make them outstanding friends. Friends who provide stability and thoughtful guidance.

CAPRICORN AND FAMILY DYNAMICS

In the context of family dynamics, individuals born under the Capricorn sign often play a pivotal role. One that is characterized by their sense of responsibility, traditional values and a pragmatic approach to family matters. Understanding how Capricorns interact within the family setting reveals much about their values, priorities and the unique strengths they bring to familial relationships.

- **Responsible** Capricorns are often seen as the pillars of their families. They take their familial responsibilities seriously. Whether as parents, siblings, or children. They are the ones family members often turn to for support and guidance due to their reliable and responsible nature.
- **Traditional and Conservative**: Many Capricorns hold traditional values close to their heart. They respect family traditions and often play a key role in maintaining family customs. Be it through organizing gatherings or keeping alive certain rituals and practices.
- **Providing Stability and Security:** As natural providers, Capricorns strive to create a stable and secure environment for their family. They are often focused on ensuring that the practical needs of the family are met. From financial security to creating a structured home life.
- **Practical Problem-Solvers**: In family conflicts or challenges, Capricorns tend to be pragmatic problem-solvers. They approach issues with a level head, often helping to mediate and find practical solutions.
- **Emotional Reserve:** Capricorns can sometimes seem emotionally reserved, preferring to express their care and love through actions rather than words. Understanding their emotional style is key to appreciating the depth of their affection and commitment.
- **Strong Work Ethic:** Their strong work ethic is not just limited to their professional life. Capricorns often put in the effort to make sure their family life is running smoothly. Sometimes at the expense of their own relaxation and leisure.
- **Role Models:** Capricorns often serve as role models within the family, especially for younger members. They exemplify traits like discipline, hard work and determination.
- **Parental Approach:** As parents, Capricorns are usually strict but fair. They emphasize discipline, education and the importance of hard work. As parents they encourage their children to be independent and self-reliant.
- **Need for Personal Space:** While deeply committed to their family, Capricorns also value their personal space and time for solitude. They appreciate when this need is respected by family members.

- **Long-Term Planning:** Capricorns are often the family members who think ahead. They are likely to plan for the family's future. Whether it's saving for children's education or planning family investments.

In conclusion, Capricorns bring a sense of strength, stability and responsibility to family dynamics. Their practical nature, combined with a deep sense of duty towards family members, makes them invaluable within the family unit. Understanding and respecting their need for structure, traditional values and occasional emotional reserve can lead to harmonious family relationships.

CHALLENGES IN FRIENDSHIPS AND FAMILY RELATIONSHIPS

While Capricorns can be loyal, dependable friends and steadfast family members, they also face specific challenges in these personal relationships. Understanding these challenges can provide insights into how Capricorns navigate their social and familial worlds and how they might work towards healthier, more fulfilling relationships.

CHALLENGES IN FRIENDSHIPS

- **Difficulty in Expressing Emotions:** Capricorns are often reserved and may struggle to express their emotions openly. This can sometimes lead to misunderstandings with friends who might perceive them as aloof or uncaring.
- **Balancing Work and Social Life:** Given their ambitious nature and focus on career, Capricorns might find it challenging to balance their work life with their social commitments. Potentially this can lead to neglected friendships.
- **Reluctance to Venture Out of Comfort Zones:** Capricorns tend to stick to routines and might be hesitant to try new activities or meet new people. This can limit the expansion of their social circle.
- **High Expectations:** They often have high standards for themselves and others. This can sometimes lead to disappointment or frustration when friends don't meet these expectations.
- **Overly Cautious Approach**: Their cautious nature might make them slow to trust and open up to new friendships, potentially missing out on meaningful connections.

CHALLENGES IN FAMILY RELATIONS

- **Overly Authoritative or Controlling:** In their desire to ensure stability and security, Capricorns can come across as controlling or overly authoritative. Especially in a family setting.
- **Struggle with Work-Family Balance:** Their dedication to career and ambition can sometimes take precedence over family time. This can lead to feelings of neglect among family members.
- **Difficulty in Emotional Vulnerability:** Similar to their friendships, Capricorns may struggle to show vulnerability within their family. This can hinder deep emotional connections.
- **Resistance to Change:** Capricorns often prefer tradition and may resist changes in family dynamics or routines. This can be challenging in evolving family structures.
- **Tendency to Take on Too Much Responsibility:** They often take on the role of the provider or problem-solver in the family. This can be overwhelming and lead to stress.

To overcome these challenges Capricorns can focus on expressing their emotions honestly in both friendships and family relationships. It is important for them to find a balance between work and personal life so as to learn how to relax their high standards and control impulsive tendencies. Embracing change and new experiences can also bring fulfillment to their connections. By acknowledging and addressing these obstacles Capricorns have the potential to develop meaningful bonds with friends and family.

As we wrap up this chapter, it becomes evident that developing relationships with Capricorns, be it friendships or familial bonds, requires patience and empathy. Acknowledging and appreciating their need for stability, respect for tradition and occasional reserved nature can contribute to rewarding connections. For Capricorns themselves, finding a balance between their sense of responsibility and the importance of vulnerability can enhance the quality of their personal relationships.

CHAPTER 4: CAREER AND MONEY

Capricorns are often propelled by a drive for success, stability and accomplishments in their careers. This chapter aims to explore the attributes that enable Capricorns to thrive in professional settings. We'll delve into their career paths and the challenges they often face on their journey towards professional excellence. Additionally we'll examine how their pragmatic and strategic nature influences decisions regarding finances, investment strategies and overall wealth management.

Come join us as we delve into the realms of careers and money, from a Capricorn's perspective. Together we will uncover their strategies, strengths and challenges that shape their unique approach to these aspects of life.

CAPRICORN CAREER PREFERENCES AND PROFESSIONAL ASPIRATIONS

Capricorns, known for their practicality, ambition and discipline, have distinct preferences when it comes to their careers. Their approach to work is often marked by determination, a strong work ethic and a focus on long-term goals. Understanding the professional world of a Capricorn reveals much about their values and what they seek in a career.

- **Structure and Stability:** Capricorns thrive in careers that offer stability and structure. They prefer well-established organizations with clear hierarchies and well defined career paths. As such they are often drawn to traditional fields like finance, management and administration where their organizational skills can be fully utilized.
- **Ambitious**: Capricorns are highly ambitious and often set lofty goals for themselves. They are willing to put in the hard work and dedication required to climb the professional ladder. Leadership roles, where they can exercise control and implement their vision, are particularly appealing to them.
- **Methodical and Detail-Oriented Approach:** They excel in careers that require attention to detail and a methodical approach. Professions in accounting, human resources and it are notable positions for them to excel in.
- **Strong Sense of Responsibility:** A strong sense of responsibility and duty often drives Capricorns in their professional choices. They are dependable and take their work commitments seriously. Overall this makes them reliable employees and managers.
- **Preference for Traditional and Practical Fields:** Capricorns often gravitate towards fields that offer tangible results and practical applications. This can include industries like construction, architecture and real estate.
- **Long-Term Career Vision:** Capricorns typically have a long-term view of their career trajectory. They like to plan their professional journey meticulously, often aiming for positions that promise higher status and security over time.
- **Need for Achievement and Recognition:** Recognition for their hard work and achievements is important to Capricorns. They strive for positions that not only offer financial rewards but also confer respect and authority.
- **Entrepreneurial Tendencies:** Some Capricorns may be drawn to entrepreneurial ventures. Their discipline and strategic planning skills make them well-suited to the challenges of starting and running a business.
- **Balancing Work with Personal Life:** Despite their career focus, Capricorns also understand the importance of balancing work with personal life. They seek careers that, while demanding, also allow them time to enjoy their personal lives.
- **Continuous Learning and Growth:** Finally, Capricorns value careers that offer opportunities for continuous learning and growth. They are always seeking to improve their skills and knowledge, often through additional training or higher education.

In conclusion, Capricorns bring a unique combination of ambition, practicality and discipline to their professional lives. They are drawn to careers that offer stability, structure and the opportunity for long-term growth. Their commitment to their work, coupled with their ability to plan and execute, often leads them to achieve high levels of success in their chosen fields.

STRENGTHS OF CAPRICORN INDIVIDUALS IN THE WORKPLACE

Capricorn individuals bring a unique set of strengths to the workplace, often propelling them to excel in their professional endeavors. Their natural traits align well with many aspects of a successful career. Overall this makes them valuable assets in various work environments. Here are some key strengths that typically allow Capricorns to thrive professionally.

- **Strong Work Ethic:** Capricorns are known for their exceptional work ethic. They are hardworking, dedicated and committed to their tasks. As such they can often be found going above and beyond what is required to ensure that the job is done to the best of their abilities.
- **Leadership Qualities:** With their natural inclination towards responsibility and reliability, Capricorns often make excellent leaders. They are capable of taking charge, setting goals and motivating others to achieve collective objectives.
- **Organizational Skills:** Capricorns possess remarkable organizational skills. They are adept at planning, structuring and executing projects efficiently. This makes them excellent managers and coordinators.
- **Practical and Analytical Mindset:** A practical and analytical approach to problems is another hallmark of Capricorns. They are able to assess situations logically and come up with realistic, workable solutions.
- **Ambitious and Goal-Oriented:** Their ambition drives them to set high goals for themselves and their determination ensures they persist until these goals are achieved. This trait often leads them to top positions within their chosen fields.
- **Dependability:** Capricorns are known for their dependability. Colleagues and superiors know they can rely on them to get the job done, meet deadlines and uphold commitments.
- **Attention to Detail:** They have a keen eye for detail, which is crucial in many professional settings. This meticulousness ensures that their work is of high quality and accuracy.

- **Patience and Persistence**: Capricorns are patient and not deterred by challenges or setbacks. They are willing to put in the time and effort required to see a project through to completion.
- **Professionalism:** They maintain a high level of professionalism in the workplace. Capricorns are respectful, tactful and usually adhere to workplace etiquette, contributing positively to the work environment.
- **Financial Acumen:** Many Capricorns have a natural understanding of financial matters, making them adept in roles that involve budgeting, finance, or resource management.

In summary, the combination of a strong work ethic, leadership, organizational skills and a practical mindset makes Capricorns highly effective and respected in the workplace. These traits not only help them excel in their careers but also often lead them to take on influential roles in their professional environments.

CHALLENGES CAPRICORNS MAY FACE IN THEIR CAREERS AND STRATEGIES TO OVERCOME THEM

While Capricorns have many strengths that make them successful in their professional lives, like all individuals, they also face certain challenges in their careers. Understanding these challenges and adopting effective strategies to overcome them can help Capricorns maximize their potential and achieve greater satisfaction in their work.

- **Tendency to Be Workaholic;** Capricorns' strong work ethic can sometimes lead to workaholism. They may struggle to maintain a healthy work-life balance, which can lead to burnout. Actively schedule downtime and hobbies outside of work. Prioritize tasks and delegate when necessary to manage workload effectively.
- **Difficulty in Adapting to Change;** Capricorns often prefer traditional methods and may resist new ways of working or innovative approaches, which can hinder adaptability in a fast-evolving workplace. Embrace a mindset of continuous learning and be open to new ideas. Participating in workshops or training sessions can help stay updated with current trends.
- **Reluctance to Express Emotions;** Capricorns might find it challenging to express their feelings, especially in a work environment. This can sometimes lead to misunderstandings with colleagues or a perception of being too distant. Work on communication skills. Especially in expressing appreciation, concerns, or feedback in a constructive manner.
- **Risk-Averse Nature;** Their cautious nature might lead them to avoid taking necessary risks that could lead to significant professional growth. Learn to evaluate risks logically and understand that calculated risks are an essential part of career growth. Seek advice from mentors to gain different perspectives.
- **Perfectionism;** Capricorns' attention to detail can turn into perfectionism. This can lead to unnecessary stress and unrealistic expectations of themselves and others. Set realistic standards and timelines. Practice self-compassion and recognize that making mistakes is part of the learning process.
- **Struggle with Networking;** Their reserved nature can sometimes make networking and building professional relationships challenging. Set specific networking goals and attend industry events. Practice conversation starters and follow up with contacts regularly.
- **Overemphasis on Career Goals;** Capricorns' focus on career success might lead to neglecting other aspects of life, impacting personal relationships and overall well being. Cultivate interests and relationships

outside of work. Recognize the importance of a holistic approach to life for long-term success and happiness.

- **Difficulty Accepting Help;** Their independent nature can make it hard for them to seek or accept help, which can limit their growth and increase workload. Acknowledge the benefits of collaboration and teamwork. Be open to support from colleagues and superiors.

In summary, by recognizing these obstacles and implementing strategies to tackle them, Capricorns can enhance their satisfaction and performance in their careers. By finding a balance between their inclinations and adaptability they can effectively leverage their strengths while mitigating challenges along their professional journey.

As we conclude this chapter one thing becomes clear. For Capricorns, careers and money are more than measures of success or stability. They serve as channels through which they express their identity, values and aspirations. Recognizing this deeper connection empowers Capricorns to make choices that bring fulfillment in these aspects of life.

CHAPTER 5: SELF-IMPROVEMENT

In this chapter we will dive into the world of Capricorns and their unwavering dedication to self improvement. Capricorns, who are born under the ambitious sign of the mountain goat are renowned for their determination, practicality and strong work ethic. They possess a set of qualities that drive them towards growth and development.

Within the pages of this chapter we will explore both the strengths and weaknesses associated with this zodiac sign. We will shed light on how Capricorns harness their characteristics to achieve their goals. We'll delve into their determination, practical mindset and deep sense of responsibility while examining how these traits contribute to their journey of self improvement. Moreover we will address challenges that Capricorns might encounter such as stubbornness, pessimism and the quest for work life balance. This chapter provides insights and strategies for Capricorns to overcome these obstacles and further enhance their growth.

Join us on a voyage of discovery as we explore the qualities that make Capricorns so adept, at self improvement. We'll also uncover strategies they can employ to sustain their pursuit of excellence in all facets of life.

PERSONAL GROWTH AND DEVELOPMENT

Personal growth and self improvement play an important role in the lives of individuals born under the zodiac sign Capricorn. Those represented by the ambitious mountain goat are recognized for their steadfastness, responsibility and strong work ethic. They possess an inclination to strive for success and are motivated by their desire to conquer life's challenges. Let's delve deeper into the topic of growth and development, for Capricorns.

- **Goal Setting and Achievement**; Capricorns excel at setting goals and accomplishing them. Their practicality allows them to achieve highly in many aspects of their lives. Personal growth often begins with identifying ambitions followed by creating plans to attain them. Continuously striving to better themselves and their circumstances is ingrained in their nature.
- **Embracing Discipline;** Discipline serves as a foundation for growth in Capricorn's lives. They possess an ability to remain focused on their goals despite challenges or distractions that may arise along the way. This enables them to develop self control and resilience during times.
- **Nurturing Patience**; While Capricorns are renowned for their adaptive nature they also recognize the value of patience when it comes to growth. They understand that achieving success often requires time and are willing to patiently wait. This helps them develop resilience and maintain a sense of purpose when faced with setbacks.
- **Embracing Change**; While they may have a preference for tradition and stability they acknowledge that growth often necessitates adapting to circumstances and seizing opportunities. As such, Capricorns strike a balance between their caution and a willingness to take calculated risks when needed.
- **Developing Emotional Intelligence**; Although Capricorns are commonly perceived as reserved and pragmatic, growth for them also entails nurturing intelligence. One must learn how to express their emotions, empathize with

others feelings and cultivate connections with people. This not only leads to meaningful relationships but also enhances their leadership abilities by enabling them to better understand and motivate those they work with.

- **Balancing Work and Personal Life**; Capricorn's strong work ethic can occasionally cause an imbalance between their work and personal lives. It is important for them to find ways to strike an equilibrium ensuring they don't neglect their well being, relationships or leisure time.
- **Continuous learning;** Capricorns are often open to receiving mentorship and help. They recognize the importance of learning from those who have already achieved success in their fields. Engaging with mentors can expedite their personal growth journey and help them to make informed decisions.

To summarize Capricorns believe that personal growth and development require a combination of discipline, patience, ambition and adaptability. They are motivated by their aspiration to succeed and are willing to put in the effort to achieve their goals. By embracing change, nurturing intelligence and seeking balance, Capricorns can continue to evolve and flourish both personally and professionally.

HARNESSING CAPRICORN STRENGTHS AND OVERCOMING WEAKNESSES

Capricorns possess a unique set of strengths and weaknesses that shape their personality and influence their approach to life. To achieve personal growth and success, it's essential for individuals born under this zodiac sign to harness their strengths while actively working on overcoming their weaknesses. Here's a closer look at how Capricorns can do just that.

HARNESSING CAPRICORN STRENGTHS

- **Determination and Ambition**: Capricorns are renowned for their unwavering determination and ambition. They set their sights high and are willing to put in the necessary effort to achieve their goals. To harness this strength effectively, Capricorns should continuously set and update their goals. Both short-term and long-term. By maintaining a clear vision and a solid work ethic, they can steadily climb the ladder of success.
- **Discipline**: Capricorns are masters of discipline. This enables them to stay focused and organized. They should leverage this strength by creating structured routines and schedules. By adhering to a well-organized plan, they can efficiently manage their time and tasks. Ultimately leading to increased productivity and personal growth.
- **Practicality**: Capricorns possess a practical mindset that allows them to make sound decisions. This strength can be used to their advantage by thoroughly analyzing situations, weighing pros and cons and considering the long-term consequences. This will help them avoid impulsive decisions and steer clear of unnecessary risks.
- **Patience**: Patience is a valuable asset for Capricorns. They should embrace this strength when faced with setbacks or delays in their pursuits. Recognizing that success often requires time and persistence can help them maintain a positive attitude and stay committed to their goals.
- **Reliability**: Capricorns are known for their dependability and strong sense of responsibility. They should continue to cultivate this strength by fulfilling their commitments and supporting others when needed. Building trust and maintaining a solid reputation for reliability can open doors to new opportunities and collaborations.

OVERCOMING CAPRICORN WEAKNESSES:

- **Stubbornness**: Capricorns' determination can sometimes border on stubbornness. To overcome this weakness, they should practice flexibility and be open to alternative viewpoints. Learning to adapt to changing circumstances and considering different perspectives can help them make more well-rounded decisions.
- **Pessimism**: Capricorns may have a tendency to focus on potential obstacles or setbacks. To overcome this weakness, they should work on developing a more optimistic outlook. Practicing gratitude, positive affirmations and visualizing success can help them cultivate a more positive mindset.
- **Work-Life Balance**: Capricorns' strong work ethic can lead to neglecting their personal lives. To address this weakness, they should prioritize self-care, leisure activities and spending quality time with loved ones. Setting boundaries and allocating time for relaxation is crucial for maintaining a healthy work-life balance.
- **Rigidity**: Capricorns may sometimes become too rigid in their routines and expectations. They can overcome this weakness by consciously introducing variety into their lives, trying new experiences and embracing change as a natural part of personal growth.
- **Fear of Failure**: Capricorns' fear of failure can hold them back from taking necessary risks. To conquer this weakness, they should remind themselves that failure is often a stepping stone to success. Embracing setbacks as valuable learning experiences can help them build resilience and face challenges with greater confidence.

To sum up Capricorns have excellent qualities that when effectively utilized can lead to significant personal growth and success. However it's crucial for them to address their weaknesses in order to become rounded individuals. By embracing change, practicing flexibility and maintaining a positive mindset, Capricorns can strike a balance between their strengths and weaknesses. In doing so the potential for success and fulfillment becomes limitless.

CHAPTER 6:
THE YEAR AHEAD

Welcome to a fresh new chapter, where we are about to delve into events and influences that will shape the lives of Capricorn individuals in the year ahead. We will analyze how celestial movements can impact aspects of Capricorn's lives including matters of the heart, relationships, career prospects, finances, health, wellness, personal growth, self discovery and much more. By understanding these currents and harnessing their energies you can make better decisions and embark on a journey of growth, fulfillment and success in the year ahead. Join us as we unveil the roadmap for the year ahead!

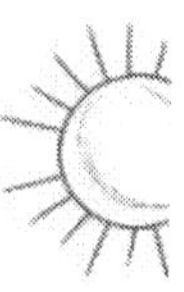

HOROSCOPE GUIDE FOR CAPRICORN INDIVIDUALS

Welcome, Capricorn! As you embark on the journey of the year ahead, the stars, bodies and planets have aligned to provide insights into the opportunities and challenges that may come your way. Here's your horoscope guide for the upcoming year.

- **Aries (March 21 - April 19)** - Career and Ambition, Your ambition and strong work ethic will shine. During this time your career is in focus. New responsibilities or considering a change will be apparent. Keep your goals clear, stay disciplined and don't be afraid to seek mentorship. Ultimately your determination will pave the way for profound, professional success.
- **Taurus (April 20 - May 20)** - Finances and Stability, Financial stability is a key theme for Capricorns this year. It's a good time to review your budget and make wise investments. Your practical nature will help you make sound financial decisions. Be patient and stay focused on long-term financial goals.
- **Gemini (May 21 - June 20) - Communication and Relationships -** Communication skills will be essential in your relationships this year. Be open and honest with your loved ones. Make an effort to understand their perspectives. Strengthening your connections will bring harmony and growth in your personal life.
- **Cancer (June 21 - July 22) - Self-Care and Well-Being-** Capricorns, remember to take care of your physical and emotional well-being. Your hardworking nature can sometimes lead to neglecting self-care. Prioritize relaxation, exercise and a balanced diet to maintain your health and vitality.
- **Leo (July 23 - August 22) - Creativity and Hobbies -** This year, explore your creative side, Capricorn. Engage in hobbies or activities that bring you joy and allow your imagination to flourish. Creative outlets can provide a much-needed escape from the daily grind.
- **Virgo (August 23 - September 22) - Relationships and Partnerships -** Your practicality and attention to detail will be assets in your relationships. If you're in a committed partnership, focus on teamwork and communication. Single Capricorns may find opportunities for meaningful connections. Keep an open heart.
- **Libra (September 23 - October 22) - Learning and Growth -** This year, expand your knowledge and skills, Capricorn. Whether it's through formal education, self-study, or workshops. Embrace opportunities for personal growth. Your willingness to learn will lead to new horizons.
- **Scorpio (October 23 - November 21) - Family and Home Life -** Family matters will be a priority in the coming year. Spend quality time with loved

ones, and resolve any lingering family issues. Creating a harmonious home environment will bring you comfort and peace.

- **Sagittarius (November 22 - December 21) - Networking and Social Connections -** Now is time to expand your social circle. Networking can lead to exciting opportunities both personally and professionally. Attend social events and connect with like-minded individuals who share your goals and values.
- **Capricorn (December 22 - January 19) - Self-Reflection and Goal Setting** - As a Capricorn, this is the perfect time to reflect on your life path and set new goals. Take stock of your achievements and make adjustments as needed. Your determination will drive you towards success in your endeavors.
- **Aquarius (January 20 - February 18) - Travel and Adventure -** Consider planning a trip or an adventure, Capricorn. Break away from routine and explore new horizons. Travel can broaden your perspective and bring fresh inspiration to your life.
- **Pisces (February 19 - March 20) - Finances and Investments -** Financial opportunities may come your way this year. Consider investments or financial strategies that align with your long-term goals. Your practical approach will serve you well in managing your resources.

Ultimately as a Capricorn, your strong sense of discipline and ambition will continue to drive you towards success in various aspects of your life. Remember to balance your determination with self-care and nurturing your personal relationships. With the guidance of the stars, you can make the most of the year ahead and continue your journey towards personal growth and fulfillment.

KEY ASTROLOGICAL EVENTS AND THEIR IMPACT ON CAPRICORN

Throughout the year there are events that can shape your experiences and opportunities. Let's take a look at some events and how they can potentially influence Capricorn individuals.

- **Saturn Transits**; Saturn, being your ruling planet, holds a significant sway over your life as it moves through different signs and houses in your birth chart. These transits can bring both challenges and rewards. Saturn's influence often tests your patience, determination and commitment to your goals. However it also presents an opportunity for long term growth and maturity. Embrace the lessons Saturn teaches you. You'll emerge stronger and more resilient.

- **Jupiter Transits**; Jupiter, known as the planet of expansion and growth has the potential to bring opportunities and abundance to Capricorns during its transits through signs. This could manifest as career advancements, personal development breakthroughs or exciting travel prospects. Seize the chance to broaden your horizons by taking calculated risks and exploring possibilities.
- **New Moon and Full Moon Phases**; New Moons and Full Moons hold significance for Capricorns too. New Moons represent starts filled with intentions— for setting goals or initiating new projects. Full Moons on the hand often bring about a sense of culmination and clarity. It's important to pay attention to these phases as they can assist you in aligning your actions with your aspirations.
- **Solar and Lunar Eclipses**; Eclipses have the potential to be moments in your life for a Capricorn like yourself. Solar eclipses can signify beginnings while lunar eclipses often indicate endings and emotional revelations. These celestial events have the power to trigger shifts in aspects of your life such as career, relationships or personal beliefs. It's advisable to be prepared for changes and remain adaptable during eclipse seasons.
- **Mercury Retrograde**; When Mercury goes retrograde it can affect communication, technology and travel for everyone including Capricorn individuals like yourself. During these times it is crucial to double check plans, avoid signing contracts and practice patience when misunderstandings arise. This period can be utilized for introspection or revisiting projects.
- **Mars and Venus Transits**; Mars symbolizes action while Venus represents relationships. When these two planets transit through signs aligned with yours it can enhance your assertiveness. Take advantage of these periods by engaging in networking opportunities or pursuing endeavors that align with your goals.
- **Capricorn Season;** The period from December to January marks Capricorn season. A time specifically dedicated to you shining brightly. With the Sun in your sign, during this time frame you are bestowed with confidence and determination that empowers you further. Take advantage of this time to set goals, acknowledge your achievements and plan your path for the year.
- **Other planets;** Pay attention to the movements of planets, like Uranus, Neptune and Pluto. These extended transits can bring about changes in society that might indirectly affect your life. Stay adaptable and open minded during these periods allowing your perspectives to evolve.

Remember that astrology serves as a tool for self awareness and guidance but does not determine your fate. Your choices and actions ultimately shape your destiny. By staying aware of these events and their potential influences you can make informed decisions and navigate through life's challenges, with wisdom and grace as a Capricorn. Now let's explore some key areas of interest and how they will be affected in the upcoming year.

LOVE AND RELATIONSHIPS

For those born under the sign of Capricorn, the astrological events that occur throughout the year can have an impact on their love lives and relationships. It is important to take note of the following happenings.

- **Venus in Capricorn**; As Venus enters your sign in the year Capricorn it enhances your charm and magnetism. Utilize this period to connect with your loved ones. Strengthen existing relationships and embark on romantic ventures. Your practical approach to love can lead to commitments.
- **Jupiter in Pisces;** During this phase Jupiter moves into Pisces, which's your sign. This will influence your partnerships and romantic endeavors. It has the potential to bring growth and expansion in your relationships by encouraging you to explore horizons with a partner. Be open to deepening connections and embracing the aspects of love.
- **Mercury Retrograde in Air Signs;** This period of Mercury retrograde might introduce communication challenges within your relationships. Be patient and mindful of choosing your words to avoid misunderstandings.

Take this opportunity to revisit issues with compassion and a hearted approach.

- **Saturn Retrograde** Saturn, which is your ruling planet retrogrades in Aquarius, during this time period. This urges you to reassess your commitments and responsibilities within your relationships. Take this time to reflect on yourself. Ensure that your partnerships align with your long term goals. Don't avoid addressing any issues that need attention.
- **The New Moon in Capricorn;** Now is an opportunity for you to set intentions for your love life. Take a moment to think about your desires and goals in relationships Capricorn and then take steps throughout the year to bring them into reality.

FINANCES

The astrological events of the year have implications for your career and financial situation as a Capricorn. Pay attention to these milestones;

- **Saturn in Aquarius;** As Saturn continues its journey through Aquarius it emphasizes innovation and unconventional approaches in your life. Embrace change and explore progressive ideas to advance in your career.
- **Jupiter in Aries;** Jupiter's transit through Aries can ignite your ambition. This period might bring opportunities for career growth and expansion. Take initiative, make calculated risks and seize chances to climb up the ladder.
- **Mercury Retrograde**; During this period of Mercury retrograde you may encounter communication challenges at work. Make sure to double check the specifics, avoid any misunderstandings and concentrate on improving projects to increase efficiency.
- **Solar and Lunar Eclipses**; Be prepared for changes and opportunities. It's important to adapt your strategies and consider investments that align with your long term goals. Additionally the Lunar Eclipse will again put a spotlight on financial matters. This might prompt you to reevaluate your stability and make adjustments to secure your future.

HEALTH AND WELLNESS

The astrological events throughout the year can have an impact on the health and well being of Capricorn individuals. Here's what you can do to maintain your well being while minimizing any negative effects;

- **Uranus movements -** Uranus may create tension between your desire for structure and the need for innovation. To reduce stress make sure to balance your work routines with opportunities for relaxation and creativity.
- **Venus is in Capricorn;** Now it's a time for self care. Focus on pampering yourself and improving both your emotional well being. You may want to consider trying out a fitness routine or wellness practice as a way of enhancing our health.
- **Jupiter's influence in Pisces:** This may encourage growth as well as emotional development. Discover the benefits of practicing mindfulness, meditation or seeking therapy to support your emotional wellbeing.

PERSONAL GROWTH AND SELF DISCOVERY

Capricorn individuals have the opportunity to embrace events throughout the year to foster growth and self discovery. Here's how you can make the most of the year;

- **Saturn Retrograde;** During Saturn's retrograde phase take time to reflect on your long term goals. Reassess your commitments, career path and personal aspirations to ensure they align with yourself.
- **Jupiter in Aries;** Embrace the energy of Jupiter in Aries as an opportunity to broaden your horizons. Take on new challenges, explore your passions and dare to step out of your comfort zone.
- **Mercury Retrograde in Earth Signs**; Utilize this period of Mercury retrograde for self reflection and revisiting projects. Examine areas in your life that require refinement and improvement.
- **New Moon in Capricorn;** Set intentions for the upcoming year. Focus on growth, self discovery and pursuing your goals with determination and clarity.

As we come to a close in our exploration of what lies for Capricorn individuals in terms of astrology it becomes clear that the stars have aligned to present a blend of opportunities and challenges. Your unwavering determination and practicality which are qualities of being a Capricorn will serve as your companions as you navigate through celestial currents.

In the tapestry of the universe Capricorn, your unique journey tells a story of ambition, determination and development. Remember that astrology serves as a guiding light. It is ultimately your choices and actions that shape your destiny. With the insights gained from this chapter you can embark on the year with wisdom, bravery, knowing that the stars are there to support you on your path, towards fulfillment and success.

As you enter into this year embrace opportunities as they arise and face challenges head on while letting your Capricorn spirit lead you towards reaching your potential. May both the journey itself be fulfilling as reaching the destination itself rewarding. May the stars continue to guide you along this path.

CHAPTER 7: FAMOUS "CAPRICORN" PERSONALITIES

Welcome to the captivating realm of individuals, with the zodiac sign of Capricorn. In this chapter we embark on a voyage through the lives of people who share this astrological symbol. Capricorns are known for their determination, practicality and strong work ethic. Not surprisingly they have left a lasting impact on various domains such as history, entertainment, politics and more.

As we delve into the lives and accomplishments of these celebrated Capricorns we will explore the characteristics and qualities that define this zodiac sign. From their various pursuits to their influence on the world around them we will unravel the captivating stories of these exceptional individuals who truly embody what it means to be a Capricorn.

Whether you are a Capricorn seeking inspiration from your zodiac peers or simply intrigued by astrology's influence on personalities, this chapter promises an enlightening exploration of remarkable achievements and enduring legacies left behind by these iconic Capricorn figures. Join us as we embark on this journey into the captivating world of the Capricorn stars.

ELVIS PRESLEY

- Date of Birth: January 8, 1935.
- Brief Biography: Elvis Presley, often referred to as the "King of Rock and Roll," was a legendary American singer and actor. He rose to fame in the mid-1950s and became a cultural icon known for his charismatic performances and pioneering music.
- Capricorn Traits: Determination, ambition and discipline.
- Impact: Elvis revolutionized the music industry and left an enduring legacy. His influence on rock and pop music continues to be felt today.
- Personal Life: Elvis struggled with the pressures of fame and health issues. Sadly he passed away on August 16, 1977.

RICHARD NIXON

- Date of Birth: January 9, 1913.
- Brief Biography: Richard Nixon was the 37th President of the United States, serving from 1969 to 1974. He played a significant role in shaping American foreign policy during his tenure.
- Capricorn Traits: Ambition, practicality and resilience.
- Impact: Nixon's presidency was marked by achievements like opening relations with China but was also overshadowed by the Watergate scandal, leading to his resignation in 1974.
- Personal Life: Nixon's political career was marked by both success and controversy. He passed away on April 22, 1994.

BETSY ROSS

- Date of Birth: January 1, 1752.
- Brief Biography: Betsy Ross is credited with creating the first American flag with thirteen stars and thirteen stripes, representing the original colonies. She was a seamstress and a symbol of American patriotism.
- Capricorn Traits: Practicality, craftsmanship and attention to detail.
- Impact: Betsy Ross' contribution to American history as the flag's designer endures as a symbol of national pride.
- Personal Life: Betsy Ross was a skilled upholsterer and ran her own upholstery business in Philadelphia. She passed away on January 30, 1836.

GRETA THUNBERG

- Date of Birth: January 3, 2003.
- Brief Biography: Greta Thunberg is a Swedish environmental activist who gained international recognition for her efforts to combat climate change.
- Capricorn Traits: Determination, resilience and leadership.
- Impact: Greta's activism has sparked a global movement, raising awareness about climate change and advocating for urgent action.
- Personal Life: Greta continues her advocacy work and is recognized as a prominent voice for climate action.

MARLENE DIETRICH

- Date of Birth: December 27, 1901.
- Brief Biography: Marlene Dietrich was a German-American actress and singer known for her glamorous Hollywood career. She starred in iconic films such as "The Blue Angel" and "Destry Rides Again."
- Capricorn Traits: Ambition, elegance and discipline.
- Impact: Marlene's beauty and talent made her an international star. She challenged gender norms with her androgynous style and bold persona.
- Personal Life: Marlene had a long and successful career, but she also faced personal challenges. She passed away on May 6, 1992.

DAVID BOWIE

- Date of Birth: January 8, 1947.
- Brief Biography: David Bowie was a British musician and actor known for his innovative and ever-evolving music style. He was a pioneer of glam rock and experimented with various genres throughout his career.
- Capricorn Traits: Creativity, versatility and ambition.
- Impact: Bowie's contributions to music and fashion continue to influence artists across generations. His hits include "Space Oddity" and "Heroes."
- Personal Life: Bowie enjoyed a successful music career and acted in films. He passed away on January 10, 2016.

KIM JONG-UN

- Date of Birth: January 8, 1983.

- Brief Biography: Kim Jong-un is the Supreme Leader of North Korea, succeeding his father, Kim Jong-il. He has been a controversial figure in global politics, leading a reclusive regime.
- Capricorn Traits: Ambition, leadership and secrecy.
- Impact: Kim Jong-un's leadership has had a significant impact on North Korea's policies and international relations, often resulting in tensions.
- Personal Life: Much of Kim Jong-un's life remains shrouded in secrecy. His regime has been criticized for human rights abuses.

JOAN OF ARC

- Date of Birth: January 6, 1412.
- Brief Biography: Joan of Arc, also known as the Maid of Orleans, was a French military leader and a heroine of the Hundred Years' War. She played a crucial role in securing French victories.
- Capricorn Traits: Determination, courage and resilience.
- Impact: Joan of Arc's bravery and leadership inspired her troops and contributed to turning the tide of the war in favor of the French.
- Personal Life: Joan of Arc faced trials and was eventually executed by the English on May 30, 1431.

DOLLY PARTON

- Date of Birth: January 19, 1946.
- Brief Biography: Dolly Parton is a celebrated American singer, songwriter, and actress known for her country music career and hits like "Jolene" and "I Will Always Love You."
- Capricorn Traits: Determination, authenticity and creativity.
- Impact: Dolly's contribution to country music has earned her numerous awards, and her philanthropic efforts, including supporting literacy, have left a lasting impact.
- Personal Life: Dolly continues to perform and is an advocate for various charitable causes.

ROWAN ATKINSON

- Date of Birth: January 6, 1955.

- Brief Biography: Rowan Atkinson is a British comedian and actor famous for his roles in "Mr. Bean" and "Blackadder." His comedic talent has made him an international star.
- Capricorn Traits: Practicality, humor and versatility.
- Impact: Rowan Atkinson's iconic character, Mr. Bean, has entertained audiences worldwide for decades, making him one of the most recognized comedians.
- Personal Life: Rowan Atkinson continues to work in comedy and acting, delighting audiences with his wit and humor.

MARY TYLER MOORE

- Date of Birth: December 29, 1936.
- Brief Biography: Mary Tyler Moore was an American actress known for her roles in "The Mary Tyler Moore Show" and "The Dick Van Dyke Show." She was a beloved television icon.
- Capricorn Traits: Ambition, professionalism and charm.
- Impact: Mary Tyler Moore's talent and charm made her a beloved figure in television history. Her work paved the way for women in the entertainment industry.
- Personal Life: Mary Tyler Moore enjoyed a successful career but also faced personal challenges. She passed away on January 25, 2017.

FAYE DUNAWAY

- Date of Birth: January 14, 1941.
- Brief Biography: Faye Dunaway is an American actress known for her roles in iconic films like "Bonnie and Clyde" and "Network." She has received critical acclaim for her work.

- Capricorn Traits: Determination, elegance and versatility.
- Impact: Faye Dunaway's performances have earned her numerous awards, including an Academy Award for her role in "Network."
- Personal Life: Faye Dunaway continues to be a respected figure in the film industry.

The above, famous Capricorn individuals have all left their mark on various fields, showcasing the determination, ambition, and resilience. Such traits are the true characteristic of this zodiac sign. As we draw this chapter to a close it serves as a reminder of the enduring impact and significant contributions made by Capricorn individuals to society, culture and the world as a whole. Their narratives bear testament to the power of determination, hard work and an enduring spirit that characterizes those born under Capricorn's influence.

As we bid farewell to this chapter may you find inspiration and admiration in these personalities associated with Capricorn. Their legacies continue to radiate, serving as a reminder that with perseverance and practicality the stars are indeed attainable, for those born under this remarkable zodiac sign.

CONCLUSION

As we conclude our exploration of the Capricorn star sign, it's first important to reflect on the key insights and themes that have emerged throughout our chapters. After this summary of chapters we will wrap up all that we have discovered and give some valuable takeaways.

Each chapter has delved deeply into different aspects of Capricorn, revealing a complex and multifaceted sign. Let's take a moment to summarize what we discover in each chapter.

- **Chapter 1: History and Mythology** - This chapter explored the historical and mythological roots of the Capricorn sign. We discovered how ancient civilizations perceived Capricorn and how these perceptions have evolved over time. This historical perspective provided a foundation for understanding the enduring traits and symbols associated with Capricorn.
- **Chapter 2: Love & Compatibility** - In this chapter, we examined the romantic side of Capricorn. We explored how Capricorn's qualities influence their love life and relationships. The chapter also provided insights into Capricorn's compatibility with other zodiac signs, offering guidance for harmonious partnerships.
- **Chapter 3: Friends And Family** - This chapter focused on the social and family aspects of Capricorn. It delved into how Capricorns interact with friends and family. Furthermore we looked at their loyalty, protective nature and how they express love and support in close relationships.
- **Chapter 4: Career And Money** - Capricorn's professional life and financial management were the focus of this chapter. We explored how their traits like ambition, discipline and pragmatism shape their career choices and approach to finances.
- **Chapter 5: Self-Improvement** - Here, we delved into the ways Capricorns can pursue personal growth and self-improvement. The chapter provided strategies for Capricorns to leverage their strengths and address their challenges for a more fulfilling life.
- **Chapter 6: The Year Ahead** - This chapter provided a forward-looking analysis, offering predictions and guidance for Capricorns in the coming

year. We discussed potential challenges and opportunities that await them in various aspects of life.

- **Chapter 7: Famous "Capricorn" Personalities** - In the final chapter, we explored the lives and achievements of famous Capricorn individuals. This chapter highlighted how Capricorn traits have manifested in these personalities. One can find inspiration and insights into the potential of this star sign.

In conclusion the journey through the world of Capricorn has been truly enlightening. It has revealed a star sign that possesses depth and diversity. From its ancient origins to its modern expressions, Capricorns embody a unique blend of discipline, ambition and practicality that sets them apart. As we bring this book to a close our hope is that readers have gained a deep understanding of Capricorn and are equipped with the knowledge to navigate the intricacies of this zodiac sign.

The central focus of this book is a profound exploration into the realm of Capricorn astrology. Throughout our exploration we have delved into many aspects such as history, mythology, personal relationships, career development and self improvement in order to unravel the multi-faceted nature of Capricorns. Our objective was to provide readers with insights into the strengths, challenges and potentials associated with being a Capricorn.

We stand by our commitment. We have successfully fulfilled it by examining each dimension of a Capricorn's life. From tracing their roots and unveiling symbolism to offering practical advice on love relationships, family dynamics, professional growth opportunities and much more. We have presented a well rounded perspective on what it means to be a Capricorn. Additionally our analysis of individuals born under this sign along with predictions for the upcoming year further enriches our understanding by showcasing how astrological traits can manifest in real world contexts.

The main takeaway we hope readers grasp is the depth and intricate nature of the Capricorn sign. Capricorns are not solely defined by ambition and discipline. They encompass resilience, loyalty and practical wisdom. Overall they possess a unique approach to facing life's challenges and embracing opportunities.

We encourage individuals who identify as Capricorns to embrace their qualities. Your strength, determination and practicality are assets that can lead to great accomplishments and to foster deep meaningful relationships. Your journey through life guided by these attributes is not only about success but also a testament to the enduring power of your signs' characteristics.

As we conclude this book, it has comprehensively delved into what it means to embody the essence of being a Capricorn. From ancient times until now Capricorns have proven themselves to be more than their star sign. Ultimately they are individuals with vibrant lives shaped by celestial influences yet firmly rooted, in the realities of our world. We sincerely hope that the wisdom and understanding you have gained here will serve as inspiration and guidance, for anyone looking to delve into this zodiac sign. Best wishes!

AQUARIUS:

A COMPLETE GUIDE TO THE AQUARIUS ASTROLOGY STAR SIGN

Contents

INTRODUCTION ---------- **1**

Overview of the Aquarius Zodiac Sign ---------- 2

CHAPTER 1: HISTORY AND MYTHOLOGY ---------- **5**

Historical & Mythological Origins of the Aquarius Constellation ---------- 5

Historical Events Under the Aquarius Season ---------- 7

Historical Figures Born Under Aquarius ---------- 7

CHAPTER 2: LOVE & COMPATIBILITY ---------- **10**

Aquarius and the Realm of Love and Romance ---------- 11

Aquarius Compatibility with Other Zodiac Signs ---------- 12

Tips for Dating and Maintaining Relationships with Aquarius Individuals -- 15

CHAPTER 3: FRIENDS AND FAMILY ---------- **18**

Aquarius as a Friend ---------- 19

Aquarius and Family Dynamics ---------- 20

CHAPTER 4: CAREER AND MONEY ---------- **24**

Aquarius Career Preferences and Professional Aspirations ---------- 25

Strengths of Aquarius Individuals in the Workplace ---------- 27

Aquarius Career Challenges and Strategies to Overcome Them ---------- 28

Strategies to Overcome Career Challenges ---------- 29

CHAPTER 5: SELF-IMPROVEMENT ---------- **31**

Personal Development for Aquarius Individuals ---------- 31

Leveraging Aquarius Strengths and Addressing Weaknesses ---------- 32

CHAPTER 6: THE YEAR AHEAD ---------- **36**

Aquarius Horoscope Guide for the Year Ahead ---------- 36

Key Astrological Events and Their Impact on Aquarius ---------------------- 41

CHAPTER 7: FAMOUS "AQUARIUS" PERSONALITIES ------------ 44

Abraham Lincoln -- 44

Thomas Edison -- 45

Shakira -- 45

Leontyne Price --- 46

Farrah Fawcett --- 46

Alicia Keys -- 47

Michael Jordan --- 47

XXXTentacion -- 47

Ed Sheeran --- 47

Kelly Hu --- 48

Virginia Woolf --- 48

Megan Thee Stallion -- 48

Oprah Winfrey -- 48

CONCLUSION -- 50

INTRODUCTION

Astrology has been practiced for thousands of years. It revolves around the belief that the positions of stars, planets and other celestial entities at the time of a person's birth can impact their personality traits, relationships and life events. The zodiac plays a key role in astrology. It consists of twelve signs, each corresponding to constellations. These serve as a reference point for predicting and interpreting various aspects of a person's life. What makes astrology so intriguing is its fusion of science, art and philosophy allowing us to gain insights into the complexities of nature and fate.

This book focuses on Aquarius, the eleventh sign in the zodiac. It is known for its advocacy of innovation, celebration of individuality and unending quest for a peaceful world. Aquarius represents qualities like originality, independence and humanitarianism. This book has been written to provide guidance for individuals born under the Aquarius zodiac sign who are looking to gain an understanding of themselves. Additionally it aims to offer insights into how being an Aquarius can impact growth, relationships, life decisions and much more. Come along with us on an exploration as we uncover the enigmatic and captivating zodiac of Aquarius.

OVERVIEW OF THE AQUARIUS ZODIAC SIGN

Aquarius is an intriguing and multifaceted zodiac sign. This overview will shed light on its key aspects. Those include its symbolic representation, elemental association, ruling planet, and the characteristics that define those born under this sign.

1. **Date of Star Sign:** January 20th to February 18th.
2. **Symbol**: The Water Bearer, symbolizing the sharing of wisdom and insight. It is often depicted as an individual pouring water from a vessel.
3. **Element**: Air, aligning with qualities of intellect, communication, and an expansive view of the world.
4. **Ruling Planet**: Uranus. The planet of innovation, revolution, and unexpected changes. Aquarius's unique and unconventional nature reflects this.
5. **Color**: Electric blue and turquoise. Such colors represent vibrancy and clarity.

PERSONALITY TRAITS

1. **Innovative**: Aquarians are forward-thinkers. They are often ahead of their time in their ideas and views.
2. **Independent**: They cherish their freedom and autonomy. This makes them somewhat resistant to conventional norms.
3. **Humanitarian**: Aquarians possess a strong sense of social justice. As such they often engage in activities aimed at making the world a better place.

STRENGTHS

1. **Intellectual**: Aquarians are highly intelligent and love intellectual stimulation.
2. **Creative**: They are exceptionally creative and inventive.
3. **Altruistic**: They are genuinely concerned about the welfare of others and are often involved in social causes.

WEAKNESSES

1. **Unpredictable**: Their desire for independence can sometimes make them seem distant or emotionally unavailable.

2. **Stubborn**: Once they have formed an opinion, it can be challenging for them to see alternative viewpoints.
3. **Aloof**: Aquarians can appear detached or unemotional, especially in personal relationships.

COMPATIBILITY

1. **Most Compatible Signs;** Gemini and Libra are considered good matches for Aquarius due to their shared air element.
2. **Good Compatibility**; Aries and Sagittarius also make good partners for Aquarius as they provide a blend of independence and a sense of adventure.

In this book's introduction we have embarked on an exploration into the captivating world of astrology. The spotlight is specifically placed on Aquarius. Aquarius truly stands out in the realm of astrology. With its combination of intellect, creativity and a rooted commitment to humanitarian causes. Individuals born under this sign are often seen as trailblazers leading the way with innovative thinking and driving change. With their unique perspective on life Aquarians not only dream big but also take action to bring their visions into reality. Now, moving beyond the introduction this book will delve deeper into various aspects of the Aquarius sign. These include the following and much more.

1. **Historical and Mythological Background;** Discover ancient history and mythological stories associated with Aquarius. These will add depth to understanding this sign's significance.
2. **In Depth Analysis of Personality;** Readers will find detailed examinations of Aquarians complex traits. In addition to how they can navigate both their inner and outer worlds.
3. **Aquarius in Relationships;** Insights into how Aquarians form and maintain types of relationships. In addition to their approach to love and friendship.
4. **Career and finances;** Explore career paths and finances for Aquarians focusing on utilizing their strengths across various professional settings.
5. **Health and Wellness;** Discussions on strategies for maintaining mental well being and health that resonate with those born under the Aquarius sign.
6. **Practical Tips for Aquarians;** Advice tailored specifically to help individuals born under the sign of Aquarius. The purpose is to help navigate life's challenges and to unleash their full potential.

Whether you are an Aquarius or simply curious, about the qualities associated with this zodiac sign this book offers enlightening insights and enriching perspectives. Let's begin our exploration.

CHAPTER 1:
HISTORY AND MYTHOLOGY

Welcome to a journey, through the realms of time and imagination. Here we embark on an exploration of the historical and mythological tapestry surrounding the Aquarius zodiac sign. In this chapter you are invited to delve into the origins, enduring legends and historical narratives that have shaped our understanding of this astrological symbol. Let us start by tracing the earliest observations of the Aquarius constellation. From ancient Babylonians to Greeks, each culture bestowed their own interpretations, weaving it intricately into their cultural fabric and spiritual beliefs.

Transitioning from mythology to reality, this chapter also shines a light on figures who were born under the sign of Aquarius. This in addition to significant events that occurred during the Aquarius season. These insights provide a glimpse into how Aquarians have shaped history highlighting their association with innovation, leadership and social change. So without further ado, let's embark on this exploration!

HISTORICAL & MYTHOLOGICAL ORIGINS OF THE AQUARIUS CONSTELLATION

The Aquarius constellation holds a significant place in the night sky and human history. Its origins and representations have been varied and profound across various cultures and eras. These are the earliest observations and recordings.

1. **Babylonian Astronomy:** One of the earliest known recordings of the Aquarius constellation dates back to ancient Babylon. The Babylonians identified this constellation as "the Great One" in their star catalogs. It was associated with the god Ea. This deity was often depicted holding an overflowing vase or jug, symbolizing the outpouring of water.
2. **Ancient Egypt**: In Egyptian astronomy, Aquarius was associated with the annual flooding of the Nile River. This was crucial for their

agriculture. The Egyptians believed that the Water Bearer's jar poured forth the waters that nourished their lands.

3. **Ancient Greece**: The ancient Greeks incorporated Aquarius into their mythology. Often they attributed it to the legend of Ganymede, a beautiful youth who was taken to Olympus by Zeus in the form of an eagle. Ganymede was given the honorable position of cupbearer to the gods. The constellation was said to represent him pouring nectar from a celestial jug.
4. **Chinese Astronomy**: In Chinese star maps, the stars of Aquarius were incorporated into two different constellations. One represented a soldier or official. The other depicted a stream of water, reflecting the dual nature of the constellation as both human and element.
5. **Indian Astronomy:** In Indian Vedic astrology, or Jyotisha, parts of the Aquarius constellation are included in the Kumbha rashi. This translates to "water pitcher". It reflects a similar understanding of Aquarius as a bearer or dispenser of water.
6. **Middle Eastern Traditions**: In various Middle Eastern cultures, Aquarius was seen as a significant astrological sign. It was often associated with the deluge or great floods in their myths and folklore.

In modern astronomy, Aquarius continues to be a point of fascination and is integral to astrological studies. Initially Aquarius was mainly associated with the flooding of rivers and the arrival of rains. It symbolized regeneration and fertility. Towards the Middle Ages, Aquarius started to acquire characteristics related to personality. It was often portrayed as a symbol of wisdom and an agent of transformation.

In modern times Aquarius is viewed in terms of individualism, innovation and a compassionate worldview. The focus has shifted towards understanding the sign through personality traits and psychological profiles.

HISTORICAL EVENTS UNDER THE AQUARIUS SEASON

1. **Scientific Advancements:** The Aquarius season has often coincided with breakthroughs in science and technology. Such happenings align with Aquarius's association with innovation and forward-thinking. For instance, the first successful test of a telephone (Alexander Graham Bell) and notable space missions have occurred during this period.
2. **Political Movements**: Significant political movements and events have occurred during the Aquarius season. For example the ratification of important treaties and the inception of progressive policies. This reflects the Aquarian traits of humanitarianism and a desire for societal advancement.
3. **Cultural Shifts:** Major cultural events, like influential art exhibitions or the release of groundbreaking music and literature, have also been noted during this time. Overall these reflect the creative and unconventional nature of Aquarius.

HISTORICAL FIGURES BORN UNDER AQUARIUS

1. **Inventors and Scientists:** Thomas Edison and Galileo Galilei, both Aquarians, revolutionized our understanding of the world through their inventions and discoveries.
2. **Political Leaders and Activists:** Abraham Lincoln, known for his leadership and emancipation proclamation. Rosa Parks, an icon of the

civil rights movement, was also born under this sign. Both reflect the Aquarian qualities of leadership and a drive for social change.

3. **Artists and Writers:** The literary and artistic genius of Charles Dickens and Wolfgang Amadeus Mozart, born in the Aquarius season, showcase the sign's creativity and originality.

As we wrap up this chapter, let's take a moment to ponder the diverse tapestry of stories, history and symbolism associated with the Aquarius zodiac sign. This journey through time has unveiled the facets of Aquarius from its origins to its modern interpretations, in astrology. Aquarius represented by the Water Bearer has always stood for innovation, humanitarianism and intellectual brilliance throughout history.

In present day astrology, the significance of the Aquarius sign remains strong. It serves as a symbol of hope. A reminder of our resilience as being and our unwavering pursuit, for knowledge and self improvement. The ideals encompassed by Aquarius. Progression, freedom and compassion, hold as much relevance today as they did in ancient times. Ultimately they continue to guide us towards a future that is enlightened and inclusive.

FURTHER READING AND REFERENCES

For those intrigued by the history and mythology of Aquarius and wishing to explore further, the following resources offer a wealth of information:

Primary Ancient Texts:

1. **"Tetrabiblos"** by Claudius Ptolemy: An essential work in the history of astrology, offering insights into the classical understanding of zodiac signs.
2. **"Poeticon Astronomicon"** by Gaius Julius Hyginus: A compilation of mythological tales, including those related to the constellations.

Astrological Classics:

1. **"The Astrology Book"** by James R. Lewis: A comprehensive guide to astrological signs, planets, and historical perspectives.
2. **"Parker's Astrology"** by Julia and Derek Parker: A detailed and visually engaging guide to astrology, including the history and significance of each sign.

Modern Interpretations and Analyses:

1. **"The Only Astrology Book You'll Ever Need"** by Joanna Martine Woolfolk: A modern, accessible approach to understanding astrology and zodiac signs.
2. **"Aquarius: Harness the Power of the Zodiac"** by Stella Andromeda: An in-depth look at the Aquarius sign, with contemporary insights and personality analysis.

CHAPTER 2:
LOVE & COMPATIBILITY

In this chapter we delve into the Aquarius, realm of love, romance and relationships. By understanding how Aquarius navigates love, romance and interacts with other zodiac signs we gain a captivating glimpse into their approach to matters of the heart. We begin our exploration by delving into the qualities that define Aquarius wnhen it comes to love. Understanding these characteristics is crucial in grasping how Aquarius forms and sustains relationships.

Moving on we will explore which signs are highly compatible with Aquarius and explore why that is so. Additionally we discuss which relationships may require effort to navigate through effectively. Overall we shall thoroughly analyze each pairing to gain insights into how these relationships function in the world. This involves considering aspects such as communication styles, emotional bonds, lifestyle preferences and more. In addition to exploring compatibility this chapter provides tips for individuals who are dating or already in a relationship with an Aquarius. The aim is to help partners understand their loved ones better and establish connections.

Throughout this chapter our goal is to offer an empathetic understanding of how Aquarians experience love. Whether you're an Aquarius seeking insights into your love life, or a partner looking to strengthen your relationship with an Aquarius. This chapter promises guidance and a deeper appreciation for the unique qualities that Aquarians bring to love and relationships. So let's embark on this journey together as we unravel the mysteries of the Aquarius heart.

AQUARIUS AND THE REALM OF LOVE AND ROMANCE

When it comes to love and romance, those born under the Aquarius sign approach relationships in a way that is as unique and unconventional as their personalities. Understanding an Aquarian's approach to love involves delving into their core traits, let’s take a closer look.

1. **Intellectual Connection**: For Aquarians, a strong mental connection is often the precursor to romance. They are drawn to partners who stimulate their intellect. For example, partners who are able to engage in deep, meaningful conversations. This need for mental stimulation means that relationships with Aquarians often blossom from friendships. Here a foundation of shared interests and intellectual pursuits has already been laid.

2. **Independence and Space:** One of the most distinctive traits of Aquarians in relationships is their fierce independence. They value their personal space and freedom. As such they seek partners who respect this need.
3. **Unconventional Romance:** Aquarians are known for their unconventional and sometimes rebellious streaks. This trait usually extends to their approach to love and romance. Overall they may shy away from societal norms when it comes to love. As such, their idea of romance might not always align with traditional expectations, as they seek to create a unique bond that resonates with their ideals and personality.
4. **Emotional Depth:** Despite their outwardly cool demeanor, Aquarians possess a deep emotional capacity. They may not be the most demonstrative lovers. They often express their feelings in more subtle, intellectual ways. Ultimately Aquarians need time to build trust and open up emotionally. But once they do, they are loyal and committed partners.
5. **Humanitarian Love:** Aquarians have a broad love for humanity. However this can sometimes overshadow their personal relationships. They may be more focused on larger societal issues or group dynamics. This can sometimes lead to their partners feeling neglected. However, a partner who shares their humanitarian outlook will find a deeply fulfilling connection.
6. **Challenges in Love -** Aquarians sometimes struggle with the more practical aspects of a relationship. Their need for independence and their unconventional approach can lead to misunderstandings. Especially with partners who value traditional expressions of love and commitment. Communication is key in navigating these challenges.

In summary, love and romance in the world of an Aquarian are as unique and multifaceted as the sign itself. A relationship with an Aquarius offers intellectual depth and respect for individuality. It is a non-traditional approach to love. Understanding and embracing their qualities is key to a harmonious and lasting relationship with an Aquarian.

AQUARIUS COMPATIBILITY WITH OTHER ZODIAC SIGNS

AQUARIUS AND ARIES

1. Compatibility: High.

2. Dynamics: Aries and Aquarius share a natural rapport and a love for adventure. Both are independent. Aries appreciates Aquarius's vision. Meanwhile Aquarius admires Aries' initiative.
3. Challenges: Aries's impulsive nature might clash with Aquarius's more calculated approach. Communication and patience are key.

AQUARIUS AND TAURUS

1. Compatibility: Moderate.
2. Dynamics: This pairing might face challenges due to their different approaches to life. Taurus values stability and tradition. Aquarius cherishes freedom and innovation.
3. Challenges: The key is to find a balance between Taurus's need for security and Aquarius's need for independence.

AQUARIUS AND GEMINI

1. Compatibility: High.
2. Dynamics: Both air signs, Aquarius and Gemini, have a lot in common. This includes a love for intellectual conversation, social activities and creativity.
3. Challenges: They need to ensure they don't get too caught up in the mental realm and neglect emotional or practical aspects of their relationship.

AQUARIUS AND CANCER

1. Compatibility: Low to moderate.
2. Dynamics: Cancer's need for emotional connection and home life can be quite different from Aquarius's love for freedom and independence.
3. Challenges: If they can respect and understand each other's needs, they can find a middle ground. From there they can build a happy relationship.

AQUARIUS AND LEO

1. Compatibility: Moderate to high.
2. Dynamics: There is a natural attraction as both are opposites on the zodiac wheel. Leo's warmth and passion can intrigue Aquarius. Aquarius's originality and unconventionality can draw in Leo.

3. Challenges: They need to balance Leo's need for attention with Aquarius's quest for independence.

AQUARIUS AND VIRGO

1. Compatibility: Moderate.
2. Dynamics: Virgo's detail-oriented approach contrasts with Aquarius's big-picture thinking. However, both share a love for intellectual pursuits.
3. Challenges: To make it work, they must respect their different approaches and learn from each other.

AQUARIUS AND LIBRA

1. Compatibility: High.
2. Dynamics: Both being air signs. Therefore, there is a natural understanding and a similar approach to life. They both love socializing, engaging in intellectual discussions, and value fairness.
3. Challenges: They need to be careful not to become too detached from emotional aspects of a relationship.

AQUARIUS AND SCORPIO

1. Compatibility: Moderate.
2. Dynamics: This is a relationship of intrigue and fascination. Scorpio's intensity and depth can draw Aquarius in. Aquarius's uniqueness and detachment can be appealing to Scorpio.
3. Challenges: The key is balancing Scorpios emotional depth with Aquarius's intellectual breadth.

AQUARIUS AND SAGITTARIUS

1. Compatibility: High.
2. Dynamics: Both love freedom and adventure. They are seekers of truth and knowledge. They complement each other well. Overall they can have a dynamic and exciting relationship.
3. Challenges: They must ensure they take time to build emotional depth and understanding.

AQUARIUS AND CAPRICORN

1. Compatibility: Moderate.
2. Dynamics: They have contrasting approaches. Capricorn is traditional and practical. Meanwhile Aquarius is innovative and unconventional. However, they can learn a lot from each other.
3. Challenges: Mutual respect and understanding of each other's strengths are crucial.

AQUARIUS AND AQUARIUS

1. Compatibility: High.
2. Dynamics: Sharing the same sign, they understand each other well. They both enjoy intellectual discussions, social activism, and creative pursuits.
3. Challenges: They need to be cautious about becoming too emotionally detached or neglecting their partner's needs.

AQUARIUS AND PISCES

1. Compatibility: Moderate.
2. Dynamics: Pisces can bring a sense of spirituality and emotional depth to the relationship.Aquarius brings innovation and a social conscience.
3. Challenges: They need to balance Aquarius's intellectual approach with Pisces's emotional one.

In summary, Aquarius can find compatibility with various signs. Although provided there is mutual understanding, respect, and willingness to embrace each other's differences.

TIPS FOR DATING AND MAINTAINING RELATIONSHIPS WITH AQUARIUS INDIVIDUALS

FOR DATING AQUARIUS MEN

1. **Appreciate His Independence**: Aquarius men value their freedom. Show that you respect his need for space and independence.
2. **Engage His Intellect:** Stimulate his mind with interesting conversations, debates, and intellectual challenges.

3. **Be Open to Adventure:** He's likely to be intrigued by new and unconventional activities. Be open to spontaneous adventures and unique experiences.
4. **Avoid Emotional Overload**: Aquarius men might be uncomfortable with overly emotional displays. Communicate your feelings honestly but respect his need for a more rational approach.
5. **Embrace His Social Circle:** He likely has a wide and varied group of friends. Show interest and be comfortable in social settings with him.
6. **Support His Humanitarian Interests:** Many Aquarius men are driven by social causes. Show genuine interest and support for his humanitarian efforts.
7. **Be Yourself:** Aquarius men appreciate authenticity. Be genuine in your interactions with him.

FOR DATING AQUARIUS WOMEN

1. **Respect Her Independence:** An Aquarius woman cherishes her freedom and autonomy. Show that you understand and respect her need to be her own person.
2. **Stimulate Her Mind:** Intellectual stimulation is key. Engage her in conversations about new ideas, world events, and creative pursuits.
3. **Be Open-Minded**: Aquarius women appreciate open-mindedness. Especially in discussions about unconventional or avant-garde topics.
4. **Give Her Space:** She might need time alone or to be with her friends. Understand and respect her need for personal space without feeling threatened.
5. **Show Your Humanitarian Side**: Many Aquarius women are passionate about making the world a better place. Participate in or support her causes and initiatives.
6. **Appreciate Her Uniqueness:** Aquarius women pride themselves on their individuality. Celebrate her unique qualities and perspectives.
7. **Emotional Balance:** While she might not be overly emotional, it's important to create a balance where emotions can be expressed healthily and respectfully.

Remember that in any relationship with an Aquarius it is essential to understand their need for independence and intellectual stimulation. Remember to also nurture connection and shared values.

As we conclude this exploration of "Aquarius Love and Compatibility " we have delved into the landscape of romance and relationships through the lens of an Aquarius. This chapter has shed light on the complexities of an Aquarian's love experiences and interactions with others. We have seen how crucial intellectual connection and independence are for Aquarians, in relationships. Their approach to love is characterized by a desire for stimulation and a sense of independence. When examining Aquarius compatibility with each zodiac sign it becomes evident that diverse dynamics can arise. While some signs align harmoniously with Aquarius nature others present potentially rewarding connections.

Aquarius teaches us about the beauty of embracing our uniqueness and staying true to ourselves in both love and life. As we wrap up this chapter, I want to emphasize the impact that Aquarius has on the realm of love and compatibility. Whether you identify as an Aquarian navigating the complexities of romance or simply find this zodiac sign fascinating, the wisdom shared here aims to enhance your comprehension and encounters with love.

CHAPTER 3: FRIENDS AND FAMILY

This chapter is dedicated to exploring the fascinating aspects of how Aquarians navigate their relationships with friends and family members. Gaining an understanding of Aquarius in these dynamics provides key insights into their character and how they engage with those who are closest to them. First we will delve into Aquarians as friends. We will explore the qualities that make them great companions. Moving on we shall shift our focus to the role of an Aquarian within a family unit.

Throughout this chapter we will also explore the complexities that arise in friendships and family relationships for those born under the Aquarius zodiac sign. Ultimately the goal of this chapter is to provide an understanding of how Aquarians establish and nurture these relationships while highlighting the qualities that enhance their interactions with loved ones. Join us on this journey as we dive into the world of Aquarius within the context of friendships and family dynamics unraveling the dynamics that shape these relationships.

AQUARIUS AS A FRIEND

When it comes to friendships, individuals born under the Aquarius sign bring a unique and refreshing dynamic to their social circles. They make for intriguing and loyal friends, albeit with some distinctive characteristics.

THE HALLMARKS OF AQUARIUS FRIENDSHIPS

1. **Intellectual Stimulation:** Aquarians thrive in friendships that offer intellectual stimulation. They are drawn to people who share their curiosity and love for learning. Discussions with them usually cover a wide range of topics. From the latest scientific discoveries to societal issues.
2. **Independent yet Social:** While they cherish their independence, they sometimes require alone time to recharge. Aquarians are also inherently social and enjoy being part of a group. Due to their varied nature, they often have a diverse set of friends from various backgrounds.
3. **Loyalty and Honesty:** Aquarians are fiercely loyal to their friends and value honesty in their relationships. They are the type of friends who will stand by you in challenging times. Furthermore they will often be brutally honest, believing that truth is a cornerstone of a genuine friendship.
4. **Non-Conformity and Uniqueness:** Aquarians are known for their non-conformist attitudes. They are not afraid to be different and often encourage their friends to embrace their individuality. In an Aquarian's company, you are likely to feel more at ease expressing your true self.
5. **Humanitarian and Altruistic:** Given their humanitarian nature, Aquarians are often involved in causes or movements. They appreciate friends who are also socially conscious and willing to make a difference in the world.
6. **Innovative and Future-Oriented:** Always thinking ahead, Aquarians bring a unique perspective to their friendships. They are the ones who introduce their friends to the latest trends, ideas, or technologies.

CHALLENGES IN AQUARIUS FRIENDSHIPS

1. **Emotional Distance:** Aquarians can come off as emotionally detached or aloof. Their focus on intellectual pursuits can make them

seem distant in emotional matters. This might be misconstrued as a lack of care or empathy.

2. **Unpredictability**: Aquarians can be unpredictable, changing plans or ideas suddenly. This trait can be exciting but also a bit unsettling for those who prefer more consistency in their friendships.

NURTURING FRIENDSHIPS WITH AQUARIUS

1. **Respect Their Need for Independence:** Understanding and respecting their need for alone time is crucial in maintaining a healthy friendship with an Aquarius.
2. **Engage in Intellectual Conversations:** Keep them engaged with stimulating discussions and be open to exploring new ideas together.
3. **Embrace Their Unconventional Nature:** Appreciate their uniqueness and be open to the unconventional experiences they bring into the friendship.

In summary, friendships with Aquarians can be intellectually enriching, socially diverse, and refreshingly honest. They push the boundaries of conventional thinking and bring a perspective that is both innovative and altruistic. While there may be challenges, especially on an emotional level, the unique bond formed with an Aquarius friend is often strong and enduring. Ultimately it is filled with growth and discovery.

AQUARIUS AND FAMILY DYNAMICS

Aquarians bring distinctive qualities to family dynamics. Understanding how they interact within the family unit provides insight into their role as family members and how they influence the familial atmosphere.

KEY CHARACTERISTICS OF AQUARIANS IN FAMILY SETTINGS

1. **Independent Spirit:** Aquarians value their independence. Even within the family context. They often seek personal space and may sometimes appear detached from family affairs. However, this independence is not a sign of disinterest but rather a reflection of their need for autonomy.
2. **Intellectual and Open-Minded:** Aquarians often encourage open and progressive discussions within the family. They are the ones who

introduce new ideas and perspectives. Overall they create an environment where learning and curiosity are valued.

3. **Non-Conformist Attitude:** Inclined towards non-conformity, Aquarians may challenge traditional family norms or expectations. They are often the advocates for change and modernization within the family structure.
4. **Humanitarian Outlook:** Aquarians are known for their humanitarianism, and this extends to their family life. They are often involved in social causes and may encourage their family members to participate in community service or charitable activities.
5. **Supportive yet Detached:** While Aquarians are supportive and wish the best for their family members, they might not always express their affection in conventional ways. Their support often comes through in their encouragement of each family member's individuality and independence.

CHALLENGES IN FAMILY DYNAMICS

1. **Emotional Expression:** Aquarians might struggle with expressing emotions. This can sometimes be misconstrued as aloofness or lack of empathy, especially in close-knit family settings.
2. **Need for Personal Space:** Their need for personal space and independence can sometimes create a sense of distance within the family. It's important for family members to understand and respect this trait.

BUILDING HARMONIOUS FAMILY RELATIONSHIPS

1. **Communication**: Open and honest communication is key. Discussing individual needs and boundaries can help in understanding the Aquarian family member better.

2. **Respect for Individuality**: Embracing the unique traits of the Aquarian family members, including their non-conformist views and independence, strengthens family bonds.
3. **Involvement in Shared Causes:** Engaging in activities or causes that resonate with the Aquarian's humanitarian spirit can be a way to connect and build stronger family relationships.
4. **Patience and Understanding:** Being patient and trying to understand the Aquarian's perspective, especially regarding their approach to emotional expression and need for space, is crucial.

To sum up, Aquarians bring a blend of intellect, innovation and compassion to their family life. While there may be challenges, in understanding their expressions and their desire for independence, embracing these qualities can lead to a harmonious and fulfilling family dynamic. Overall with an Aquarian in the family you'll often find a mix of individuality thinking ideas and a collective aspiration to make contributions to the world around them.

As we wrap up our exploration of "Aquarius. Friends and Family " we reflect on the captivating dynamics that Aquarians bring into their relationships. This journey has provided us with an understanding of how individuals born under the Aquarius sign interact, connect and shape their bonds with friends and loved ones. We've witnessed how Aquarius individuals cultivate friendships based on stimulating conversations and creative interactions. Within family dynamics we've observed how Aquarians often emerge as the voice advocating for progressiveness and modernization.Their tendency to go against the norm and their independent nature can sometimes challenge family structures. However it also brings a fresh perspective and new ideas.

If you have an Aquarius in your life whether they are a friend or a family member embracing their qualities of innovation, intellect and humanitarianism can add depth to your relationship. It is important to honor their need for independence while valuing the wisdom they bring to the table. By celebrating the distinctiveness of Aquarius in friendships and family ties we acknowledge the role they play in enriching the lives of those around them. Through understanding and embracing the spirit of an Aquarius individual, friends and family members can cultivate bonds that are more meaningful and mutually respectful, with their beloved Aquarians.

As we come to the end of this chapter we are presented with an image of how an Aquarian contributes to the realms of friendship and family. Their approach to these relationships characterized by their depth, independence and future oriented outlook not only shapes their interactions but also brings a distinct element to the lives they impact.

CHAPTER 4:
CAREER AND MONEY

Welcome to this chapter dedicated to exploring the relationship between Aquarius individuals and their careers and finances. In this chapter we delve into the traits and characteristics of Aquarians shedding light on how these qualities shape their professional choices and financial approach. By understanding how Aquarians navigate the realms of work and money we gain a glimpse into their values, aspirations and the obstacles they may encounter along the way.

Let's start by examining the career preferences of Aquarians. We'll explore their inclination towards roles that offer stimulation, innovation and opportunities for making a positive impact on society. Whether it's thriving in creative fields or being driven by philanthropy we'll uncover the types of professional environments where Aquarians truly shine and how their strengths contribute to their success.

Moving on to financial matters we'll discuss how Aquarians manage their money, approach security. We'll see how their independent nature and visionary outlook influences their financial decisions. This section will provide insights into an Aquarian's attitude towards wealth, investments. It will also show how to find a balance between financial stability and pursuing altruistic goals.

Addressing challenges is a part of this chapter as well. Inside we'll explore some of the obstacles that Aquarians may encounter in the workplace while offering guidance on how they can overcome them. By the end of this chapter readers will have a complete understanding of how to leverage the qualities of Aquarius in the professional world while effectively managing any challenges that may arise. This knowledge will contribute towards a career journey and a balanced approach to decision making. Join us as we explore the relationship between the sign of Aquarius and its impact on career choices, workplace dynamics and financial decision making.

AQUARIUS CAREER PREFERENCES AND PROFESSIONAL ASPIRATIONS

Aquarians are known for their innovative minds, humanitarian instincts, and a strong desire for intellectual stimulation. These traits significantly influence their career choices and professional aspirations.

KEY CAREER PREFERENCES FOR AQUARIUS

1. **Innovation and Creativity:** Aquarians thrive in careers that allow them to think outside the box. Here they can bring innovative solutions to the table. For example they tend to excel in fields like technology, engineering, and design. Here they can leverage their creativity and forward-thinking.
2. **Independence and Autonomy:** Preferring to work under their own terms, Aquarians are drawn to professions that offer a degree of autonomy and freedom. Freelancing, entrepreneurship, or roles that allow for a flexible work schedule are often the most appealing.
3. **Social Impact and Humanitarianism:** With a natural inclination towards helping others, Aquarians often find fulfillment in careers that make a positive impact on society. This could lead them to roles in non-profit organizations, social work, environmental advocacy, or humanitarian efforts.

4. **Intellectual Stimulation:** Jobs that provide continuous learning opportunities and intellectual challenges are highly attractive to Aquarians. They might be inclined towards academia, research, or careers in science and technology.
5. **Communication and Expression:** Aquarians are effective communicators. As such they are often drawn to careers in writing, journalism, public speaking, or digital media. Here they can express their ideas and thoughts.

PROFESSIONAL ASPIRATIONS OF AQUARIANS

1. **Leadership Roles:** Many Aquarians aspire to be in positions where they can lead and implement progressive changes. They are visionaries who want to influence and shape the future.
2. **Making a Difference:** Professional success for an Aquarian includes making a significant impact on society or a particular field. Their aspirations are frequently tied to the greater good rather than just personal gain.
3. **Continuous Growth:** Aquarians seek careers that offer opportunities for personal and professional growth. They are lifelong learners and always look for ways to expand their knowledge and skills.

CHALLENGES IN PROFESSIONAL LIFE

1. **Conformity:** Aquarians may struggle in traditional, hierarchical organizations where conformity is expected. They prefer environments where their unique perspectives and unconventional methods are valued.
2. **Emotional Detachment:** Their tendency towards emotional detachment can sometimes be misinterpreted as a lack of passion or commitment in professional settings.

In conclusion, the career path of an Aquarius is often as unconventional as they are. It is marked by a desire for innovation, independence, and making a meaningful contribution to the world. Their ideal professional environment is one that values creativity, offers autonomy, and aligns with their humanitarian values. By finding the right balance between their need for independence and the demands of teamwork, Aquarians can achieve remarkable success and find fulfillment in their careers.

STRENGTHS OF AQUARIUS INDIVIDUALS IN THE WORKPLACE

Aquarius individuals are recognized for their strengths that set them apart and contribute to their success, in professional environments. Their exceptional blend of brilliance, innovative thinking and compassion enables them to thrive in the workplace. Here are some key strengths of Aquarius individuals that drive their achievements.

1. **Natural Innovators;** Aquarians are exceptional problem solvers. Particularly in roles that demand creative solutions.
2. **Forward Thinking;** They often have a foresight that surpasses their time and brings cutting edge ideas to the table. This quality makes them highly valuable in evolving industries like technology and science.
3. **Intellectual Curiosity;** Aquarius individuals exhibit a curiosity and an insatiable desire to learn and explore new concepts. This keeps them well informed and at the forefront of their fields.
4. **Analytical Skills;** They possess robust analytical capabilities enabling them to deconstruct intricate problems and formulate logical and efficient solutions.
5. **Self Motivation;** Aquarians are inherently self driven functioning effectively without supervision or guidance. They proactively take initiative in their work.
6. **Autonomous Work Style;** Aquarians thrive in roles where they can take charge and manage their projects thanks to their preference for autonomy.
7. **Empathy;** Despite being perceived as detached, Aquarians are highly empathetic and compassionate. Such qualities help to foster team cohesion and boost morale.
8. **Excellent communicators;** Aquarians excel in communication oriented roles such as relations, writing and advocacy due to their social nature. They have a knack for expressing ideas persuasively. Furthermore their open mindedness enables them to listen and collaborate with others where valuing other perspectives is crucial in team settings.
9. **Adaptability;** Their adaptability is remarkable; Aquarians effortlessly adjust to new challenges and environments. This trait proves valuable, in industries characterized by change.
10. **Resilience;** Additionally they possess resilience. When faced with setbacks they refuse to be discouraged. Such perseverance helps them in navigating through challenging times.

11. **Leadership;** Aquarius individuals possess a visionary outlook that fuels their leadership abilities. When taking on leadership positions they have the power to inspire and motivate others. As such they often set an example within their teams.

In summary Aquarius individuals bring key strengths to the workplace. These include their mindset, intellectual capacity, humanitarian nature and effective communication skills. Their knack for offering fresh perspectives along with their balanced principles and resilience make them well suited for success, in various professional roles.

AQUARIUS CAREER CHALLENGES AND STRATEGIES TO OVERCOME THEM

While Aquarius individuals possess many strengths that contribute to their success in the workplace, like all zodiac signs, they also face specific challenges. Understanding these challenges and implementing effective strategies can help Aquarians navigate their professional lives more successfully.

CHALLENGES FACED BY AQUARIUS IN THE WORKPLACE

1. **Resistance to Conformity**: Aquarians often struggle in rigid, traditional corporate environments. Their non-conformist nature might clash with conventional workplace norms and hierarchies.
2. **Perceived Emotional Detachment**: Due to their preference for intellectual over emotional expression, Aquarians may sometimes be perceived as aloof or uncaring. This can negatively affect workplace relationships.

3. **Difficulty with Routine**: Aquarians often seek variety and innovation. As such they may find routine or mundane tasks uninspiring.
4. **Impatience with Slow Processes:** Their forward-thinking nature can lead to impatience with slower, more methodical processes or resistance to change within organizations.
5. **Struggle with Authority:** Their independent nature might make it challenging for Aquarians to deal with authoritative figures or highly structured management.

STRATEGIES TO OVERCOME CAREER CHALLENGES

EMBRACING FLEXIBILITY AND ADAPTABILITY

1. **Seek Out Innovative Environments:** Aquarians should aim for careers or companies that value innovation and creativity. Here their non-conformist approach will be appreciated.
2. **Flexible Work Arrangements:** Pursuing roles that offer flexible working conditions can help satisfy their need for independence and variety.

ENHANCING EMOTIONAL INTELLIGENCE AND COMMUNICATION

1. **Develop Emotional Intelligence:** Working on emotional intelligence can help Aquarians better understand and connect with their colleagues. Overall it will enhance teamwork and collaboration.
2. **Effective Communication:** Practicing clear and empathetic communication can mitigate misunderstandings related to their perceived emotional detachment.

FINDING MEANING IN ROUTINE

1. **Discover Purpose in Small Tasks:** Finding a deeper purpose or understanding the bigger picture behind routine tasks can make them more engaging for Aquarians.
2. **Incorporate Creativity:** Injecting creativity into mundane tasks can make them more interesting and bearable.

PATIENCE AND UNDERSTANDING ORGANIZATIONAL DYNAMICS

1. **Developing Patience:** Learning to be patient, especially with processes that take time to evolve, can be beneficial. Mindfulness techniques can be helpful in cultivating this patience.
2. **Understanding Organizational Structures:** Gaining a better understanding of why certain structures or hierarchies exist in the workplace can help Aquarians navigate them more effectively.

NAVIGATING HIERARCHIES AND AUTHORITY

1. **Positive Authority Relationships:** Building positive relationships with superiors and understanding the value of different management styles can improve workplace harmony.
2. **Seeking Leadership Roles:** Aquarians should aim for leadership positions where they can be agents of change and implement their ideas more freely.

In conclusion Aquarians may encounter challenges in their lives. However with these strategies they can overcome these obstacles

As we wrap up the chapter we have explored the landscape and financial mindset of individuals born under the Aquarius sign. This exploration has provided us with key insights into how Aquarians navigate their careers and manage their finances. We have observed that Aquarians excel in careers that allow them to express their creativity, independence and humanitarian ideals. Their strengths in innovation, intellectualism and visionary thinking make them valuable assets in the workplace.

Throughout this chapter our aim has been to provide an understanding of how Aquarians can maximize their potential in their careers while effectively handling their finances. The distinctive qualities of Aquarius, not only shape how they approach career decisions and manage money but also enrich the professional world with their unique perspectives and contributions. Ultimately the way Aquarians approach their careers and finances is as diverse and individualistic as they are. By embracing their abilities and acknowledging their obstacles, Aquarians can confidently navigate the realms of work and money. From this they can make significant positive contributions to society through their understanding and exceptional skills.

CHAPTER 5: SELF-IMPROVEMENT

Welcome into the realm of self improvement through the perspective of individuals born under the Aquarius star sign. This chapter is dedicated to gaining an understanding of Aquarians and utilizing their traits for personal development. Here I will provide insights and strategies for self improvement both for Aquarians themselves and those seeking a better understanding of them. Ultimately my aim is to help Aquarians understand and utilize their strengths while effectively navigating through their challenges. By embracing their individuality and striving for improvement, Aquarians can find fulfillment and make meaningful contributions to the world around them. So join us as we embark on an exploration of self improvement specifically tailored for those with an Aquarius birth sign.

PERSONAL DEVELOPMENT FOR AQUARIUS INDIVIDUALS

For those who are born as Aquarians, personal development often revolves around finding harmony between their inclination towards innovation, intellectualism and humanitarianism. By understanding and harnessing these qualities profound self improvement and fulfillment can be achieved. Let's take a closer look.

1. **Continuous Learning;** Aquarians possess a desire for acquiring knowledge and exploring new ideas. Embracing this inclination through education whether through traditional ways or self directed study can result in significant personal growth.
2. **Exploring Diverse Interests;** Curiosity is encouraged by engaging in subjects or hobbies that can further enrich depth and foster creativity. Keep an open mind.
3. **Recognizing Emotional Intelligence;** Known for their exceptional skills, it's essential for individuals born under the Aquarius sign to recognize and nurture their emotional intelligence. This development can significantly enhance personal relationships and self-awareness.

4. **Communication skills**; Improving communication skills in expressing emotions and understanding others is crucial for Aquarians to foster better connections.
5. **Community**; While independence is a trait, striking a balance with interdependence can strengthen professional relationships for Aquarians. Engaging in community projects and activities can help Aquarians appreciate the value of teamwork and shared goals.
6. **Contribution;** Aquarians naturally have a desire to contribute to society. Getting involved in volunteer work or social causes will bring fulfillment and a sense of purpose. Incorporating sustainable practices into their professional lives aligns perfectly with the humanitarian nature of Aquarians.
7. **Health;** Maintaining great health through exercise and adopting a healthy lifestyle is essential. Aquarians might find enjoyment in sports or fitness routines that match their preferences. To manage their tendency towards overactivity and stress Aquarians can benefit from practicing mindfulness techniques and relaxation methods.
8. **Creativity;** Finding outlets for creativity is crucial for satisfaction among Aquarians. This could involve taking up art, writing, designing or any other form of expression that resonates with them personally.
9. **Build resilience;** Building resilience is vital when facing challenges, for Aquarians. Being able to confront life's challenges is extremely important. Overall this entails gaining wisdom from failures and perceiving setbacks as opportunities for growth.
10. **Adapting to Change;** Embracing change and learning to adjust can empower Aquarians to thrive in circumstances.

In summary, personal development of an Aquarius involves nurturing their creative abilities, cultivating intelligence, engaging in social endeavors and prioritizing their own well being. By embracing these elements Aquarians can embark on a rewarding journey of self improvement.

LEVERAGING AQUARIUS STRENGTHS AND ADDRESSING WEAKNESSES

Aquarius boasts a wide range of strengths that can be tapped into for enhanced personal and professional success. However like all zodiac signs Aquarians also encounter weaknesses. By acknowledging and working on these areas Aquarians can attain a fulfilling life.

LEVERAGING AQUARIUS STRENGTHS

1. **Innovative Mindset;** Aquarians are innovative. Encouraging them to pursue careers or hobbies that allow for problem solving or creative thinking can result in significant contributions within creative, technological or social realms.
2. **Intellectual Curiosity;** Their thirst for knowledge makes them diligent learners. Aquarians should be encouraged to explore areas of interest and engage in intellectual pursuits. This will help them stay motivated and mentally sharp.
3. **Caring for Others;** Aquarians have an inclination towards finding fulfillment in activities that contribute to the greater good. Engaging in volunteering, activism or pursuing careers focused on change can be particularly rewarding for them.
4. **Embracing Independence;** Aquarians highly value their independence. They thrive when they have the freedom to make their choices and follow self directed paths leading to increased satisfaction and productivity.

5. **Communication;** Aquarians possess excellent communication skills especially when it comes to discussing new ideas and concepts. Overall they excel in roles that require persuasive communication abilities.

ADDRESSING AQUARIUS CHALLENGES

1. **Expressing Emotions**; Sometimes Aquarians may find it challenging to express their emotions. Practices like mindfulness, counseling sessions or conversations about feelings can help to improve in this area.
2. **Overcoming Perceived Aloofness;** Due to their reserved nature Aquarians might come across as aloof or detached at times. They can work on showcasing their compassionate side by engaging more deeply in personal relationships.
3. **Balancing Non Conformity with Structure;** While non conformity is considered a strength for Aquarians there are situations where some level of structure is necessary. Striking a balance between expressing individuality and adhering to frameworks can help them succeed.
4. **Cultivate patience;** Aquarians have the potential to strike a balance, between maintaining their individuality and embracing established norms when necessary. However their eagerness for progress can sometimes lead to impatience. It would be beneficial for Aquarians to cultivate patience and realize that certain changes take time.
5. **Self reflection;** Regular self reflection can help them become more aware of how their traits impact themselves and others. This will foster growth. Seeking feedback from trusted individuals such as friends, family or colleagues can also provide insights for areas of improvement. Additionally being open minded and adaptable to other perspectives can help mitigate some of the weaknesses associated with being an Aquarius.

As we wrap up this chapter we want to leave Aquarians with a message of hope and motivation. The path of self improvement is not something that has an endpoint but an ongoing journey that keeps evolving. This perfectly aligns with the nature of Aquarius individuals who are always forward thinking and ready to embrace change. With their combination of visionary thinking and compassionate hearts Aquarians are destined for a life filled with fulfillment, innovation and profound personal growth.

Ultimately the journey of an Aquarian revolves around finding harmony between their ideas and practical solutions balancing their idealism with action. It's about utilizing their strengths while acknowledging their weaknesses as they move forward, driven by ambition and guided by a mind that recognizes the possibilities within the universe.

CHAPTER 6:
THE YEAR AHEAD

This chapter is designed to guide Aquarians through the year ahead by examining key astrological events and their expected impact on various aspects of life. As an Aquarius it is crucial to comprehend the influences that await you throughout the year in order to navigate challenges and seize opportunities. Thus the purpose of this chapter is to lay out a roadmap for what lies ahead this year for Aquarius. It is a road map that highlights the planetary movements and alignments that will play a pivotal role in your life as an Aquarius. But this chapter isn't just about predicting the future. Think of it as your toolkit for empowerment and self awareness. By understanding the influences at play as an Aquarius you can make better decisions, adapt to changes and utilize your inherent strengths to have a fulfilling year.

AQUARIUS HOROSCOPE GUIDE FOR THE YEAR AHEAD

As an Aquarius, the year ahead promises a blend of challenges and opportunities, allowing for significant personal growth and progress in various aspects of life. Here is your guide to navigate the upcoming year. One that highlights key themes, potential challenges and opportunities.

OVERALL OUTLOOK

This year is mainly about balance and growth for Aquarians. You will find yourself focusing on both personal development. Along with your contributions to the larger community. Expect periods of introspection followed by bursts of social activity. Balancing these aspects will be key to your success and happiness. Below are a few key points.

1. **Self-Discovery:** The year is ripe for self-discovery. Explore new interests, hobbies, and learning opportunities.
2. **Emotional Intelligence**: Focus on developing emotional intelligence, which will enhance both your personal and professional relationships.

3. **Mindfulness and Wellbeing**: Prioritize your mental and physical wellbeing. Practices like yoga, meditation, or regular exercise will be beneficial.

Challenges to Overcome

1. **Dealing with Change:** You may face changes in various aspects of your life. Embrace these changes as opportunities for growth.
2. **Managing Stress:** Be mindful of stress levels, especially during busy periods. Regular self-care and relaxation will be key.

CAREER AND PROFESSIONAL LIFE

The year's astrological events suggest a dynamic period for career and finances for Aquarius individuals. Planetary movements, particularly those of Jupiter and Saturn, will have a substantial influence. Let's break it down.

1. **Jupiter's Prosperity:** Jupiter's transit may bring opportunities for expansion and growth in your career. This could manifest as promotions, new job offers, or successful completion of important projects.
2. **Saturn's Lessons:** Saturn might test your professional resilience. It's a time for hard work and discipline, which will lay the foundation for future success.
3. **Critical Times:** Pay attention to the periods when Jupiter and Saturn form significant aspects with Aquarius. These will be crucial for your career and financial decisions.

Strategies

1. **Seize Opportunities:** Be ready to seize opportunities for growth and advancement in your career.
2. **Financial Planning:** Practice prudent financial planning, especially during any turbulent astrological periods. Ones that may impact financial stability.
3. **Innovation and Opportunities:** Your career will be marked by opportunities to showcase your innovative ideas. Be ready to take on new projects or roles that challenge your creativity.
4. **Collaboration and Independence:** While independent projects will thrive, don't overlook the benefits of collaboration. Mid-year might bring opportunities for significant teamwork, leading to valuable connections and achievements.

5. **Leadership:** The latter part of the year may present opportunities for leadership roles or initiatives. Embrace these to expand your professional influence.

Financial Management

1. **Smart Investments:** Financially, this is a year to make smart investments. Look for opportunities that align with your long-term goals.
2. **Budgeting and Planning:** Be mindful of your spending habits. Mid-year might require some budgeting and financial planning.

HEALTH AND WELLNESS

Health and wellness for Aquarius this year may be influenced by various planetary aspects. Particularly those affecting stress and mental well-being. Let's explore further.

1. **Stress Management:** Times of intense astrological activity, such as Mercury Retrograde or eclipses, may bring added stress.
2. **Mental Health Focus**: Planetary alignments may emphasize the importance of mental health and emotional well-being.
3. **Regular Exercise:** Incorporate physical activity into your routine to manage stress effectively.
4. **Mindfulness Practices:** Engage in mindfulness practices like meditation or yoga to maintain mental and emotional balance.

LOVE AND RELATIONSHIPS

The astrological events of the year bring a mix of challenges and opportunities in the realm of love and relationships for Aquarius individuals. Key planetary movements, particularly those involving Venus, will play a significant role. Let's take a closer look.

1. **Venus Transits:** Look out for Venus transits. They will greatly influence romantic connections. These periods can bring harmony and deepen existing relationships or could attract new love interests.
2. **Significant Periods:** Mid-year may be particularly important when Venus enters a sign that harmonizes well with Aquarius. This will fostering understanding and intimacy in relationships.

Advice

1. **Communication:** Prioritize open and honest communication. Especially during periods of potential misunderstandings due to Mercury Retrograde.
2. **Embrace Change:** Be open to the transformations in relationships brought about by eclipses. These can be times of significant growth and deepening of bonds.

3. **Deepening Connections:** For those in relationships, this year is a time to deepen connections. Communicate openly and embrace shared experiences.
4. **New Encounters:** Single Aquarians might find new romantic interests, particularly in social settings or through community projects.
5. **Balancing Independence:** Remember to balance your need for independence with your partner's needs. Honest communication will be crucial.

PERSONAL GROWTH AND DEVELOPMENT

The astrological events of the year provide fertile ground for personal growth and self-discovery for Aquarius individuals. Let's take a closer look.

1. **Self-Reflection**: Eclipses and significant planetary transits are ideal times for introspection and reevaluating personal goals and values.
2. **Embracing Change:** The year's cosmic activity encourages embracing change and growth. Particularly in areas of life that may have felt stagnant.

Growth Strategies

1. **Explore New Interests:** Use this year to explore new hobbies or learning opportunities, aligning with the Aquarian love for knowledge.
2. **Emotional Development:** Focus on developing emotional intelligence and deepening your understanding of yourself. In addition to your relationships with others.

Travel and Exploration

1. **Adventurous Travels:** Travel opportunities may arise, offering chances for adventure and new experiences. These trips could also provide deeper insights into your own life and goals.
2. **Learning Journeys:** Consider travels that are not just vacations but also learning experiences. These will align with your natural curiosity.

Social Life and Community Engagement

1. **Active Social Life:** Expect an active social life this year. Your network may expand, bringing interesting new contacts.
2. **Community Projects:** Involvement in community projects or social causes will be fulfilling and could lead to significant personal growth.

Overall for Aquarius individuals, the year ahead is rich with opportunities for growth in love, career, health, personal development and much more. By being mindful of the key astrological events and their potential impacts, Aquarians can navigate the year with confidence and make the most of the opportunities. Embrace your innovative spirit, focus on building deeper connections, and stay open to learning from every experience. Remember, balance is your mantra for the year ahead.

KEY ASTROLOGICAL EVENTS AND THEIR IMPACT ON AQUARIUS

As an Aquarius, certain astrological events throughout the year can have a significant impact on various aspects of your life. Understanding these events and their potential influence can help you navigate the year more effectively. Here's a guide to some key astrological events and how they may affect you as an Aquarius.

MERCURY RETROGRADE

1. **Impact:** During Mercury Retrograde periods, you may find communication more challenging than usual. There might be misunderstandings or delays in your plans. Especially those involving technology or travel.
2. **Advice:** Use this time to review and revise plans rather than starting new projects. Be patient and clear in your communications.

SOLAR AND LUNAR ECLIPSES

1. **Impact:** Eclipses often bring significant changes and revelations. For Aquarius, these could relate to personal identity, career, or important relationships.
2. **Advice:** Be open to change and self-discovery. Eclipses are powerful times for growth. Even if they initially bring uncertainty.

AQUARIUS NEW MOON

1. **Impact:** The New Moon in Aquarius is a potent time for setting intentions and starting new projects. Particularly those aligned with your true self and personal aspirations.

2. **Advice:** Reflect on your goals and desires. Use this energy to initiate changes or projects that are deeply meaningful to you.

JUPITER TRANSIT

1. **Impact:** Jupiter's transit can bring expansion and growth in the areas it touches. For Aquarius, this could mean opportunities for advancement in education, travel, or spiritual exploration.
2. **Advice:** Embrace opportunities for growth and learning. Be open to exploring new philosophies or broadening your horizons.

SATURN TRANSIT

1. **Impact:** Saturn's influence often involves lessons and challenges. For Aquarius, this may manifest as a need to restructure certain areas of life, possibly relating to career or personal responsibilities.
2. **Advice:** Face challenges with patience and determination. This is a time for building foundations and long-term planning.

URANUS SQUARES AND OPPOSITIONS

1. **Impact:** Uranus can bring sudden changes or upheavals. As an Aquarius, you might find yourself desiring more freedom or experiencing unexpected shifts in your life path.
2. **Advice:** Stay flexible and adaptable. Use these changes as opportunities for innovation and personal liberation.

VENUS TRANSIT

1. **Impact:** Venus governs relationships and finances. Its transit can highlight these areas, bringing harmony or challenges, depending on its aspect.
2. **Advice:** Focus on balancing your personal relationships and financial matters. It's a good time to address any imbalances or issues in these areas.

Ultimately every astrological occurrence brings forth its own set of possibilities and difficulties. As an Aquarius, being aware of these influences enables you to align your actions with the energies of the cosmos. Your aim is to foster growth while minimizing obstacles. Remember that astrology serves as guidance rather than a path. Ultimately your free will and choices shape your own unique journey.

Having concluded our exploration in the chapter "Aquarius in the Year Ahead " we have traversed through the landscape of astrological influences understanding how they intertwine with the life of an Aquarius. This journey has provided a guide to the opportunities and challenges that lie ahead. My aim has been to equip Aquarians with insights to navigate the year confidently and gracefully. Armed with an understanding of the forecast Aquarians can embrace the future with optimism.

As we conclude this chapter Aquarians are encouraged to move into the year prepared to welcome the experiences and teachings it brings. Equip yourselves with the wisdom and understanding acquired here. May the voyage lead you to a year filled with exploration and happiness.

CHAPTER 7:
FAMOUS "AQUARIUS" PERSONALITIES

Within this chapter we aim to highlight the lives and achievements of a few famous individuals who were born under the Aquarius zodiac. Through their captivating stories we will gain insights into the qualities and potential that Aquarius embodies across various domains including politics, science, arts, sports and entertainment. From the brilliance of Abraham Lincoln, to Thomas Edison's genius; Shakiras artistic allure; and Michael Jordans athletic prowess. This chapter presents a rich tapestry of personalities that illuminate different aspects of the Aquarius sign.

Aquarians are renowned for their brilliant ideas, progressive nature and strong sense of individuality. In this chapter we delve into how these remarkable characteristics have manifested in the lives of some famous Aquarians. We witness how their visionary perspectives, talents and dedication to progress have left an enduring impact on our world. These profiles not only serve as a source of inspiration but also showcase the various ways in which Aquarian traits can be expressed and celebrated.

Through our exploration of the lives of these individuals we will uncover the obstacles they encountered, the triumphs they achieved and the profound impact they had. Their journeys offer lessons and insights for Aquarians and anyone fascinated by this zodiac sign. Ultimately their stories exemplify how Aquarians can utilize their qualities to attain greatness and positively influence the world. So come along and embark on this captivating voyage as we delve into the lives of Aquarians. This chapter guarantees an illuminating exploration into the hearts and minds of some of history's greatest personalities born at the season of Aquarius.

ABRAHAM LINCOLN

1. Date of Birth: February 12, 1809.

2. Brief Biography: The 16th President of the United States, Lincoln is best known for leading the nation through the Civil War and abolishing slavery.
3. Aquarius Traits: Visionary leadership and commitment to principles.
4. Impact: Preserved the Union and redefined the U.S. Constitution.
5. Personal Life: Known for his humility and deep moral convictions.

THOMAS EDISON

1. Date of Birth: February 11, 1847.
2. Brief Biography: An American inventor and businessman. He developed many devices like the phonograph and the electric light bulb.
3. Aquarius Traits: Innovative, intellectual and forward-thinking.
4. Impact: His inventions have significantly impacted modern life.
5. Personal Life: Edison was known for his tireless work ethic and creativity.

SHAKIRA

1. Date of Birth: February 2, 1977.
2. Brief Biography: A Colombian singer, songwriter, and dancer known for hits like "Hips Don't Lie" and "Waka Waka."
3. Aquarius Traits: Charismatic, humanitarian and originator.
4. Impact: Global pop icon and active in philanthropic endeavors.

5. Personal Life: Engages in significant charity work, particularly in education.

LEONTYNE PRICE

1. Date of Birth: February 10, 1927.
2. Brief Biography: An acclaimed American soprano. She was one of the first African Americans to become a leading artist at the Metropolitan Opera.
3. Aquarius Traits: Trailblazing, passionate and strong-willed.
4. Impact: Broke racial barriers in the world of opera.
5. Personal Life: Known for her dignity and grace. Both onstage and off.

FARRAH FAWCETT

1. Date of Birth: February 2, 1947.
2. Brief Biography: An American actress and model. She is famous for her role in the TV series "Charlie's Angels."
3. Aquarius Traits: Charismatic, independent and innovative.
4. Impact: Icon of the 1970s and a pop culture figure.
5. Personal Life: Fawcett was also known for her battle with cancer and activism.

ALICIA KEYS

1. Date of Birth: January 25, 1981.
2. Brief Biography: An American musician, singer, and songwriter. She is known for her soulful music and hits like "Fallin'."
3. Aquarius Traits: Artistic, passionate and humanitarian.
4. Impact: 15-time Grammy Award-winning artist and a significant cultural influence.
5. Personal Life: Involved in various philanthropic activities, including HIV/AIDS awareness.

MICHAEL JORDAN

1. Date of Birth: February 17, 1963.
2. Brief Biography: Widely regarded as the greatest basketball player of all time. He is well known for his time with the Chicago Bulls.
3. Aquarius Traits: Competitive, innovative and a leader.
4. Impact: Transformed professional basketball and became a global icon.
5. Personal Life: His competitive nature extends to his business ventures and philanthropy.

XXXTENTACION

1. Date of Birth: January 23, 1998.
2. Brief Biography: An American rapper, singer, and songwriter. He was known for his deep and emotive music.
3. Aquarius Traits: Artistic, intense and complex.
4. Impact: Influenced a younger generation of music artists and fans.
5. Personal Life: His life was marked by legal issues and a tragic early death.

ED SHEERAN

1. Date of Birth: February 17, 1991.
2. Brief Biography: An English singer-songwriter known for hits like "Shape of You" and "Thinking Out Loud."
3. Aquarius Traits: Creative, empathetic and original.
4. Impact: One of the world's best-selling music artists.
5. Personal Life: Actively involved in charitable causes. He is known for his down-to-earth personality.

KELLY HU

1. Date of Birth: February 13, 1968.
2. Brief Biography: An American actress and former fashion model, known for her roles in "The Scorpion King" and "X2."
3. Aquarius Traits: Versatile, strong and independent.
4. Impact: A prominent Asian-American actress in Hollywood.
5. Personal Life: Actively involved in various charity organizations.

VIRGINIA WOOLF

1. Date of Birth: January 25, 1882.
2. Brief Biography: An English writer. She is considered one of the most important modernist 20th-century authors.
3. Aquarius Traits: Intellectual, innovative and complex.
4. Impact: A major figure in the literary world, known for her novels and essays.
5. Personal Life: Her life and work were significantly influenced by her mental health struggles.

MEGAN THEE STALLION

1. Date of Birth: February 15, 1995.
2. Brief Biography: An American rapper, singer, and songwriter. She is famous for her confident and bold persona.
3. Aquarius Traits: Charismatic, independent and assertive.
4. Impact: A rising star in the music industry, known for empowering women.
5. Personal Life: Actively involved in promoting education and social issues.

OPRAH WINFREY

1. Date of Birth: January 29, 1954
2. Brief Biography: Oprah Winfrey is a renowned American media executive, actress, talk show host, television producer, and philanthropist. She is best known for her talk show, "The Oprah Winfrey Show," which was the highest-rated television program of its kind and was nationally syndicated from 1986 to 2011.

3. Aquarius Traits: Oprah Winfrey embodies many of the quintessential traits of an Aquarius. She is highly charismatic, independent, and assertive.
4. Impact: Oprah's impact on the media industry and society at large is profound. She has been a champion for women, advocating for their empowerment and self-worth.
5. Personal Life: Beyond her professional achievements, Oprah is deeply involved in social and educational causes. She has established scholarships, funded school projects, and is actively engaged in various charitable endeavors.

Each of these individuals personify characteristics commonly found in Aquarius individuals. They utilize their visionary, innovative and humanitarian qualities to create impacts in their fields. Their stories consistently highlight their ability to think ahead, innovate and approach things from a perspective. Whether it is politics, science, arts or sports. Their talent for looking beyond boundaries has been instrumental in their accomplishments.

Many of these personalities have utilized their influence for the good. A reflection of Aquarius humanitarian trait. Their contributions extend beyond achievements as they actively engage in societal issues and philanthropic endeavors. The range of fields and approaches among these Aquarians underscores this sign's association with individuality and nonconformity. Overall they serve as reminders that staying true to oneself can be a path towards success and influence.

Ultimately the stories of these individuals serve as a source of inspiration for Aquarians and others encouraging them to embrace their qualities. By embracing their individuality and caring for the community remarkable achievements can be attained. As we conclude this chapter Aquarians are encouraged to embrace their unique attributes and utilize them as a solid foundation for their endeavors. The stories shared by these personalities demonstrate that staying true to one's nature can lead to a fulfilling life. One that can have significant, positive impact. In conclusion, these accounts serve as a reminder of the potential inherent in being an Aquarius individual.

CONCLUSION

As we reach the conclusion of this comprehensive book about the Aquarius star sign, it's time to reflect on the journey. A journey we've taken to understand the unique characteristics, strengths, and challenges of those born under this innovative and humanitarian zodiac sign. Through the various chapters, we have delved into the historical, personal, professional, and astrological aspects of the Aquarius sign. From these we have found insights and guidance for Aquarians and those who wish to understand them better. Below is a summarization of Key Points found in the chapters about Aquarius.

Chapter 1: History and Mythology

1. **Insights Gained**: Explored the ancient origins and mythological stories of the Aquarius constellation. Revealing how these historical narratives have shaped the sign's modern interpretation.
2. **Key Takeaway:** Aquarius has been historically symbolized as a bearer of wisdom and change. These reflect the sign's innovative and progressive spirit.

Chapter 2: Love & Compatibility

1. **Insights Gained:** Focused on the romantic inclinations and compatibility of Aquarius with other zodiac signs. Highlighted how their need for intellectual stimulation and independence plays a key role in relationships.
2. **Key Takeaway:** In love, Aquarians seek deep intellectual connections and value their autonomy. This makes them compatible with signs that respect their space and share their visionary outlook.

Chapter 3: Friends And Family

1. **Insights Gained:** Discussed the dynamics of Aquarius in friendships and family relationships. Emphasized their loyalty, but sometimes emotionally detached nature.

2. **Key Takeaway:** Aquarians are supportive yet independent in their personal relationships. They cherish intellectual connections and respect individuality.

Chapter 4: Career And Money

1. **Insights Gained:** Analyzed the career preferences and financial habits of Aquarians. Noticeably their inclination towards innovative and humanitarian fields.
2. **Key Takeaway:** In professional life, Aquarians excel in roles that allow for creativity and independence. Overall they approach their finances with a blend of idealism and pragmatism.

Chapter 5: Self-Improvement

1. **Insights Gained**: Explored the avenues for personal growth and development for Aquarians. Focus was on enhancing emotional intelligence and embracing their unique traits.
2. **Key Takeaway:** Self-improvement for Aquarians involves nurturing their intellectual and creative talents. Meanwhile, balancing their emotional expression.

Chapter 6: The Year Ahead

1. **Insights Gained:** Provided a forecast of the upcoming year for Aquarians. Highlighted how astrological events may influence various aspects of their life.
2. **Key Takeaway:** The year ahead holds opportunities for growth and challenges. These require Aquarians to adapt and utilize their innovative thinking.

Chapter 7: Famous "Aquarius" Personalities

1. **Insights Gained:** Showcased the lives of famous Aquarians. Illustrated how their traits have manifested in diverse ways to achieve success and impact.
2. **Key Takeaway:** The stories of these individuals underscore the potential of Aquarians to use their visionary and humanitarian qualities. In doing so they will make significant contributions.

The core message conveyed in this book is to explore the characteristics of individuals born under the Aquarius star sign. We have delved into the historical origins, mythology and their modern day expressions across various aspects of life. My aim was to provide readers with an understanding of what it means to be an Aquarian.

Throughout this book my commitment was completed by delving into facets that shape an Aquarius personality. We explored topics such as love, compatibility, friendships, family dynamics, career aspirations and financial tendencies along with strategies for growth. Each chapter was designed to offer valuable insights tailored specifically for an Aquarius, serving as a valuable guide, for navigating life's diverse arenas.

The main thing to remember from this book is the appreciation and celebration of Aquarius' unique characteristics. Their forward thinking mentality, compassion for humanity and their progressive approach to life. These qualities aren't only traits. They are also strengths that when embraced can result in remarkable accomplishments and fulfilling lives.

The significance of astrology lies in its capacity to provide insights into our personalities and life journeys. Understanding one's zodiac sign can be a tool for self discovery and personal development. The Aquarius sign, with its symbolism and distinct qualities offers a captivating perspective through which we can perceive the world and our role within it.

In wrapping things up this book has taken us on a journey exploring the essence of the Aquarius sign. We've uncovered the qualities that make Aquarians stand out and provided guidance on how to harness these qualities for a fulfilling life. Whether it's, in our relationships, career paths or personal growth endeavors. Understanding the spirit of an Aquarian can lead to a sense of self appreciation and a more intentional approach to life.

To all the Aquarius individuals reading this book. Embrace your attributes. Your innovative thinking, your passion for change and your unwavering individuality aren't just rare but essential in this world. Dream big, for you have the potential to inspire transformations in both your own life as well as those around you. Keep your heads in the stars while staying grounded. You possess the ability to envision and manifest a brilliant future. May you continue embracing your individuality and let your unique Aquarian light shine brightly.

PISCES:

A COMPLETE GUIDE TO THE PISCES ASTROLOGY STAR SIGN

Contents

INTRODUCTION -- 1

Overview of Pisces Zodiac Sign -- 2

CHAPTER 1: HISTORY AND MYTHOLOGY -- 4

Historical Origins -- 4

Historical events associated with Pisces -- 6

The Evolution of Pisces over Time -- 7

Additional Readings and References -- 8

CHAPTER 2: LOVE & COMPATIBILITY -- 9

Love and relationships -- 9

Compatibility of Pisces with other Zodiac Signs -- 10

Relationships with Pisces Individuals -- 14

CHAPTER 3: FRIENDS AND FAMILY -- 16

Pisces as a friend -- 17

Pisces in Family Dynamics -- 18

Challenges, in Friendships and Family Relationships -- 19

Nurturing Relationships; A Guide, for Pisces -- 21

CHAPTER 4: CAREER AND AMBITIONS -- 23

Professional Aspirations of Pisces -- 24

Strengths That Propel Pisces Individuals in the Workplace -- 25

Challenges Faced by Pisces in Their Careers and Strategies to Overcome Them -- 27

CHAPTER 5: SELF-IMPROVEMENT -- 29

Harnessing Strengths and Overcoming Weaknesses -- 29

Exercises for self awareness tailored specifically for Pisces -- 31

CHAPTER 6: PISCES IN THE YEAR AHEAD -------------------- 34
Discover what awaits Pisces in the year ahead------------------------------------ 35
Astrological Events That Influence Pisces and Their Effects ------------------ 36
Love and Relationships-- 38
Career prospects and financial situations -- 39
Self discovery--- 40
CHAPTER 7: FAMOUS PISCES PERSONALITIES----------------- 42
CONCLUSION --- 48

INTRODUCTION

Astrology, a practice that seeks to understand how celestial bodies influence our lives has intrigued people for countless generations. This timeless tradition has given individuals insights into their personalities, relationships and life journeys through studying the positions of planets and stars at the time of their birth. At its core astrology divides the sky into twelve sections, each associated with a zodiac. In this book we embark on an enthralling voyage through the realm of astrology focusing specifically on one aspect, the Pisces star sign.

If your birthday falls between "February 19 and March 20" you possess the imprint of Pisces. The purpose of this book is to help you gain an understanding of its qualities, strengths and challenges. Whether you are a Piscean seeking self awareness or simply someone intrigued by this sign. This book will offer insights into Pisces personality traits as well as its impact on love and relationships, career choices and much more. So let's dive into the world of Pisces and uncover the mysteries that reside within this captivating astrological sign.

OVERVIEW OF PISCES ZODIAC SIGN

- **Date**: February 19 to March 20.
- **Symbol:** Symbolized by two fish swimming in opposite directions. This dual fish emblem signifies the inherent duality often found within Pisces. personalities.
- **Element**: Belonging to the water element, individuals under Pisces are deeply emotional, intuitive and empathetic. Water signs are renowned for their sensitivity and receptiveness towards currents and energies in our world.
- **Planet**: Neptune governs over Pisces, as its ruling planet. Neptune is often associated with the realm of imagination, spirituality and the world of dreams. This connection further strengthens Pisces affinity for the ethereal aspects of life.
- **Personality Traits**: Pisceans are renowned for their diverse personalities. They display a level of empathy, compassion and artistic flair. Their minds are filled with imagination. Guided by their instincts Pisceans rely on their intuition to navigate life's challenges with finesse. They are also recognized for their kindness and unwavering willingness to assist others.
- **Color**; light green

STRENGTHS

- **Compassion**; Pisceans possess an inclination to care deeply for others while providing support.
- **Creativity**; They harbor an inclination towards artistry and creativity.
- **Intuition**; The intuitive nature of Pisces individuals serves as a guiding force in decision making.
- **Adaptability**; They possess an ability to effortlessly adapt to situations while being perceived as flexible individuals.

WEAKNESSES

- **Heightened Sensitivity**; The heightened sensitivity of Pisceans renders them vulnerable to hurt feelings.
- **Tendency Towards Escapism**; The dreamlike tendencies inherent in Pisces may lead them towards seeking an escape from reality. Usually through means such as daydreaming.

In this book's introduction we embarked on a journey into the timeless practice of astrology which delves into how celestial bodies influence our lives. The purpose of this book is to provide an exploration of Pisces offering insights into its personality traits, strengths, weaknesses, compatibility and more. As we embark on an exploration of this book you can anticipate gaining an understanding of what it truly means to embody the qualities of a Piscean individual. We will delve into the nuances that define Pisces personality traits delving into their strengths and weaknesses. How these attributes shape their relationships, career choices and life journey. Additionally we will discuss Pisces compatibility with zodiac signs.

Throughout this book you will uncover the captivating complexities that make up Pisces, equipping you with knowledge and insights to embrace your Piscean essence or to better understand those in your life who identify as Pisceans. So now let us immerse ourselves in the realm of Pisces as we uncover the mysteries inherent in this astrological sign.

CHAPTER 1: HISTORY AND MYTHOLOGY

The constellation of Pisces, holds a past deeply rooted in ancient civilizations. Different cultures across the globe have documented this constellation each interpreting its pattern in their own distinctive manner. The early observations of Pisces often incorporated tales, myths and significant symbols contributing to the constellations' captivating legacy. It is a legacy that continues to astronomers and star enthusiasts in the present day. Let's explore the beginnings.

HISTORICAL ORIGINS

ANCIENT MESOPOTAMIA

One of the earliest references to the Pisces constellation comes from Mesopotamia. Specifically from the Sumerians and Babylonians. They associated this constellation with two fish connected by a cord. This closely resembles how Pisces is depicted today. In their records they referred to this constellation as the "Tails" or "Fish."

ANCIENT GREEK AND ROMAN

The ancient Greeks adopted and further developed many of the constellations, including Pisces. In Greek mythology Pisces is often linked to the tale of Aphrodite and her son Eros (known as Venus and Cupid in mythology) who transformed into fish to escape from the monstrous Typhon. This story is connected to the representation of Pisces, as two fish that saved them from danger. The Greeks and later Romans incorporated this narrative into their star charts.

CHINESE ASTRONOMY

In Chinese astronomy Pisces is associated with the "Northern River," which forms part of a system of constellations related to celestial rivers. In this context Pisces is not depicted as a fish but as a component of a broader aquatic theme.

ARABIC AND ISLAMIC ASTRONOMY

During the Islamic Golden Age Arab, astronomers played a role in advancing the understanding of celestial objects. They referred to Pisces as "Al Hut " meaning "the fish." The influence of culture helped. Transmit knowledge about this constellation to later civilizations in Europe.

INDIAN ASTRONOMY

In Indian astronomy, the Pisces constellation is known as "Meena," which translates to "fish." In Hindu mythology it is associated with the Matsya Avatar, where Lord Vishnu assumed the form of a fish to rescue the world from a flood.

Over time these different cultural interpretations and representations of Pisces influenced one another contributing to the development of the constellation we recognize today. The history of the Pisces constellation is diverse and captivating, reflecting humanity's enduring fascination with the night sky and our timeless quest for connections within its tapestry. Whether perceived as two interlinked fish symbolizing love or as part of a narrative, Pisces has left its indelible mark throughout history.

HISTORICAL EVENTS ASSOCIATED WITH PISCES

Throughout history there have been various events that took place during the time when the Pisces constellation held sway. These occurrences have sparked interest and curiosity about their significance. Here are a few noteworthy historical events associated with Pisces.

EMERGENCE OF CHRISTIANITY

One of the most notable events that unfolded during the Pisces era was the rise of Christianity within the Roman Empire. Pisces is often linked to spirituality and its symbol, two fish bear resemblance to the symbol known as Ichthy. This is a representation of faith and salvation.

RENAISSANCE PERIOD

The Renaissance period, characterized by a revival of art, science and culture, in Europe coincided with the dominance of Pisces. The creative and imaginative qualities attributed to Pisces can be seen in the artistry, literature and scientific progress achieved during this time.

WORLD WAR II

Both the outbreak and eventual end of World War II occurred under the influence of Pisces. Known for its nature representing unity as well as division this constellation seems to mirror both global conflicts and subsequent efforts at reconciliation.

Throughout history there have been notable individuals who were born under the Pisces sign. Let's explore a few of them.

- **Michelangelo**; This renowned Italian artist, sculptor and painter created breathtaking masterpieces, like the Sistine Chapel ceiling. This showcases the creative talents commonly associated with Pisces.

- **Albert Einstein**; Known as a physicist Einstein revolutionized our understanding of the universe through his theory of relativity. His deep imagination aligns with the traits often associated with Pisces.
- **George Washington**; As the first President of the United States, Washington's leadership and integrity reflect Pisces qualities of empathy and moral strength.

THE EVOLUTION OF PISCES OVER TIME

The perception and interpretation of Pisces have evolved over centuries. From old times to modern astrology we can observe changes in how it has been understood.

- **Ancient Interpretations**; In ancient times Pisces was intertwined with tales involving fish such as Aphrodite and Eros. These stories emphasized its connection to themes, like love, sacrifice and protection.
- **Medieval and Renaissance**; During the Middle Ages and Renaissance eras Pisces became associated with spiritual symbolism. It was seen as an age that brought forth enlightenment.
- **Modern Astrology**; In modern astrology Pisces is viewed from a perspective focusing on traits such as empathy, intuition, creativity and adaptability. Than solely relying on narratives, contemporary astrologers delve into the nuanced personality characteristics of Pisces individuals. The perception of Pisces has shifted over time from a mythological viewpoint to one that incorporates psychological and personality based interpretations. This change reflects the continued fascination with the cosmos and its impact on human affairs.

As we wrap up this chapter we find ourselves fully immersed in the tapestry of tales and historical significance surrounding the Pisces zodiac sign. From myths centered around Aphrodite and Eros to the representation of fish found in diverse cultural narratives. Pisces has transcended time and geographical boundaries to become a symbol of unity, spirituality and salvation. The lasting impact that Pisces has had on consciousness stands as a testament to its universally recognized significance.

Pisces continues to hold a place as a sign associated with intuition, empathy, creativity and adaptability. While the fascinating origins of Pisces, in mythology continue to captivate us, modern astrologers now explore the personality traits and life patterns associated with individuals born under this zodiac sign. The

Piscean archetype has evolved from a symbolic and mythological representation to a framework that delves into psychology and personalities.

For those interested to delve into the history and mythology of Pisces there are a plethora of ancient texts and contemporary writings available. Below are some recommended references for readers interested in exploring further into the world of Pisces.

ADDITIONAL READINGS AND REFERENCES

- **"The Greek Myths"** by Robert Graves; This comprehensive source covers Greek mythology extensively including stories related to Aphrodite, Eros and other figures associated with Pisces.
- **"The Bible"** (Genesis 6 9); For readers intrigued by biblical flood narratives you can find the story of Noah's Ark in the Book of Genesis.
- **"The Secret Teachings of All Ages"** by Manly P. Hall; A timeless work that explores knowledge encompassing symbolism and its historical significance.
- **"The Inner Sky"** by Steven Forrest; A astrology book that delves into the aspects not only specific to Pisces but also other zodiac signs. It offers insights, for growth and self discovery.

As we continue our journey into the world of Pisces we encourage you to delve into this transformative zodiac sign. Allow its timeless wisdom to ignite your curiosity, about the universe and the depths of the spirit.

CHAPTER 2: LOVE & COMPATIBILITY

In this chapter we embark on a journey into the aspects of love, intimacy and compatibility within the Piscean realm. Pisces is well known for its emotional sensitivity, empathy and romantic nature. It's a sign that craves connections and has an approach to matters of the heart. Within these pages we will uncover the way Pisceans approach love and romance. We will explore their yearning for connections and their passion for creativity. Additionally we will navigate through the dynamics of Pisces compatibility with zodiac signs. We'll discover what makes some unions harmonious while others require balancing acts.

As we venture into the world of Pisces in matters of love and intimacy we invite you to explore their emotions, desires and their distinctive way of expressing love and affection. Whether you are a Piscean seeking understanding about your tendencies or simply a curious reader intrigued by the intricacies of Pisces relationships. This chapter promises to be an enlightening exploration into love, sex and compatibility, under the enchanting constellation of Pisces.

LOVE AND RELATIONSHIPS

Pisces is often associated with being deeply sensitive, empathetic and having an inclination towards romance. When it comes to love and romance Pisces individuals have an captivating approach to relationships. Let's explore how.

- **A Profound Emotional Bond**; Pisceans are known for their ability to form deep, emotional connections with their partners. They approach love with a heart openly expressing their emotions. This profound emotional bond allows them to truly understand and empathize with their partners feelings and experiences.
- **Idealism and Romance**; Pisces individuals are romantics. They believe in fairy tale love stories. They are often attracted to gestures and expressions

of affection. Love is seen as an experience for them as they seek a partner who can match their vision of romance.

- **Empathy and Compassion**; The empathy and compassion of Pisces make them supportive partners. They have an understanding of their loved ones needs. Are always ready to listen or offer support when needed. They are attuned to their partners' well being, striving for harmony in the relationship.
- **Creativity and Imagination**; Pisces individuals tend to bring creativity and imagination into their relationships. They enjoy indulging in daydreams, about shared adventures or simply immersing themselves in each other's worlds. This imaginative approach keeps the romance alive and ensures that their love continuously evolves into something
- **Selflessness and Sacrifice**; Pisces individuals are known for their willingness to go above and beyond to make their partners happy. Their selfless nature and readiness to make sacrifices for the sake of love can be both a strength and a challenge. While it makes them partners they also need to ensure that they maintain a sense of self identity throughout the process.
- **Vulnerability and Sensitivity**; The vulnerability and sensitivity of Pisces individuals can sometimes leave them open to emotional struggles within relationships. They may be more easily hurt by criticism or perceive rejection more intensely than others. Therefore it's crucial for their partners to handle their feelings with care.
- **Seeking a Spiritual Connection**; Pisceans often seek a soulful connection in their romantic relationships. They believe in the concept of soulmates. They are drawn towards partners who can provide them with a sense of fulfillment as well as emotional depth.

In conclusion when it comes to love and romance Pisces approaches it with a blend of idealism, empathy and creativity. Their profound emotional bond coupled with their sensitive nature makes them highly devoted and nurturing partners. While dealing with their sensitivity and vulnerability may present challenges to individuals. Overall, Pisces traits bring a captivating perspective to love often leading to fulfilling and spiritually significant relationships.

COMPATIBILITY OF PISCES WITH OTHER ZODIAC SIGNS

Pisces being a water sign is known for their profound emotional nature, empathy and artistic sensibilities. When it comes to compatibility with zodiac signs Pisceans have the potential to form loving connections with various partners. However there are signs that naturally harmonize better with their characteristics and preferences. Let's look at how Pisces interacts with zodiac signs.

PISCES AND ARIES

Initially Pisces and Aries may appear as a mismatch due to the contrasting fiery and impulsive nature of Aries compared to the sensitive disposition of Pisces. However when they find a balance between Aries assertiveness and Pisces empathy their differences can actually complement each other. Although it requires effort and understanding from both sides, a relationship between these two signs can be passionate and dynamic.

PISCES AND TAURUS

Taurus represents an earth sign that can offer the stability and security that Pisceans desire in a relationship. These signs share a love for the arts as well as an appreciation for life's sensual pleasures. Taurus grounded nature can help balance out Pisces dreaminess. The result is in an affectionate partnership.

PISCES AND GEMINI

When it comes to Pisces and Gemini their communication styles and priorities often differ. This can sometimes lead to misunderstandings. Pisces values depth and connection. Gemini craves stimulation and variety. However if both partners are open to compromise and appreciate each other's differences they can find a balance that combines insight with intellectual curiosity, in their relationship.

PISCES AND CANCER

In the case of Pisces and Cancer both are water signs which share an understanding of emotions. Both have nurturing qualities. This natural compatibility between them leads to an intuitive connection. They effortlessly comprehend each other's needs making them compatible partners in both love and friendship.

PISCES AND LEO

Pisces and Leo possess contrasting personalities; Leo is extroverted while Pisces tends to be more introverted and sensitive. Although challenges may arise due to these differences there is an attraction between them. If Leo learns to appreciate Pisces depth of character and creativity. While Pisces admires Leo's charisma and confidence, they can establish a bond that transcends their dissimilarities.

PISCES AND VIRGO

When it comes to Pisces and Virgo they may face some challenges due to their alternative approaches to life. Virgo's practical nature can sometimes clash with Pisces' dreamy disposition. However if both partners are open to learning from each other Pisces has the potential to inspire Virgo's imagination. Meanwhile Virgo can provide grounding and structure for Pisces.

PISCES AND LIBRA

Pisces and Libra are both signs that appreciate romance and artistry sharing a love for beauty and harmony. They can connect on an intellectual level. This forms the foundation of a loving and balanced relationship. Pisces finds charm and diplomacy in Libra admirable. Meanwhile Libra greatly admires the empathy and creativity of Pisces.

PISCES AND SCORPIO

The bond between Pisces and Scorpio is characterized by intensity and a shared understanding of the intricacies of human emotions. Their connection often goes beyond the surface level leading to transformations in their lives. Both signs possess intuition which fosters a bond filled with spirituality.

PISCES AND SAGITTARIUS

In terms of priorities and perspectives, Pisces differs from Sagittarius. Sagittarius values freedom and adventure, Pisces seeks depth and security. While there may be challenges, Pisces and Sagittarius can learn from each other's perspectives. Sagittarius encourages Pisces to explore horizons. Meanwhile Pisces helps Sagittarius connect on an emotional level.

PISCES AND CAPRICORN

When it comes to the relationship between Pisces and Capricorn they may face some difficulties due to their contrasting traits. Capricorn's practicality and ambition might seem different from Pisces' dreaminess. However if they work together they can create a balanced partnership that combines Pisces creativity with Capricorn's determination.

PISCES AND AQUARIUS

Pisces and Aquarius have approaches to life. While Pisces values depth Aquarius prioritizes pursuits and independence. Despite these differences, if they can find ground and respect each other's individuality they have the potential to form a loving partnership.

PISCES AND PISCES

When two individuals with the sign of Pisces come together there is often a connection and an intuitive understanding of each other's feelings. They can create an empathetic partnership. However it is important for them to be cautious not to enable each other's tendencies towards escapism.

It is important to note that in astrology compatibility is influenced by factors beyond sun signs such as moon signs, rising signs and the entire birth chart. Ultimately when it comes to Pisces compatibility it's important to consider both the astrological picture and individual factors that contribute to a romantic connection.

RELATIONSHIPS WITH PISCES INDIVIDUALS

FOR MEN DATING PISCES WOMEN

- **Embrace Emotional Depth**; Pisces women are highly in touch with their emotions. They value connections. Therefore it's important to be open and supportive when discussing feelings.
- **Cultivate Creativity**; Engage in activities that nurture her creative side like visiting art exhibitions, attending concerts or exploring hobbies together.
- **Practice Patience**; Understand that Pisces women may need time to process their emotions. Give her the space she needs for introspection and be patient when she retreats into her world.

- **Show Empathy**; It's crucial to display empathy and understanding towards her feelings and concerns. Listening attentively and offering support will make a difference.
- **Create Moments**; Pisces women appreciate gestures and thoughtful surprises. Planning dates, writing notes or surprising her with small tokens of affection will undoubtedly make her feel loved.

FOR WOMEN DATING PISCES MEN

- **Support His Dreams**; Pisces men often have imaginations and follow creative pursuits. Encouraging their dreams while being a source of motivation for their endeavors is essential.
- **Be Compassionate**; Pisces men are known to be highly sensitive. They can easily be influenced by stress or negative energy. It's important to provide them with an understanding presence during difficult times.
- **Share Spiritual Connections**; Many Pisces men have a spiritual side. Engaging in discussions about spirituality or philosophy can significantly strengthen your bond with them.
- **Create Emotional Security**; Establishing a space where Pisces men feel comfortable expressing their emotions without fear of judgement is crucial. Building trust is key for them to fully open up.
- **Nurture Their Intuition**; Pisces men often possess intuition. Encouraging them to trust their instincts and supporting their decision making process can greatly empower them.

In this chapter we've explored how Pisces approaches love and romance. We've delved into their romantic tendencies. Such as their love for creativity, imagination and craving for strong emotional bonds. We've also examined how Pisces gets along with zodiac signs. From this we discovered what makes some pairings harmonious while others require a balancing act.

In conclusion, love is like a canvas for Pisces! They paint their emotions in intricate strokes. For them intimacy is an art form through which they can express their desires and vulnerabilities. Their unique perspective on matters of the heart showcases their nature. Longing for connections that are profound. As we continue our journey through the stars, may we all be inspired to seek and nurture connections that enrich our lives with enduring beauty and complexity.

CHAPTER 3: FRIENDS AND FAMILY

In this chapter we embark on a heartwarming journey, into the world of Pisces individuals and their distinct dynamics in friendships and family connections. Inside we will explore how Pisces individuals navigate the tapestry of emotions, bonds and responsibilities that come with being part of both chosen friendships and inherited families. We will delve into their natural ability to cultivate friendships and their role as emotional anchors within their families.

As we venture into the realm of Pisces within the context of friends and family we invite you to discover the influence that Pisces individuals have on those around them. Whether you are a Piscean seeking insights into your relationships or an inquisitive reader eager to explore the unique qualities exhibited by Pisces. This chapter guarantees an enlightening exploration of Pisces individuals within their treasured friendships and family relationships.

PISCES AS A FRIEND

Having a Pisces friend is like having a soulful and understanding companion by your side. They bring unique qualities to their friendships that make them cherished companions. Let's take a look at what it's like to have a Pisces, as a friend and what you can expect from these individuals.

- **Compassion and Empathy;** Pisces friends are known for their compassion and empathy. They possess an ability to understand and connect with your emotions and experiences making you feel heard and supported during times.
- **Creativity and Imagination**; Pisces often have a creative inclination, which they bring into their friendships. They may suggest engaging in activities, exploring new artistic endeavors collectively or simply add an imaginative touch to your conversations.
- **Supportive Listeners**; Pisceans excel at being listeners who genuinely care about your thoughts and concerns. They create a haven where you can openly express your feelings and ideas without fear of judgment knowing that they will provide understanding support.
- **Loyalty and Devotion**; A Pisces friend is fiercely loyal and devoted. They are the kind of friends who will stand by you through thick and thin to lend a helping hand or offer emotional support when you need it most.
- **Intuitive**; Pisces individuals possess a high level of intuition. They possess the ability to sense and understand your emotions. Even when you don't express them verbally. Overall this leads to stronger bonds and deeper understanding.
- **Conflict avoidance**; When it comes to conflicts Pisces folks tend to shy from confrontations. Maintaining harmony is a priority. They are peacekeepers who rely on diplomacy and empathy to resolve disagreements.
- **Motivational**; One of the qualities of Pisces friends is their motivated nature. This can serve as a wellspring of inspiration and motivation for those around them. They have this talent for encouraging others to explore their dreams and unleash their inner creativity.
- **Spiritual**; Pisces often have an interest in spirituality or mysticism. They may introduce you to practices like meditation or engage you in philosophical discussions that help foster a profound spiritual connection between friends.

To sum it up, having a friend who is a Pisces means having an understanding and imaginative companion who brings depth and emotional richness to your life. They have an ability to connect with others on a level and offer unwavering support making them extraordinary friends who enhance your life just by being in it.

PISCES IN FAMILY DYNAMICS

Pisces brings unique qualities and sensitivities that shape their role within their families. They are known for their emotions, empathy and artistic inclinations. Here's a closer look at how Pisces individuals contribute to family dynamics.

- **Emotional Pillars**; Pisces individuals often serve as pillars within their families. They are quick to provide comfort and support during times. Their empathetic nature allows them to understand the emotions of family members and lend an ear when needed.
- **Compassionate Conflict Solvers**; Pisces family members excel at approaching family issues with compassion and understanding. They strive to find resolutions to conflicts and're willing mediators who bring diplomacy and empathy into disputes.
- **Nurturers and Protectors**; Pisces individuals naturally have an inclination, towards nurturing and taking care of their loved ones.They take on the role of caretakers ensuring that their family members feel loved, protected and well cared for. This characteristic is particularly evident in mothers and fathers.
- **Engaging Family Activities**; Pisces creativity and imagination often manifest in the form of family activities. They enjoy organizing art projects, movie nights or imaginative games that bring the family together and create memories.
- **Empathetic Sibling Bonds;** Pisces siblings are known for their connections with their brothers and sisters. They are understanding and supportive making them great confidants for their siblings.
- **Awareness of Family Dynamics**; Pisces individuals are highly sensitive to the dynamics within their families. They have a knack for picking up on underlying tensions or unexpressed emotions, which may prompt them to intervene or offer comfort to those in distress.
- **Spiritual and Mystical Interests**; Many Pisces individuals have an interest in spirituality or mysticism that they may introduce to their families. They may encourage family members to explore meditation, yoga or engage in discussions that deepen the bond within the family.
- **Vulnerability in Relationships**; Due to their vulnerability Pisces individuals can be more susceptible to being affected by conflicts or tensions

within the family. During times of strife they may require emotional support from their loved ones.

- **Bridging Generational Gaps through Empathy**; Pisces individuals often serve as bridges across generations, within their families.Pisces individuals effortlessly establish connections, with family members from generations promoting unity and understanding across age groups.

To summarize, Pisces individuals play an important role in family dynamics by bringing compassion, creativity and emotional support to their loved ones. Their empathetic and nurturing nature helps build bonds within the family unit making them contributors to overall harmony and well being at home.

CHALLENGES, IN FRIENDSHIPS AND FAMILY RELATIONSHIPS

While Pisces individuals bring qualities to their friendships and family relationships they also encounter specific challenges due to their unique personality traits and sensitivities. It's important for both Pisces individuals and their loved ones to understand these challenges. Here are some common difficulties that Pisces may face in their friendships and family relationships.

- **Dealing with Emotions**; Pisces individuals often absorb the emotions of those around them. This empathetic nature can sometimes lead to feeling overwhelmed especially when family members or friends are going through times. It can be challenging for Pisces to separate their feelings from the emotions of others.
- **Establishing Boundaries and Assertiveness**; Setting boundaries can be a struggle for Pisces individuals. They may find it difficult to say "no" when they feel obligated to help or support someone even if it means compromising their well being.
- **Escapism**; When confronted with emotions or stressful situations Pisces individuals may turn to escapism as a way of coping. This can manifest as daydreaming overindulging in habits or withdrawing from responsibilities. However these tendencies can strain both friendships and family relations.
- **Idealistic Expectations**; Pisces individuals often have romantic notions about relationships. Sometimes Pisces individuals have unrealistic expectations for their friends and family. This can lead them to end up feeling disappointed when reality doesn't align with their visions.

- **Manipulation**; Pisces trusting nature and their desire to please others can make them susceptible to manipulation by individuals. It's important for them to exercise caution in choosing whom they trust and confide in.
- **Avoidance**; Pisces often prefer to avoid confrontations or conflicts even if it means neglecting their needs or compromising the health of their relationships. By suppressing their concerns they risk leaving issues that can impact both friendships and family dynamics.
- **Reflection**; Regular periods of solitude are essential for Pisces individuals to recharge and reflect. However this need for time might be misunderstood by friends and family as being distant or withdrawn potentially leading to misunderstandings.
- **Overthinking**; Pisces tend to overthink things and experience anxiety. This tendency may affect their ability to maintain relationships as they ruminate on events or excessively worry about the future.

To overcome these challenges and build relationships Pisces individuals can benefit from developing a sense of self awareness, setting clear boundaries and practicing assertiveness. Seeking support from friends, family members or therapists can also be instrumental in navigating these difficulties. Understanding and compassion from those close to them play a role in supporting Pisces individuals.

NURTURING RELATIONSHIPS; A GUIDE, FOR PISCES

If you're a Pisces you possess a sensitivity, an empathetic nature and a creative spirit that naturally makes you a caring individual in your relationships. You derive joy from offering support and building connections with your loved ones. To help you cultivate and nurture fulfilling relationships here's a guide that highlights your qualities and provides insights into your approach to love and connection.

- **Embrace Your Empathy**; As a Pisces one of your strengths lies in your ability to feel deeply and connect emotionally with others. Embracing this empathy allows you to understand the feelings and needs of your loved ones on a level. Your genuine compassion and support serve as gifts to those around you.
- **Communicate Openly**; Although you possess an understanding of others emotions remember that open communication is crucial for nurturing any relationship. Don't hesitate to express your thoughts and feelings as it builds trust and encourages your loved ones to reciprocate with their vulnerability.
- **Establish Healthy Boundaries**; Pisces individuals often face challenges when it comes to setting boundaries due to their inclination to assist others at all costs. However, learning how to establish and maintain boundaries is vital in order to prevent exhaustion and maintain balance within your relationships. Recognize that it's perfectly alright to say "no" when it is necessary.
- **Make Self Care a Priority**; Building relationships begins with taking care of yourself. Dedicate time to self care. Prioritize your well being. When you are emotionally and physically healthy you can be a supportive partner, friend or family member.
- **Embrace Creativity**; Pisces innate creativity can inject excitement and inspiration into relationships. Embrace shared endeavors with your loved ones whether it involves pursuits exploring new hobbies together or simply infusing everyday life with imaginative ideas.
- **Surround Yourself with Like Minded Individuals**; Surround yourself with friends and partners who value and appreciate your sensitivity and artistic nature. Seek out kindred spirits who can understand and celebrate your qualities as they are more likely to support and nurture your well being.
- **Practice Patience**; Patience is a virtue when it comes to nurturing relationships. Not everyone may. Respond to emotions deeply as you do. Allow your loved ones the time and space they need to express themselves in their way.

- **Maintain Your Independence**; While you highly value connections remember the importance of maintaining your independence and sense of self. Don't get too caught up in relationships. Make sure you strike a balance, between being together and maintaining your individuality.

As we come to an end in our exploration of "Pisces; Friends and Family " we have delved into the realm inhabited by Pisces individuals and their remarkable roles, within friendships and family relationships. Pisces, the sign of the zodiac has graciously shared with us their qualities of empathy, emotional sensitivity and creative brilliance. These characteristics shape their interactions and relationships, with those they hold dear. As we continue our exploration of the Pisces star sign may we all be inspired by the enduring warmth and empathy that Pisces individuals bring forth. Let us cherish and nurture our relationships that make lifes journey so beautifully profound.

CHAPTER 4:
CAREER AND AMBITIONS

Pisces brings a combination of creativity, empathy and sensitivity to their work and financial choices. This chapter takes you on a journey, through their career preferences, strengths and challenges. We also delve into their relationship with money including how they spend and what financial matters are important to them.

Whether you are a Pisces seeking insights into your career path and financial decisions or simply curious about how Pisceans navigate work and manage finances this chapter aims to provide you with an understanding of Pisces career goals, strengths and attitudes towards money.

PROFESSIONAL ASPIRATIONS OF PISCES

- **Roles of Compassion**; Due to their compassionate nature Pisces individuals are often drawn towards careers that involve helping and supporting others. They excel in professions such as counseling, psychology, social work, nursing or healthcare. Here their ability to connect with people is highly valued.
- **Healing and Well being**; Pisces have a desire to make contributions to the well being of others. They may be inclined towards careers in healing practices, alternative medicine fields, yoga instruction or spiritual counseling where they can promote emotional healing.
- **Environmental Conservation**; The deep connection that Pisces individuals feel with the world often leads them towards careers related to environmental conservation efforts like biology or animal welfare.
- **Charitable Work**; Many Pisceans are driven by a sense of purpose and an innate desire to make the world a better place. They frequently involve themselves in organizations, charity work initiatives or humanitarian efforts where their compassion and unwavering dedication shine through.
- **Storytelling and Communication**; People born under the Pisces zodiac sign possess a talent for storytelling and communication. They often excel in professions such as journalism, writing, filmmaking or public speaking. Here they can utilize their words and creative abilities to inspire and educate others.
- **Entrepreneurship**; The artistic inclination and visionary mindset of Pisces individuals often drive them towards entrepreneurship. They may embark on business ventures within fields like fashion, design or the arts infusing their work with their style and creativity.
- **Music and Entertainment**; Those born under Pisces frequently share a connection with music and the performing arts. Many choose careers as musicians, actors or performers to express their emotions and showcase their talents to an audience.
- **Philanthropy and Social Causes;** Pisces individuals are commonly drawn to philanthropic work and social causes. They may support organizations that align with their values allowing them to contribute positively towards change.
- **Flexibility and Autonomy**; Pisces individuals highly value flexibility and autonomy in their professional lives. They thrive in environments that grant them the freedom to follow their intuition while working on projects that resonate with their passions and personal values.

Although career preferences among those born under Pisces vary widely they all share a desire to make an impact by expressing their creativity along with forming emotional connections with others. They derive satisfaction from pursuing careers that align with their core values enabling them to utilize their talents for the betterment of society.

STRENGTHS THAT PROPEL PISCES INDIVIDUALS IN THE WORKPLACE

Pisces individuals possess a set of strengths and attributes that empower them to thrive in an array of professional roles and settings. Their imaginative, compassionate and artistic nature is complemented by a range of qualities that make them highly sought after employees. Here are some key strengths that distinguish Pisces individuals in their lives.

- **Empathy and Compassion**; Those with Pisces traits possess a capacity to comprehend and connect with the emotions and needs of their colleagues and clients. Their innate empathy enables them to foster work environments making them exceptional team players well as effective leaders.

- **Creativity and Imagination**; The inclination and vibrant imagination of Pisces individuals prove invaluable in problem solving, innovation and brainstorming. They consistently bring perspectives infused with ideas to projects, inspiring creativity, among their peers.
- **Adaptability**; Pisces individuals display adaptability and embrace change gracefully rendering them well suited for dynamic work environments.They have the ability to adapt to changing priorities, embrace technologies and excel in situations that demand flexibility.
- **Intuition and Gut Instincts**; Pisces individuals often rely on their nature when making decisions. They possess a sense of what feels right or wrong. Overall this guides them in making choices throughout their careers.
- **Dedication and Commitment**; Pisceans show commitment to their work. They are willing to put in extra effort to achieve their goals. Their dedication ensures that they consistently deliver high quality results in their projects and tasks.
- **Strong Communication Skills**; Many Pisces individuals have a talent for both written and verbal communication. They possess the ability to express ideas with clarity and eloquence. This valuable skill greatly benefits roles that require communication.
- **Conflict Resolution**; Although Pisces individuals may avoid conflict they are adept at resolving disputes through diplomacy and sensitivity. They have the ability to diffuse situations and mediate conflicts effectively.
- **Attention to Detail;** While Pisces individuals are often associated with creativity they also demonstrate attention to detail when necessary. This combination of creativity and precision proves advantageous across professions.
- **Emotional Resilience**; Pisces individuals capacity for processing and managing emotions makes them emotionally resilient, in the workplace. They have an ability to handle stress and difficult situations, with grace often offering support to their colleagues during times.
- **Holistic Thinking**; Pisces individuals tend to have a perspective. They can see how different pieces fit together. This holistic thinking is beneficial in areas such as planning, project management and organizational development.
- **Strong Work Ethic**; Pisceans take their responsibilities seriously. They are dedicated to delivering their best. They are known for being reliable, responsible and becoming trusted members of their teams.
- **Supportive Leadership**; When in leadership roles Pisces individuals lead with an understanding approach. They motivate their teams by appreciating each member's contributions and fostering a work environment.

In summary Pisces individuals bring a range of strengths to the workplace. From empathy and creativity to adaptability and dedication. Their ability to connect emotionally with others while encouraging creativity often leads them to careers in fields. These strengths make them valuable assets for any organization as they contribute not within the boundaries of their job titles but beyond.

CHALLENGES FACED BY PISCES IN THEIR CAREERS AND STRATEGIES TO OVERCOME THEM

While Pisces individuals possess strengths that make them employees they also encounter certain challenges in their careers due to the unique aspects of their personality traits. Recognizing and addressing these challenges can greatly benefit Pisces individuals in their lives. Below are some career obstacles faced by Pisces and effective strategies to overcome them.

- **Sensitive to Feedback**; Pisces individuals tend to be highly sensitive. They may take constructive criticism personally. To overcome this it is important for them to build resilience by focusing on the opportunity for growth rather than dwelling on feedback.
- **Distraction**; Due to their nature Pisces individuals may struggle with getting easily distracted. To stay on track it is helpful for them to set goals, break tasks into steps and establish a structured work environment.
- **Difficulty with Assertiveness**; Asserting themselves in the workplace can be challenging for Pisces individuals. Developing assertiveness skills through communication and setting boundaries can empower them to advocate for their needs and ideas.
- **Maintaining Boundaries**; Pisces inclination to help others sometimes leads to violations of their boundaries. Establishing and maintaining professional boundaries is crucial in order to avoid overextending oneself.
- **Indecisiveness**; Relying on intuition can occasionally result in indecisiveness for Pisces individuals. They can overcome this by weighing the pros and cons of decisions while seeking input, from trusted colleagues or mentors.
- **Feeling overwhelmed**; People born under the Pisces zodiac sign often have many connections with others. This can sometimes lead to feeling overwhelmed. It's important for them to prioritize self care, establish boundaries and seek support when necessary.

- **Restlessness with routine**; Pisces individuals may easily become bored with tasks. They can explore opportunities for creativity and variety within their positions or projects as a means of maintaining their enthusiasm.
- **Struggles with time management**; Due to their perception of time Pisces individuals may encounter difficulties in managing it. Utilizing calendars, making use of to do lists and employing time management apps can assist them in meeting deadlines.
- **Overextending oneself**; The inclination of Pisces individuals to help others often leads them to push themselves beyond their limits. However this can negatively impact their well being. Learning how to prioritize responsibilities and being comfortable saying "no" when necessary is crucial in avoiding burnout.
- **Uncertainty about career direction**; Individuals born under the Pisces zodiac sign may find it challenging to identify a career path due to having many interests. Career guidance, mentorship and self reflection can assist individuals in discovering their passions and aspirations.

To sum up Pisces individuals possess both strengths and obstacles, in their professional journeys. By acknowledging these challenges and employing strategies to overcome them, they can effectively utilize their qualities, find fulfillment in their careers. Furthermore they can easily overcome any hurdles on the path to success.

Reflecting on Pisces within the realm of career and finances reminds us of the importance of aligning one's trajectory and financial choices with values and passions. As we continue our exploration of the Pisces star sign may those who fall under this sign continue to embrace their strengths and sensitivities. Let this pave the way for fulfilling careers and impactful contributions.

CHAPTER 5: SELF-IMPROVEMENT

In this chapter we will dive into the exploration of self-improvement, through the lens of Pisces individuals. Pisces brings a blend of creativity, empathy and sensitivity to their journey of self improvement. This chapter will explore strategies and approaches that Pisces individuals can adopt to enrich their lives, nurture their strengths and tackle challenges they may encounter.

Whether you are a Pisces seeking insights into your path of self improvement or simply a curious reader interested in understanding how Pisceans perceive personal growth this chapter aims to provide guidance and inspiration. It embarks on an expedition of self discovery and self enhancement guided by the qualities that define Pisces as they pursue growth and strive for improvement.

HARNESSING STRENGTHS AND OVERCOMING WEAKNESSES

Pisces individuals possess an array of strengths as well as many areas where they face challenges. Understanding how to leverage their strengths while addressing these challenges is crucial for achieving success. Here's a guide that can help Pisces individuals capitalize on their strengths and address their weaknesses.

STRENGTHS

- **Empathy and Compassion**; Utilize your ability to empathize with others on an emotional level. This strength can be highly valuable. Particularly in professions like counseling, healthcare or social work where supporting and assisting people is crucial.
- **Creativity and Imagination**; Embrace your creative side. Allow your creativity to flow freely. Consider pursuing a career that allows you to

express your ideas. Whether it's through art, writing, music or any other creative outlet you enjoy.

- **Adaptability;** Embrace change and new experiences by leveraging your adaptability. This quality makes you a valuable asset in dynamic work environments that require flexibility.
- **Intuition**; Trust your intuition when making decisions both personally and professionally. Your innate sense of what feels right will guide you along the way.
- **Commitment**; Continue to dedicate yourself to growth well as professional endeavors. Your commitment often leads to recognition and success in your chosen field.
- **Communication Skills**; Leverage your communication skills to effectively convey ideas and build strong relationships with colleagues and clients alike.
- **Conflict Resolution**; Utilize your expertise in conflict resolution to foster environments and effectively resolve disputes in a manner.
- **Emotional Resilience**; Focus on developing resilience allowing you to gracefully handle stress and adversity while also being there to offer support to others when they require it.
- **Holistic Thinking**; Leverage your ability to consider the picture as an advantage in planning, project management and decision making processes.

WEAKNESSES

- **Sensitive to Criticism**; Work towards building a mindset that allows you to embrace criticism rather than taking it personally.
- **Procrastination**; Cultivate effective time management skills. Discipline yourself to minimize distractions, ensuring focus on tasks at hand.
- **Difficulty with Assertiveness**; Enhance your assertiveness abilities in order to confidently communicate your needs and opinions.
- **Boundary Issues**; Establish boundaries that prevent overextending yourself promoting a balance between work and personal life.
- **Indecisiveness**; Take the time to weigh your options thoroughly. Avoid prolonged indecision by setting deadlines for making decisions.
- **Escapism**; Channel any tendencies towards escapism into stress relief activities such as exercise, meditation or engaging hobbies.
- **Feeling Overwhelmed**; Learn how to prioritize tasks and seek support when emotions or responsibilities become overwhelming.
- **Impatience with Routine**; Embrace the power of establishing routines in order to achieve your objectives and maintain a sense of enthusiasm for your work.

By acknowledging and embracing their strengths while actively addressing areas for growth Pisces individuals can lead fulfilling lives both personally and professionally.

EXERCISES FOR SELF AWARENESS TAILORED SPECIFICALLY FOR PISCES

Developing self awareness is a skill that can assist Pisces individuals in navigating their distinct personality traits and emotions effectively. Here are some exercises designed specifically for Pisces to help them gain insight into themselves and their inner worlds.

- **Journaling**; Regularly journaling can greatly benefit Pisces individuals. Here they can explore their thoughts, emotions and dreams. Write about your experiences, feelings and sources of inspiration. This practice will enable you to identify recurring patterns and gain clarity regarding your desires and aspirations.
- **Meditation and Mindfulness**; Embrace mindfulness meditation as a means to become more attuned with your emotions and physical sensations. Observe your thoughts without judgment, noticing how they impact your

feelings and actions. This practice will help you cultivate presence in the moment.

- **Self Reflective Questions**; Take time for self reflection. Ask questions to yourself. For instance you can ask yourself questions, like "What're the values that matter most to me?". What brings me the greatest happiness?" By reflecting on these inquiries you can gain an understanding of your motivations and priorities.
- **Tracking Emotions**; Keep a journal where you record your experiences throughout the day. Take note of what triggers emotions and how you respond to them. This practice can help you identify patterns in your emotions and develop strategies for managing them.
- **Expressing Creativity**; Utilize your abilities to express your world. Whether it's through painting, writing, music or any other creative outlet. Channel your emotions and thoughts into your artwork. This can serve as a method for processing feelings and gaining self awareness.
- **Seeking Feedback**; Ask trusted friends, family members or colleagues for feedback on both your strengths and weaknesses. Their perspectives can provide insights into your behaviors and how others perceive you.
- **Exploring Dreams**; Pay attention to the symbolism in your dreams. Keep a dream journal where you document your dreams upon waking up. Analyze recurring themes, symbols and emotions. Allow the process to delve deeper into understanding your mind.
- **Setting Positive Intentions**; Before embarking on each day establish intentions regarding how you want to feel and behave. Take a moment to reflect on your aspirations and the principles you hold dear. This habit can assist you in staying true to yourself throughout the day.
- **Immerse Yourself in Nature**; Dedicate time to being in surroundings as a way to rejuvenate and connect with yourself. Nature offers a grounding atmosphere that fosters introspection and self examination.
- **Consider Therapy**; If navigating your emotions or dealing with matters becomes challenging it might be beneficial to seek guidance from a therapist or counselor. Professional support can offer insights and tools for developing self awareness.

By engaging in exercises that promote self awareness individuals born under Pisces can deepen their understanding of their emotions, motivations and inner worlds. This heightened sense of self awareness can pave the way for better relationships, personal growth and a stronger connection with their unique strengths..

Ultimately personal growth and development, for Pisces individuals involves a journey of self exploration and self acceptance. Throughout this chapter we have uncovered the strategies and approaches that Pisces individuals can employ to nurture their strengths, address their challenges and embark on a path of self discovery. We have observed how embracing creativity fostering resilience, establishing targets and maintaining equilibrium can contribute to their individual progression.

As we contemplate Pisces within the context of personal development we are reminded of the significance of self awareness and self acceptance. Pisces individuals exemplify the importance of comprehending one's emotions while nurturing one's creativity as fostering meaningful connections, in pursuit of personal growth.

As we continue our exploration of the Pisces zodiac sign may those who identify as Pisces always embrace the power of self improvement. May they inspire us all to embark on our paths of personal growth, self awareness and self enhancement.

CHAPTER 6: PISCES IN THE YEAR AHEAD

Now we are about to set off on an adventure that sheds light on what lies ahead for individuals born under the sign of Pisces. This chapter provides an examination of how the changing cosmic forces will impact various aspects of Pisces individuals lives in the upcoming year. With their sensitivity, creativity and intuition Pisces individuals have a deep connection to the cosmic energies that shape their destinies. As we delve into the events and alignments that lie ahead we will uncover insights into love and relationships, career and finances, health and much more.

This chapter serves as a roadmap offering Pisces individuals a glimpse into the opportunities, challenges and transformative moments that await them. Whether you're a Pisces seeking guidance for the coming year or an intrigued reader. This chapter acts as your guiding star to navigate through it all with wisdom and understanding. So let's embark on this voyage together!

DISCOVER WHAT AWAITS PISCES IN THE YEAR AHEAD

Welcome, Pisces! This yearly horoscope guide is here to give you insights into the influences that might shape your journey in the year ahead. The stars have much to reveal to you.

- **Aries Season (March 21. April 19)**; The year starts off with an energetic Aries season encouraging you to take charge and assert yourself. Embrace your inner warrior and approach projects with confidence. This is a time to set goals and lay the foundation for your dreams.
- **Taurus Season (April 20. May 20);** As Taurus season unfolds focus on achieving stability and ensuring material security. Consider budgeting and saving for endeavors. You may also find joy in taking care of your well being, through a diet and regular exercise.
- **Gemini Season (May 21. June 20)**; During Gemini season communication and networking become factors. Your natural adaptability allows you to connect with a range of people effectively. Engage in thought provoking conversations and explore opportunities for collaboration.
- **Cancer Season (June 21. July 22)**; As a water sign Cancer season truly resonates with your emotions. Take some time for introspection. Focus on nurturing your well being. It's the moment to strengthen your bonds with loved ones and create a harmonious home environment.
- **Leo Season (July 23. August 22)**; Get ready for a surge of energy and self expression during Leo season. Embrace your performer. Let your talents shine. Dive into pursuits and share your passions. Enjoy being in the spotlight.
- **Virgo Season (August 23. September 22)**; Virgo season encourages you to prioritize organization and self care. Take charge of any lingering tasks. Declutter your life for a renewed sense of order. Pay attention to your well being by adopting an approach to taking care of yourself.
- **Libra Season (September 23. October 22)**; During Libra season relationships take stage. Strive for balance and harmony in all your connections. This is a time for diplomacy negotiation skills and strengthening the bonds you have with others.
- **Scorpio Season (October 23. November 21)**; Scorpio season invites you to delve into yourself through introspection. Explore your passions, undergo transformations and embrace your mystic while trusting in the power of intuition.
- **Sagittarius Season (November 22. December 21)**; During the Sagittarius season you'll feel a sense of adventure. Embrace opportunities to explore

places, expand your knowledge and widen your perspectives. It's a time to seek wisdom and broaden your outlook.

- **Capricorn Season (December 22. January 19)**l; Capricorn season puts the spotlight on your career and long term goals. Focus on your ambitions, put plans into action and work diligently towards achieving success. Your hard work will pay off.
- **Aquarius Season (January 20. February 18)** ; As Aquarius season unfolds your interests, causes and humanitarian efforts take stage. Engage in group activities and lend support to causes. Connect with like minded individuals who share your vision for positive change.
- **Pisces Season (February 19. March 20);** The year comes to an end with Pisces season—the time to embrace your compassionate nature. Reflect on your growth, trust your instincts, set intentions for the year and continue channeling your creativity.

Throughout the year don't forget to embrace your gifts of empathy, creativity and intuition. They are like guiding stars in your life's journey. Trust yourself to gracefully navigate through life's ups and downs, with sensitivity. May your exploration of self and personal development be guided by the vastness of the universe. May the upcoming year bring you a sense of harmony and transformation enriching your Piscean narrative with connections to the world that surrounds you.

ASTROLOGICAL EVENTS THAT INFLUENCE PISCES AND THEIR EFFECTS

Astrology provides a perspective on how celestial happenings can impact the lives of those born under zodiac signs, including Pisces. While every event in the calendar holds significance, there are key astrological occurrences that can particularly affect individuals with Pisces traits. Here are some notable events and their potential influences.

- **New Moon in Pisces**; The annual New Moon in Pisces holds power for those with this zodiac sign. It's a time when they can set intentions, embark on projects and deepen their spiritual practices. This lunar alignment resonates with their imaginative nature enabling them to tap into its energy for self reflection and personal growth.
- **Mercury Retrograde in Water Signs**; When Mercury goes retrograde in water signs like Pisces it can enhance abilities. However, it may also lead to

misunderstandings and challenges. During these periods it's advisable to practice patience and strive for clarity in their interactions.

- **Jupiter in Pisces**; The arrival of Jupiter into Pisces brings forth opportunities for growth, creative pursuits and emotional healing. It's a time to feel more inspired, generous and open hearted.
- **Moon in Pisces**; The Full Moon occurring within the realm of Pisces has the potential to intensify experiences. It's a time to let go, forgive and release baggage. It can also bring moments of intuition and vivid dreams.
- **Neptune's Influence**; Neptune, which rules over Pisces often has an impact on the lives of Pisces individuals. Its movements can inspire awakenings, artistic breakthroughs or moments of confusion. Strive for clarity and discernment.
- **Saturn Opposition**; When Saturn opposes its position, Pisces individuals may experience a period of self reflection and evaluation. This can lead to life changes as they align with values and pursue ambitions.
- **Solar Eclipses in the Pisces Virgo Axis**; Solar eclipses occurring in the Pisces Virgo axis often mark moments for Pisces individuals. These events frequently bring about shifts in their routines, health or work life balance. Remain adaptable and open to change.
- **Pisces Birthdays**; Paying attention to events happening around their birthdays is particularly important for Pisces individuals. These events provide valuable insights into their personal growth journey.
- **Venus in Pisces;** When Venus passes through Pisces it heightens artistic sensibilities, for those born under this sign. Now is a time to strengthen relationships, explore your side and express love and affection.
- **Mars enters Pisces;** When Mars enters Pisces it brings a sense of dreaminess and creative energy to Pisces individuals. It's the moment to start projects and pursue passions but it's important to avoid procrastination as well.
- **Lunar eclipses;** Lunar eclipses, in water signs can bring about experiences for Pisces. These events may lead to introspection. Require individuals born under Pisces to confront their emotions and make significant decisions.

Each astrological event holds its energy and potential impact on Pisces individuals. By staying aware of these occurrences and how they align with their birth charts, those born under Pisces can harness the cosmic energies to navigate life's ups and downs, deepen self awareness and continue their journey of personal growth.

LOVE AND RELATIONSHIPS

In the year those born under Pisces can expect a journey in their romantic lives and relationships influenced by significant astrological events. The positions of Venus, Mars and other celestial bodies will greatly shape the landscape.

- **Venus transits through Pisces;** When Venus transits through Pisces it is a time where those born under Pisces thrive romantically. During these periods Pisces individuals tend to value connections, experience heightened sensitivity and seek soulful and compassionate partnerships. It's a time for Pisces to express their love and affection.
- **The movements of Jupiter;** The movements of Jupiter can have an impact on Pisces relationships. Keep an eye out for when Jupiter enters water signs like Cancer and Scorpio. These specific periods can bring developments in love, such as relationships, engagements or stronger bonds.
- **Lunar and solar eclipses;** Both lunar and solar eclipses can play a role in shaping Pisces relationships. Lunar eclipses occurring in water signs may trigger revelations while solar eclipses symbolize new beginnings. Pay attention to the eclipses that fall within your relationship houses in your birth chart for insights into potential relationship changes.

- **Mars transits;** When Mars transits through water signs it tends to ignite emotions and passions within Pisces romantic lives. These periods occur throughout the year. Often leads to increased intimacy and desire. However it's important for Pisces individuals to be mindful of conflicts that may arise from emotions.

CAREER PROSPECTS AND FINANCIAL SITUATIONS

Looking ahead at career prospects and financial situations, for Pisces individuals there are possibilities of shifts and opportunities influenced by events that drive ambition and prosperity.

- **Saturn and Jupiter;** When Saturn and Jupiter align it can have an impact on your career. Especially if these planets form connections with your birth chart. Keep an eye on their positions in the areas of your chart related to work and professional growth. This alignment could bring opportunities for promotions, job prospects or recognition in your field.
- **Mars enters Pisces;** As Mars enters Pisces bringing a surge of energy and ambition to those born under this sign. Take advantage of this time to start projects, assert yourself professionally and make moves in your career.
- **Mercury retrograde;** During Mercury retrogrades it's important to proceed with caution as they can create communication challenges that might impact work relationships or financial matters. Be sure to double check contracts and agreements. Avoid making financial decisions during these periods.
- **Saturn;** The influence of Saturn in the house of finances may inspire Pisces individuals to adopt a disciplined approach to money management. Consider setting up a budget, saving money regularly and exploring long term investment options for stability.

HEALTH AND WELLBEING

It's crucial for Pisces individuals to prioritize their health and well being in the year. Astrological events can have an effect on both emotional states so self care should be a priority.

- **Neptune;** As Neptune is the ruling planet for Pisces individuals its transits can significantly impact well being. Stay attuned to how Neptunes movement, through areas of your chart may affect you While Neptune encourages creativity and intuition it can also make one emotionally sensitive. To maintain balance it is beneficial to practice techniques, like grounding, meditation and mindfulness.

- **Lunar eclipses**; Lunar eclipses have the potential to intensify emotions and impact well being. It would be helpful to prioritize self care routines, maintain a lifestyle and seek support when needed. Pisces individuals can find holistic health practices like yoga, meditation and energy healing beneficial. These practices align with your spiritual nature while helping you stay centered. It's also important to pay attention to your health during challenging events. Seeking therapy or counseling can assist in processing emotions. Gaining clarity during times.

SELF DISCOVERY

In the year ahead, Pisces individuals will encounter opportunities for personal growth and self discovery through astrological events that encourage introspection and personal development.

- **Jupiters Expansive Energy**; Jupiter's influence can expand your horizons by encouraging exploration of interests and experiences. Consider enrolling in courses traveling or delving into studies to broaden your knowledge and perspective.
- **New Moon in Pisces**; The annual New Moon in Pisces presents a time for setting intentions related to growth and self awareness. Make the most of this time by engaging in endeavors reflecting on yourself deeply and practicing spirituality.
- **Chiron Healing**; Chiron, who is referred to as the "wounded healer " might motivate you to address wounds and focus on self healing. Consider methods, like working with your child or exploring your shadow self to facilitate personal growth and emotional well being.
- **Embrace Intuition**; Your natural intuition and connection to the realms are your strengths. Embrace practices that can enhance your abilities such as meditation, analyzing dreams and energy work. These practices will help you delve deeper into your journey of self discovery.

As a Pisces individual yourself you possess a gift for navigating life's ups and downs with intuitive understanding. Trust in your wisdom while also embracing guidance offered by celestial bodies. Open yourself up to possibilities in love connections, career progressions, self discovery journeys and overall holistic well being that are presented by the cosmos.

Remember that astrology serves as a tool for self awareness and guidance, rather than a fixed script dictating your destiny. You hold the power to shape your future through choices you make along your chosen path. The knowledge acquired through this journey into astrology aims to empower you as you strive for growth, fulfillment and a deeper self awareness.

May the upcoming year bring about transformations and meaningful experiences in your life's narrative as a Pisces. Embrace the energies that encompass you, stay authentic, to your creative essence and embark on this new chapter, with the guidance of the stars illuminating your path.

CHAPTER 7: FAMOUS PISCES PERSONALITIES

Now we embark on a journey, through the life stories and accomplishments of people who share the zodiac sign, Pisces. This chapter celebrates the talents and remarkable contributions made by individuals born under this mystical sign across various fields. From musicians and visionary artists to groundbreaking scientists and influential leaders. Personalities with a Pisces background have left an imprint on our world through their creativity, compassion and forward thinking. We will delve into their biographies, career highlights and explore how their distinct Piscean traits have shaped their journeys towards fame and success.

Whether you are a Piscean seeking inspiration from kindred spirits or simply an intrigued reader interested in understanding how astrological signs influence figures, this chapter provides a glimpse into the unique qualities that define Pisces as well as celebrating the extraordinary achievements of those who share this astrological placement. Join us as we dive into the lives of these individuals born under the sign of Pisces and celebrate their lasting legacies.

STEVE JOBS

- Date of Birth; February 24th, 1955.
- Brief Biography; Steve Jobs was one of the co-founders behind Apple Inc., an technology company that has become an icon worldwide. He played a role in transforming the personal computer, music and mobile phone industries.
- Pisces Traits; Known for being visionary and innovative.
- Impact; The innovations brought about by Steve Jobs revolutionized how people communicate, work and enjoy music. His influence on technology and design is still felt today.
- Personal Life; Steve Jobs was known for his unwavering dedication to his work. He also had periods of introspection and spiritual exploration in his life.

ALBERT EINSTEIN

- Date of Birth; March 14 1879.
- Brief Biography; Albert Einstein was an acclaimed physicist and mathematician renowned for his theory of relativity. He received the Nobel Prize in Physics in 1921. Einstein developed the theory of relativity along with the equation $E=mc^2$. His contributions to quantum mechanics were also remarkable.
- Pisces Traits; intelligent, imaginative, curious and empathetic.
- Impact; Einstein's theories completely transformed our understanding of the universe. Laid the groundwork for physics as we know it today.
- Personal Life; Einstein was well known for his commitment to pacifism and efforts. He became a figure due to his advocacy for peace and social justice.

RIHANNA

- Date of Birth; February 20 1988.
- Brief Biography; Rihanna is a singer, songwriter and successful businesswoman, from Barbados. She has achieved success in the music industry. In addition to her music endeavors Rihanna also established the renowned cosmetics brand Fenty Beauty.
- Pisces Traits; Known for her prowess, depth, adaptability and charisma.
- Impact; Rihanna's impact extends beyond just music. She has become an icon through her contributions to fashion. The launch of Fenty Beauty

brought about a revolution in the cosmetics industry with its approach and diverse range of products.

- Personal Life; Beyond her talent and achievements in the entertainment world Rihanna is highly regarded for her efforts and advocacy for various social and political causes.

ELIZABETH TAYLOR

- Date of Birth; February 27 1932.
- Brief Biography; Elizabeth Taylor was an actress renowned for both her beauty and extraordinary talent. She graced timeless films throughout her career and received two Academy Awards for Best Actress.
- Pisces Traits; Romantic, charming and artistically inclined.
- Impact; Taylors captivating beauty and exceptional acting skills have established her as a timeless Hollywood icon. Moreover her tireless dedication to causes and active involvement in AIDS advocacy have left a mark on society.
- Personal Life; When it comes to Taylors life she is notable for her marriages and unwavering commitment to philanthropy particularly in the field of AIDS research.

JUSTIN BIEBER

- Date of Birth; March 1 1994.
- Brief Biography; Justin Bieber, a singer and songwriter skyrocketed to fame as an adolescent sensation and quickly became an international phenomenon in the pop music scene. Career Highlights; He has released albums such as "My World 2.0 " "Purpose," and "Changes."
- Pisces Traits; Known for being sensitive, artistic, compassionate and creative.
- Impact; Justin Bieber has amassed a fan base through his music and is widely acknowledged as one of the most influential pop artists of his generation.

- Personal Life; Justin is married to Hailey Rhode Bieber, an American model and media personality.

CAMILA CABELLO

- Date of Birth; March 3 1997.
- Brief Biography; Camila Cabello is a singer songwriter who initially gained recognition as a member of the girl group Fifth Harmony before embarking on a successful solo career. Cabello has released solo albums such as "Camila" and "Romance," gaining recognition for chart topping hits like "Havana" and "Senorita."
- Pisces Traits; Dreamy, artistic, compassionate and emotionally expressive.
- Impact; Cabellos music has received acclaim with her Mexican heritage serving as a wellspring of inspiration that is celebrated by many.
- Personal Life; Apart from her achievements Cabello is known for championing health awareness and her romantic relationship with fellow musician Shawn Mendes.

NEVILLE CHAMBERLAIN

- Date of Birth; March 18 1869.
- Brief Biography; Neville Chamberlain was a regarded statesman who held the position of Prime Minister of the United Kingdom from 1937 to 1940. He played a role in the stages of World War II.
- Pisces Traits; Diplomatic, empathetic and possessing negotiation skills.
- Impact; The decisions made by Chamberlain leading up to World War II had consequences that continue to be extensively debated in historical discourse.
- Personal Life; Alongside his political endeavors focused on maintaining peace Chamberlain scrutiny regarding his handling of Adolf Hitlers actions.

KURT COBAIN

- Date of Birth; February 20 1967.
- Brief Biography; Kurt Cobain was the lead singer and guitarist of the rock band Nirvana. He is considered one of the most legendary musicians in rock music history.
- Pisces Traits; Artistic, introspective, sensitive and creative.
- Impact; Cobains music and lyrics deeply connected with a generation and his contributions to the grunge movement revolutionized the music industry.
- Personal life; Unfortunately Cobain faced struggles with addiction and mental health problems that tragically led to his passing in 1994.

JESSICA BIEL

- Date of Birth; Born on March 3 1982.
- Brief Biography; Jessica Biel is an actress known for her performances in both movies and television. She gained recognition through her role in the TV series "7th Heaven."
- Pisces Traits; Compassionate, artistic, adaptable and empathetic.
- Impact; Biels acting talent and versatility have earned her acclaim along with a loyal fan base.
- Personal life; She is happily married to the actor and musician Justin Timberlake and together they have a son.

NINA SIMONE

- Date of Birth; February 21 1933
- Brief Biography; Nina Simone was a singer, songwriter and advocate for civil rights. Her unique voice and incredible musical abilities made her an icon.
- Pisces Traits; Expressive and visionary with a strong sense of social awareness.
- Impact; Simone's music went beyond boundaries. Became a voice during the civil rights movement fighting for equality.
- Personal Life; Nina Simone's unwavering commitment to both civil rights activism and her passion for music left an imprint on the industry as well as the pursuit of equality.

These profiles exemplify the talent and contributions that Pisceans have offered in various domains ranging from music and entertainment to science and politics. Their inherent Pisces qualities, like creativity, empathy and sensitivity significantly influenced their careers trajectories while leaving behind enduring legacies.

As we come to the end of our exploration into the lives of "Famous Pisces Personalities " we have embarked on a journey, through the captivating stories and legacies of individuals born under this enchanting zodiac sign. From musicians who stirred our souls with their melodies to scientists who expanded our knowledge of the universe and from artists who painted worlds to leaders who shaped history Pisceans have graced us with their creativity, empathy and visionary thinking.

These renowned Pisces individuals not only made an impact in their respective fields but also served as a source of inspiration for countless others. They are a testament to the traits associated with Pisces, such as sensitivity, adaptability and artistic brilliance that have played a role in shaping human history. May the tales of these Pisces personalities motivate us to embrace our innate qualities as Pisceans. Let them encourage us to dream fearlessly, create passionately and empathize profoundly with the world around us.

CONCLUSION

As we approach the end of our exploration into the realm of Pisces it's a time to ponder the aspects that have illuminated this book. Pisces, has revealed itself as a constellation embodying depth, empathy and boundless creativity. We've delved into its mythological origins and discussed matters concerning love, family, career and much more. Additionally we've caught a glimpse of the tapestry that shapes what lies ahead in the coming year and celebrated individuals with Pisces traits.

Now let us transition into the core of our conclusion where we unite all that we've explored during this odyssey. In the tapestry of Pisces we have embarked on a journey that has unfolded throughout the pages of this book. As we near the concluding chapters it is time to bring together the threads that have intertwined themselves through our exploration of the essence of Pisces. Here is a short summary of the chapters.

- **Chapter 1; History and Mythology**; In our first chapter we ventured back in time to uncover the origins and mythical stories that have infused Pisces. From ancient civilizations to diverse cultures, Pisces has left a mark on humanity's collective imagination. Overall serving as a constant reminder of the enduring presence of celestial influences in our earthly narratives.
- **Chapter 2; Love & Compatibility;** When it comes to matters of the heart we delved deeply into Pisces Romantic nature. We explored the depths of love, intricacies of attraction and complexities of compatibility with zodiac signs. Pisces your empathetic approach to love is truly a gift deserving profound appreciation.
- **Chapter 3; Friends and Family;** Within the bonds of friendship and family connections we uncovered the compassionate aspects in Pisces individuals. Your ability to cultivate nurturing relationships and serve as a peacemaker, within your circles enriches the lives of those enough to be connected with you. These connections represent the stars that guide you through the challenges of life.
- **Chapter 4; Career and Finance;** We delved into your pursuit of work and the financial stability you desire in your career. Your creativity, adaptability

and intuition are like guiding lights as you navigate the world. Remember that your artistic nature can bring light to paths.

- **Chapter 5; Self Improvement;** The journey of self discovery and personal growth lies at the core of Pisces evolution. Your sensitivity, combined with your strength acts as a compass that leads you toward self awareness and emotional well being. Embrace the beauty of your journey and the endless possibilities within yourself.
- **Chapter 6; The Year Ahead;** Our exploration into insights for the year revealed the magic held by astrology. As a Pisces you are attuned to the rhythms of forces. These insights serve as tools to help you navigate life's currents and harness cosmic energy around you.
- **Chapter 7; " Famous Pisces Personalities;** We honored the individuals born as Pisces who have made a lasting impact on the world. Their journeys remind us of the power that Pisces individuals possess to shape destinies and inspire generations. You too are a shining star in this universe and your presence plays a significant role in the ever evolving story of our world.

Throughout these pages we have embarked on a journey to uncover the qualities of Pisces and understand the impact of astrology. Our commitment was to unravel the tapestry of Pisces providing insights into its origins, relationships, career paths and the cosmic forces that shape its path. We have fulfilled this commitment by shedding light on the role Pisces has played in history and mythology. We have unraveled the mysteries surrounding love and compatibility, delving into the dynamics of friendships and family connections. Onwards we have guided you through career choices and personal growth opportunities and revealing insights for the upcoming year. We have also celebrated personalities born under Pisces who have made a lasting impact on our world.

As we reach the end of this exploration through Pisces, always remember that you are a collection of dreams. A tapestry woven into the fabric of existence and a beacon of compassion. Your journey is a testament to the nature of our universe and astrology's beauty. Embrace your qualities, follow your path illuminated by stars and continue to discover the cosmos within yourself and around you.

Ultimately what we hope you take away from this book is an understanding that as a Pisces individual you're an extraordinary creation born out of cosmic marvels. An embodiment of dreams and an illuminating force shaping lifes grand narrative. With the stars above, as your companions may your light shine brightly radiate and gracefully dance through life's seas.

In conclusion we invite you to continue exploring astrology as a tool that unveils patterns and influences our lives. To deepen your understanding of astrology and Pisces further we recommend reading materials and resources that will allow you to delve into the captivating world of the zodiac and its cosmic wonders. The stars, planets and infinite cosmos eagerly await your exploration. The magic of astrology is a journey that promises revelations.

May you always hold onto this wisdom as you journey through life and may the mystical forces of Pisces forever lead you towards the realms of dreams, empathy and boundless opportunities.